THE HISTORY OF
LEICESTERSHIRE
COUNTY
CRICKET CLUB

Dennis Lambert

With a personal view by
MIKE TURNER

CHRISTOPHER HELM
London

© 1992 Dennis Lambert and Mike Turner
Christopher Helm (Publishers) Ltd, a subsidiary of
A & C Black (Publishers) Ltd, 35 Bedford Row,
London WCIR 4JH

The authors wish to acknowledge the debt they owe to Eric Snow, formerly
the County Club historian, whose diligent researches over more than 50 years
he kindly put at their disposal.

ISBN 0-7136-8091-1

A CIP catalogue record for this book is available
from the British Library

Typeset by Rowland Phototypesetting Ltd, Bury St Edmunds, Suffolk
Printed and bound in Great Britain by Biddles Ltd, Guildford and King's Lynn

CONTENTS

A PERSONAL VIEW
Mike Turner

I CONSIDER MYSELF EXTREMELY fortunate that I have been able to devote my entire working life so far to the game and Club I love and, as a result of this, I have been able to derive enormous job satisfaction and career fulfilment out of my work.

For most of this period I have lived within 100 yards of the Grace Road pavilion and quite often in the evening I stroll round the ground in complete solitude. To me, there is a special peacefulness and I often stand by the Hawkesbury Road scoreboard – close to where my father died in 1977 – and I look across to the pavilion and reflect on the changes that have taken place since I joined the club as a young player in 1951.

It is true to say that when I became Secretary in 1960 the ground did not exist in its present form although, of course, the game was played within its perimeter. The land was owned by the Leicester City Council (Education Authority) and during term time the pupils of the City of Leicester Boys' Grammar School (where I was a pupil until 1950) played soccer and cricket there. During the holidays the Leicestershire team played most of their matches there. In fact, during term time the Club were allowed to play only four matches and this is why out games were played at Ashby-de-la-Zouch, Hinckley, Coalville and Loughborough.

When I joined the Club the only buildings on the ground were a dilapidated wooden pavilion and dining room, a brick stable (formerly for the horse which pulled the heavy roller) and the semi-underground air raid shelters which covered the whole of the present car park and the terraced area in the north-east corner of the ground.

It is nice for me to reflect that almost everything that is on the ground today – the balconied pavilion, the sponsors' suites, dining room, roof stands, offices, terraces, the Geary Stand, scoreboards, The Meet and even the rose bushes and trees have all been built or planted since I became Secretary.

When I decide to retire – or when the Committee decides not to offer me another contract – I will at least have the considerable personal satisfaction of having been largely instrumental in building a new foundation for the Club and creating something for the future which did not exist before.

The fact that I have been able to look out of my office window and each year see visible signs of progress has been a great motivation and in my final working years with the Club my ambition is to make even more progress both on and off the field of play.

It now all seems a far cry since my schoolboy days when I was football and cricket mad and dreamed of playing for Leicester City at soccer and for the County at cricket. However, when the invitation to join the staff came from Charles Palmer, the Club's Secretary and captain, my parents were not at all enthusiastic as they hoped that I would want to continue with my studies, go on to University and

1

only then, if I had the talent, turn my attention to the sporting scene. My own views and ambitions were rather different because in those days two years National Service had to be completed and I reasoned that I could enjoy two years of cricket before going into the army and then, after National Service, I could decide on my future career.

With these thoughts in mind I accepted the invitation to join the playing staff for the princely sum of £150 a year. I still have the contract letter from Charles Palmer addressed in the style of the day: 'Dear Turner . . .'

I can clearly remember reporting at the Aylestone Road Ground on the first day of April in 1951 for pre-season training. Although the Club had moved away from Aylestone Road after the War Office requisitioned the ground at the start of the Second World War, the old wooden indoor cricket school was still used for the pre-season practice. During the winter, prior to joining the staff, I had attended the school for coaching with Maurice Tompkin and Gerry Lester and it was Gerry who had recommended that I should join the staff.

It was the first day for other young hopefuls such as the Australian Murray Sargent, Bob Gardner and Freddie Foulds.

I cannot honestly say that I looked out on the ground and visualised the great players who had trod on the hallowed turf because somehow I had never related the Electricity Sports Ground to county cricket. The pavilion – painted black and white – reminded me of a country railway station and although the outfield and square were well tended, the ground was completely spoiled by two enormous cooling towers that had been erected on the old practice ground and which stood behind the bowler's arm and overshadowed the whole ground.

The outstanding memory of that first day was meeting Alec Skelding, who sat huddled by the large coke stove and in his deep gravel voice was telling stories about the county circuit. Alec was one of the great characters of cricket who played for Leicestershire before and after the First World War and was a first-class umpire from 1931 to 1958. He was a wonderful raconteur and was always in demand at cricket club dinners, where he often delivered his speech in rhyme. One particularly well known verse entitled 'The Duties, Trials and Troubles of County Umpires' or 'The Umpires' Lament' was very popular and began:

> Oh! Multitudinous scintillations,
> Where, midst thy bevy of constellations,
> With the group whose known occupations
> Are those of the cricket umpires?

I played cricket for two years and then, presumably because of my cricketing ability, I was pre-selected for the Royal Army Education Corps where I qualified as an army school teacher. I spent my two years National Service firstly teaching Royal Artillery Band Boys at Green Hills School, Woolwich and then teaching preliminary education at the Brigade of Guards Training Depot at Caterham, Surrey.

I really enjoyed my two years in the army. Apart from playing an immense amount of sport I was also given some real responsibility for the first time and this, coupled with the self discipline required by the Guards, provided experience which was a good foundation for my future career.

At this stage I was still uncertain about which direction my career would take but after deliberation I chose to rejoin the County Club when I left the army instead of going to Loughborough Colleges where I had the opportunity to take a teaching course in physical education.

Cricket in those days with Leicestershire was far from being a bed of roses and many older Leicestershire supporters will recall those struggling years when a County victory was a rarity. Even so, Leicestershire had their personalities – Les Berry's career only overlapped by one year with my own but there were other good players such as Jack Walsh, Vic Jackson, Maurice Tompkin and Charles Palmer. Maurice Hallam's career also started to blossom in the 1950s.

Palmer played a vital role during this period. Apart from being a batsman of international calibre, he was also a first-class administrator and, under his guidance, the Club's fortunes began to improve. Charles came to Leicester from Worcestershire in 1950 and in 1953 led the team to third in the Championship, which was the Club's highest ever position at that time. He played for the County with great distinction, scoring 33 centuries during his first-class career and taking 365 wickets – including his famous analysis of eight wickets for seven runs against the mighty Surrey in their Championship-winning days.

After retiring as Secretary-captain in 1957 he was immediately elected to the Committee as joint Honorary Secretary and he was elected Chairman in 1964. He was Chairman of the Club for 25 years and during this period he was elected President of MCC and Chairman of ICC; he was also Chairman of the Cricket Council and Chairman of the TCCB. Finally, he was elected President of Leicestershire in 1986.

During these years I had nurtured hopes of having a successful playing career but although I had reasonable success playing Minor Counties cricket my cricketing dreams were really dashed when Willie Watson – who succeeded Charles Palmer as captain – told me that in his opinion there was no place for a leg-spinner in the modern game because the emphasis was on containment. I had great respect for Willie's cricketing opinions and his future analysis of county cricket has proved to be very accurate with the demise of the spin bowler.

Needless to say, I took his advice very seriously and because of this – and also because I had married my childhood sweetheart Patricia – I decided to 'retire' from the game and go into industry.

Nevertheless, the Club offered me another playing contract or, alternatively, the Committee invited me to join the administrative staff if I was genuinely determined to leave the game as a player. Obviously, I chose the latter course of action and was extremely lucky when the Committee – under the Chairmanship of Neville Dowen – allowed me to attend a day course at the Leicester Colleges of Art and Technology. Consequently, instead of working full time in the office I went

3

off to College to study economics, the basic rudiments of English law, company law and accountancy.

I progressed from being Club Cashier to Assistant Secretary and then 'out of the blue' the Club Secretary resigned and to my surprise I was selected from 87 candidates and appointed Secretary in 1960. At 25 years of age I was the youngest ever County Cricket Club Secretary – this is still a record – and in my view the Committee took a great risk, especially as I had little administrative or commercial experience.

However, I did have a high-calibre Committee. William Bentley MBE was the newly appointed President, and after my own appointment he summoned me to his boardroom and almost his first words were: 'I want you to know that I am accustomed to being associated with success'.

For 25 years I had two splendid working partners in Bill Bentley as President and Charles Palmer as Chairman and they gave me great support and strength in trying to shape the future success of the Club. There is no doubt that Bill Bentley brought a new dimension to the thinking within the Committee room. As Chairman and Managing Director of the Bentley Engineering Group of Companies and as Chairman of the British Knitting Machine Association he had extensive business operations, and the Club was fortunate that he gave time to the game.

Other very valuable and dedicated Committee men at this time were Billy Butler, who raised many thousands of pounds through the football Competition; Sydney Hickling and Alfred Broughton, two successive Honorary Treasurers who helped with their wise guidance over the Club's financial affairs; and Eric Snow, who wrote two histories of Leicestershire Cricket.

My ambitions after my appointment were fairly straightforward – I wanted to improve the playing side of the Club and I wanted the Club to have its own headquarters and own the ground.

County cricket generally was in the doldrums in the early 1960s and it was because of this that I was lucky enough to make my mark nationally very early in my Secretarial career when in 1962 I initiated the Midland Counties Knock Out Cup. This was the first ever one-day county cricket knock-out competition played on a limited-overs basis, and was the forerunner of the Gillette Cup and the other one-day competitions. Little was it realised at the time that this type of cricket would prove to be the financial saviour of county cricket, as it attracted large crowds and national sponsorship.

The game was entering a period of change and this was particularly true at Leicestershire. Although the Club's playing record was the worst of all counties in the 20 years after the end of the Second World War, the attitude at the Club was of great optimism. Firstly, negotiations were completed to purchase the County Ground and, secondly, there was a noticeable change in the policy relating to the recruitment of players.

Contracts were exchanged with the local authorities for the purchase of the Grace Road Ground in December 1965 and the new players' pavilion was built on the same site as the old wooden pavilion. The building was completed before the start of the 1966 season. Probably the highlight of that season was the opening ceremony of the new pavilion by the Club's Patron, the Lord Bishop of Leicester, the Rt Rev R. R. Williams DD, who began his speech in a typical way with the words 'Pavilioned in Splendour and Girded in Praise'. He finished by saying that it had always been his ambition to 'open for Leicestershire' and then proceeded to open the pavilion door with a specially made gold key.

The Lord Bishop was a great supporter of cricket and he advised me during the great debate about whether county cricket should be played on Sundays. It is difficult to appreciate now the strong feelings and deep divisions of opinion which existed about the introduction of county cricket on Sundays. In 1966 Leicestershire were the first Midlands county to play Championship cricket on the Sabbath.

We had been able to purchase the ground primarily because of the shrewd financial management of the Club. The football competition had been extremely successful for a number of years and even in the mid-1960s there were still over 14,000 Ground Members who each paid ten shillings to join the competition each year and then paid a shilling for each entry in the weekly competition. Through the scheme the profit generated amounted to over £100,000. The Club paid £24,500 for the purchase of the ground and then allocated £80,000 for the first stages of an extensive ground improvement scheme which embraced the new pavilion and a complete conversion of the Richards Stand into a new spectator area which included glass-fronted bars and refreshment areas overlooking the playing area. The upstairs room, which was for members only, was very spacious and was also used for hiring out to local clubs for social functions.

Better facilities enabled me to recruit players – at last we had a home of our own. The importance of having good facilities for players had been brought home to me when I had been negotiating with Tom Graveney after he announced that he was leaving Gloucestershire. When he decided against joining Leicestershire he had written to me to tell me that he had been tempted by the County's offer and he would have liked to come to Leicester to captain the side – but he just couldn't face changing every day in the old pavilion and getting splinters in his feet when he went to the showers!

The recruitment policy changed quite dramatically and Leicestershire set a precedent by recruiting a high percentage of players from other counties. To a certain extent this policy had begun with the signing of players like Alan Wharton and Willie Watson but this trend accelerated very considerably. It is worth noting that in the 1950s 17 Leicestershire-born players played for the County, while only six played in the 1960s, four in the 1970s and five in the 1980s.

In 1965 Bill Ashdown, the former Kent opening bat and Leicestershire's coach for many years, was appointed chief scout and this in itself was a clear indication of the policy change. The ethics of this style of recruitment were queried by several counties but there was no doubt in my mind that if the County were ever going to be a force in the Championship then the playing staff had to be strengthened by substantial recruitment from outside Leicestershire, including overseas players.

It was, of course, important to do everything possible within the financial limitations of the Club to produce Leicestershire-born cricketers, but to concentrate all our recruitment resources on a Leicestershire youth development policy was idealistic and not realistic.

This is equally true today because although we have one of the most extensive youth development programmes in the country and we do everything possible to develop our own players, unfortunately the standard of club cricket in the county is so poor that the future well-being of the club will depend upon the success of the recruitment of both young and experienced players from elsewhere.

The outstanding signing which probably transformed the County more than any other was the acquisition of Tony Lock, who had been a friend of mine for a number of years. This great left-arm spinner, formerly of Surrey and England, had emigrated to Australia but was persuaded to return to English county cricket in 1965. Because he had a contract with a Lancashire League Club (a fact that was unknown to us at the time he signed the contract – we were threatened with legal action!) he played only in midweek matches in his first season but he captained the side in the following two summers.

The performances of the side improved and the advent of Lock as captain brought a much more determined approach by the team. There have been few cricketers who can have such a compulsive effect both on the game and a team as G. A. R. Lock did for us. He was an extremely strong driving force who imbued self-confidence in the other players. In his first year as captain the team moved up the Championship table to eighth and they finished joint second in 1967. There were high hopes for the following year but, sadly, Tony Lock was unable to return owing to his wife's ill-health.

However, the Club had gained considerable momentum both on and off the field and there were major playing acquisitions in the signings of Barry Knight from Essex, Graham McKenzie, the Australian Test bowler, and Ray Illingworth from Yorkshire.

The last two were signed in 1969, which also saw the introduction of the John Player League, a 40-overs competition on Sunday afternoons. Apart from providing a much needed cash injection into the game from sponsorship, this new style of county cricket drew large crowds and the fact that the matches were televised on BBC2 attracted perimeter advertising at county grounds throughout the country.

At the inception of the competition I was invited by John Player to be a 'consultant for cricket' and also during the year I was invited to be a member of the Chairman's Advisory Committee at Lord's – subsequently the TCCB Executive Committee – a Committee on which I have served continuously to the present day. My own role also changed at Leicestershire where I was officially designated Secretary and Team Manager.

However, the most significant event of 1969 was Ray Illingworth's move from Yorkshire to captain Leicestershire which began the most successful period in the Club's history. In Illy, I felt that I had a kindred spirit because, like me, his burning ambition as captain was to create success for his adopted county and most people believed we had the basic ingredients within the team to be in contention for one of the titles in the near future.

Although Illy's appointment as Leicestershire skipper had been greeted with apprehension in some quarters, his ability was soon recognised because in his first season he was invited to captain England. This was a blow in some senses to the County's ambitions, as for the next three years he played in only half the matches as he was away on international duty. Barry Knight also played for England during this period.

I must confess that Ray Illingworth's return to international cricket had not been anticipated because the recruitment policy had been based on recruiting either young players of potential or, alternatively, signing players whose international career was over or almost over – such as Tony Lock, Barry Knight and later, Ken Higgs.

However, 22 July 1972 was a real red letter day in the annals of Leicestershire cricket when the County beat Yorkshire by five wickets, and won the first Benson & Hedges Cup. It was a wonderful moment for Illy and myself to stand on the balcony at Lord's holding the trophy aloft in front of many thousands of jubilant Leicestershire supporters.

Apart from winning the cup the team were runners-up in the John Player League, finished sixth in the Championship and throughout this wonderful summer played magnificent cricket.

During the next few years the team won the Benson & Hedges Cup for the second time and were also losing finalists, they won the John Player League twice and were runners-up twice and in 1975 Leicestershire not only won the County Championship for the first time but also won the Benson & Hedges Cup – and as the Second XI won the Warwick Pool Under-25 Competition, it was a season to remember! At this point it was the first time a County had won two major trophies in one season, and to complete the triumph the Australians were also beaten by the County for the first time since 1888.

Of course, the credit for much of the success goes to Ray Illingworth. For the ten years he was the Club skipper we had a wonderful working relationship and they were the vintage years of Leicestershire cricket. There is no doubt that during this decade we had several star performers but basically success was achieved through good captaincy and all-round teamwork both on and off the field, because generally we worked with a small staff so that the budget was well-balanced.

One of Ray Illingworth's great advantages was that the team grew up and matured together, and players such as Roger Tolchard, Brian Davison, Barry Dudleston, John Steele, Jack Birkenshaw and Chris Balderstone all developed into top-class cricketers. Terry Spencer, cricketer/footballer Graham Cross, Norman McVicker and Mickey Norman also played a vital part.

Unfortunately, as the team matured together so they grew old together and after Ray Illingworth departed to take up the post of team manager back at his native Yorkshire the Club entered into a difficult period of transition.

Nevertheless, Andy Roberts, the West Indian and former Hampshire star, was recruited and David Gower, whom I signed as a 16-year-old player when he was playing for Loughborough Town, soon graduated to international status. Of all the players I have signed I think that David has given me more pleasure as a batsman than any other.

He joined the staff in 1975 and had two periods of captaincy – 1983–86 and 1988–89. He has played in 114 Tests and scored 8,081 runs and he is the only England captain ever to lead a team to a series win in India after being one match down. He also led England to a resounding Ashes win in 1985. During his career with the Club he played in 196 matches and scored 10,685 first-class runs for the County.

David Gower's contribution to cricket in Leicestershire and for England was outstanding and his grace and elegance at the crease gave spectators enormous pleasure. He is a world-class cricketer and a friend and I was deeply sorry when he decided to leave the Club for personal reasons at the end of the 1988 season.

In 1985 under his captaincy we won the Benson & Hedges Trophy for the third time after a match-winning innings by Peter Willey. This was the last title won by the Club and under David's captaincy there was a period of unrest in the dressing

room which culminated in several players leaving. Because of this the Committee decided to reorganise the administrative structure of the Club and appoint a Cricket Manager to be specifically responsible for all aspects of the playing of the game including the retention and recruitment of staff. It was believed that such an appointment would reinforce David Gower's authority as captain and also stop the movement of high-calibre players away from the Club. Unfortunately, the appointment of the Australian coach Bob Simpson as Cricket Manager was not a success and during his two years with the Club David Gower, Winston Benjamin, Chris Lewis, Jon Agnew and Peter Willey all departed for various reasons.

In spite of these set-backs I believe we can still look forward to the next decade and there are some exciting plans on the drawing board.

The Club has really good foundations – during the last 20 years the average position in the championship has been sixth, the ground has been completely redeveloped into one of the best county grounds in the country and there are substantial capital reserves.

I have had a wonderful career with Leicestershire and I can look back for over 40 years and truly say that I have enjoyed my work immensely. Throughout all this time I have been able to look forward to the future with optimism – and I am now looking forward to more success in the not too distant future.

(Patrick Eagar)

A SLOW START

'ON SALE, THE ARTICLES of the Game of Cricket as settled by the several Cricket Clubs particularly that of the Star and Garter in Pall Mall (with a neat Copperplate of the Representation of the Game), Price 6d.'

This advertisement appeared in the *Leicester and Nottingham Journal* of 20 August 1774 and is the first known reference to cricket in the local Leicester press. The advertisement goes on to state that the articles are available from J. Gregory and J. Ireland in Leicester. Gregory was the publisher of the newspaper in which the advertisement appeared and Ireland a Leicester bookseller.

The first reference to a match in the county comes two years later when a fixture between Barrow (on Soar) and Mountsorrel is announced, to be played at Barrow on 9 September. No score of this match was published in the press.

The first mention of cricket in the two counties bordering Leicestershire on its southern side had been somewhat earlier – Northamptonshire in 1741 and Warwickshire in 1751. This sequence is in line with the general pattern of cricket's spread northwards from its beginnings in the South East of the country 150 years before, but the development of cricket in Leicestershire itself did not build up from south to north. Rather did it flourish in the towns and villages north of the county town, whilst those to the south remained backwaters.

The reason for this was the speed at which cricket took root in Nottingham and a great rivalry developed not only between Nottingham and Leicester, but amongst the villages on either side of the Notts–Leics border.

Both Leicestershire and Nottinghamshire had a large hosiery industry, which was based on framework knitters having machines in their homes. This gave the potential cricket players more flexibility in their working hours than their opposite numbers engaged as agricultural labourers, so the framework knitters became more adept at cricket. Thus Nottinghamshire and Leicestershire improved their standard of cricket beyond that of the more agriculturally based neighbouring counties.

In the South of England the top cricketers had received encouragement and, indeed, in the more illustrious cases, employment with the cricket-loving landed gentry, the Dukes of Richmond and Dorset and the Earl of Tankerville being three such in Sussex, Kent and Surrey. Although neither Leicestershire nor Nottinghamshire were so fortunate in their landowners, their little neighbour, Rutland, had a famous cricketing peer, the Earl of Winchilsea, whose country seat was at Burley on the Hill, just outside Oakham.

George Finch, the 9th Earl of Winchilsea, was born in London in 1752 and was educated at Eton. In the 1770s he was involved in the American War of Independence and it was not until the following decade that his name appears in the great matches of the day. In 1786 he was elected a member of the Hambledon Club and in 1787 was the main supporter of Thomas Lord when the latter laid out his cricket ground. In July 1790 he brought many of the famous cricketers of the day, including the heroes of Hambledon, to Burley and on his private ground there staged an All England *v* Hampshire match. The fixture was repeated in 1791, when two further games were played, Old Etonians *v* MCC and MCC *v* Leicestershire.

This last game was the first in which a team entitled specifically 'Leicestershire' took the field. The eleven were: W. Clarke, R. Stringer, W. Barsby, – Judd, – Line, – Davis, J. Rowell, – Graham, T. Neill, – Barrett, T. Watts. (Another version gives T. Nutt in place of T. Neill). The local county lost by an innings. The Earl himself turned out for the MCC. Haygarth in his brief biography of the Earl in *Scores & Biographies* (Vol 1, p.63) does not make any comment on the ability of the Earl, apart from the fact that he made some good scores in the best matches. Likewise Pycroft in *The Cricket Field*, though mentioning Winchilsea several times gives no detail as to his style.

In July 1792 another week of cricket was arranged at Burley, commencing again with England *v* Hampshire, followed by MCC *v* XXII Of Nottingham and finishing with Nottingham *v* Leicestershire and Rutland. Leicestershire and Rutland won by four wickets, despite the fact that Nottingham gained a first-innings lead. Mark Graham hit 49 in the winners' second innings. The Earl, who had played in the two matches earlier in the week, did not appear in this game. In 1793 the cricket week started with England *v* Surrey, the Earl turning out for Surrey and when this game finished in the middle of the third day, a match, the Earl's XI *v* R. Leigh's XI was played which lasted three and a half days – there was no Leicestershire match.

After this matches at Burley continued on a more parochial scale and the 9th Earl died in 1826.

In so far as any bona fide cricket club existed in the county, the first report of one occurs as early as 1780, when the press announced: 'A meeting of a Cricket Club in Leicester on May 29'.

Later in the same year, the town of Leicester features in a reported match for the first time, playing Loughborough on St Margaret's Pasture in Leicester. The Leicester Club seems to have been firmly based, for in 1781 it played matches against Melton Mowbray, which they lost by 16 runs, and in September Nottingham. The Nottingham side were dismissed for 50 and the contemporary report continues:

> . . . the Nottingham Club then began to bowl what are called Sheffield Bowls, which every lover of the game have complained of as unmanly in the extreme. The Leicester Club having no chance of giving the same in return thought of an expedient which they conceived would make them return to that manly mode of play which was shown by both clubs the first day to the satisfaction of every spectator. On the first ball being delivered on Tuesday morning the Leicester batsman fell with a leg on each side the stumps of his wicket and the ball passed wide of his leg at the distance of a yard and of the wicket at least a yard and a half, upon which the Nottingham umpire declared the man out, the Leicester umpire declared him in, the law was appealed to, notwithstanding which the Nottingham umpire persisted in his declaration; both umpires then called play, and at length the Nottingham Club refused to bowl any more against the youth who had been declared . . . thus ended the match.

Sheffield bowls are, it is presumed, wides, which at that time did not incur a run penalty.

In 1782 Nottingham issued a challenge to any neighbouring clubs and Leicester replied that they would play if Nottingham paid the debt owed from the 1781 Loughborough game. A meeting was arranged and terms were agreed, one of which was that each side name 15 men from whom the eventual eleven would be chosen. Leicester in the event named only 13, leaving two blanks. On the day arranged for the match – at Nottingham – Leicester arrived and the Nottingham backers found that the best five of their 15 were unable to come. Nottingham asked that they could pick an extra man to make up the eleven. Leicester refused. Nottingham then said they would play ten *v* eleven; Leicester again refused and the Nottingham supporters suggested that Leicester were only too glad to use any excuse to avoid losing. The match therefore did not take place.

The following year Melton Mowbray, rather than Leicester, played Nottingham. Melton lost both home and away. The match in Nottingham on 11 September began just after 9.00 am and finished at 4.00 pm. The Nottingham players wore green jackets, Melton wore white. 'An incredible number of spectators were present who conducted themselves with becoming propriety, and to the honour of both parties the utmost harmony prevailed,' commented the *Nottingham Journal*, probably having a dig at the disharmony between Leicester and Nottingham during the two previous summers.

Haines (no initial known) carried his bat through the Melton second innings to score 16 not out, having been the not out batsman at the end of the first innings.

The Leicester Club played Syston in 1785 – no matches were reported in the county in 1784 – and the only game recorded in 1786 was against Oakham, which Leicester won by an innings.

Still ignoring Nottingham, Leicester arranged a match with Coventry in 1787. The game was played at Hinckley and after very low scoring in the first two innings – Coventry made 23, Leicester only 13, Leicester hit 132 in their second and won by 45 runs. The Coventry supporters, or at least a gang of them from Nuneaton and Bedworth, went on the rampage. Fighting broke out in the centre of Hinckley and the shopkeepers put shutters up at their windows. The *Birmingham Gazette* ended its dramatic report with: 'At present we have not heard of any lives being lost, though the weapons used in the contest were the most dangerous and alarming.'

When the Leicester players returned to their home town they were met by great crowds and the horses were unhitched from the carriages, so that the crowd itself could pull the conveyances into the market place.

The Leicester triumph was short lived – a month later Leicester were beaten by an innings by Melton Mowbray and the Birmingham press printed some sarcastic lines contrasting the manner in which the defeated Leicester cricketers arrived in Leicester after this reverse, compared with the reception when they beat Coventry.

Nottingham sent a challenge to Leicester in 1788, but Leicester would only agree to a match at home, so the challenge went unheeded. The Leicester Club also challenged the rest of Leicestershire, but this came to nothing. However, despite the riot of 1787, Leicester did arrange a match with Coventry. The match, at Walcote, near Lutterworth on 22, 23 and 24 September was ruined by umpiring disputes. John Nedham, presumably the Leicester captain, hurled abuse at his own umpire for wrongful decisions – the umpire resigned and a fresh man was appointed, who was not as efficient. William Clarke, Leicester's best batsman was given out 'hit ball twice', though he was defending his own wicket when he struck the ball a second time. Nedham ordered him to continue batting. The match temporarily ended, but was resumed a few weeks later – the authorities agreed that Clarke could continue his innings and Leicester eventually won by 28 runs.

John Nedham, who caused much of the controversy, was a well-known satirist and writer and, it seems, wrote much of the cricket reportage printed in the *Leicester Journal* about this time. He died in 1791 aged 30.

After a break of seven years, Leicester resumed their fixture with Nottingham in 1789. Two matches were arranged, both to take place at Loughborough. Leicester were beaten in the first game by an innings, not a single Leicester batsman reaching double figures. The return began on 5 October. After two days a dispute broke out, but on 2 November the incomplete game was continued and Leicester won by one run. For years after it was considered the most exciting match ever staged and was recalled as 'The Odd Notch Match.' The player mainly responsible for the victory was Mark Graham, who not only took the vital final Nottingham wicket, but captured four others in the last innings, as well as having a catch and stumping (the names of the bowlers in this latter case not being given).

Apart from the matches already mentioned at Burley, little Leicester cricket was reported during the 1790s and the next important match outside those arranged by the Earl of Winchilsea was the Leicester *v* Nottingham game of 1800.

This game, played on St Margaret's Pasture, Leicester, was a disaster for the home club, who were dismissed for 15 and 8, the latter total being the lowest ever recorded in a match of such standing. Nottingham won by an innings. Mark Graham was still in the Leicester side, but no batsmen of stature had been found to replace William Clarke, John Nedham and William Barsby. The morale of Leicestershire cricket was further dented later in the same year when the Nottingham town of Bingham easily out-played Melton Mowbray, the game taking place at Hose, mid-way between the two towns.

Matters for the Leicester Club did not improve in 1801. Major Morgan on behalf of the Mountsorrel Club challenged the Leicester Club and the village team won by four wickets; Morgan however engaged William Chapman of Nottingham and it was Chapman who was the architect of Mountsorrel's victory. Whilst it would appear that the standard of Leicester cricket was falling in relation to that of Nottingham, a test of the latter in 1803 showed that the Midlands were still a long way behind the cricketers of the South.

Major Morgan took it upon himself to arrange a match against Hampshire at Lord's in July – Morgan is reputed to have backed his side for 1,000 guineas. Morgan picked eight Nottingham men, including William Chapman, two Leicester players, namely himself and Robert Stringer, and finally Lord Frederick Beauclerk, the leading all-rounder in England. Beauclerk made the highest individual score, 74, but the combined Nottingham and Leicester side lost by an innings.

The two main matches of the Leicester Club in 1803 both ended in defeat, first at the hands of the Nottingham village of Radcliffe-on-Trent and second by Loughborough.

The Napoleonic Wars caused cricket to be played much less frequently during the period from 1804 to 1810, only a handful of matches being reported in the Leicester press. In 1813 the Leicester *v* Nottingham fixture was revived. Leicester fielded a genuinely county side, and Nottingham were over-optimistic in allowing Leicester 22 men against 11. Leicester won by an innings and the places from which the various Leicester players came were recorded. To give an idea of the towns and villages which contributed to the victory, the complete list of players is as follows:

Barrow on Soar: J. Dix; W. Sharpe; W. Lovett.

Hoton: W. Clarke.

Leicester: J. Wale; R. Newton; W. Harris; C. Anderson; J. Moore; J. Dent.

Loughborough: W. Jennings; J. Clarke; R. Eddowes; W. Wilkins.

Mountsorrel: J. Boam; J. Antill.

Quordon: J. Phipps.

Seagrave: W. Bakewell.

Sileby: J. Taylor; W. Taylor.

Whitwick: W. Moore; W. Ainsworth.

J. Moore of Leicester made the highest score for the Twenty-two and also took most wickets. He had first played for Leicester against Barrow in 1810 and was to continue in local matches for about 20 years.

There was another cricket festival at Burley in 1814, the principal match being Rutland *v* Nottingham; Rutland lost by an innings. Nottingham also played Barrow in the same year, Nottingham again proving victorious.

In 1815 Barrow combined with Mountsorrel to play Nottingham and the combination were allowed fifteen men, but were still unable to get the upper hand. The only local to come out of the game with much credit was J. Antill, who took eight Nottingham wickets in their first innings. The match was played at Bunny, the Notts village on the Loughborough road.

The Leicester Club with W. Sharpe of Barrow played a combined eleven of Radcliffe on Trent and Cropwell Bishop on The Forest at Nottingham in 1816. Sharpe with innings of 45 and 16 not out was easily the best bat, whilst J. Moore took most wickets; Leicester won by seven wickets.

There was a cricket festival at Burley and a note in the press states that Lord Winchilsea (aged 64) played in a match in place of an absentee – this was the last recorded appearance of one of cricket's most famous patrons as an active player. Of equal interest, the *Stamford Mercury* records at Burley a match between Oakham School and Uppingham School. Uppingham at that time had some 50 boys only and by agreement Oakham's two best players were barred, but Uppingham won and Oakham immediately challenged them to a return. Uppingham declined – in such a manner that the editor of the *Mercury* refused to publish their comments, saying they would cause ill-feeling.

The great history of Uppingham Cricket written by W. S. Patterson and published in 1909 makes no definite mention of any Uppingham matches before the 1830s, but clearly this cricketing public school was earlier on the scene. Uppingham School again fielded an eleven at Burley in 1817, so the match against Oakham was not an isolated example.

The Leicester Club seems to have been in disarray about this period and several of the other clubs in the county could boast of sides as strong, if not stronger, than that of the county town. No documents seem to have survived which give any details of the Leicester Club of this era and in 1818 the press speaks of a 'New Leicester Club'; one assumes the old organisation collapsed. Around the same year a County Gentlemen's Cricket Club seems to have appeared, or re-appeared.

In 1820 the County Gentlemen played both Barrow and the New Leicester Town Club. The Gentlemen lost both matches, but their side contains several cricketers of some note. Captain Richard Cheslyn of Langley Priory, aged 22, was in the 7th Hussars. A useful all-round cricketer at local level, he promoted many matches, including the famous North *v* South match at Leicester in 1836. Although from a well-to-do family he failed to prosper financially, perhaps through his cricket, and came down in the world. He died in 1858 in Shelford Hills, Newton, near Radcliffe on Trent.

The highest scorer for the Gentlemen in their game with the town was John Earl, a left-handed batsman from Quordon. He moved to Manchester and his name is later found in the Manchester team. Three members of the Packe family of Prestwold Hall also appeared for the Gentlemen. The family were to continue to be strong supporters of the county's cricket for many years to come.

The *Nottingham Journal* of 14 July 1820 notes: 'The admirers of this noble game will be highly gratified to hear that a County Club has been formed at Loughborough comprising among its members, Lord Grey, Mr Packe jun of Prestwold, Mr Osbaldeston, Mr Cheslyn etc. They meet twice a week in a close adjoining this town.'

This is clearly the County Gentlemen's Club referred to above. At this point therefore Leicestershire cricket, with two new organisations seemed to be set for a prosperous future.

Nottingham however were not too impressed and in 1821 when Leicester challenged their northern neighbour, Nottingham allowed Leicester 16 men to 11. The match was played in Leicester, but not on the usual field, Abbey Meadow being used instead. The match which 'excited much interest', was won by the home side with an innings to spare. Leicester immediately challenged Nottingham to a return, on even terms. Nottingham accepted, then withdrew and no contest took place.

No external matches were played in 1822, though the two clubs played each other twice – the Gentlemen won the first, John Earl making the highest score, whilst the Town Club won the return by an innings, Henry Davis of Groby hitting 42. In the autumn came another notice concerning the formation of a new club, 'on the principles of Marylebone and similar to the Notts Club lately established. Should they succeed, it is supposed that Earl Howe will take the lead.'

The return with Nottingham finally took place in August 1823 on The Forest for 60 guineas. Leicester fielded 14 men, and were 20 behind on first innings, then a brilliant innings by Joseph Dennis for Nottingham, scoring an unbeaten 50 in three hours, put his side in the lead by 157 and Leicester lost by exactly 100 runs.

Not put off by this reverse, Leicester went further afield and in 1824 played Sheffield for the first time, Sheffield having long been rivals of Nottingham. The match was on the Darnall Ground at Sheffield, which at this time was probably the best laid out venue in the north. The four-day game ended in victory for Leicester by a single run, John Earl once more being the highest scorer for his side.

Perhaps inspired by this victory and the arrangements they found at Darnall, yet another new County Club was set up and laid out a ground at Wharf Street in Leicester. This ground was to be used for over 30 years. On 20 June 1825 the opening game at the new venue was the County Club *v* Leicester, and then the County Club went to Nottingham to oppose the Sherwood Forest Club for 200 sovereigns. Leicester lost this fixture, but won the return. In August Sheffield came to Leicester and with E. Vincent making 114 not out won by an innings; Leicester however proved victorious when they went to Darnall.

The Leicester Club engaged the Hampshire cricketer, T. C. Howard, as a coach. Howard, in his mid-forties, was one of the best all-rounders of his day and was 'indefatigable in his endeavours to eradicate the old systems and bring them as near perfection as possible.'

Nottingham in 1826 decided to challenge the combined forces of Sheffield and Leicester. There were six Sheffielders in the side and five from Leicester: Shelton, G. Owston, W. Squires, H. Davis and Tom Gamble. The last named was the younger brother of William Gamble, born in Leicester in 1800. He made 61, but the whole of the match was dwarfed by Tom Marsden of Sheffield who scored 227 out of 379. The Nottingham Club was overwhelmed by this incredible total.

A cricket song was written to celebrate the event and the last of thirteen verses links Leicester's Gamble with Marsden:

> For Marsden and Gamble we filled up our glasses,
> As brimful as when we toast favourite lasses,
> And then drank success to all Cricketers true,
> Who with honour this noble diversion pursue.

In September a combined Sheffield and Leicester XXII opposed XI of England at Darnall. Leicester had just four representatives: W. Shelton, G. Owston, T. Gamble and J. Thomas. The XXII won by six wickets, but the Leicester four played little part in the victory. On the way to Sheffield, the England side had played at Wharf Street, when 16 Leicester players had been in the XXII and Tom Gamble had scored 31, with the home side winning by an innings.

The Leicester Club engaged George Brown, the Sussex cricketer, to coach them in 1827. Brown was a fast under-arm bowler, as well as a capable batsman. There were no matches with either Sheffield or Nottingham that season, but one significant event was the first recorded century by a Leicester cricketer. G. W.

Owston of the Leicester Club hit 118 in about seven hours against a combined Belgrave and Thurmaston XI. Owston had been born in the county town in 1801 and was Governor of the Borough Gaol. He died in 1848.

When Leicester resumed fixtures with Sheffield in 1828, they engaged Fuller Pilch as a 'given man', perhaps to counteract the brilliance of Tom Marsden. Pilch, the Norfolk-born batsman, was then aged 25 and playing for Bury St Edmunds was beginning to build up his reputation. In the 1830s he was regarded as the best batsman in England. Not only did he make a major contribution with the bat in both matches, but took most wickets. Marsden hit 86 in the return at Darnall, but Leicester won both games. The season also saw the first North *v* South match (though the title was Yorkshire, Leicester and Nottingham *v* England). Leicester had two representatives, W. Shelton and W. Gamble, and H. Davis was also picked but failed to appear, Charles Dearman of Yorkshire taking his place. The South (or England) won by a large margin.

The victories over Sheffield, and the fact that Sheffield, mainly through Marsden's batting, beat Nottingham twice, encouraged Leicester to challenge the Nottingham Club in 1829, but without employing Pilch. Defeats were suffered in both matches – by 123 runs at Wharf Street and 73 on The Forest. Arthur Haygarth in *Scores & Biographies* notes after the second defeat: 'After 1829, the veteran Leicester club never played together for various reasons.' E. E. Snow makes the same comment in his history, but does not elaborate.

The County Gentlemen's Club continued its existence, but the type of professional set-up which flourished both in Sheffield and Nottingham was no longer encouraged in Leicester. William Whitehead, who had taken over the management of the Wharf Street Ground in 1828, hired out the facilities to amateur sides and for various social functions. The rather dubious reputations of many professional cricketers, who made money betting on individual performances and match results, no doubt made the respectable middle class steer clear of such company.

In July 1836, the Rev John Bradshaw scored 198 not out for the County Gentlemen *v* Stamford, carrying his bat through the whole innings and being on the field throughout the match – this was a new record score for the Wharf Street Ground. Bradshaw came from Barrow on Soar and was in the Cambridge Eleven in 1833 and 1834 – his innings was against inferior bowling, but even so deserves recording.

A fortnight before Bradshaw's innings, the North had played

the South at Lord's for the first time. No Leicester players had been included in the Northern side, but Captain Cheslyn signed an agreement with the MCC that a return match would be played on the Wharf Street Ground. When news of this agreement became known, the Nottingham cricketing fraternity were up in arms – six Nottingham players had turned out for the North, the team being completed by two Yorkshiremen, two from Cambridge and Pilch of Norfolk. A public protest meeting was held in Nottingham, but the MCC would not go back on their agreement with Captain Cheslyn and the fact that the Wharf Street ground was better appointed than the public racecourse at Nottingham did nothing to further the Nottingham claim.

The match duly took place on 22, 23, 24 and 25 August 1836, the South winning mainly due to an incredible century by Alfred Mynn, the Kent amateur. He went in in the second innings with the score 91 for three and carried out his bat for 125, but was so injured by repeatedly being hit about the legs from the fast bowling of Sam Redgate, that it was touch and go whether he would have to have his leg amputated – he returned to London strapped on top of the stage coach and missed the whole of the 1837 season.

No Leicester cricketers played in this game, but Captain Cheslyn was greatly to be admired for his efforts in arranging it and apart from the Nottingham spectators everyone was delighted with the whole affair. It might be said that, even though over 150 years have gone by, this is still the most famous cricket match played in the county.

It was a pity that Captain Cheslyn seemed unable to motivate the leading cricketers of the county, for both 1837 and 1838 were blank years so far as 'inter-county' Leicestershire cricket was concerned. In 1839 home and away games took place against Sheffield – Cheslyn played in the first, on the Hyde Park Ground at Sheffield, scoring 1 and 0, but not in the return. There were several cricketers of note in the Leicester side, but three of them were imports from the Burton on Trent Club. Abram Bass was a 35-year-old solicitor from Burton and a great patron of cricket in that town; G. M. Kettle was born in Leicestershire, at Overseal, but most of his cricket was with Burton and he was also a member of MCC; the professional, A. Girling, also came from Burton and later made his name in Manchester cricket. John Hall, who played at Sheffield, was Nottingham born, but moved to Leicester at the age of 12 – he was to move on to Bradford and many years later played for Yorkshire. However one genuine Leicester player did distinguish himself, making the highest score for his side in both matches, Sam Dakin. Born in Sileby in 1808, he was a very useful all-rounder and Leicestershire cricket would have benefited to a large degree if a patron had been able to pay to keep his talent within the county. Unfortunately this was not the case. For four years, including the one in question, he was with the South Derbyshire Club. He was four years in Gloucestershire and then was with the MCC at Lord's from 1847 to 1855. From about 1850 onwards he lived in Cambridge and was latterly a coach at the university.

Leicester lost the game at Hyde Park, but were victorious at Wharf Street, their best bowler being Henry Deacon. When the Northern Counties opposed MCC at Lord's in 1840, Deacon, together with Dakin and Kettle, represented the Counties, as did Bass, and there was an amusing incident whilst Bass and Dakin were batting. Dakin hit the ball which was fielded and thrown back, but dislodged Bass's hat in the process. The ball disappeared, and was found in the lining of the hat!

Despite being well represented in this game, Leicester failed to arrange any major matches either in 1840 or the following summer.

Aside from Kettle, Dakin and Deacon, several other worthwhile native cricketers emerged during the 1840s, among them the Rev Edward Elmhirst of Enderby, an excellent wicketkeeper and powerful batsman, and the Rev Richard Seddon, born in the county town. Both represented Cambridge, as did E. S. E. Hartopp of Thurnby, whose country seat was at Clipsham Hall, near Oakham. Seddon and Hartopp were both good enough to appear in the powerful Notts side of the 1840s. T. C. Goodrich was perhaps even more talented. He was born at Stamford in 1823 and became the best amateur lob bowler of his day and played for the Free Foresters as well as the Leicestershire Gentlemen.

In theory therefore Leicestershire in the 1840s could put a 'firstclass' side into the field. William Barker had taken the lease of the Wharf Street Ground in 1840 and was apparently keen to stage good quality cricket matches there, but a Leicestershire side failed to materialise, except in a very haphazard manner. Home and away games were arranged with Nottingham Amateurs in 1845 and Leicester won the fixture at Wharf Street due to the batting of William Garrat who hit 66 not out – Garrat was a Nottingham batsman, presumably helping Leicester as a given man.

The major visitor of the season at Wharf Street for several summers was MCC, playing either Midland Counties or Northern Counties, and the Leicestershire representatives, such as

Dakin, Seddon and Hartopp usually gave a good account of themselves.

In 1846, the Nottingham bowler, William Clarke, founded his All England Eleven and for more than a decade this powerful wandering troupe captured the public's imagination, taking the interest away from inter-county cricket. The side visited Wharf Street during August 1847 and beat Twenty of Leicestershire by an innings. George Parr, who was to become the leading batsman in the country hit a century for the visitors.

The Leicester Club did venture onto new ground in 1848, playing two matches against Manchester. Away from home, Leicester found themselves so far in arrears on first innings that they gave up the match; in the game at Wharf Street they fared much better and won by three runs.

The Rev R. T. King and Elmhirst both played for the Gentlemen v Players at Lord's in 1848 and both made useful contributions to their side's victory. R. T. King was born in Melton Mowbray and at this time was in the Cambridge Eleven. A brilliant fieldsman at point, he was also a hard-hitting batsman and fast round-arm bowler. In 1849 he made his debut for Leicestershire and though his appearances in major matches at Lord's ceased when he took holy orders, he played regularly for Leicestershire Gentlemen. He was also a founder member of the Cambridge Quidnuncs.

For the first time in the 19th century, Leicestershire opposed MCC in 1851, the county being reinforced by three given men, F. Tinley, W. Buttress and Butler Parr. Each side claimed a victory.

The twins, Alfred and Arthur Payne, made occasional appearances in Leicestershire matches during the 1850s. Both obtained their blues at Oxford, Alfred captaining the University in 1856. Born in Leicester, Alfred obtained an appointment as Secretary to the Earl of Stamford at Enville – the Earl being a very keen patron of cricket. Arthur spent much of his time in France, where he was interested in painting.

Apart from Barker's ground at Wharf Street, a second 'professional' ground was set up in the 1850s. This was Tyler's Ground at Loughborough and both grounds were in regular use for the All England Eleven and its rival (created in 1852) the United All England Eleven. Throughout the decade these Odds matches were the principal cricket fixtures staged in the county. The County Gentlemen's Club played about half a dozen matches a year against opponents from outside the shire – South Derbyshire and Gentlemen of Notts being the major opposition. The beginnings of the modern County Championship were struggling into life, due to the very powerful club being built up at The Oval. Sussex and Kent, the two counties with histories going back to the 1820s in a continuous thread, were the main contenders against Surrey. Of the Midland counties only Nottinghamshire and Cambridgeshire were capable of making a realistic challenge, whilst Yorkshire and Lancashire, based on Sheffield and Manchester, were evolving slowly into County Clubs of importance. For the rest, most were, like Leicestershire, Gentlemen's County Clubs with weak organisations who were generally satisfied when they played their immediate neighbours.

As mentioned before the one real cricketing asset the county possessed was the Wharf Street Ground run by William Barker. In 1860 even this was to vanish. Barker gave up the lease in the winter of 1859–60 and Edward Murrell took over the running of the ground, but in November 1860 the ground and adjoining land was put up for sale and fell prey to the builders as the town of Leicester expanded.

The last match played on the ground was Leicestershire *v* All England, the county fielding 22 men. The home side won by an innings, with the Rev Alfred Payne making the highest score, but F. P. Miller, the Surrey amateur, who was playing for Leicestershire without any qualification, took twelve wickets. R. A. H. Mitchell, the Etonian cricketer, appeared in the Leicester side. A brilliant batsman, he went on to Oxford and captained the University for three years. Born at Enderby Hall he would have proved an enormous asset to Leicestershire cricket, but took up a post at Eton in 1866 and remained there for some 30 years.

Apart from the occasional visit of the All England Eleven, Leicestershire cricket assumed a very parochial stance through the 1860s – in *Lillywhite's Cricketers' Companion* of 1867, for example, not a single Leicester club is featured. In *Lillywhite's Cricketers' Annual* of 1873, when many more local clubs have their details entered, only Market Harborough CC is given. The Gentlemen of Leicestershire Club was resuscitated about 1868 but its matches were few. Victoria Park, which was principally used as a racecourse, became the main Leicester cricket ground in 1866 and a sign of better times ahead for the county's cricket came in 1873 when Leicestershire opposed MCC at Victoria Park, after the county had played at Lord's with all their expenses paid by the premier club.

The men behind these matches were F. W. Gardiner (Secretary of Leicester CC) and R. Clements (Secretary of the Leicester Cricket Association). Both matches resulted in victories by the county, the Lord's win being by a single wicket and that at Victoria Park by seven wickets.

The two bowlers who were mainly responsible for Leicestershire's creditable performances against MCC were the professionals, Bishop and Randon. At 41, George Bishop was coming to the end of his career. A round-arm bowler who could vary his pace, he had spent some seasons as a professional in Lancashire, but was a native of Loughborough and he represented his town against the All England Eleven for some 20 years. Randon – known as Frederick J., though the initial was used only to distinguish him from another of the same name – was born in Nottinghamshire but had moved to Hathern as a youth. He had had trials for his native county in 1869, 1870 and 1871 and made his debut for the Notts 1st XI in the last-named year. In 1873 he was the coach at Wellington College. His fast bowling for Leicestershire so impressed MCC that he was offered an engagement at Lord's for 1874, where he remained until 1880. In 1881 he met with a serious accident from which he never recovered and he died at Hathern in 1883 aged 37. His brother, Charles, was also a useful player and appeared for Leicestershire, as did his son, Fred.

Batting honours in the 1873 MCC matches went to the brothers Marriott from Cotesbach near Lutterworth. The elder of the two was Charles, who had been in the Winchester XI of 1867 and obtained his blue at Oxford in 1871, when he was described as 'a steady and good bat with strong defence; a splendid field and catch at leg. Has been known to bowl slow-round with success.' Charles Marriott captained the 1873 county side and continued as its leader until 1885. He later became President of the County Club and for several years served on the MCC Committee. J. M. Marriott was five years younger than Charles; he went to Winchester and Oxford, but failed to obtain his blue. A third brother, G.S., was at Winchester in 1873, and was to make his debut for Leicestershire the following year. He was awarded his blue in 1878.

When MCC came to Leicester in 1874 they were again defeated, Randon, Bishop and Charles Marriott being the architects of victory. E. Holmes was now the Secretary of the Leicestershire Cricket Association; he was later to be Chief Constable of the County. Under his leadership, in 1875, the county arranged home and away matches with Lancashire. *Lillywhite's Companion* notes in a brief feature on Leicestershire: 'A new aspirant to county cricket fame, and one not devoid of amateur talent, nor yet of pluck, as evinced by the following opening matches.'

Apart from Leicestershire, the only counties featured in the

Companion that year were the 'first-class' counties, namely Nottinghamshire, Yorkshire, Sussex, Lancashire, Gloucestershire, Surrey, Kent, Middlesex, Derbyshire and Hampshire, in that order. The rival *Lillywhite's Annual* includes the ten 'first-class' counties and then under a section headed 'Minor Counties' gives Leicestershire, Northamptonshire and Warwickshire.

The first match with Lancashire, staged on Leicester Racecourse was drawn, but when they went to Old Trafford, Leicestershire lost by an innings. *Wisden's Almanack* does not have a feature on Leicestershire in its 1876 edition, but it includes the full scores of both games under 'Lancashire' and comments after the Old Trafford defeat: 'but that (defeat) is no reason why Leicestershire men should not try to lick the Lancastrians in 1876.' The journalists of the day were keen to encourage counties to build strong county cricket clubs.

Arnold 'Bobby' Rylott first represented Leicestershire at Manchester. A fast left-arm bowler he was a native of Grantham, but had qualified for Leicester by residence and in 1875 was on the staff at Lord's. He was to prove one of the leading figures for the county right through the 1880s and turned in some excellent performances for MCC. His complete first-class record of 456 wickets at 11.69 runs each stands testament to his ability and no doubt he would have reached 1,000 wickets if Leicestershire had been in the County Championship during his career. A second professional appearing for the county against Lancashire was John Parnham of Bottesford. Like Rylott he bowled left-arm, but slow to medium. Aged 18, he was more than 17 years younger than Rylott, whom he joined on the MCC staff in 1883 following a sensational first-class debut. He played for the United England XI against the Australians in 1882 and took 12 wickets in the match. Four years later he hit the headlines by helping to add 157 runs for the last wicket for North *v* South at Lord's.

The encouragement the Leicester authorities received from the press was outweighed however by the lack of a good enclosed venue. When the centre of the Racecourse in Victoria Park was used the only way gate money could be taken was by surrounding the playing area with canvas fencing, which was not ideal. However the county possessed a very enthusiastic cricket patron, A. J. Hamel, who was a leading light in the formation of the Leicestershire Cricket Ground Company, which was floated with 2,000 £10 shares for the specific purpose of building a cricket ground in Leicester. The company purchased 16 acres of land from the Duke of Rutland's estate at Grace Road, laid out a cricket ground, cycle and running tracks and erected a hotel, known as

Charles Marriott was captain of Leicestershire for 15 years prior to the County achieving first-class status. He was on the MCC Committee.

The Reverend George Strickland Marriott, the brother of Charles, played against the Australians at Grace Road in 1878 during his career with Leicestershire.

the Cricket Ground Hotel. A large members' stand was built, but initially no pavilion as such.

The purchase took place in September 1877 and by the following spring the ground was ready for use. M. Hawksworth was engaged as the groundsman and the Leicestershire Cricket Association, under the secretaryship of W. H. Bearman, arranged home and away matches with Northants and Notts, and home matches with Bedfordshire and the visiting Australians. This was much in advance of any other previous 'inter-county' fixture list organised by Leicestershire. Bearman began his season by copying his two northern neighbours and arranging a Colts Trial on Easter Monday.

It was very ambitious of Leicestershire to oppose Notts and the results were defeats by ten wickets at Trent Bridge and an innings at Grace Road; of the Leicestershire batsmen only John Wheeler came out of the games with any credit, opening the batting and being last out in the second innings at Leicester. Against Northants, Leicestershire fared much better, winning away and having the better of a draw at home. The Bedfordshire game was also drawn.

LEICESTERSHIRE *v* AUSTRALIANS

Played at Grace Road, Leicester, 15, 16 and 17 July 1878

AUSTRALIANS WON BY EIGHT WICKETS

LEICESTERSHIRE	FIRST INNINGS		SECOND INNINGS	
J. Wheeler	c Boyle b Spofforth	60	c Blackham b Spofforth	65
Mr A. Sankey	b Garrett	70	retired hurt	0
G. Panter	c Gregory b Garrett	20	b Bailey	32
Rev. G. S. Marriott	c Horan b Garrett	7	b Blackham	18
Mr J. Collier	not out	20	lbw b Boyle	6
J. Parnham	c Garrett b Spofforth	0	c Gregory b Garrett	0
J. Rodwell	b Garrett	4	c Bailey b Spofforth	6
H. Walter	c Allan b Spofforth	2	c Boyle b Spofforth	0
A. Rylott	run out	4	b Garrett	0
F. Randon	b Spofforth	2	lbw b Spofforth	0
G. Bishop	b Spofforth	0	not out	10
Extras	lb	4	b 5, lb 3	8
Total		193		145

BOWLING	O	M	R	W	O	M	R	W
Spofforth	27	4	60	5	8.1	2	26	4
Allan	24	9	44	0	11	4	23	0
Garrett	22	10	30	4	8	3	28	2
Boyle	18	8	27	0	16	8	21	1
Bailey	10	6	13	0	11	3	19	1
Horan	6	1	15	0	6	2	16	0
Blackham					3	1	4	1

AUSTRALIANS	FIRST INNINGS		SECOND INNINGS	
W. L. Murdoch	b Rylott	16	b Parnham	24
C. Bannerman	c Bishop b Rylott	15	run out	133
T. P. Horan	run out	1	not out	40
★D. W. Gregory	c Bishop b Parnham	23	not out	3
T. W. Garrett	b Randon	7		
F. R. Spofforth	c Marriott b Randon	7		
G. H. Bailey	c Panter b Randon	0		
F. E. Allan	c Rodwell b Parnham	5		
†J. McC. Blackham	not out	24		
J. Conway	c Bishop b Parnham	12		
H. F. Boyle	b Rylott	8		
Extras	b 8, lb 4	12	b 8, nb 2	10
Total		130	(2 wkts)	210

BOWLING	O	M	R	W	O	M	R	W
Rylott	42.3	25	45	3	30	11	66	0
Randon	27	14	39	3	12	4	30	0
Parnham	15	3	34	3	19	6	40	1
Bishop					6.2	3	12	0
Collier					4	1	6	0
Wheeler					4	0	26	0
Panter					3	0	20	0

★Captain; †Wicketkeeper

The major match however was clearly the one against the Australians and so keen were the Leicester authorities to set up the match that they were the first club to make a fixture with the tourists and to guarantee a lump sum in payment. The latter must have been a very courageous step by, presumably, the Cricket Ground Company. Fortunately for them the weather was kind. Nearly 12,000 spectators came on the first day and, winning the toss, the county made a brilliant start, Wheeler and Sankey adding 113 for the first wicket. The rest did little, but even so the Australians were 63 in arrears in the first innings. The tourists required 209 to win in the final innings and with Charles Bannerman batting well and reaching a century after a little over two hours at the wicket, the visitors won by an unexpectedly large margin.

Lillywhite's Annual printed the Leicestershire averages for the first time in its 1879 edition, covering 1878. Rylott, Randon and Parnham were the principal wicket-takers, Rylott's 30 wickets costing 13 runs each. All three have been noted previously; on the other hand the three batsmen to hit over 100 runs and average more than 20 were until now not so well known. John Wheeler was born in Sutton Bonington in 1844 and had no less than four trials in the Easter Colts match of his native county, Notts. He had moved to Loughborough as a boy and after failing to achieve much with Notts, made his Leicestershire debut against MCC in 1876, having been engaged with the Phoenix Park Club in Dublin between 1870 and 1875. In 1878 he was taken on the staff at Lord's and remained there for 31 years. He was to be one of Leicestershire's main batsmen through the 1880s and also a useful wicketkeeper. The second batsman was George Panter, who had spent some years as a professional in Scotland and was now aged 40 – he had played in the Colts match at Lord's in 1873, though he was aged 34. Born in Earl Shilton his appearances in Leicestershire cricket had been very restricted due to his professional engagements, but in Scottish cricket he had scored many runs, including 146 not out for the Players of Scotland in 1870. The third run-maker was the amateur Arthur Sankey, son of the rector of Stoney Stanton. *Lillywhite's Annual* describes him as 'a good steady bat and first-class field.' His membership of the Liverpool Stock Exchange prevented him making more than the occasional appearance for his county.

THE PRESENT COUNTY CLUB IS ESTABLISHED

ANXIOUS TO MAKE THE Grace Road Ground financially viable, the Company running the ground held a meeting on 25 February 1879 to form a 'Leicester Club', as distinct from the Leicester Town Club. The result of this meeting was a second gathering, on 25 March, which proposed and agreed to form 'Leicestershire County Cricket Club'. Edward Miles of Leicester was elected Honorary Secretary and C. T. Freer of Billesdon Coplow the Honorary Treasurer. Freer had played in important matches in the 1840s and was aged 73; of Miles little seems to be known.

The new County Club began its first year with a Colts Trial and arranged home and away fixtures with three counties – Sussex, Northants and Bedfordshire. The results, five wins and one loss were encouraging. On paper, to beat Sussex twice certainly looked impressive, that county being the only one of the three regarded as 'first-class'. *Lillywhite's Companion* in its notes on Sussex cricket of 1879, comments:

> The other (Sussex) contests – those with Leicestershire and Hertfordshire – are not ranked as first-class. Possibly in another year the classification of matches will have to be altered, for certainly the claims of Leicestershire to a regular place among the counties are entitled to consideration.

The first win over Sussex, at Grace Road, was due to the bowling of Rylott and Bottomore, who took nine and eight wickets respectively. William Bottomore, a fast right-arm bowler from Shepshed, was 34. He had had professional engagements all over Great Britain and for this reason was rarely available for his County. During the 1880s he went to America for a season or two and thus was unable to help Leicestershire. The County were forced to follow on by Sussex, but Alfred Buswell, the wicketkeeper, made an excellent 60 and when Sussex collapsed in their final innings, victory came by 45 runs. Buswell was the father of the Northants cricketer, W. A. Buswell.

In the return at Hove, the County were without Rylott, but Parnham took ten wickets and Charles Marriott, the captain hit 75, the only individual score above fifty in the entire game.

Rylott was largely responsible for the double success over Northants, with 12 wickets at Northampton and 11 at Leicester –

Rylott's 45 wickets in the season cost only 6 runs each, as did Parnham's 39. Of the regular players only the captain had a batting average above 17; he hit 338 in 9 completed innings, including a match against Uppingham Rovers.

Despite the five victories, the public showed only passing interest in the new County Club, their opponents were only modest and did not possess the drawing power of the top half-dozen sides: W. G. Grace's Gloucestershire was the most attractive county of the day, followed by Yorkshire, Notts and Lancashire. One of Leicestershire's problems from a financial viewpoint was that their side contained six or seven professionals, who needed paying, whereas the other lesser counties – Hertfordshire, Essex or Suffolk for example – got by with one or two, or at most three paid players, and therefore did not need money through the gate to keep afloat. Leicestershire were reported to have lost £1,000 in their first summer.

In 1880 the Australians came for their second visit. A definite decision to tour had not been made until the major counties had arranged their fixtures, so Leicestershire were very happy to oblige the Australians and fix a match for mid-July. After the great success of the 1878 visit it was to be hoped that this plum

Leicestershire in 1879, the year the present County Club was formed. Left to right, back: J. H. Wheeler, A. Buswell, N. J. Hughes-Hallett, Rev G. S. Marriott, G. Chamberlain (scorer). Front: J. Parnham, G. Panter, R. W. G. Stainton, C. Marriott, W. H. Hay, W. Bottomore, F. J. Randon.

fixture would improve the County's finances considerably. Unfortunately Charles Marriott was unavailable all summer and the wicketkeeper-batsman, Buswell, couldn't turn out against the tourists, so the County side was weak. To make matters worse, rain ruined the second and third days and the game was drawn much in favour of the visitors.

The two Sussex fixtures saw a victory to each side at home. Rylott and Parnham bowled unchanged through both innings at Grace Road, each having nine wickets. At the seaside good all-round cricket by Bottomore – 79 and 16 as well as five wickets – could not prevent an innings defeat. Somerset, who like Leicestershire were trying to break into first-class Championship cricket, came to Grace Road and beat the home side with ease, the Leicestershire batting being exceedingly poor; in the first innings not a single batsman reached double figures. There was no return match and Leicestershire's only other major game was at Lord's against MCC, another defeat due to poor batting. Rylott, Bottomore and Parnham were the only players to finish the summer with respectable figures.

The 1880 results combined with the financial restrictions to allow only one inter-county game in 1881 and that against the very modest Bedfordshire side. It was drawn due to rain. MCC were opposed home and away; at Lord's, for once, Leicestershire's batting came off, the County making 405 in their second innings. A. W. Crofts, the opening batsman, a native of the county town, hit 90 in excellent style with 13 fours. The 30-year-old Crofts had played for the County since 1872. Parnham, coming in low down, made 79. The match was drawn and when MCC came to Grace Road in August it was back to the more familiar pattern of batting collapse – Leicestershire all out for 76 and 89. Parnham made over half the runs in the second innings and he also picked up five wickets.

A development which the Leicester County Ground Company must have viewed with concern was the building of a second sports ground in Leicester. Extending to some ten acres it was situated in Belgrave Road and like the Grace Road ground had a running track surrounding the cricket pitch. The new ground was briefly home to the Tigers rugby club and Leicester Fosse FC, but was sold for building in 1901. In 1881 the All England Eleven opposed 16 of the county there, but the days when the AEE was a major attraction had gone.

The hopes of Leicestershire joining the County Championship dimmed further in 1882. The Club managed just a single inter-county game, against Norfolk. *Lillywhite's Annual* did not bother to give the Leicestershire averages any more and its usual feature on county cricket did not mention Leicestershire: even Rutland is given preference!

The Australians on their third visit to England came to Grace Road and found the County's batting as feeble as ever – all out 43, with Charles Marriott making 17, though it must be noted that Palmer and Spofforth, who destroyed Leicestershire, meted out similar treatment to counties with much more vaunted reputations. Both matches against MCC were drawn in favour of the premier club; at Lord's the County bowling suffered as William Barnes and William Midwinter created a new world record, adding 454 for the third wicket. Barnes' innings of 266 was the second highest, up to that date, ever made at Lord's and the 546 total was the highest ever by MCC at home. When MCC came to Grace Road (it should be noted that in *Wisden*, the venue is given as 'Aylestone Road' and reporters frequently described the Grace Road Ground as such, but it should not be confused with the later Aylestone Road Ground, not laid out at this time) matters were more even, only five runs separating the teams after the first innings. Leicestershire needed 44 to win with three wickets to fall when the two-day match ended.

Thomas Warren made his debut as a batsman for Leicestershire *v* Australians and failed to score in either innings; he was however to develop into the best run-getter in the County. A native of Hathern, he was the professional for Soar Valley CC in 1882. Later he spent three seasons in Lancashire and in 1887 was engaged at Grace Road. The magazine *Cricket* noted in 1889: 'Full of confidence, he stands up to every kind of bowling without fear, and when set is a dangerous batsman, hitting all round with equal freedom.' Warren was to continue with Leicestershire until the mid-1890s. In his old age he acted as one of the gatemen at County matches.

Thomas Burdett, a banker in Leicester, and R. W. Gillespie-Stainton of Bitteswell Hall (he assumed the additional name Stainton in 1873) took over the running of the County Club in 1883. Gillespie-Stainton had been in the Harrow XI in 1861. Matches were arranged for the first time against both Yorkshire and Surrey: *Lillywhite's Companion* comments approvingly: 'This rising County Club made strenuous efforts to assert its right to a place among the leading counties.'

The new order opened its inter-county campaign with a splendid victory over Surrey at Grace Road by just seven runs. Charles Marriott scored 46 and 46, Parnham took 11 wickets and Rylott seven. Surrey were not quite at full strength and Pooley their wicketkeeper was unable to field in the second innings due to a hand injury, but nevertheless this was a major victory. Leicestershire drew the two Yorkshire matches and then Surrey had their revenge at The Oval.

The batting once more was Leicestershire's weakness; apart from Charles Marriott and to a lesser extent Wheeler and Warren no one was reliable and several of the batsman had single-figure averages. Parnham and Rylott were the leading wicket-takers, but the amateur, H. T. Arnall, the Rugby captain in 1882 and now up at Oxford, bowled his slow left-arm spin to some effect, taking 24 wickets at 15 runs each. He assumed the name Arnall-Thompson in 1885 and led the County from 1886 to 1889. In the 1883 home match against Yorkshire he performed the hat-trick.

Another amateur to make his debut for the County in 1883 was John Alfred Turner. He was in his first year at Cambridge, and is described in *Lillywhite's Annual* of 1884 as: 'Fair slow round-arm bowler; capital field anywhere; not very successful as a bat, being rather nervous at starting.' He certainly improved on this as a batsman and when the loss of an eye ended his cricket in 1892, he had two first-class centuries to his name and over 1,000 first-class runs.

An 18-year-old fast bowler made his mark in the early weeks of the following season and was to become one of the leading bowlers of his time. A. D. Pougher (pronounced 'Puffer') turned out for Leicester Town Colts *v* County Colts and returned figures of 19-12-12-9. He did not make his County debut until 1885, and joined the Lord's staff in 1887, remaining there 23 years.

Seven matches against 'first-class' opposition were arranged for 1884 – home and away with Surrey, Lancashire and MCC, and a single game against the Australians. The County was vying with Hampshire and Somerset in the grey area between first-class and minor county status. Hampshire, more for sentimental reasons than cricketing strength, was accorded first-class status by *Wisden's Almanack* and Somerset also crept in under the tape, but Leicestershire remained in the cold. In terms of results there was very little to choose between the three and in fact Derbyshire, which had been regarded as 'first-class' for more than a decade, had an identical record to Leicestershire – a single 'first-class' victory over a very moderate MCC side.

Leicestershire beat MCC at Grace Road in June, Rylott picking up 12 wickets for 69, but some idea of the premier club's strength can be gauged by the fact that one of their opening batsmen, indeed the one who made the highest score for MCC, was the Leicestershire Treasurer, R. W. Gillespie-Stainton! A brief glance at the reverses suffered shows the continuing weakness of the County's batting. In the five matches against Lancashire, Surrey and the Australians Leicestershire were dismissed ten times for totals under 200; in fact the only time that figure was reached was against Norfolk in a drawn game.

Warwickshire were met for the first time and Leicestershire at least demonstrated that they were superior to that minor county with victories of an innings at Coventry and 120 runs at Grace Road, H. T. Arnall taking ten for 70 in the latter success.

The Uppingham all-rounder, C. C. Stone, made his County debut in 1884, but his bowling was scarcely used and his batting did not add greatly to the run-getting powers of the side. He toured the West Indies with the 1896–97 English side and appeared intermittently for the County until 1896 – he was a regular army officer.

The financial situation was no better than it had been in the first year or two. The magazine *Cricket* reported in the early summer of 1885:

> The poor support for county cricket in Leicestershire was the cause for much concern. A meeting of secretaries of local clubs was held early in May at Grace Road to consider what steps could be taken to secure better support. No definite conclusions were achieved, but a public meeting for the same purpose was arranged for May 14th at the Temperance Hall, to be presided over by the Mayor, Alderman Hart. (At this latter meeting) it was stated that the arrangements with the Cricket Ground Company were that they (the Company) should take all receipts from whatever source and indemnify the Club from any loss. The result had been that the Club had suffered financial loss each year, and could not carry on in the same way. After much discussion, a resolution was passed re-electing the old Committee with power to add to their number, and calling on them to take measures to make the club self-supporting for the future.

The Lancashire fixture of 1884 was not renewed, so Surrey was the only first-class county met in 1885. Leicestershire were overwhelmed in the match at The Oval and were badly mauled in the drawn return game at Grace Road; two bright spots in London were the fine bowling of Pougher on his County debut and an excellent 107 (out of 185 all out) by Wheeler in the second innings. The three minor counties opposed were Warwickshire, Cheshire and Norfolk, but the only victory was at home against Cheshire, an innings margin with Rylott picking up ten for 78.

Pougher topped the bowling table with 42 wickets at a cost of 643 runs, with Rylott, whose figures included matches with Harrow Wanderers and Uppingham Rovers, taking 39 at slightly greater cost. The batting remained feeble, only Warren having a respectable average.

Two important changes came at the Annual General Meeting in the spring of 1886. Charles Marriott relinquished the captaincy in favour of Arnall-Thompson, and W. Billings took over as Honorary Treasurer. A new agreement was reached with the Ground Company on better terms.

Late June and early July, in a period of 18 days, Leicestershire claimed the attention of the cricket press. On 26 June Warwickshire were beaten by eight wickets, Rylott and Pougher bowling out their opponents for 76 and 91. The match was at Grace Road and the next visitors to the ground were Surrey, who fared even worse than Warwickshire, being dismissed for 26 and 83, Pougher took six for 10 in the first innings and seven for 44 in the second. The magazine *Cricket* commented:

> Pougher, the destroying angel of the Surrey eleven, has been having a very enjoyable time of it during the last week. He came, he saw and he conquered a strongish eleven of Surrey on Thursday, at Leicester, as the supporters of the County are not likely to forget, I should fancy, for some little time. His performance on this occasion was indeed a remarkable one, as he not only got thirteen of the nineteen wickets which fell to the Leicestershire bowlers – at the expense of only 54 runs – off his own bowling, but caught three others from Rylott.

The report then continues by describing what happened three days later when Leicestershire travelled to Edgbaston. Warwickshire were dismissed for 30 and 82, Pougher taking twelve for 45.

By a coincidence in the same week, the parliamentary constituency of Market Harborough returned T. K. Tapling as its MP; Tapling played first-class cricket in 1886 for MCC, but was born in Surrey!

So Pougher took 25 wickets for 99 in a week. The rest of the season was not so dramatic. The two games with Cheshire were drawn and when the County went to The Oval in August, Surrey were much more determined. Pougher took seven wickets, but they cost him 116 runs, Walter Read hit an unbeaten 157 and Surrey reached 415 on the first day. On the second day Leicestershire's batsmen, with a perfect wicket, failed to make much headway, Lohmann and Bowley dismissing them twice for

LEICESTERSHIRE *v* SURREY

Played at Grace Road, Leicester, 8 and 9 July 1886

LEICESTERSHIRE WON BY TEN WICKETS

SURREY	FIRST INNINGS		SECOND INNINGS	
Mr K. J. Key	c sub b Pougher	0	c Wheeler b Pougher	14
R. Abel	b Rylott	0	b Rylott	8
E. J. Diver	c Pougher b Rylott	1	b Pougher	1
Mr W. W. Read	c Wheeler b Pougher	3	c Pougher b Rylott	3
J. M. Read	c Wheeler b Pougher	4	c Turner b Pougher	29
Mr M. P. Bowden	run out	10	lbw b Pougher	0
W. Brockwell	c Pougher b Rylott	0	b Pougher	0
G. A. Lohmann	c Hill b Pougher	3	c Rylott b Pougher	9
†H. Wood	b Pougher	0	b Rylott	2
G. G. Jones	b Pougher	2	b Pougher	5
T. Bowley	not out	3	not out	12
Extras		0		0
Total		26		83

BOWLING	O	M	R	W	O	M	R	W
Pougher	11.1	6	10	6	35	18	44	7
Rylott	11	5	16	3	34.1	17	39	3

LEICESTERSHIRE	FIRST INNINGS		SECOND INNINGS	
J. Wheeler	b Bowley	1	not out	4
Mr E. Hill	b Lohmann	8		
T. Warren	b Jones	52	not out	0
Mr J. A. Turner	b Bowley	3		
F. Turner	c Diver b Bowley	4		
Mr C. C. Stone	b Lohmann	4		
J. Parnham	c Wood b Lohmann	5		
A. D. Pougher	b Lohmann	0		
★Mr H. T. Arnall-Thompson	c Wood b Bowley	6		
W. Colver	not out	20		
A. Rylott	c J. M. Read b Jones	0		
Extras	b	4		
Total		107	(0 wkt)	4

BOWLING	O	M	R	W	O	M	R	W
Bowley	44	21	49	4	1	0	4	0
Lohmann	43	23	44	4	1	1	0	0
Jones	7.3	3	10	2				

Toss: Surrey. Close of play: Surrey (2) 45-4
★Captain; †Wicketkeeper

120 and 121. The only visitor to shine was the former captain, Charles Marriott, who made 44. The County did slightly better in their only other important match – at Lord's *v* MCC – when two defensive innings by Wheeler forced a draw.

Pougher finished the season with 78 wickets at less than 10 runs each and Rylott took 40 wickets at a slightly larger cost; the only other bowler to take ten wickets was the captain. The figures include matches *v* Harrow Wanderers and Uppingham Rovers.

Along with the other 'minor counties' Leicestershire were growing frustrated by the arbitrary way counties had been divided into 'first-class' and 'minor'. In December 1885, Burdett, the Leicestershire Secretary, had represented the County at a meeting of the minor counties organised by the Warwickshire Secretary, to encourage more fixtures between the first-class counties and the rest. In December 1886, Burdett again represented Leicestershire at a meeting in London, this time to discuss Lord Harris's proposal to reduce the length of residential qualification from two years to one. The opponents of the proposal, including Leicestershire, argued that it would drain talent from the minor counties to the strongest ones and in fact a counter-proposal was mooted to increase residential qualification to three years. Lord Harris's motion failed by 14 votes to three. In contrast to the present-day system whereby the first-class counties virtually control cricket, in 1886 every county with a county cricket club could send a representative to the annual meeting and each county, regardless of status, had a single vote.

The County Committee were determined on expansion and improvement for the 1887 season. Not only were Colts Trials fixed for Market Harborough, Melton, Hinckley and Lutterworth, but matches with Yorkshire resumed and a single match was arranged for the first time *v* Derbyshire. To accommodate this increase two old-standing minor fixtures were dropped, against Uppingham Rovers and Harrow Wanderers. In some reports the County team for these matches had been styled 'Gentlemen of Leicestershire', but in almost all the games three professionals had been included on the County side, so, though of lesser significance, these matches ought to rank as genuine Leicestershire CCC 1st XI fixtures.

A summary of results for 1887 reveals five wins, six losses and a draw. This, in the eyes of the Editor of *Wisden*, was very creditable and that Almanack puts Leicestershire first in its section headed 'Minor Counties' – the counties are listed in merit, rather than alphabetical order, though no summary table of results is printed. Leicestershire beat Warwickshire twice – the first meeting due to

Pougher's bowling, in the second to Warren's batting. Cheshire and Essex were beaten once each, Warren making another 100 in the latter game, and the only defeat by a minor county was against Essex at Grace Road by only two wickets. No other minor county suffered so few defeats at the hands of their brethren, so *Wisden*'s judgment on the merit of Leicestershire was justified.

The gap between minor and first-class was still large and Leicestershire lost all five matches against their superiors. No minor county, not even Somerset, beat a first-class side in 1887, so Leicestershire were not alone. The defeats were by relatively large margins except in the case of the Derbyshire match when Leicestershire's bowlers let them down. Leicestershire made 216 and then Derbyshire were dismissed for 127, but following on Derbyshire improved, and with the tail-enders making too many runs Leicestershire needed 191 to win, a total they never looked like achieving.

The County Cricket Council was formed in July 1887. Burdett represented Leicestershire and was quite vocal during the first meeting. When Middlesex proposed that the first-class counties should frame the county qualification laws, Burdett pointed out that Leicestershire considered itself equal to some of the first-class counties and he was supported by Warwickshire in saying that all the counties ought to have a say in the framing of the rules. When another delegate from the first-class counties implied that the minor counties would want the residential rules made more lenient, Burdett was the first to deny the idea and stated that Leicestershire wanted a three-year qualification.

As he had suggested in the 1888 edition of the *Almanack*, the editor of *Wisden* decided to divide the minor counties (i.e. those not first-class) into two sections, 'second class' counties and the rest. The *Almanack* published for the first time a league table of results for the 'second-class' which appeared as follows:

	P	W	L	D
1. Leicestershire	5	4	1	0
2. Somersetshire	9	5	2	2
3. Warwickshire	6	3	1	2
4. Essex	10	3	4	3
5. Staffordshire	10	2	3	5
6. Hampshire	6	1	2	3
7. Hertfordshire	8	2	4	1
8. Norfolk	4	1	1	1
9. Derbyshire	3	1	2	0
10. Northamptonshire	4	0	3	1

The table is a little hard on Derbyshire, who had been relegated from the first-class championship, but still played mainly first-class sides. Leicestershire however thoroughly deserved their position, for not included in the table were their two victories over Surrey and the Australians. Pougher and Rylott again proved to be the downfall of Surrey. The pair, as in 1886, bowled unchanged through both innings as Surrey were dismissed for 81 and 98, Pougher taking 13 for 104 and Rylott 6 for 54 – the victory was not quite as brilliant as its predecessor since the five Surrey amateurs, Shuter, Read, Roller, Key and Bowden were playing for the Gentlemen *v* Australians on the same days, but Surrey were the 1888 County Champions and ought to have been able to overcome these absentees.

The success over the tourists was thoroughly deserved. The wicket at Grace Road was poor, but Warren, opening the batting for the County, made 42 and this proved to be the only substantial individual innings in the entire match. Leicestershire were all out for 119; Australia managed 62, with Pougher and Arnall-Thompson bowling unchanged. The County fared even worse in their second attempt – 50 all out – but Australia never looked likely to make the 108 required for victory. Pougher took six for 40, making ten for 71 in the match and the margin of the success was 20 runs.

The Leicestershire side which beat the Australian tourists in 1888. Left to right, back: W. Atkins, A. W. Crofts, J. H. Wheeler, J. Collier. Middle: C. C. Stone, C. Marriott, H. T. Arnall-Thompson, C. E. de Trafford. Front: T. Warren, A. D. Pougher, W Tomlin.

AUSTRALIANS *v* LEICESTERSHIRE

Played at Leicester, 5, 6 July 1888

LEICESTERSHIRE WON BY 20 RUNS

LEICESTERSHIRE	FIRST INNINGS		SECOND INNINGS	
J. Wheeler	c Trott b Turner	0	b Turner	11
T. Warren	c Blackham b Trott	42	lbw b Turner	0
W. Tomlin	c Jarvis b Trott	14	c Trott b Turner	2
Mr C. Marriott	b Turner	5	c Worrall b Ferris	12
Mr C. E. de Trafford	c Trott b Boyle	7	run out	1
Mr C. C. Stone	c Blackham b Turner	8	c Trott b Ferris	0
A. D. Pougher	c Worrall b Turner	18	c Lyons b Turner	11
Mr A. W. Crofts	b Turner	0	b Turner	3
Mr J. Collier	not out	11	b Ferris	1
Mr H. T. Arnall-Thompson	b Turner	0	c and b Ferris	2
W. Atkins	b Trott	9	not out	4
Extras	lb	5	b	3
Total		119		50

BOWLING	O	M	R	W	O	M	R	W
Turner	32	16	44	6	23	16	20	5
Worrall	6	3	6	0				
Ferris	9	5	11	0	22.3	12	27	4
Boyle	18	7	35	1				
Trott	16.3	7	18	3				

AUSTRALIANS	FIRST INNINGS		SECOND INNINGS	
A. C. Bannerman	c Crofts b Pougher	2	c Crofts b Pougher	20
†J. M'C. Blackham	c Crofts b Arnall-Thompson	2	lbw b Pougher	3
★G. H. S. Trott	c de Trafford b Arnall-Thompson	0	c Wheeler b Atkins	19
G. J. Bonnor	c and b Pougher	21	b Arnall-Thompson	0
A. H. Jarvis	b Arnall-Thompson	16	c Stone b Pougher	8
P. S. M'Donnell	b Arnall-Thompson	1	c Arnall-Thompson b Pougher	12
C. T. B. Turner	c Collier b Pougher	8	c Stone b Arnall-Thompson	3
J. J. Lyons	c Pougher b Arnall-Thompson	0	c de Trafford b Pougher	9
J. Worrall	b Pougher	0	c and b Pougher	0
J. J. Ferris	c Warren b Arnall-Thompson	6	c Warren b Arnall-Thompson	7
H. F. Boyle	not out	6	not out	0
Extras			b	6
Total		62		87

BOWLING	O	M	R	W	O	M	R	W
Pougher	23	11	31	4	33	13	40	6
Arnall-Thompson	22.1	11	31	6	24	10	34	3
Atkins					9	6	7	1

Umpires: Farrands and Bishop

★Captain; †Wicketkeeper

The 'first-class' averages for 1888 give a very false picture of Pougher's ability – he is shown in *Wisden* as taking 31 wickets costing 15 runs each, but he took another 22 wickets in Leicestershire matches against first-class opposition, which victims were not included. Pougher had in fact been a member of Arthur Shrewsbury's side that toured Australia the previous winter and his record in all matches on the tour had been 78 wickets at 6 runs each.

At the meeting of the County Cricket Council to discuss alterations to the lbw law, Leicestershire were represented by Burdett and Arnall-Thompson and voted for the alterations, but at the meeting to discuss county qualifications, J. Bonnor represented Leicestershire and he does not seem to have taken an active part in the debate.

Despite the playing successes of 1888, the County Club was still in financial difficulties and lost £120 on the season. There were 372 members of the Club, whereas neighbouring Warwickshire had nearly three times that number. The Committee still determined to expand and an ambitious programme of 14 matches, six against first-class counties, was arranged for 1889. Only Warwickshire among the other minor counties had such an extensive fixture list; Derbyshire played only 11 games and Essex and Hampshire ten each.

The season turned out to be one of total disaster; not a single victory and ten of the 14 matches lost. The batting, as usual, was woefully inadequate, but to this could be now added a weakness in the bowling. Parnham had gone; Rylott, now aged 50, played in every match, but no longer had the pace of former days and his wickets cost nearly 20 runs each. Pougher missed three matches through injury and though he took 52 wickets was also more expensive. Arnall-Thompson fell away; he missed half the matches and took only 12 wickets at 26 runs each. A doctor from Markfield, S. R. Wright, was the other bowler to take more than ten wickets. He also batted usefully, but his appearances in county cricket were very restricted.

Rylott was awarded the MCC match at Grace Road for his benefit and received a total of £125. A new pavilion was built on the Leicester ground and it was to survive until 1966.

Depressing though the results of 1889 must have been to followers of Leicestershire that summer they could not draw comfort from the appearance, in the final match, against Lancashire at Old Trafford, of Arthur Woodcock. He batted last, made 0 and 1 not out and bowled 5 overs for 9 runs. The County lost by an innings and 69 runs, the game being all over in a single day. But Woodcock, aged 23, was to become one of the best fast bowlers of his day. He was born in Northampton, but moved to Billesdon when a month old. As a teenager he had much success with the Billesdon Club, but did not turn professional until 1887, when he was engaged by Mitcham CC in Surrey. In 1888 he accepted a coaching engagement at Haverford College in the United States and remained there until 1894. Because of this engagement he could play for Leicestershire only during the second half of the season. In 1895 the magazine *Cricket Field* commences its article on him with: 'In the opinion of nearly all the batsmen who have played against him, Woodcock, the good tempered Leicestershire professional, is the fastest bowler in England.'

A cartoon in 1895 shows him perched on a stool turning the crank of a Gatling gun and balls spraying out of the barrel sent wickets, bats and indeed, batsmen flying in all directions. His most effective delivery was the fast yorker. Woodcock was to play for Leicestershire until 1908. His best summer was 1895 when he took in all first-class matches 102 wickets and his best analysis was nine for 28 against MCC in 1899. He made a final fleeting appearance for the County in 1908, but died in very unusual circumstances two years later. On Saturday 13 May 1910, he returned home very late, asked his sister to kiss him and said he had come home to die. It turned out that he had taken a fatal dose of poison and though a doctor was summoned, Woodcock died at 3.00 am on the Sunday morning, aged 44.

Another bowler who later became one of the leading cricketers in England made his Leicestershire debut in 1889. Albert William Hallam, known as 'Darkie' due to his complexion, took two wickets for 26 runs in his single match. Born in East Leake, Nottinghamshire, he moved to Loughborough about 1886 and was thus qualified for the County by residence. A right-arm medium pace bowler, he appeared occasionally until 1893, when he moved to Manchester with a view to qualifying for Lancashire. In 1897 he helped that county win the Championship, taking 100 wickets. Ill-health dogged him, but he again switched counties, moving to Nottinghamshire, and in 1907 again took 100 wickets helping his native side to capture the Championship title. By the time he retired from first-class cricket he had taken more than 1,000 wickets – none unfortunately for Leicestershire. He returned to Loughborough and in his later days acted as coach to the local grammar school.

The attractive fixtures of 1889 did, despite the end results, encourage people to join the County Club and membership exceeded 500 for the first time, and the increase in subscription levels meant that there was a profit for the year – only £8 however!

The 1890 season began with a change of captaincy, C. E. de Trafford taking over the helm from Arnall-Thompson. His first match was not one he would wish to remember. Leicestershire travelled to London and were defeated in a day by Surrey – thus, having lost in a day to Lancashire in the last match of 1889, Leicestershire can claim the dubious distinction of successive one-day defeats.

As in 1889, 14 matches were played, but the Lancashire fixture was dropped in favour of Somerset, so only two first-class counties were met. There were four wins to balance against ten defeats – not an outstanding record but much improved on the previous summer.

Charles Edmund de Trafford, as his name suggests, was a native of Lancashire and was born at Trafford Park, Manchester. At the age of 20 he made a solitary appearance for the county of his birth, but he failed to score and there followed several seasons of club cricket. In 1887 he hit very effectively for MCC and in 1888 made his first appearance for Leicestershire, having a residence in the county. He was a fast-footed hitter and although he made plenty of runs in minor matches, in first-class cricket superior field-placing often had him caught in the deep. He led the County with great enthusiasm until 1906, thereafter appearing at irregular intervals until 1920.

Another amateur who turned out for the County in 1890 was T. S. Pearson, who was born at Barwell in 1851; like de Trafford he was an attacking batsman, but unlike the captain he already had much experience of first-class cricket, turning out for Oxford University in 1872 and fairly often for Middlesex between 1878 and 1885. Now reaching the veteran stage he stood in as captain for Leicestershire in some matches.

When Surrey came to Grace Road in early June for the return match, the home side lacked Pougher and two of their regular amateur batsmen, J. A. Turner and S. R. Wright. It was not thought that Leicestershire would put up much of a fight and indeed they looked in a hopeless position after the first two innings, being almost 200 in arrears. Alexander Lorrimer, who had been dismissed without scoring in the first innings, this being his County debut, came to the rescue and in a brilliant display of cricket scored 109 out of 187 in 160 minutes. He gave only one chance and not only saved the innings defeat but left Surrey with 76 to make. This the visitors achieved without loss.

Lorrimer was the first Leicestershire cricketer to make a hun-

Arthur Dick Pougher, the County's best bowler in the 1880s and 1890s. He toured Australia and South Africa and played in a Test in 1891–2. (NCCC)

dred on his debut and the feat was not to be equalled until 1984. A hosiery manufacturer in Leicester, he was a member of Leicester Town Club and already over 30 when he began in county cricket. He became one of the leading business men in the county and rarely had time for three-day cricket, though appearing on occasion until 1896; his younger brother, David, also represented the County in some matches.

The bowling for 1890 was very much in the hands of Pougher (84 wickets at 14.93 each) and Woodcock (44 at 13.34). Rylott's day was done – his single victim cost 186 runs and after the third match he was omitted from the side. Warren with 723 runs was easily the most effective batsman. He hit 142 against Essex and with Wheeler added 186 for the first wicket, the largest stand recorded to date for the County; he also carried his bat through the completed second innings of the match with Derbyshire at Derby.

The second-class counties table for 1891 read:

		P	W	L	D	Pts
1.	Leicestershire	10	6	3	1	3
2.	Essex	8	4	2	2	2
3.	Derbyshire	6	3	2	1	1
4.	Cheshire	4	2	1	1	1
5.	Hampshire	6	2	3	1	−1
6.	Staffordshire	6	1	3	2	−2
7.	Warwickshire	8	1	5	2	−4

This was the version published in *Wisden*, the editor of whom was one of the leading figures in trying to force an organised 'league' system on the counties, but when the matter was debated by the County Cricket Council in December 1890, the debate became so fraught that the Council was suspended 'sine die' and never again met. It will be noticed that Somerset do not feature in the 1891 table given above, the reason being that they had gained entry into the first-class County Championship simply by making fixtures with six of the eight existing first-class counties and thereby forcing their way in – in fact they had won all eight matches against their second-class opponents in 1890.

The Leicestershire Committee were no doubt encouraged by Somerset's success. Five professionals were engaged at Grace Road for 1891, William Finney, a 24-year-old medium fast bowler from Montgomeryshire, Alick Handford, another medium fast bowler, from Wilford near Nottingham, Moule of Cambridge and the two regular county players, Warren and Woodcock. Improvements had been made to the pavilion during the winter and a telephone service laid on.

The season began with a visit to The Oval, where Surrey reigned as the County Champions. Some splendid batting by de Trafford enabled Leicestershire to gain a first-innings lead and though Surrey fought back to win the game, the report noted: 'Looking at the disparity of strength between the two elevens, the game reflected as much credit on the losers as the winners.' The form shown by the captain in this initial game was to continue through the summer. The high point of his batting was 136 *v* Staffordshire and he ended the summer top of the County's batting table with 868 runs at an average of 27.12. Although they failed to beat Surrey (the return was also lost), Leicestershire did inflict defeat on Yorkshire. This was the most exciting contest of the season. When the last Leicestershire batsman, George Walton, joined Woodcock 22 runs were required – four wickets having fallen for the addition of a single – and the pair obtained the runs. Early in the innings de Trafford had hit 60 in 55 minutes.

The victories by largest margins were inflicted on Derbyshire and Staffordshire. In the former match Pougher made a chanceless 135, his maiden hundred for the County. He had a quite brilliant season with the ball, taking 127 wickets at 14 runs each, as well as scoring 666 runs, the third highest aggregate. Woodcock took 76 with a slightly better average than Pougher and in the early matches, when Woodcock was still in America, Walton bowled destructively – 27 wickets in the first three games and 47 in all. He was a fast bowler, but somewhat erratic. The only other bowler to take more than 20 wickets was W. E. Arnall-Thompson, the brother of the former captain; he was a useful all-rounder, but his appearances were infrequent.

An attacking left-hand batsman from the Ivanhoe Club, Albert Goadby hit 63 on his debut *v* Staffordshire and followed this up with seven wickets in the second innings – he had been regarded as something of an infant prodigy in Leicester club cricket, but for some reason he never pursued a career in county cricket.

None of the seven 'second-class' counties managed a victory against their seniors in 1892. In the table of results among themselves, Leicestershire came third, behind Warwickshire and Derbyshire, but the club was the only one to arrange fixtures against all six second-class opponents, both Warwickshire and Derbyshire playing against only four each. This really made a bit of a nonsense of the table in terms of quality rating. Pougher as in 1891 was the outstanding player, with over 100 wickets and 500 runs – no other second-class county possessed a bowler taking 100 wickets. Four times Pougher took ten wickets in a match and against Essex had an innings analysis of eight for 48, whilst at Stoke on Trent his figures read: 24-18-9-7. Woodcock, missing the early games with Walton again acting as his stand-in, took 73 wickets, but was more expensive than the previous summer.

De Trafford unfortunately had to miss nearly half the season and this seriously weakened the rather suspect batting. Warren made the only century during John Wheeler's benefit match against Derbyshire, and also had the best run aggregate.

A curiosity of the season was John Holland's dismissal against Essex at Grace Road. A defensive opening batsman from Nant-wich he played for Leicestershire from 1889 to 1896, without any outstanding success, and then moved to Lancashire and qualified for that county. Holland hit a ball from Taberer twice and then immediately started off for a run, this before any runs had been scored in Leicestershire's second innings. The umpire was appealed to and gave him out 'hit the ball twice'.

Of the newcomers in 1892, F. W. Stocks, the Denstone schoolboy, was left-handed both as a batsman and bowler. He went up to Oxford in 1896, gaining a blue for both hockey and cricket. His chief asset was his medium pace bowling, but he was also a very fine field, both close to the wicket and in the deep. He turned in some fine analyses for the County, but whilst at Oxford his appearances were of course limited and after coming down he joined the teaching profession which meant he was available only in the holidays. His final appearance was in 1903.

Hassall, from the same Cheshire town as Holland, was tried as a batsman, but made little impression and went to the leagues as a professional, as did Edwin Riley, whose son was later to represent the County – Riley came from Stoney Stanton.

Two alterations at Grace Road in the spring of 1893 were first the appointment of the former County player, A. W. Crofts, as the first paid Secretary – Burdett remained as Honorary Secretary – and the 'retirement' of George Panter as groundsman, with Ted Horne of Gloucestershire taking on the position. In fact Panter had lasted only a single year and his work had been far from satisfactory.

Fixtures with the old enemy Nottinghamshire were arranged for the first time since 1878 and Leicestershire had the satisfaction of winning by 57 runs, after being 84 behind on first innings. The reliable Pougher took ten wickets and in the second innings Tomlin scored his maiden hundred for the County, though now in his seventh season. Billy Tomlin was an attractive, free-scoring batsman who was to reach three-figures several more times before his career ended for disciplinary reasons in 1899. Not satisfied with the success over Notts, Leicestershire also beat Surrey, Pougher this time taking eleven wickets in a very low scoring game: Surrey were dismissed for 34 and 64, whilst Leicestershire made 43 and 56 for five. Pougher also made the highest score in the match, a vital 24 not out in the final innings.

In the 'second-class' counties competition, Leicestershire again came third, with Derbyshire and Warwickshire ahead of them. Pougher took 98 wickets and scored 480 runs, being the outstanding personality in the side. Finney had one or two good matches with the ball and ended with a better average than Pougher, but less than half the wickets. Woodcock was as effective as before. A new name in the bowling table was an all-round sportsman, G. W. Hillyard. A naval officer he was better known on the tennis courts. In 1886 he had had a cricket trial with Middlesex, but achieved little and virtually gave up the game in favour of tennis. In 1893 he was qualified by residence for Leicestershire and tried with the Colts as a bowler; this was quite successful and his fast medium bowling was used by the county until 1896. In 1908 he represented England at tennis in the Olympic Games; in addition he was a noted golfer. In later years he acted as Secretary to the All England Lawn Tennis Club at Wimbledon, retiring in 1925.

The main talking point in County cricket remained the division of the counties into first and second class. The mania for creating 'leagues' in sporting circles had come over from America and had been introduced into soccer in 1888, and in some of the midland and northern counties at cricket soon afterwards. There was a strong body of opinion against county cricket being organised on a league basis – the MCC resolutely maintained that all county clubs were equal – but the public (according to the press) wanted leagues and this further divided the cricket authorities.

Leicestershire were naturally very interested in all the informal remarks which filled many columns of the sporting press. When the County Secretaries had their traditional Lord's fixture meeting in December 1893, the Yorkshire representative, M. J. Ellison, without any prior notification proposed: 'That for the purposes of classification there should be no distinction drawn between counties who play out and home three-day matches with not less than six other counties.'

Derbyshire, still smarting from its removal by the press from first-class status, seconded Mr Ellison's motion, but the resulting debate meant that nothing could be decided until the County representatives had consulted their counties, and thus Leicestershire along with the other first-class aspirants had to wait until the spring of 1894.

FIRST-CLASS STATUS

THE CHALLENGE WHICH IN EFFECT the Yorkshire delegate threw down at the December 1893 Secretaries Meeting, when he put his proposal regarding the future classification of the counties, did not result in the expected meeting in January. By and large the counties with no interest in 'first-class' status and those who already possessed that accolade were not motivated to organise such a meeting – of 24 counties at the December Meeting only six or seven, at most, were keen to take the initiative.

On Monday 30 April, the captains of the nine first-class counties agreed that the following resolution be put to the MCC at the club's Annual General Meeting:

> That the matches played by the following four counties: Derbyshire, Warwickshire, Essex and Leicestershire, against the nine counties at present styled first-class, and also against one another and against the MCC should be regarded as first-class matches, and the records of the players engaged in these matches shall be included in the list of first-class averages.

The following day eight of the nine counties (Gloucestershire being the absentee) with representatives of Hampshire, Leicestershire, Warwickshire, Derbyshire and Essex, met to discuss the postponed decision on Yorkshire's resolution of the previous December. T. Burdett and G. W. Hillyard represented Leicestershire and the latter seconded Mr Ellison's proposal. However before a vote was taken, Mr Denison (Notts) proposed an amendment: 'That the MCC be requested to consider and advise upon the whole question of the classification of the counties.' This was seconded by Mr Murray Anderdon (Somerset) and carried unanimously; Mr Ellison withdrawing his proposition.

On 2 May, the MCC Annual General Meeting approved the resolution of the nine first-class counties' captains and the following Monday the Committee of the MCC put its seal on the matter. The question of who should run county cricket was still uppermost in many minds, but on 14 May Leicestershire began their first 'first-class' match at Leyton and had the satisfaction of achieving victory. The match was a triumph for Pougher. Not only did he take 14 wickets for 89 runs, but his unbeaten 109 was quite outstanding in that he did not make a false stroke until he reached three figures, though he batted only 140 minutes. It was to be 60 years before another Leicestershire player achieved the match 'double' for the County.

Having won their first match, the County gained victories in four of the next six matches including a victory by 47 runs over Yorkshire at Grace Road, when the all-powerful Pougher took another ten wickets and de Trafford hit 92. Hillyard captured the other ten and apart from one over, the pair bowled unchanged throughout the match. Unfortunately the County had a poor time in August – Pougher missed three of these matches and though Woodcock was back from America his form was not as formidable as his colleague. The final bowling table reinforces the point; Pougher 64 wickets at 9 runs each; Woodcock 48 at 16 runs each. Hillyard came third with 57 wickets at 17 runs each. These figures include five non-first-class matches.

C. E. de Trafford captained Leicestershire from 1890 to 1906, and was therefore captain in the County's first first-class match in 1894, a victory over Essex at Leyton. (NCCC)

ESSEX *v* LEICESTERSHIRE

Played on the County Ground, Leyton, 14, 15 and 16 May 1894

LEICESTERSHIRE WON BY 68 RUNS

LEICESTERSHIRE	FIRST INNINGS		SECOND INNINGS	
*Mr C. E. de Trafford	c Kortright b Mead	70	run out	8
T. Warren	run out	0	lbw b Burns	21
J. Holland	b Kortright	12	b Burns	50
W. Tomlin	b Kortright	1	c Mead b Kortright	14
A. D. Pougher	b Mead	5	(6) not out	109
F. Hassall	c and b Mead	0	(7) c Russell b Pickett	13
M. Chapman	c Burns b Mead	34	(5) b Burns	15
W. Finney	b Mead	0	b Kortright	0
Mr F. W. Stocks	b Kortright	0	b Kortright	0
†J. P. Whiteside	not out	4	b Pickett	27
F. Randon jun	b Mead	5	c Hailey b Pickett	0
Extras		0	b 9, lb 1	10
Total		131		267

1st inns: 1-0, 2-28, 3-30, 4-37, 5-37, 6-121, 7-121, 8-122, 9-124
2nd inns: 1-12, 2-48, 3-77, 4-104, 5-149, 6-170, 7-175, 8-175, 9-265

BOWLING	O	M	R	W	O	M	R	W
Kortright	18	2	41	3	28	3	90	3
Mead	19.3	6	49	6	39	15	70	0
Pickett	9	1	18	0	23.3	5	44	3
Burns	7	0	23	0	18	5	24	3
Carpenter					9	5	10	0
Owen					1	0	4	0
Lucas					3	0	15	0

ESSEX	FIRST INNINGS		SECOND INNINGS	
H. A. Carpenter	b Pougher	20	b Pougher	0
J. A. Burns	b Pougher	0	b Randon	36
Mr H. Hailey	b Randon	7	(5) c Pougher b Finney	35
*Mr A. P. Lucas	b Finney	6	b Pougher	7
Mr H. G. P. Owen	b Randon	5	(3) b Pougher	76
†T. M. Russell	b Pougher	7	lbw b Pougher	26
E. C. Freeman	b Pougher	0	c Tomlin b Pougher	12
Mr C. P. McGahey	st Whiteside b Pougher	3	b Pougher	20
Mr C. J. Kortright	c Holland b Pougher	7	c Chapman b Pougher	25
W. Mead	b Randon	1	c Chapman b Pougher	14
H. Pickett	not out	0	not out	20
Extras	lb	1	b 1, lb 1	2
Total		57		273

1st inns: 1-3, 2-20, 3-34, 4-38, 5-46, 6-46, 7-48, 8-56, 9-57
2nd inns: 1-2, 2-97, 3-119, 4-126, 5-169, 6-185, 7-199, 8-239, 9-242

BOWLING	O	M	R	W	O	M	R	W
Pougher	18	7	29	6	40.3	19	60	8
Randon	15.3	6	20	3	36	9	98	1
Finney	2	0	7	1	14	3	55	1
Stocks					7	1	33	0
Hassall					3	0	25	0

Umpires: W. F. Collishaw and H. Holmes
Leicestershire won the toss
*Captain; †Wicketkeeper

Apart from Yorkshire, Leicestershire had the satisfaction of beating both Notts and Surrey, of the nine old first-class counties. In the Surrey game, Pougher claimed another 11 victims, but equally responsible for the success was Holland who carried his bat through the innings for 95 not out. When Notts came to Grace Road, Woodcock produced his best figures of the summer with 15 for 136 – Pougher injured his hand and was unable to bowl and did not bat in the second innings. Notts had a slight lead after the first innings, but de Trafford's hitting – he made 89 with only one chance – gave Woodcock enough runs to bowl at in the final innings.

Although it was agreed that the four new first-class counties should not compete in the County Championship in 1894, nevertheless the press issued a Championship table which included the four. Leicestershire came seventh equal with Kent out of the 13 and therefore justified their elevated status – the bottom three clubs were all from the original nine: Notts, Sussex and Gloucestershire, though Essex only avoided the lowest position because they played insufficient matches.

In addition to the programme of first-class matches, Leicestershire also played home and away against Hampshire and Cheshire, as well as a single fixture against the South Africans. A total of 19 three-day games were thus played, so no less than 30 days' cricket was planned for Grace Road. This fixture list was more ambitious than that of several of the nine old counties and of the four new, only Warwickshire had a more extensive programme. The County Club was full of enthusiasm and under the continuing leadership of C. E. de Trafford ready for its first season in the County Championship. With Woodcock having a place on the MCC staff and the two amateurs, G. W. Hillyard and F. W. Stocks to bolster Woodcock and Pougher the attack looked very capable. In addition Geeson, a native of Redmile, but until now playing for Lincolnshire, had joined his native county. The batting remained of doubtful quality.

The County went down to London to play matches against MCC and Surrey at the beginning of May. The MCC match was lost, but the debut match in the Championship was won by four wickets. The victory was all the more pleasing because Surrey gained a first-innings lead of 63 and Leicestershire fought back in a most creditable manner: Woodcock took 6 for 44 as Surrey were dismissed for 113, then Tomlin made 106 not out as his side reached 177 for six and victory. Returning to Grace Road, Leicestershire inflicted a two-day defeat on neighbours Notts. Woodcock and Pougher took 19 wickets between them and

Geeson, on his debut, made an undefeated 49, batting 160 minutes without an error. So the new recruits, Leicestershire, had played two Championship matches, both against the old counties, and won two. If a Championship table had been issued so early in the season, Leicestershire would have topped it.

Defeat at Old Trafford however quickly brought the team down a peg; Woodcock bowled badly in the first innings and with Mold and Briggs in excellent form, the Leicestershire batsmen were unable to repair the damage, so that despite some much better bowling in the second innings, with Woodcock taking six for 77, Lancashire's victory was by 177 runs.

The Whitsun Bank Holiday saw Leicestershire at Leyton and Woodcock found easy pickings among the moderate Essex batsmen; 12 wickets came his way and Leicestershire notched a third victory.

After that the summer was all downhill. Woodcock seemed to lose his pace; Pougher was unwell and Hillyard proved expensive. Stocks could only play infrequently, but was erratic when he did appear. This was not the whole story and a paragraph in *Wisden*'s review of the season throws some light on the underlying flaw in the side:

> It was a matter of common knowledge that there was a lack of discipline among the professionals, and it is fair to assume that much of the ill-success attending the later efforts of the eleven can be attributed to this cause. The committee even went to the length of leaving one or two men out of matches. It is to be hoped the punishment, light as it was, will have taught the delinquents the error of their ways before another season opens; otherwise even more drastic measures may have to be taken to prevent a recurrence of what was really a scandal.

Sixteen matches were required to qualify for the Championship. Leicestershire obtained the three early wins, of the rest they lost ten and drew three. This summary placed them third from bottom. The two other matches played were the initial game *v* MCC and a fixture with Dublin University, in which Tomlin scored a century and the Irish batsman, L. H. Gwynn, hit 153 not out, carrying his bat through the completed University first innings – the County won the game by 126 runs. A youngster who also made runs in the match was Albert Knight – 34 not out and 81. It was the 22-year-old professional's first season on the Leicestershire staff and he was to develop into one of the stalwarts of the side, as was a second debutant, John King, a Lutterworth Grammar School product, who was taken onto the County staff in 1895. It was several years before King secured a regular place in the Leicestershire side.

The strongest eleven in this first Championship year consisted of the two amateurs, de Trafford and Hillyard, eight pros, Tomlin, Pougher, Holland, Knight, Geeson, Chapman, Woodcock and the wicketkeeper, Whiteside, and then one of eight players who appeared in three to six matches, of whom Stocks played most. The one important point that should be made is that virtually all the players were either born or brought up in the county.

In the winter of 1895–96, the County Ground Company offered to sell Grace Road to the County Club. The Club refused to buy, but entered into a new agreement whereby they paid £275 for the year, rather than 20 per cent of the gross receipts, plus an amount for using the ground for practice. The attendances in the first Championship year had not been up to expectation and the cause, it was generally thought, was the distance from the centre of Leicester and the main line station in particular. The County Club were therefore looking for a site nearer to the town centre and did not wish to commit themselves to the present location. The club lost £51 on the year's workings.

The committee were not too depressed by the general results of 1895 and for 1896 nine players were engaged for the season, among them L. Brown, S. Coe, A. Cobley, A. E. Knight, T. Poole and C. J. B. Wood. Woodcock, Geeson, Pougher and Whiteside were all engaged by MCC, but released for county matches.

The 1896 season proved even more disappointing than its predecessor, only two matches ending in favourable results and those by the narrow margins of one wicket (*v* Warwickshire) and 21 runs (*v* Hampshire). Both Pougher and Woodcock were much more expensive than in 1895 and with Hillyard only making occasional appearances they had reasonable support from just one colleague – Geeson. Pougher had a good summer with the bat and in all first-class matches completed 1,000 runs. De Trafford's faults were becoming more apparent to the opposition and if it had not been for his 113 against Lancashire, made out of 138, his average would have been a very moderate one. A. E. Knight, very defensive, came second in the batting table and looked very much a player with a future, but H. H. Marriott had another terrible season. Marriott, a Malvern schoolboy, was not related to the former captain, Charles Marriott, but came from a Kibworth family. He gained a blue at Cambridge in 1895 as a stylish right-hand batsman; in 1896 he again played against Oxford, but the contrast between his averages for Cambridge and for the County in these two seasons was quite extraordinary. For the university he hit 899 runs, averaging 37 per innings, and for the County 104 runs at 7 per innings. After leaving Cambridge he became a Director of William Joy & Sons Ltd, Oil Refiners, and played only occasionally in Championship matches until 1902.

Two youngsters, who were to serve the County well, made their debuts in 1896. Sam Coe, a 22-year-old from Earl Shilton, left-handed both as a batsman and bowler, quickly established a permanent place in the side, batting in the middle order and capable of scoring all round the wicket. In addition his medium to slow bowling increased in value as the years went by and he vied with King as the County's leading all-rounder. He played until 1923 and from 1931 to 1949 acted as County scorer; in December 1951 he was made an Honorary Life member of the Club.

C. J. B. Wood, educated at Wellingborough School, was two years younger than Coe. He had played in a few matches as an amateur for Northants in 1895, but in 1896 was living in Market Harborough and was taken on the Grace Road groundstaff. In contrast to Coe he was a stubborn, defensive opening batsman. In 1897 he gained a regular place in the side. He reached 1,000 runs 13 times, going on to 2,000 once in all first-class matches. His career ended in the same year as Coe's; he captained the County each side of the First World War and in the Second World War acted as Secretary for two years.

Of the others who were tried in 1896, Ralph Joyce was only 17 and a member of the Bedford Grammar School side. He went up to Oxford and though tried in the Freshmen's and later in the Seniors' matches failed to appear for the university. An attractive batsman he made 48 appearances for the County spread over 12 seasons. Lewis Brown, a professional, played somewhat more frequently than Joyce, and opening the batting he had some days of success.

In the winter of 1896–97 negotiations between the Leicester Corporation and the County Club for a lease of land on Aylestone Road were completed and the County Club began the work of getting the new venue fit for county cricket – it was to be 1901 before the Club finally took up residence.

Whilst practising before the first 1897 match, Pougher met with an accident, which kept him out of the eleven for almost the whole summer. This deprived the team of its best bowler and leading all-rounder. The effect was quite alarming. The first three matches were all lost by an innings and though victory was then achieved at the expense of MCC, by the middle of the campaign, when Leicestershire had played seven out of their 14 Championship games, they had lost six by an innings and drawn one. The results seemed to depress the captain, whose batting form disappeared, and he dropped out of quite a number of matches. Without Pougher, Woodcock was not so effective, though F. W. Stocks, during the vacation, bowled better and provided the County with their sole victory – over Derbyshire at Grace Road by five wickets. Stocks took eight wickets in the match and bowled unchanged with Woodcock through the first innings.

Top of Leicestershire's batting table, though only with averages of 20.89 and 19.52, were Wood and Knight; Coe also made some runs. So, even if the present looked very grim, the three young recruits appeared to be fulfilling their promise.

An interesting footnote to the season was that William Bestwick from Derbyshire had been taken on the staff. He remained only for the one season, but later had a long and chequered career with his native county, achieving a modicum of fame with his bowling and even more notoriety from his drinking prowess. His career has been the subject of several graphic essays.

The 1898 season saw no improvement in the position of the County – again they occupied a lowly berth and managed only one victory, that being once more against Derbyshire. Pougher began the season still hampered by the old ankle injury of twelve months ago and later cut his hand so badly that he had to miss several matches – when he did play he showed very little form with either bat or ball. The attack relied very much on Geeson and Woodcock, but neither held much terror for the opposing batsmen.

H. H. Marriott topped the batting, but played in only five games and owed a lot to a single brilliant innings of 103 against Hampshire. Wood, Knight and Lewis Brown were the first three in the order for many matches and all three had quite reasonable returns. King was given a further trial in six games and looked promising. Overall it was now the bowling, rather than the batting, which let the side down, though criticism was also levelled at the outcricket.

Harry Whitehead played in five Championship matches. A right-hand batsman, usually opening, he was inclined to be impetuous, but was to have many days of success in the years ahead, hitting over 15,000 runs for the County in a career which lasted until 1922 – he also improved the fielding standards, being equally alert in the slips or the deep. His medium pace bowling was of occasional use. Lewis Brown's brother, J.H., was given a trial, as was Charles Agar of Birstall, but neither made much of a mark in county cricket.

Leicestershire tied with Somerset in the penultimate position in the 1899 Championship table. Fine weather and hard wickets produced more draws in general – Leicestershire had eight and eight losses, but they also managed two wins, the same number as four other counties, so at least on paper the weaker sides were much of a muchness. There were quite a number of excellent individual performances by members of the side in the course of the summer. Knight hit three hundreds, the most satisfying of which was against Yorkshire at Bramall Lane. Both De Trafford and Pougher, after some years of little account, hit two hundreds; whilst Marriott's only three-figure innings almost brought victory over Hampshire, when Leicestershire needed 237 in 160 minutes and reached 203 for 2, Knight 69 and Marriott not out 101.

The team's major success was much more a combined effort – no one made a hundred and no one took five wickets in an innings, but Lancashire were beaten at Old Trafford by 79 runs – no less than six Leicestershire bowlers shared the wickets and there were eight scores over 30, with Knight's 59 being the highest. The two counties had played in all 19 matches and this was the first time Leicestershire had won. The fact that Woodcock was absent through injury balanced the absence of Tyldesley, the Lancastrian who was taking part in the first Test.

Immediately following the Old Trafford match, Leicestershire met Worcestershire in a first-class encounter for the first time at Grace Road. Stocks took eight for 56 in the first innings and five more wickets in the second, enabling Leicestershire to win by eight wickets.

Several records fell during the year. Leicestershire's total of 476 at Bournemouth was a new highest team total; Knight's aggregate of 1,246 runs (average 34.61) was another record. Woodcock took nine for 28 against MCC at Lord's, the first time a Leicestershire bowler had captured as many wickets in a single innings. Woodcock, however, missed much of the season through injury. On the reverse side, Essex hit 673 against the County, which beat the previous record of 660 by Yorkshire three years before.

A special meeting was held in June to appeal for funds in order to complete the building of the new ground. The estimated expenditure was £4,200 and £3,120 was promised. The total size of the ground was to be 10 acres, of which two acres were for a practice area.

James King, brother of John, played a few matches for the

County starting in 1899, as did G. Grewcock, but of more interest were two debutant amateurs, G. H. S. Fowke and Dr R. Mac-Donald. The former was a regular army officer who had the misfortune to be captured by the enemy in both the Boer and the First World War. He played odd matches in county cricket whilst on leave, then in 1922, at the age of 41, he plunged into regular Championship cricket, as Leicestershire's captain. At the time of his debut he had just left Uppingham, where he had topped the batting averages.

Dr Robert Macdonald might be described as Leicestershire's first overseas cricketer. A native of Melbourne, Australia, he had moved to Queensland and made his debut for that colony in 1893. He came over to England on holiday and whilst staying in the county appeared fairly often for three seasons. He later set up a dental practice in Leicester and in 1922 became Hon Secretary of the County Club.

When the Annual General Meeting was held on 17 March 1900, the Committee were able to report that the fund for the new ground was progressing satisfactorily and an inspection by G. G. Hearne, the acknowledged expert, had drawn a favourable response concerning the suitability of the site. The general finances of the Club however were not so pleasing and a deficit of £71 was announced.

In spite of the lack of finance, the Committee arranged no less than 23 first-class matches, as well as a game against the West Indies; this was the largest programme on which the County had embarked. It was ambitious, but those in control must have been rather downhearted when every one of the first seven games ended in defeat – eight wickets being the smallest margin. There followed in succession two fixtures against Worcestershire (the county promoted to first-class in 1899). In the first, at Grace Road, Woodcock and King bowled out the visitors for 98, giving a lead of 94. Rain interrupted play, but in their second innings Leicestershire hit out and de Trafford bravely declared setting a target of 179. King and Woodcock again bowled well and the score fell to 37 for seven. A victory at last seemed assured, but after the eighth wicket fell, the rain returned and the game was drawn. The fixture at Worcester was equally interesting. Wood-cock and King again had Worcestershire struggling and in the final innings Leicestershire required 113. The score progressed to 40 for two, but Wilson, the Worcester fast bowler returned figures of 7.5-4-8-4 and Leicestershire failed by 10 runs. In these two matches King took 17 wickets and Woodcock 16. These two close encounters encouraged the eleven and on the following three days they posted their first win, beating Middlesex by the satisfactory margin of 199 runs. It was a thorough team effort, though Sam Coe, making the highest score in the match, 80, was singled out for particular praise.

That victory was at Grace Road. It was a fortnight before the next home match and this produced a glut of batting records. Leicestershire made 609 for eight declared, the highest County total to date with Knight batting 240 minutes for 182, another record; opponents Sussex spent the rest of the match scoring 686 for eight, another record. The Indian prince, Ranjitsinhji, made 275, the highest against Leicestershire to date.

By mid-August, with just the single win against Middlesex, Leicestershire appeared very forlorn, but two victories in the last three games made the overall picture a little more cheerful. Hampshire were beaten even though they gained a first innings lead of 79, King and Geeson bowling them out in their second innings for 100 before King then helped Wood in a second-wicket stand of 109 to put victory within reach. That was at Southampton. The County then came back to Grace Road for what was billed as the final Championship game on the ground. It proved a triumph, with Derbyshire going down to an innings defeat. Wood and Knight replied to a Derbyshire total of 285 with an opening stand of 128; the former went on to 147 and a declaration was made 123 runs ahead. Derbyshire collapsed in their second innings – all out 89, Woodcock five for 24, Geeson four for 29.

This fillip in the County's record came too late to make any difference to their standing in the Championship and the penultimate position remained theirs. A glance at the first-class averages soon reveals Leicestershire's problem – only one batsman in the top 40 and the two leading bowlers, King and Geeson, stood 27th and 28th in the table.

Cecil Wood hit 1,537 runs, average 39.41; Knight was the other batsman to top 1,000, but King proved the most useful man in the side, making 940 runs and taking 76 wickets, though Geeson was not far behind with 641 runs and 70 wickets. In the case of King he was to continue his all-round form for many years, but Geeson's effort was to prove his best.

Very little was seen of Pougher, though he turned out in his Benefit Match against Yorkshire; ill-health was ending his career.

The finances remained somewhat unhealthy but the following paragraph from *Cricket* of 20 December 1900 shows that the enthusiasm for county cricket still bloomed:

The financial condition of the Leicestershire County CC was

the subject of an animated discussion at Leicester on December 8th. It was pointed out that there was a loss of about a thousand pounds on last season's matches, while £2,000 was still required to make the new cricket ground complete. The meeting was enthusiastic, and it was unanimously resolved to ask members to double their annual subscription; no fears were expressed that the committee will not be able to tide over their difficulties.

When *Wisden's Almanack* appeared, its review was equally optimistic:

> With the new premises should come a period of greater prosperity for Leicestershire. They are comparatively near to the city, so that if any of the rising talent continues to improve, much larger crowds are sure to watch the cricket than hitherto, and then the position of the county will be advanced in every way.

When the financial details emerged, the loss was only £860, and £300 had been donated to pay off some of the debt. Pougher received just £228 for his benefit – the Yorkshire batsman, J. T. Brown, received ten times that figure in 1901.

The official ceremony to open the new ground at Aylestone Road took place on Monday 13 May 1901 – the first day of the first Championship match, with Surrey as the opponents. A large crowd turned out and saw Leicestershire make 359 for seven, Wood, King, Pougher and Coe all making fifties. Surrey however made even better use of the new pitch and, as only King managed to score runs in the second innings, Surrey won by ten wickets.

The new ground was leased from the Leicester Corporation for 21 years. The total cost of its layout ended at £7,400 and the County Club had only £4,500 in its ground fund when the Surrey game was staged, but the local *Daily Post* launched a 'Shilling Fund' which raised 15,000 shillings (£750) and a bazaar produced a profit of £1,300. The pavilion was still being completed, but provided much better accommodation than at Grace Road and though the actual playing area – 145 yards by 135 yards – was somewhat smaller, there was additional room for practice nets.

The population of the county fulfilled the expectations of the committee – all but £700 of the £7,400 for the new ground was donated by the end of the year and a profit was made on the 1901 season as a whole. Just as important, the membership rose to 1,500, so the club now had a sound financial base from subscriptions.

For two or three years there had been comments about the promising youngsters who would improve the playing fortunes of the club, but the final results had remained very modest. In 1901 not only did the promising youngsters begin to mature in earnest, but the table of results made more pleasant reading. Of the 23 first-class matches, six ended in victory, four being in the Championship. The most satisfying of the successes was the first win at Aylestone Road, when Notts were overcome in two days, play being extended on the second evening to allow Leicestershire to make the necessary runs. King had match figures of 13 for 73 and the batting prize went to de Trafford, who hit a brilliant 67 in the first innings and 35 in the second.

The three other Championship wins were against Warwickshire, Derbyshire and Worcestershire. In the Warwickshire match, a 19-year-old amateur, W. W. Odell, caused a great surprise. Brought up in Birmingham he had played frequently for Warwickshire Club and Ground and for the Old Edwardians without any startling results, but his family moved to Leicester and with Woodcock away injured, Odell was given a trial. His medium pace bowling took ten wickets and Leicester won by 218 runs.

The victory over Derbyshire was even more pronounced. The game was played at Glossop. King, MacDonald and Geeson all hit hundreds in Leicestershire's total of 541 for four declared. It was Geeson's first and last Championship century. Geeson then took 12 wickets to complete the match double and defeat the home club by an innings and 20 runs. At Worcester, Leicestershire appeared in danger of a thrashing – all out 234 with Worcester 200 for one. Pougher, who was now playing as a batsman, was put on as a seventh bowler and took seven wickets, which restricted Worcestershire's eventual lead to 70. Wood made a faultless 156 in the second innings and Worcestershire never looked like obtaining the 266 needed on the final day. They lost by 79 runs.

These victories moved Leicestershire only two places up the Championship table. Of the other first-class fixtures, the South Africans were beaten by nine wickets after de Trafford took a risk and put the tourists in to bat. There was an innings victory over W. G. Grace's London County; the latter fielded a poor side and both King and MacDonald took advantage, hitting hundreds.

Of the debutants of 1901, Odell played fairly often until 1908; Arthur Davis, an amateur from the Ivanhoe Club, deputised for Whiteside behind the stumps and played regularly in 1903; R. T.

Crawford, who had played for Surrey 2nd XI in 1900 and was the brother of V. F. S. Crawford, the brilliant Surrey batsman, was qualified for Leicestershire by birth and made his debut in the opening home match against Surrey, his brother playing for the opposition. Reggie Crawford averaged about ten matches a year over a decade and proved a useful all-rounder. He had the great disadvantage of a club-foot and his appearances were also limited by professional engagements as a singer.

The weather was quite abominable in 1902. Of the 20 County Championship games Leicestershire arranged only six produced a definite result – two wins and four defeats. Since all counties were similarly affected this seemingly modest record pushed Leicestershire slightly further up the table to eleventh position. It was found that the clay subsoil under a portion of the new ground tended to retain the frequent downpours longer than desirable and caused unnecessary delays in the resumption of play after rain – in the following winter this defect was remedied.

The first of the two 1902 successes was a match of great contrast – Leicestershire made 92, then bowled out Worcestershire for 98, Odell and Woodcock being unchanged. On the second day everything changed. Knight and King hit hundreds and 377 was the total. The bowlers then took charge again and victory was by 175 runs. That was in May; the County had to wait until mid-August for a second taste of victory, Hampshire being beaten in the final home match by six wickets, despite the whole of the first day being lost to rain. Odell took seven for 33 in the second innings and in all captured 88 first-class wickets during the summer – not bad for a player who was regarded as second rate 18 months before. It was just as well he proved so destructive, because Woodcock strained a knee early in the campaign and could turn out in only eight Championship matches, whilst Geeson's leg-breaks no longer seemed to bother anyone. Tom Marlow of Anstey, a slow left-arm bowler was given another try; he had played one or twice in 1900 and 1901. He twice took five wickets in an innings. His action was good, but somehow he never developed further and after 1903 left the County Club. Arthur Emmett, the son of the old Yorkshire professional, Tom, was given a trial in three games, without success. A right-arm medium pace bowler, he played for Leicester Town and for that club against Oakham in 1905 bowled the first four batsmen with his first four deliveries, ending by clean bowling all ten for just 14 runs.

Four friendly first-class fixtures were also played in 1902 and in the home match with London County Albert Knight reached 190 not out at close of play on the second day, but failed to become Leicestershire's first double-centurion because the final day was washed out.

Knight and Wood were the only batsmen to complete 1,000 runs, though King managed 949 – King was the only bowler apart from Odell to reach 50 wickets.

The previews for 1903 were very optimistic. Not only was it hoped that the young players would improve further, but two established first-class county players were engaged. The first was V. F. S. Crawford, brother of R. T. Crawford. V. F. S. Crawford had been a schoolboy prodigy at Whitgift and in 1902 was regarded as the hardest hitting batsman in county cricket – in 1899 he had actually hit a hundred in 19 minutes and reached 180 out of a total of 215. In another local game in Surrey he made 75 out of 77! When he joined Leicestershire as Secretary, having been Assistant Secretary at The Oval, he had been appearing for Surrey since 1896 and his best summer had been 1901 when he completed over 1,500 runs. He was qualified by birth for Leicestershire as was the other recruit, George Gill, the Somerset professional. A fast-medium bowler, Gill had been playing for Somerset since 1897 and in the season just past had taken 79 wickets at 18 runs each. He was also a useful batsman.

In the event, the 1903 season was to prove one of the worst in the County's history – because so much had been expected, perhaps it might be considered the worst of all. The County shared bottom place with Hampshire, both clubs having one victory and ten defeats. Apologists could point to the total breakdown of Woodcock – he played two matches only – and the disappearance of Geeson, but the latter was over 40 and each of his wickets in 1902 had cost 47 runs each. The bowling could be described as innocuous. Gill had the best figures, but his 36 Championship wickets cost 26 runs each. King and Odell were less effective than in 1902 and R. T. Crawford, who had picked up 37 wickets at 22 runs the previous year, now had 33 at 29.

Looking at the batting, R. T. Crawford and V. F. S. Crawford both had very moderate figures. Coe did so badly that he was dropped from the side. King and Wood remained the same as in 1902, so the one bright spot was Albert Knight. In Leicestershire games he hit 1,553 runs, average 45.68 and was selected for the Players *v* Gentlemen, scored a century, which brought him more prominently to the public eye and was selected for the MCC tour to Australia. He also hit the first Leicestershire double century – 229 not out at Worcester.

By some odd chance, the single Championship win came when

Knight was away representing the Players and Gill was also absent. The opponents were Derbyshire, who gained a first-innings lead of 70, but Wood, Whitehead and King all batted well in the second knock, King hitting 167 and Odell took six wickets to dismiss Derbyshire on the final afternoon.

The defeats should be quickly dealt with. Of the ten, three were by an innings, and the closest was at The Oval, where Leicestershire seemed to be heading for victory, having a first-innings lead of 124, and setting Surrey 280 in the last innings in 225 minutes. Surrey won by three wickets with five minutes to spare. Knight was almost entirely responsible for the narrowness of this defeat – he made 144 out of 312 in the first innings and 91 out of 155 in the second. The latter was not out, so Knight was unlucky not to complete a century in each innings.

One of the drawn games demands attention. At Trent Bridge Notts hit 739 for seven declared off the Leicestershire bowlers, four of whom conceded more than 100 runs. It was the highest total made against Leicestershire and the partnership of 369 between John and William Gunn was a world first-class record for the third wicket. John Gunn hit 294. After the first innings Leicestershire were 508 in arrears, but following on, Knight and King both hit hundreds and put on 241 for the second wicket to save the match.

Apart from Gill and V. F. S. Crawford, two other cricketers made their debut in 1903: Thomas Allsopp, a slow left-arm bowler, and Thomas Jayes, a fast bowler from Ratby. Allsopp played for three seasons with some success, but then moved to Norfolk and did well in minor counties cricket. Jayes was soon to develop into one of the best fast bowlers in England and just missed playing against Australia in 1909; ill-health, however, caused him to give up cricket early in 1911 and he died in April 1913.

On 15 June 1904, Leicestershire beat Derbyshire at Derby by six wickets. The Championship table published the following day showed Leicestershire in second place, only Lancashire being ahead of them. This was the County's fifth victory, including two over London County. The next two matches provided two more wins at the expense of MCC and Hampshire and this was immediately followed by victory over Worcestershire, keeping the County hard on the heels of Lancashire. The turnround in the side's fortunes was thus quite dramatic. The successes were very much team efforts. Wood, Knight and King had the best figures, but most of the side made useful contributions. The sudden run of good fortune seemed to evaporate as quickly as it had arrived. In the second half of the campaign only one further Championship victory was garnered and that against a very feeble Hampshire side. The immediate reason for the decline was the injury which Knight suffered whilst playing for the Players at Lord's in early July. In this match, King, who was selected at the last moment, had the distinction of a century in each innings.

The results in July and August meant that Leicestershire fell out of the race for the title and had to settle for seventh place. This was the best result the County had achieved so far in ten years of Championship cricket. Five batsmen completed 1,000 first-class runs for the side, Knight, Wood, King, Coe and Whitehead, the last two for the first time. Vivian Crawford, in his second summer, again failed to reproduce the form he had shown for Surrey.

On the whole the bowling was expensive, all four of the main bowlers, Gill, Allsopp, King and Odell averaging between 24 and 28 runs per wicket. It was Allsopp's one season of success at first-class level. The fielding came in for considerable criticism,

The Leicestershire team in 1905, when the County enjoyed their most successful season till then, finishing fifth in the Championship. Left to right, back: G. C. Gill, A. E. Davis, H. Whitehead, A. E. Knight, T. Jayes. Middle: C. J. B. Wood, R. T. Crawford, C. E. de Trafford, V. F. S. Crawford, W. W. O'Dell. Front: S. Coe.

though Vivian Crawford held 25 catches, his brother 24 and Whitehead the same number.

With one change in the regular eleven for 1905, the introduction of the fast bowler, Jayes, Leicestershire not only consolidated their newly acquired place in the Championship, but four consecutive wins, all at Aylestone Road, beginning in late July, took the County up to fifth position. This result was not to be bettered until 1953. Jayes made all the difference to the attack, taking 102 wickets at 23.52. At times he was very fast – in fact he did sacrifice accuracy for speed in some instances – but it was as much his whole attitude to the game that seemed to put the rest of his colleagues on their toes and the outcricket improved immensely.

Despite the success of Leicestershire, the difference between the strength of the top four counties – Yorkshire, Lancashire, Sussex and Surrey – and the rest, particularly those raised to Championship status in 1895, remained quite large. Leicestershire failed to beat any of the four noted above. The difference was to remain more or less unaltered until after the Second World War. The County beat Hampshire, Derbyshire and Essex twice and Warwickshire at Edgbaston and Northants at Leicester. The successes against Hampshire were mainly the work of Wood and Knight as batsmen and the bowling of Jayes. In the fixture at Aylestone Road, Wood completed his first double century, Knight made 96 and Jayes took eight wickets, an innings victory being obtained inside two days. This was not completely to the advantage of Knight, who had chosen the game for his Benefit. The away match was also an innings victory. Knight made 177, Wood 119 and Jayes again took eight wickets.

Another innings win was achieved at Chesterfield. Wood made exactly 100 and Odell returned match figures of 11 for 44 – Derbyshire were all out for 36 and 80. At Aylestone Road the game was more even and Leicestershire's success owed almost everything to Jayes. He came in to bat with the total 27 for five and hit 74, then in the final innings took nine for 78 to finish off the game before lunch on the third day; this proved most fortunate since the rain arrived in the afternoon.

The double over Essex was achieved by an innings at Leyton and six wickets at Leicester. De Trafford hit his first hundred for six years at Leyton – in 95 minutes – and Jayes took ten wickets. At home Whitehead made 137 and a lead of 218 was gained on first innings, which meant that Essex followed on and despite an improved second innings, left Leicester only 105 to make.

Wood headed the batting table with 1,663 runs, average 44.95; Knight and Whitehead also topped 1,000. Vivian Crawford at last looked something like the player he had been at The Oval, but missed much of the second half of the season. His brother was rarely available. Gill took 22 wickets in the first three matches, including an innings analysis of nine for 89 at Edgbaston, then could manage only eight more Championship victims in ten matches. In contrast Coe's bowling took on a new dimension and he actually topped the Championship averages with 49 wickets at 22 runs each.

It should be noted that the amateur 'G. B. W. Brown' who turned out at Bramall Lane was in fact the professional J. H. Brown, who had played occasionally commencing 1898.

Leicestershire's good season on the field was echoed by an excellent year financially with both membership and turnstiles receipts on the increase. The Aylestone Road ground had been further improved and the facilities were appreciated by the local supporters.

From the relative success of the previous two summers, Leicestershire plummeted down to the penultimate post in 1906. The Committee were quite alarmed by this change and set up a committee of inquiry. The report of this sub-committee made the following pronouncement: 'slackness in the field, a lack of grit and determination on critical occasions, an absence of esprit de corps in the team, and neglect by players in certain instances to travel with the rest of the team overnight.'

The Committee suggested that the ground staff should be increased, a local coach be employed as head of the groundstaff and that the general running of the groundstaff should be based on the system used by Kent.

Whilst this was unfolding in the aftermath of the season, de Trafford announced that he wished to resign as captain. His leadership had, in fact, been the subject of a barrage of criticism. Another sub-committee was appointed to advise on the subject of the captaincy.

The Committee could not be blamed for being dilatory. The first sub-committee produced its report by mid-September and the announcement of a new captain came before the end of November.

'Teddy' Richardson, who had played for the County Club soon after its formation and whose local cricket was for Belgrave and Leicester Town, was placed in charge of the groundstaff.

Looking briefly at the results of 1906: the three Championship wins were against Derbyshire, Northants and Worcestershire, the counties which with Leicestershire occupied the four bottom places at the end of the year. Leicestershire achieved a batting

WORCESTERSHIRE *v* LEICESTERSHIRE

Played at Worcester, 19, 20 and 21 July 1906

MATCH DRAWN

WORCESTERSHIRE	FIRST INNINGS		SECOND INNINGS	
*Mr H. K. Foster	b King	52	c R. T. Crawford b Jayes	18
F. Bowley	b Odell	10	not out	167
E. Arnold	b King	18	c and b Whitehead	112
Mr W. E. C. Hutchings	c Shields b R. T. Crawford	0	not out	25
J. A. Cuffe	b Jayes	11		
Mr W. B. Burns	c V. F. S. Crawford b Coe	87		
F. Pearson	lbw b Jayes	95		
G. Wheldon	c Wood b Odell	17		
G. A. Wilson	c Wood b R. T. Crawford	66		
R. Burrows	b Jayes	15		
†J. Ainley	not out	0		
Extras	b	9	b 14, lb 3, w 5	22
Total		380	(2 wkts)	344

BOWLING	O	M	R	W	O	M	R	W
Jayes	30	2	161	3	18	3	57	1
Odell	23	5	72	2	9	3	16	0
King	21	5	58	2	8	1	12	0
Crawford	16.3	2	54	2	8	2	24	0
Coe	7	0	26	1	9	1	32	0
Wood					22	2	98	0
Whitehead					22	4	83	1

LEICESTERSHIRE	FIRST INNINGS		SECOND INNINGS
Mr C. J. B. Wood	b Wilson	225	
H. Whitehead	c Foster b Cuffe	174	
A. E. Knight	c Hutchings b Arnold	97	
S. Coe	b Burrows	50	
Mr V. F. S. Crawford	not out	102	
J. H. King	not out	14	
*Mr C. E. de Trafford			
Mr R. T. Crawford			
Mr W. W. Odell			
†Mr J. Shields			
T. Jayes			
Extras	b 25, lb 4, w 10	39	
Total	(4 wkts dec)	701	

BOWLING	O	M	R	W	O	M	R	W
Wilson	35	3	162	1				
Arnold	20	3	73	1				
Burrows	20	2	93	1				
Cuffe	42	2	165	1				
Pearson	36	3	148	0				
Burns	1	0	6	0				
Bowley	2	0	15	0				

Umpires: J. Carlin and W. A. J. West

*Captain; †Wicketkeeper

triumph in a drawn match at Worcester in July, scoring the highest total of the season, 701 for four declared. Wood made 225, his highest score, Whitehead 174 and Vivian Crawford 102 not out. But Worcestershire had made 380 in their first innings and did better in the second, when Bowley and Arnold were centurions in a total of 344 for two. Altogether 1,425 runs were scored for the loss of only 16 wickets. Wood, as a batsman, and Jayes, as a bowler, more or less maintained their figures of 1905, though both had poorer averages. Knight was much less consistent, but an unbeaten 180 against Hampshire kept his average reasonably healthy. King had a very disappointing year with both bat and ball, whilst Coe's bowling fell back. The wicketkeeper, John Whiteside, retired at the end of the summer – he was now 45 and had played since 1893.

William Ewart Benskin made his debut against Essex at Southend – the first Championship game ever played at the venue – and by taking the last three wickets in the Essex first innings marked the occasion with a hat-trick. A right-arm fast bowler, he was engaged as a professional in Scotland for some years and reappeared for Leicestershire after the First World War.

Another 'William Ewart' made his debut – W. E. Astill – and he will feature in this story until 1930, by which time he had taken 2,130 wickets for the County. His first appearance was the final match of 1906.

The *Wisden* review of the season overlooked Astill, stating that no new players of promise were seen in 1906 and it was up to the old hands to regain the ground lost during the year.

ASTILL ARRIVES

SIR ARTHUR HAZLERIGG WAS appointed captain in place of de Trafford. The new captain was 28. He had been educated at Eton and Trinity College, Cambridge, but had not played cricket for his school or university. The move by the County Committee to appoint as leader for a County Championship a cricketer with no previous experience of county cricket or indeed of cricket at any level above Country House matches, was at the time unique, though in the following 50 years it was to become, if not commonplace, certainly fairly frequent. All the counties in 1907 had amateur captains, the last full-time professional to be employed before then being Sherwin for Notts in 1888, but the number of counties had increased to 16 in the Championship and the number of talented amateurs available for an entire season was very limited. Those developed through Oxford and Cambridge by and large played for a season or two before business or the professions removed them from the county scene except when on leave or holiday.

Leicestershire, in fact, had two amateurs in their regular side – V. F. S. Crawford and W. W. Odell – so the committee presumably thought neither suitable and that the unease in the dressing room required a man in the mould of Lord Hawke, the long-serving Yorkshire captain, who had dealt with the unruly elements in that county side and turned the eleven into the strongest in England. Lord Hawke, however, had been in the eleven at Eton and obtained a blue at Cambridge before taking on the Yorkshire side.

Hazlerigg had two pieces of good luck – first the side was remarkably free from injury: five players appeared in every Championship game, another two missed one, Jayes missed two and Wood and King three each. The final member of the side was Shields, the amateur wicketkeeper. Shields, Scottish by birth, was a member of the Ashby-de-la-Zouch Club and though not an elegant wicketkeeper was effective enough; he had made his debut in 1906 and when he was absent Albert Payne deputised. Payne was regarded as a brilliant prospect, but he died of consumption in May 1908 aged 22.

The other piece of luck was the sudden blooming of Astill. Aged 19 when the season began and with just one first-class match behind him, his slow-medium deliveries captured 80 wickets at 17 runs each and he topped the Leicestershire bowling

Sir Arthur Hazlerigg, who was to become 1st Baron Hazlerigg in 1945, led Leicestershire from 1907 to 1910 and became President in 1930.

averages. If he had not begun to tire in mid-August he might well have taken 100 wickets.

Sir Arthur got off to, on paper, a dreadful start, but the fixture list was so arranged that Leicestershire met the strongest sides first – the second and third matches were both against Notts, who won the 1907 title and Leicestershire lost the away game by an innings and the home game by nine wickets; the first fixture was with Lancashire and the fourth with Surrey, two other leading sides, and both were lost. There followed Kent and Yorkshire, the first another loss and the second a draw, but much in Yorkshire's favour.

There were two non-Championship games in this period. The touring South Africans won by 98 runs, while the MCC match at Lord's proved one of the features of the season. MCC made 371 and the County replied with 239. It looked all over, but Odell and Jayes, taking five wickets apiece, dismissed MCC for 69 and this left Leicestershire 201 in the final innings. The first five wickets went for 83, then Coe and King, helped by dropped catches, increased the score to within a handful. Unfortunately wickets then fell fast and the match ended as a tie.

The run of ill-fortune ended on 12 July, when Hampshire were beaten in two days, bowled out for 89 and 58 by Odell and Astill. This was immediately followed by victory over Derbyshire, when Wood batted 260 minutes for 133 and Vivian Crawford 120 minutes for 114.

Four more wins in the second half of the season meant that the County finished in 11th place – not as good as in 1905, but quite respectable. The Championship at this time was awarded on a percentage system as the counties played a different number of matches – Surrey had 28 fixtures, Leicestershire 20 and Somerset only 18 – and counties did not have to play every other side. Leicestershire divided their fixtures equally between the top counties and the weak ones, playing home and away against five of each.

The season being wet, runs were at a premium and no Leicestershire batsman reached 1,000, though Knight made 976. Whitehead and Vivian Crawford also made over 900. Odell completed 100 wickets and with Astill, King and Jayes did the bulk of the bowling. Jayes found the wickets too slow and was more expensive, though at Maidstone against Kent he performed the hat-trick, dismissing three good batsmen in Dillon, Troughton and Woolley.

The dismal weather had an adverse effect on the finances and the club were in debt to the tune of some £1,500. A campaign led by the County's President, J. W. Logan, succeeded in wiping off the arrears and putting some money in the bank for improvements to the ground.

In order to attract more spectators, Leicestershire experimented by starting their first fixture of 1908 on a Saturday, the first time this idea had been tried in Championship cricket. A crowd of 6,000 turned out and the County appropriately were in form. Dismissed for 173, they ran through Warwickshire, Odell and Astill bowling unchanged and not a single visiting batsman reaching double figures, the total being 54. A decisive victory was gained by 173 runs. There followed a sequence of three losses and two draws before a second success, Northants losing by an innings. King and Coe hit hundreds and added 249 for the fourth wicket and with Northants failing twice the match was all over on the third morning. Nine days later Sussex were beaten at Aylestone Road, when nearly everyone in the side made a useful contribution. That was on 19 June. It seemed that the County might finish in the top half of the table, but the results in the second half of the summer were deplorable. The bowling lost its bite – at one stage the Committee even brought back the long retired Woodcock – and confidence was lost. The old complaints of poor fielding and general slackness were once more coming to the surface. Only one match was won in this period, Derbyshire being beaten at Derby, when Ewart Astill had two splendid analyses: 24.3-10-31-6 and 15-5-30-7. The County dropped two places compared with 1907.

The improved conditions meant that run-getting was easier – Coe, Wood and Crawford all completed 1,000 runs, but Knight and Whitehead did not do so well. Astill topped the bowling averages – 91 wickets at 20.43 runs each. His main support came from Odell, Jayes being more expensive as well as missing six matches through injury.

The year saw the debut of William Shipman from Ratby. A right-arm fast bowler he was to play regularly until 1914 and was the elder brother of A. W. Shipman, who played between the wars as a batsman – there was a 15-year difference between the ages of the two.

The membership of the County Club was now 1,601, bringing in subscriptions worth £1,754, whilst gate receipts for 1908 were £1,507. At the Annual General Meeting, T. Burdett was presented with a silver tea service and candelabras to signal his 30 years as Honorary Secretary.

Odell announced that owing to business he would be unable to play during 1909. This proved to be very unfortunate, since the wickets during the summer were just the sort to suit his bowling. In his absence and with little fresh talent, Leicestershire struggled. Only three wins came their way, the most satisfying being the ten-wicket victory over Notts at Aylestone Road. Jayes and King dismissed Notts for 148 and good innings by Wood and King produced a lead of 118. King again bowled well in the second innings and with three run-outs, Notts made even less than in their first outing.

Leicestershire supporters, however, had a pleasant surprise on 11 June, when the selectors named both King and Jayes for the England side in the second Test at Lord's. The critics were also caught unawares as the following comment in *Cricket* makes clear:

> A week ago the selection of King and Jayes for so important a match would have been regarded as very improbable, although the merits of the former as an all-round player have long been known to all those who follow the game at all closely. Many cricketers are of the opinion that the presence of a sound left-handed batsman is a source of strength to any side, and I, for one, was very glad when it was announced that King had been asked to be present at Lord's on Monday. He had been doing excellent work for Leicestershire, and on his occasional appearances in MCC and other matches, for several years, and the most weighty reason urged against his selection for this week's game appears to have been that he is no longer a young man. That, however, is his misfortune, and not his fault . . . Jayes has been known for the past few seasons as a very good all-round cricketer, but he had done nothing to justify his selection for so important a match. Why he should have been chosen, with Fielder, Wass and Buckenham available, is a mystery which goes to show that cricket is a game of which the 'glorious uncertainty' is not confined to the actual play.

In the event only King played – it was the first time a Leicestershire cricketer had been included for a Test in England, though Pougher and Knight had played overseas. Australia won the match by nine wickets, but King made the highest individual score for England – 60 out of 131 in 155 minutes without a chance. He never appeared again and was not even in the 14 selected for the third Test. Jayes was never to play for England.

King topped the County batting table. He averaged 30.37 and hit 1,154 runs, but without scoring a hundred; as he had only two 'not outs' to aid his average his figures showed a remarkable consistency. Knight was the other batsman to top 1,000. Vivian Crawford hit two hundreds and 922 runs; Wood and Whitehead had poor summers, as did Coe.

With regard to the bowling Jayes took 105 wickets at 20.09 runs each, his main support coming from Astill and King, though Billy Shipman had days of success, including a hat-trick against Derbyshire.

Apart from King's Test, the other honour which came was the selection of John Shields as wicketkeeper for the Gentlemen at both Lord's and The Oval. At Lord's he executed four stumpings and was complimented on his keeping. The County acquired a very useful deputy keeper in Walter Sturman, but owing to

Shields' presence his outings with the County were very restricted.

The financial situation continued to be cause for concern and in
July the whole of the Finance Sub-Committee resigned en bloc
due to an argument over expenses. There was more ill-feeling
when the Committee recommended reducing the Championship
fixtures by two in order to save money. The Hampshire matches
were dropped for 1910. An Extraordinary General Meeting
presided over by C. E. de Trafford was held in December. The
year's workings had resulted in a loss of £600 and total debts now
amounted to £1,000. It was agreed that in future Ladies' tickets
should be charged for – many counties allowed husbands to bring
their wives into the ground free of charge, if the husband was a
member. It was also decided to seek a number of guarantors for
the County Club.

Scholastic duties again prevented Odell playing in 1910 and a
further blow occurred in the spring when King injured a knee and
as a result missed practically the whole summer.

The one new player to gain a regular place in the side was A. T.
Sharp from Whitwick. He had been in the Repton Eleven in 1907
and 1908, making his County debut in the latter summer. It was a
vintage year for Repton – no less than four of the eleven going
straight into county cricket and two others being invited but
declining, whilst a seventh played for Sussex 2nd XI. Sharp was
regarded as the best bat in the school. He did not, however, make
much of an impression in Championship matches until 1911 and
his best year was 1921 when he captained the side. A member of
the legal profession, his appearances were limited for much of his
career, which continued until 1935. In 1910 Sharp averaged 18,
with a highest score of 68.

The most pleasing feature of the year was the improved
bowling of Shipman; he took 86 wickets at 21 runs each, topping
the table. His best performance came in the final match, which
had been postponed from May due to the death of King Edward
VII. Shipman returned first-innings figures of 19-2-83-9 and
Leicestershire went on to win by 63 runs – the previous week
Surrey had beaten them at Aylestone Road by an innings. It was
the end to a very odd season, for Leicestershire also beat Yorkshire, for the first time in Championship cricket, Kent and
Lancashire. Other wins against lesser opponents in Warwickshire
and Northants placed the County in 10th position.

The victory over Yorkshire was at Headingley. Leicestershire
batted first and made a laborious 278; Shipman then dismissed the
first five Yorkshire batsmen at a personal cost of 12 runs and a

ALBERT ERNEST KNIGHT

'A self-made cricketer, he is one of the most scientific batsmen in English cricket, playing a very straight bat and dealing with every ball "according to Cocker".' Thus is Knight described in the *Blue Book* of 1909. Cocker was the celebrated author of a book on arithmetic, from which pupils down the ages suffered. It is an appropriate metaphor, since Knight himself wrote a highly idiosyncratic volume, *The Complete Cricketer.*

His batting was especially strong on the off-side and his most notable stroke was the square cut.

Born in Leicester in 1872 his first-class career opened in 1895 and his best year was 1903 when he hit 1,834 runs. This form won him a place in the MCC side to Australia in 1903–04. His only Tests for England were on that tour and his innings of 70 not out in the fourth Test at Sydney enabled England to regain the Ashes – it was the highest individual innings in a low-scoring match. His career ended in 1912, by which time he had played 367 matches for Leicestershire. The following year he accepted a post as coach at Highgate School and remained there for many years.

Having moved down to London before the First World War, he died in Edmonton in 1946 aged 73. In all first-class matches he hit 19,357 runs, average 29.24, with 34 hundreds; he was a brilliant fieldsman in the covers.

(NCCC)

total of 31; Hirst saved a complete debacle, but Yorkshire were 148 in arrears. Leicestershire then hit out and declared, setting Yorkshire 405 in five hours. Jayes captured seven for 57 and the margin of victory was 259 runs. Kent, the eventual Champions, were beaten at Aylestone Road. Shipman took nine wickets and Astill six. The Lancashire match at home was remarkable in that Leicestershire gained a first-innings lead of 354, Coe making 156 in 170 minutes. Lancashire followed on and totalled 414, a splendid recovery but not enough to prevent Leicestershire winning by six wickets – Shipman took ten for 136 in the match.

Wood and Coe both made 1,000 runs; the former through consistent batting, the latter due to three centuries. Knight had another poor summer; of the others, Whitehead and Vivian Crawford were moderately successful. Crawford left the County at the end of the year to become a tea-planter in Ceylon. His brilliant reputation with Surrey had only occasionally been seen whilst he played for his native county. He died in 1922 aged 43, his health having been badly affected while serving in the First World War. His colleague in the Surrey side, D. L. A. Jephson began a tribute to him as follows:

> To those of us who love the clean, straight bat, the full-faced drive, the low, clean, golf-tinged shot, or the shoulder swing that cleared the ground, minimum of effort, maximum of accomplishment, his passing in the very prime of manhood, came as a blow – delivered in the face.

Albert Callington, known as Albert Lord, made his debut for the county in 1910. The legend concerning this cricketing alias is that, on joining the staff and finding John KING and Albert KNIGHT, Callington thought he would elevate himself to the peerage. A sound right-hand opening batsman he played for the County until 1926 and when appearing in cricket matches always seems to have used his alias.

On 22 March 1911 the County Committee received a letter from Sir Arthur Hazlerigg resigning as captain. The Committee on 5 April were in two minds as to the appointment of a successor and finally issued a statement announcing that John Shields would lead the side 'for the first three matches'. Shields protested that he would not agree to be a captain 'on trial' and the Committee then had second thoughts: Shields was appointed for the whole season and continued, in fact, for three.

Another cause for concern was the health of two players. Jayes was sent to Bournemouth in the hope that his chest complaint would ease; A T. Sharp had an operation for appendicitis. Jayes played in the first two games of 1911, failed to take a wicket and the Club paid for him to go to Switzerland, his career at an end. Sharp played in eight 1911 Championship games, in seven he scored just 147 runs at an average of ten. In the eighth – at Chesterfield – he hit 216 with two fives and 37 fours in 250 minutes, after taking 105 minutes to reach 50.

The 1911 season in general was not one Leicestershire supporters care to remember. After 20 first-class matches had been undertaken 16 had been lost and the other four drawn. One bright spot among all this was the performance of Wood, in the match with Yorkshire at Bradford in June. Wood became only the third player to carry his bat through an innings twice in one match. He made 107 not out in Leicestershire's first innings of 309, and 117 not out in the second innings of 296. *Wisden* reported that: 'his achievement was rendered the more wonderful from the fact that in neither innings did he give a chance'. He batted eight hours and 40 minutes in all, and was, of course, on the field for the whole match. Sadly Leicestershire lost the match by five wickets. The County's first Championship win came, however, on 10 August, when Yorkshire came to Aylestone Road for the return. Shipman bowled them out for 153, taking seven for 73 and another good innings from Wood put Leicestershire in the lead by 67 runs. Yorkshire batted a second time and King produced the most remarkable spell of bowling in his long career – in 20 deliveries he took seven wickets without conceding a run. According to the experts at the time, such a spell had only been witnessed once before in Championship cricket – A. W. Mold produced the selfsame figures for Lancashire *v* Somerset in 1894. King's full innings figures were 9.5-3-17-8 and Yorkshire were all out for 47, losing by an innings.

It is sad to report that the next two, the last two, home matches were both lost by an innings. The final home fixture took the County away for Leicester for the first time, the match against Warwickshire being at Hinckley. A crowd of 5,000 attended on the Saturday and 4,000 on the Monday (the game finished in two days).

The disappearance of Jayes meant that the bowling was weakened and it was therefore even more serious that Astill, for the first time in his still young career, failed and was left out of the eleven. So the attack consisted of Shipman and King, but outside his astonishing Yorkshire match King achieved modest figures and Shipman, with 110 wickets, was the only bowler whose victims cost less than 30 runs each.

Nine new players were tried but only one, Arthur 'Pecker'

YORKSHIRE *v* LEICESTERSHIRE

Played at Bradford, 12, 13 and 14 June 1911

LEICESTERSHIRE WON BY FIVE WICKETS

LEICESTERSHIRE	**FIRST INNINGS**		**SECOND INNINGS**	
Mr C. J. B. Wood	not out	107	not out	117
A. E. Knight	c Dolphin b Hirst	12	b Hirst	14
H. Whitehead	c Dolphin b Hirst	5	c Booth b Hirst	2
A. Lord	c Hirst b Booth	43	b Hirst	4
J. H. King	b Hirst	2	b Drake	1
S. Coe	c Hirst b Rhodes	49	absent hurt	0
Mr F. M. Joyce	b Haigh	0	b Hirst	5
A. Mounteney	c Booth b Hirst	21	c Denton b Rhodes	96
W. Shipman	c Wilson b Rhodes	38	c Turner b Haigh	29
*†Mr J. Shields	c Dolphin b Rhodes	20	c Hirst b Bayes	6
W. Brown	run out	4	b Hirst	8
Extras	b 7, lb 1	8	lb 13, nb 1	14
Total		309		296

BOWLING	**O**	**M**	**R**	**W**	**O**	**M**	**R**	**W**
Hirst	29	7	77	4	29.2	8	68	5
Booth	24	6	65	1	13	1	50	0
Bayes	11	2	50	0	7	0	29	1
Haigh	9	2	22	1	15	3	40	1
Rhodes	16.3	3	47	3	12	2	58	1
Drake	10	1	40	0	16	5	37	1

YORKSHIRE	**FIRST INNINGS**		**SECOND INNINGS**	
W. Rhodes	c Whitehead b Joyce	92	c Wood b King	38
B. B. Wilson	b Shipman	21	b Joyce	16
D. Denton	c sub b Brown	27	not out	137
A. Drake	c Whitehead b Joyce	19	c sub b Shipman	25
G. H. Hirst	c sub b Joyce	20	b Shipman	10
M. W. Booth	c King b Joyce	71	c Shields b Joyce	18
A. Turner	c Mounteney b Brown	12	not out	16
E. Oldroyd	c sub b Whitehead	17		
S. Haigh	run out	39		
†A. Dolphin	b Shipman	1		
G. Bayes	not out	5		
Extras	b 4, lb 6	10	b 9, lb 1, w 1, nb 1	12
Total		334	(5 wkts)	272

BOWLING	**O**	**M**	**R**	**W**	**O**	**M**	**R**	**W**
Shipman	22	3	63	2	16	0	93	2
King	15	1	50	0	6	0	41	0
Brown	16	1	64	2	4.2	0	26	0
Wood	13	1	39	0	3	0	22	0
Joyce	20	1	70	4	13	2	48	2
Lord	1	0	1	0	2	1	1	0
Whitehead	10.4	0	37	1	5	0	29	0

Umpires: H. Bagshaw and W. Flowers

*Captain; †Wicketkeeper

Mounteney, the son of the old county cricketer, stayed long with the County. He was an attractive batsman and appeared regularly until 1923. Rather easy-going his 'laid back' nature prevented him from going as far as he might in county cricket. Like a number of his County colleagues he was a useful soccer player and appeared for Leicester Fosse.

The County ended the season last but one, only Somerset being below them. The financial situation had not improved, about £500 being lost on the year – King received £276 for his benefit.

Season 1912 produced little sign of improvement either on or off the field. The Club ended the season with the debt having grown to £1,500 and the position was deemed so serious that a Special General Meeting was held on 20 November in the County Assembly Rooms to decide what should be done. There was some straight talking at the meeting and Mr H. Logan went so far as to say that he did not consider it worth while running a County Club unless it could be run properly. Leicestershire in fact were not alone, as Somerset, Worcestershire, Derbyshire and Northants also struggled to survive and the press called for a two-division Championship to help those in financial difficulties. The local newspapers started a Shilling Fund to help the Club and the other two immediate moves were first to spread more fixtures around the county and second to have Saturday starts to matches whenever possible.

Turning to events on the field in 1912, three Championship games were won and 13 lost. The first success came in mid-June at Nuneaton when Astill and King bowled unchanged to dismiss Warwickshire for 85 and provide a first innings lead of 111. F. R. Foster then hit back and with an analysis of 19.2-11-21-7 removed Leicestershire for 90. Warwickshire needed 202 in the final innings and fortunes fluctuated wildly. Warwickshire seemed certain to win when needing only 22 with five wickets left, but a sudden collapse meant that Leicestershire won by three runs. An unknown bowler called Alec Skelding took two of the vital last five wickets. Born in Leicester in 1886, he is now remembered as an eccentric first-class umpire with very thick-lensed glasses and an aversion to dogs. The stories told concerning his days as an umpire are many – he officiated from 1931 until 1958 when he was 72. He had his own system of umpiring signals. The England batsman Joe Hardstaff, who was a particular friend of his, recalled going in to bat and Skelding telling him there would be no lbw decisions because he was wearing his reading glasses by mistake!

A very fast bowler, Skelding performed only modestly in the years up to the First World War and rather true to character did not have his best season until 1927, when he was 40 – unusual for a fast bowler!

From Nuneaton, Leicestershire went to Aylestone Road and another victory, beating Hampshire by 152 runs, with Astill taking eight wickets – after his failures in 1911, Astill regained his confidence and came second only to King as the main wicket-taker for the County.

The third and final win of 1912 came at home against Sussex in July and was very much a team effort, five bowlers sharing the wickets, whilst Knight, King, Whitehead and Curtis made the runs. Jack Curtis was a useful all-rounder, who played in 36 matches between 1906 and 1921, but preferred League cricket and spent much of his time in Lancashire.

The wet wickets meant that Shipman was largely ineffectual and, apart from Astill, the team had to rely very much on King, who ended with 114 wickets at 16 runs each, the best of his career.

Batsmen found run-making difficult, and only Wood exceeded 1,000, but the best innings of the year came from Albert Knight with 147 at Bramall Lane. He batted 290 minutes without a chance against the formidable Yorkshire attack of Rhodes, Hirst, Haigh and Booth. Knight decided at the end of the summer to retire and go as coach to Highgate School – he was only 40. Leicestershire added Ashby-de-la-Zouch to their county venues, Derbyshire being the visitors. Being near the border between the two counties it was to be a frequent meeting place for this fixture and continued to be used until 1964.

Apart from Skelding, another young player who was to become a household name made his debut, George Geary. In 1912 his performances were scarcely of note, but the 19-year-old from Barwell was to become a leading all-rounder in the 1920s, both for Leicestershire and England.

The three victories meant that Leicestershire moved into 13th place (out of 16), a slight improvement, but there was still a great gap between the lesser counties and those at the top.

Season 1912 had been the year of the ill-fated Triangular Tournament. Bad weather and a very moderate Australian team meant the experiment was not a success, but Aylestone did see both Australia and South Africa play the County. G. A. Faulkner was the man of the match when South Africa were the visitors. In a very low-scoring affair his 33 was the best by any batsman and he then took 11 for 59. The County gave a trial to a former Tonbridge School pupil, H. M. Bannister, and on his debut he took seven for 47. He came from Lutterworth and was now aged

81

The Leicestershire team in 1913. Left to right, back: J. H. King, W. E. Astill, G. Geary, W. Shipman, A. Mounteney jun., A. Skelding, A. Lord, Earl of Lanesborough (President). Front: S. C. Packer (Secretary), C. J. B. Wood, J. Shields (Captain), H. M. Bannister, H. Whitehead. (NCCC)

23, but his career in banking prevented him making any regular outings in first-class cricket.

South Africa won their match by 60 runs at tea on the second day. The Australian fixture was drawn, when rain prevented any play on the third day, saving Leicestershire from defeat.

In Ceylon, V. F. S. Crawford was proving to be the outstanding cricketer of the island. He hit over 1,000 runs in 1912 at an average above 50 and also took quite a number of wickets. He also toured Burma with the Ceylon side.

The staff at Aylestone Road for 1913 numbered just eleven: Coe, Whitehead, Shipman, Lord, Mounteney, Brown, Skelding, Preston, Geary, Osborne and Moore – King and Astill were engaged at Lord's. At the AGM a loss of £790 was announced on the 1912 season.

Coalville and Loughborough, in addition to Ashby and Hinckley, were allocated Championship matches for 1913. Each of these out venues had one match, which left seven for Aylestone Road. The Appeal Fund raised about £750 in 1912 and the good attendances at Hinckley and Ashby meant that expenses more or less equalled receipts. The immediate financial future was now secure, but in 1913 the results were as disappointing as ever. Wins increased from three to four, but as Derbyshire and Worcestershire also had improved records, the County fell from 13th to 14th place. As in 1912 it was not until mid-June that a victory was hoisted. This occurred at the new venue of Coalville, when Worcestershire went down by eight wickets. Geary dismissed eleven batsmen and Whitehead hit a brilliant 100 in two hours and then in the final innings he and King added 131 in 75 minutes for the second wicket. The second win, at Queen's Park, Chesterfield, was a quite spectacular affair. The former captain, Charles de Trafford, now aged 49, made only his second County appearance in seven years and arrived at the crease with total 8 for three; two further wickets went down to produce 41 for five, then de Trafford launched into the bowling and in 120 minutes hit 137 with 3 sixes and 17 fours. Shipman and Astill, coming in at 8 and 9 were inspired. The former knocked up 60 in 25 minutes and the latter 75 in 80 minutes. Derbyshire failed twice and victory came by an innings in two days. A fortnight later came a second two-day win, again by an innings. The venue was Hinckley and the victims Warwickshire. This time Wood was the batsman in form. He stayed throughout the innings to make 164 not out from 392 in five hours. On the second day, Shipman and Geary, plus three wickets from Skelding, removed the opposition twice to produce an easy win.

The fourth success was nothing like as emphatic, but Leicestershire turned disaster into triumph, due to King and Skelding. At New Road, Worcestershire made 463 and then dismissed Leicestershire for 286. A masterly exhibition in the follow-on by King – 146 not out in 270 minutes – forced Worcestershire to bat in the final innings needing 139 in 145 minutes on the last afternoon. Skelding bowled tremendously fast and took six wickets to bring victory by eight runs with five minutes playing time to spare.

The fast wickets of 1913 improved most of the averages of the Leicestershire batsmen compared with 1912. King, Whitehead and Wood all exceeded 1,000 runs and nine hundreds were made in Championship matches, King making two in the Northants home game. There was one new centurion, W. N. Riley the Cambridge University blue. He had made his Leicestershire debut whilst still a pupil at Atherstone Grammar School in 1911. A hard-hitting batsman and useful seam bowler, he lost a leg in action in the First World War and later moved to Sussex where he was a member of the County Club Committee.

Wickets were generally dearly bought in 1913. Geary's 79 cost 26 runs each, Shipman's 63, 27 runs and Skelding's 53, 33 runs. King and Astill had even more modest returns.

One debutant of 1913 was the wicketkeeper, Tom Sidwell. He was born in Belgrave in 1888 and both his father and grandfather had been very useful local cricketers. Neat and quiet behind the stumps, Sidwell became the regular keeper in 1914 and remained in possession until 1931; two years afterwards he came out of retirement to assist when Paddy Corrall met with a serious accident. Sidwell was also quite a useful lower-order batsman.

Cecil Wood was appointed captain of Leicestershire for 1914 and marked the start of his leadership with a victory over Essex by 239 runs in the first Championship match of the summer; in addition he scored 120 in the second innings, thus materially assisting in the success. Although the County were then trounced by Hampshire, in the third match they beat the strong Lancashire side by 34 runs at Aylestone Road. Coe made an excellent 79 – the highest knock of the match – and Geary returned the best bowling figures. Against all the official laws, Wood allowed Lancashire to replace Heap with William Tyldesley, after the former had been taken ill when fielding on the first day – Tyldesley batted in both innings and actually made Lancashire's highest score in the second. On 3 June another victory came Leicestershire's way, Northants going down by 214 runs, with Coe hitting 252 not out, the largest individual total ever made for the County. Coe batted only 240 minutes with a six, a five and 39 fours. Geary took six wickets in the first Northants innings and Skelding a similar number in the second.

The following week it was announced that Geary had been chosen for what the press described as the Test Trial at Lord's – The Rest of England *v* MCC Team that toured South Africa. *The World of Cricket* forecast that Geary would play for England, but what concerned the critics was that he was effectively Leicestershire's main bowler and for one so young would be in grave danger of being overbowled to the detriment of his long-term career.

As it turned out the County achieved only one more victory during the summer – at the Fox and Goose Ground, Coalville, against Worcestershire. Leicestershire amassed 507, John King making 227 not out, his highest score for the County. Geary picked up eleven wickets and an innings win was attained.

In the game at Ashby-de-la-Zouch against Kent, Leicestershire were set 375 to win on the final day; against Blythe, Woolley and Fielder this was a tough assignment, so Wood decided to try and bat out time. Leicestershire failed, but Wood spent four hours

LEICESTERSHIRE *v* NORTHAMPTONSHIRE

Played at Leicester, 1, 2 and 3 June 1914

LEICESTER WON BY 214 RUNS

LEICESTERSHIRE	FIRST INNINGS		SECOND INNINGS	
*Mr C. J. B. Wood	b Thompson	15	b Wells	36
H. Whitehead	c Wells b Thompson	0	c sub b Beers	52
A. Mounteney	c Haywood b Smith	55	st Buswell b Smith	26
J. H. King	run out	22	not out	41
Mr A. T. Sharp	lbw b Wells	24	c Beers b Smith	0
S. Coe	not out	252	c Woolley b Wells	7
Mr F. M. Joyce	lbw b Woolley	32	st Buswell b Smith	10
W. Shipman	b Wells	13	c Haywood b Smith	14
†T. E. Sidwell	lbw b Smith	26		
G. Geary	lbw b Smith	0		
A. Skelding	b Wells	2		
Extras	b 7, lb 3, w 1, nb 1	12	lb 3, nb 2	5
Total		453	(7 wkts dec)	191

BOWLING	O	M	R	W	O	M	R	W
Wells	30	4	126	3	15	1	66	2
Thompson	23	7	64	2				
Smith	30	9	88	3	19.4	4	52	4
Murdin	12	1	60	0	7	0	22	0
Woolley	11	2	46	1	11	2	21	0
Beers	8	0	40	0	4	0	25	1
Haywood	2	0	17	0				

NORTHAMPTONSHIRE	FIRST INNINGS		SECOND INNINGS	
*Mr G. A. T. Vials	b Geary	42	c Shipman b Skelding	16
Mr W. H. Denton	c Sharp b Geary	0	lbw b King	12
R. Haywood	b Geary	3	c Mounteney b King	53
Mr S. G. Smith	b Geary	11	b Skelding	54
G. J. Thompson	b King	52	c Skelding b Wood	32
C. N. Woolley	c Whitehead b King	41	c Sidwell b Skelding	15
Mr H. G. Beers	c Joyce b Geary	0	lbw b Skelding	2
F. Walden	lbw b King	16	b Skelding	7
W. Wells	c Shipman b Geary	7	b Skelding	6
†W. A. Buswell	not out	4	lbw b Wood	36
V. Murdin	b King	0	not out	6
Extras	lb	6	b 4, lb 3, w 1, nb 1	9
Total		182		248

BOWLING	O	M	R	W	O	M	R	W
Geary	30	2	75	6	23	6	53	0
Shipman	6	0	36	0	2	0	12	0
King	26.4	11	51	4	17	3	54	2
Skelding	6	0	12	0	27	3	85	6
Joyce	1	0	2	0				
Coe					5	0	20	0
Whitehead					2	0	6	0
Wood					2.3	1	9	2

Umpires: W. Phillips and R. G. Barlow

*Captain; †Wicketkeeper

over 66 runs and evoked the following amusing press comment: 'So stolid was Wood's defence that he made King – no very rapid scorer as a rule – seem an express train compared with a L.B. and S.C.R. local (one writes feelingly).'

Whitehead was awarded the Sussex match in July for his benefit; he had previously agreed to postpone his benefit year, in order to give preference to Tom Jayes. Unfortunately for Whitehead rain ruined his match, the second day being entirely washed out and his receipts were very moderate.

Although war was declared at the beginning of August, the county programme continued. One of the first to be called up was A. T. Sharp and this in effect lost Leicestershire the match with Northants. Sharp, having batted in the first innings, was summoned by the Army on the second day and therefore could not bat in the final innings, Leicestershire losing by four runs.

The final match, against Surrey in September, was not played because The Oval had been requisitioned.

Leicestershire's final record was four wins and 11 losses, which meant they finished 13th. Coe, King and Wood all scored three hundreds and all exceeded 1,000 runs. The bowling figures were much better than the last few seasons. Geary took 115 wickets at 20 runs each, Skelding took 72 wickets and reduced his average from 33 to 22, whilst King took 62 wickets. The surprise of the season however was Bill Brown – in 1912 he had taken five Championship wickets at 44 runs each; in 1913 another five, but at 53 runs each; this season he captured 61 at less than 20 runs each. A 26-year-old left-arm slow-medium bowler from Old Woodhouse, Brown had been on the fringe of the County side since 1910. He was in and out of the side during the first half of the summer, then at Liverpool against Lancashire took six for 80 in the first innings and from that time formed an integral part of the attack. When cricket resumed in 1919 Brown played in the first Leicestershire matches, but found no form and dropped out of county cricket.

THE TWENTIES

DURING THE FIRST WORLD WAR the Aylestone Road pavilion was used as the headquarters of the 53rd ASC Remount Depot and the luncheon pavilion housed a rifle range for the 1st Battalion Leicestershire Volunteer Regt, the ground itself being used for drill. At the beginning of 1918, the Secretary, S. C. Packer reported that many members had continued to pay their subscriptions and that the long-standing overdraft had, as a result, been paid off.

Most of the pre-war cricketers served in the armed forces – J. W. Burdett, F. M. Joyce, W. W. Odell and G. N. Wykes were each awarded the Military Cross, whilst E. L. Challenor and W. W. Jelf received the DSO. As was previously noted, G. H. S. Fowke became a prisoner of war for the second time; he was captured at Auvers on 24 October 1914. Harold Wright, a captain in the 6th Loyal North Lancashire Regiment died as a result of wounds received at Gallipoli; Private A. E. Davis, Royal Fusiliers, was killed near Albert in November 1916 and Second Lieutenant W. W. Odell was posted missing, believed killed, in October 1917.

Not long after the armistice, the county secretaries gathered to arrange a programme for 1919 and the Leicestershire Secretary stated that the Club was able to undertake the necessary number of fixtures to compete in the Championship – only Worcestershire found themselves unable to take part. The authorities agreed that matches should be restricted to two days, but with longer playing hours (an experiment that quickly proved unpopular even with those who had sponsored it).

C. J. B. Wood was reappointed as captain and the first post-war Championship match involving the County was staged at Trent Bridge on 21 and 22 May 1919. There were no new faces, but Benskin reappeared, having ceased his professional commitment in Scotland. The match, like so many in 1919, was drawn; Wood hit the County's first hundred of the new era, in, for him, quick time – 122 in 180 minutes – and the best bowling figures came, not from Geary, King or Brown, but the amateur J. S. Curtis who took seven for 75.

Leicestershire played only 14 Championship games altogether – the minimum allowed being 12 – and with three wins they finished ninth equal with Derbyshire. The first success came against Gloucestershire. The veteran (46-year-old) King took six for 36 to dismiss the western county for 86. The follow-on was enforced, 199 runs in arrears, and though Gloucestershire batted much more strongly the second time round, Leicestershire won by four wickets. The second victory was at Chesterfield, again by four wickets, but with only five minutes to spare. Benskin took 13 wickets in the match, whilst G. B. F. Rudd made the highest score, 75, in quick time. Rudd had been in the Westminster School Eleven in 1913 and made his first-class debut in the following holidays. In 1914 he was up at Oxford and played with little success in the Freshmen's Match and one or two other trials. At the start of 1919 his first-class cricket still amounted to one match, but he appeared throughout 1919 for the County and looked useful without making any major contributions, except the 75 mentioned.

The third win came in the final game at Coventry, when Benskin (six for 21) and Curtis (four for 24) dismissed their opponents for 48 and victory was by nine wickets. In the second innings W. C. M. Berridge took five wickets for the only time in his brief county career. Berridge had captained the Malvern side in 1914 and topped the College bowling averages; he followed his father into the medical profession and played 22 matches for Leicestershire spread over five seasons. He later captained the St Thomas's Hospital side.

Berridge had in fact played in 1914 and therefore despite the four-year break only two newcomers were seen in the eleven. One was Jack Burdett, the son of Thomas Burdett, the long time Honorary Secretary. The younger Burdett played only once. The other was Norman Armstrong, the Loughborough batsman, who also played once and then did not re-appear until 1926. He was to become one of the mainstays of the side.

Although 1919 had been a relatively successful season for Leicestershire the worrying aspect was the average age of the leading players. When practice began for the 1920 campaign, C. J. B. Wood was 44, J. H. King 49, H. Whitehead 45, S. Coe 46, W. E. Benskin 40 and A. Mounteney 37 – in other words half the probable 1920 side were over 35 and most of the so-called youngsters, Sharp, Astill, Sidwell, Rudd, were all over 30. Thus nearly all the County side had reached that stage in their first-class career when, all things being equal, they were not going to improve the standard of their individual performances and old age was going to show in the field. The County needed new blood desperately. Matters were not improved when the one bright star of Leicester cricket, George Geary, announced that he had signed a contract with the Lancashire League Club Nelson for

JOHN HERBERT KING

One of the backbones of Leicestershire and indeed of county cricket for more than a quarter of a century, J. H. King was a confident left-hand batsman and a very useful medium-pace bowler, who deceived the unwary with the way he flighted the ball. He was also a very reliable slip field.

Born in 1871, he was 24 before he made his first-class debut, but still managed a county career spanning 31 seasons. Outside county cricket he received very little recognition. He never toured overseas with a major English side and his Test career was limited to a single match at Lord's in the 1909 series against Australia, when he scored 60 and 4. His most famous match occurred in 1904, when he was chosen for the Players v Gentlemen at Lord's simply because he happened to be on the ground

on the morning of the match, when J. T. Tyldesley was forced to stand down at the last minute. King hit hundreds in both innings, a feat performed only once before in this historic fixture. The wicket was described as very fiery and only two other batsmen in either innings of the Players managed to reach 50, never mind 100.

King played in 502 Leicestershire matches and in his complete first-class career hit 25,122 runs, average 27.33 and took 1,204 wickets, average 25.17. He completed the 'double' in 1912 and 14 times exceeded 1,000 runs in a season. At the age of 52 he scored 205 for Leicestershire v Hampshire at Aylestone Road. He died in Denbigh, North Wales, in 1946. His brother James, and his nephew John William, both occasionally represented Leicestershire.

(NCCC)

1920: he took 95 wickets at 7 runs each and came fourth in the overall League averages. Even more embarrassing to Leicestershire supporters was that third in the same averages was J. S. Curtis, with 112 wickets at 6 runs each. Whilst the County struggled in the lower reaches of the Championship therefore, two of the top four Lancashire League bowlers hailed from the County.

Having played 14 Championship matches in 1919, Leicestershire arranged 24 games in 1920, but out matches were staged at only Hinckley and Ashby – the pitch at Loughborough had come in for some criticism in 1919.

When the 1920 season was over, one comment summed up the County: batting failure. The leading Leicestershire run-getter stood 80th in the first-class averages and only two players averaged more than 20 – Coe 23.41 and Mounteney 20.20. As a comparison, the County Champions, Middlesex, had seven batsmen with better averages than Coe!

By far the best feature of the summer was the five-wicket victory over Notts at Aylestone Road. For once the batting held together, Mounteney made 132 in 180 minutes, the best innings he had ever produced in Championship cricket, King and Coe reached fifty apiece and good bowling by King, Benskin and Astill produced a lead of over 200. Notts followed on and in the final innings Leicestershire required 88 – two wickets fell very quickly, but King and Astill added 53 for the third and prevented any embarrassment.

Somerset were beaten twice. Astill took ten wickets in a low scoring game in Leicester; at Weston, runs were again at a premium, but Astill took six for 42 in the first innings and King seven for 34, including a hat-trick, in the second. The margins of victory were 47 and 41 runs respectively.

The other four wins were at the expense of the weaker counties – Hampshire, Northants and Derbyshire. The difference in strength between the top counties and the others seemed even more marked than it had been in the pre-war days.

The bowling relied entirely on three men. King took 100 wickets at 17.65, Astill, scarcely seen in 1919, captured 97 at 19.80, his spin bowling being more accurate than in the past, and Benskin had 71 victims at 22.26. For the opponents, the bowling of Charlie Parker deserves a mention. In the two Gloucestershire matches he took 26 wickets, including an innings analysis of nine for 35 at Cheltenham, when Leicestershire were dismissed for 54 and 83.

In an effort to strengthen the side six new players were given

CECIL JOHN BURDITT WOOD

Usually known as 'C. J. B.', Wood gained the reputation as one of the most difficult batsman to dismiss in county cricket. Right-handed, he developed a stubborn defence and though his batting was unattractive to watch and his runs came in dribs and drabs he proved invaluable to a County side whose batting was unreliable. No fewer than 17 times he carried his bat through the entire innings, a record without parallel in County Championship cricket. On one famous occasion at Park Avenue, Bradford, in 1911, he performed the feat in both innings of the match and that against the powerful Yorkshire attack – the feat had only been accomplished twice before.

A native of Northampton, he had been in the XI at Wellingborough and played one or two games for Northants before moving on to Leicestershire as a professional in 1896. He later accepted the post of Assistant Treasurer of the County Club and resumed status as an amateur. He was selected for the Gentlemen against the Players on four occasions, but that was as far as he climbed in terms of official recognition. In 1914 he was appointed captain of Leicestershire and continued in that post for two seasons after the First World War. In the early years of the century he frequently turned out for London County at Crystal Palace, opening the batting with W. G. Grace.

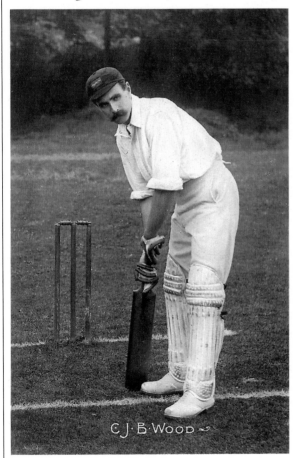

C.J.B.WOOD

Always ready to assist Leicestershire in any way he could, he served as Secretary in 1940 and 1941. He played altogether in 423 Leicestershire first-class matches and in all first-class games hit 23,879 runs, average 31.05. His slow bowling also came in useful occasionally.

C. J. B. died in Leicester in 1960, aged 84.

(NCCC)

trials in the First Eleven of whom only Frank Bale, the left-arm spinner, made any impact. He was a player who bowled in quite devastating form in the nets, but perhaps through nerves never really showed the same skill in the middle. He played until 1928 and took more than 200 wickets, spread over nine seasons.

C. J. B. Wood, whose batting form had been poor throughout 1920, retired from the captaincy for 1921 and A. T. Sharp was appointed to replace him. The County also lured Geary back from the Leagues. These were the two major changes for the new season and there did not seem any reason to be over-optimistic. The all-conquering Australians began their first-class programme at Leicester and trounced the County. Macartney and Bardsley made hundreds. The fearsome McDonald took eight for 41 in the first innings and another four in the second – victory was by an innings and 152 runs. The game was over in two days, but the attendance was very large and on the Saturday 12,000 came of whom 9,378 paid receipts of £1,053, a record for a single day at Leicester.

Sydney Smith, the Australian manager, described the tour in his book and in the pages concerning the Leicestershire match are the following comments:

Leicester was the first county we had to meet, and three trains were cancelled before I finally knew the exact time the Team would be able to leave London. But we had to make the best of it. We arrived in Leicester the day before the fixture and were met by Mr Howe, President, and Mr S. Packer, Secretary of the Leicester Club.

Leicester is noted for the socks and stockings it produces and a walk around the market square (every provincial town in England has a market square) showed that socks were being sold at 1/- per pair. We were given a reception, dinner and smoke concert in the evening. Mayor Hilton presided. We met Dr R. McDonald, the old Queensland representative, who played for Leicester for many years.

Although the Australian defeat was followed by another at the hands of Notts, Leicestershire beat Northants easily and a week later produced a much more impressive win against Sussex. The batting had more backbone than in 1920, Sharp and King made hundreds and though behind on first innings, fine bowling by Astill, Benskin and King dismissed Sussex in their second innings for 117. Another good win was at Old Trafford. King made 125 not out in the first innings and some excellent bowling in the second by Astill dismissed Lancashire for 183 of which the opener Charlie Hallows made 110 – Leicestershire won by 180 runs.

Against the lesser counties Leicestershire had a fine record and ended the summer with ten victories, the most they had ever attained in the Championship. They finished in 11th place out of 17 – Glamorgan having now joined the competition.

The new captain headed the batting averages with 879 runs, average 41.86 and four hundreds; it was a pity that due to his profession he was not available for about half the matches. Wood, the former captain, appeared in only one game, and Rudd usually led the team in Sharp's absence.

King, Astill and Coe all exceeded 1,000 runs. Astill had a remarkable summer, completing the 'double' for the first time, as well as holding 21 catches. He bowled 1,226 overs, a total more than King and Benskin combined and his bag of 153 victims was the highest attained to date by a Leicestershire bowler. Benskin took 71 wickets and King, who found that he could no longer combine the skills of batsman and bowler as well as in former years, took 55 wickets. Geary, Curtis and Skelding all remained engaged to League clubs and were only seen occasionally in the County side. No less than 34 players represented the County in Championship matches, ten being newcomers. Early in June J. A. F. M. P. de Lisle was brought in for one game when Sharp was unable to turn out and batting at number five hit 72 and 88 – the most runs scored by anyone in the match, which was v Kent at Leicester. The 29-year-old de Lisle had been in the Beaumont XI in 1907 to 1909, but went out to India in 1912 and remained there until 1926, when he returned to live at Charnwood Lodge in the county. After this single memorable debut, he played just occasionally until 1930, when he was appointed captain for one season.

The only 1921 debutant to have any lasting effect on the County's cricket was the Rutland all-rounder, H. C. Snary. An accurate medium to slow bowler his main successes were between 1930 and 1932. Of the others, perhaps the best was Christopher Gimson, who had been on the fringe of the Cambridge Eleven in 1908 and had earlier topped the Oundle batting averages. Like de Lisle he had gone out to India, remaining there for 36 years. He played just eight matches for Leicestershire, all in 1921.

Good weather in 1921 kept attendances high at county matches and the Leicestershire membership rose to 2,254. For once the season ended with a large surplus in the bank!

With A. T. Sharp unable to find the time for regular county cricket, the club changed captains for 1922, Major G. H. S. Fowke being appointed. Although his debut for the County had been in 1899, he did not appear at all in 1921 and was now aged 41. Fowke himself did better than might have been expected, narrowly missing 1,000 runs. Both Geary and Skelding were available for many more matches and the attack on paper looked one of the strongest in the Championship, but the rain produced many soft wickets and this did not suit Skelding or the two other right-arm fast bowlers, Benskin and Shipman. The work therefore devolved largely on Astill and Geary. The former achieved the 'double' for the second time with 1,168 runs and 138 wickets, while Geary took 73 wickets at 19.33 runs each, bowling half the number of overs of Astill. The difficulty was that their styles were not sufficiently contrasting.

Apart from Astill, the veterans King and Coe both completed 1,000 runs. The former was now the oldest cricketer regularly playing in Championship matches. Their ages meant that they had to be hidden in the field – one commentator noted that too many of the County's fielders tended to stop the ball with their feet rather than bending down.

Six matches were won but eleven lost and the side finished in 14th place. Not a very impressive set of figures, but an analysis shows that in several matches against the senior counties a little more luck and experience might have brought victory. In the two games with Lancashire this was very apparent. At Aylestone Road, Lancashire won by two runs, only because Sidwell and Skelding, the last pair, got into a hopeless muddle over a run and Sidwell was stranded and run out. At Old Trafford, Leicestershire fought back splendidly after being 270 behind on first innings. Mounteney made 85 and Coe 117, and with fifties from Geary and Lord, the second innings reached 436 and Lancashire had to score runs against the clock on the final afternoon. They lost six wickets before the target was reached.

The two matches with Surrey brought similar excitement. At The Oval Skelding and Astill dismissed Surrey for 130, giving Leicestershire a lead of 91. In the final innings Surrey required 247 and though Surrey won by three wickets, the Surrey batsmen stated afterwards that it was the most difficult target they had all season. At Leicester Surrey won due to a very optimistic declaration by Fowke, which set the visitors 150 in 80 minutes. He 'forgot' about Fender's remarkable batting powers and Surrey made the runs in 63 minutes with Fender 91 not out.

At Ashby, Gloucestershire were beaten by two wickets; the margin ought to have been much greater since Leicester needed only 37 in the final innings, but Charlie Parker produced figures of 9-3-18-6 and the seventh wicket fell with the total only 8. Geary and Sidwell with the help of some leg-byes then saved the day. The return with Gloucestershire was the last match of the summer and this time it was the western county's turn to attempt to reach a modest final innings target – 147. Astill and Geary bowled unchanged taking four for 37 and six for 26, bringing victory by 74 runs – the two bowlers had already bowled unchanged through the first innings. It was the first time that such a feat had been performed for the County in a first-class match, though opposition bowlers had done so on four previous occasions.

The other victories were against Glamorgan, Northants, Derbyshire and Sussex. H. T. W. Hardinge had the distinction of being on the field of play throughout the Kent game at Aylestone Road. He hit 249 not out in the first innings and on the last afternoon with the game meandering to a draw batted out time in the second.

Two very talented amateurs made their debuts in 1922. E. W. Dawson opened the batting for Eton during the summer and played in the final five matches of the programme. Aged 18 he still had another year before leaving school. In 1924 he went up to Cambridge, obtained his blue and captained the university in 1927. The following season he was appointed captain of the County, having been capped for England in the winter of 1927–28. A sound right-hand batsman he completed 1,000 first-class runs in a season six times, 1929 being his most prolific, but he was not seen in county cricket after 1934.

A second schoolboy batsman of 1922 to appear for the County in the holidays was C. H. Taylor. Topping both batting and bowling tables for Westminster School he was selected for the Public Schools at Lord's and made 56 *v* The Army and like Dawson was included in Leicestershire's closing matches. Taylor went up to Oxford in the autumn and played against Cambridge for four seasons. He appeared for Leicestershire during the vacation, but on going down he joined the Westminster staff and was lost to first-class cricket. An elegant stroke player, Taylor scored runs all round the wicket and was a delight to watch. During the Second World War he was appointed cricket master at Eton and when peace returned was occasionally found in the Buckinghamshire side.

The 1923 season can be described as very disappointing.

Geary's talents were recognised in so far as he was selected for one of the Test Trials; Sidwell's expertise was also used in one Trial. Astill performed the 'double' to reinforce his status as one of the leading all-rounders in England, but overall these factors did nothing to improve Leicestershire's Championship performance and they remained stationary in 14th place. Only five wins were recorded and there were 13 defeats. Unlike 1922, the County did not shine in many of the matches against the top counties, though Kent were beaten at Leicester by 82 runs in the game allotted to King as a second benefit. Benskin was unplayable in the first innings, taking seven for 29 and though this gave Leicestershire a lead of 172 Fowke did not enforce the follow on, possibly because it would reduce the receipts of King's benefit considerably. Leicestershire failed (King apart) in their second innings and Kent required 318 to win. Hardinge batted brilliantly so that Kent were 164 for 4 at lunch and so had a good chance of victory, but Benskin dismissed Hardinge for 85 soon after the resumption of play and Astill and Geary made certain that the lower order caused very little trouble.

The other wins of 1923 were two against Northants – at Northampton, Fowke made his only hundred in first-class cricket – and one each against Glamorgan and Hampshire.

Two veterans who made their farewell appearances during the summer were Cecil Wood, who made 66 against a formidable Notts attack and then 59 in his only other game, *v* Warwickshire, and Sam Coe, whose batting fell away and he was left out of the side in August. The other veteran, King, continued to flourish and was one of only two Leicestershire men to reach 1,000 runs, Astill being the other. King's greatest feat was his innings against Hampshire at Aylestone Road, when he was at the wicket six hours and made 205, becoming the oldest cricketer to compile a first-class double hundred, a record which he still retains.

The batting on the whole was unsatisfactory, but the bowling figures were a different story. Geary took 117 wickets at 16.92 runs each, the first time he had captured more than 100 wickets in a season, and Astill completed the 'double' for the third season running. Benskin and Shipman had very useful figures, but Skelding turned out in only four matches and was very expensive.

J. C. Bradshaw, the Uppingham Town amateur, made his debut for the County in 1923. A stylish middle-order batsman educated at Stamford School, he turned professional in 1926 and held a regular place in the side from that year until 1932. In 1929 he topped 1,000 runs. He also played hockey for the County.

Another debutant was S. S. Coulson, a steady opening batsman. He played intermittently until 1927 and afterwards took the post of professional at Gainsborough.

During a break in the Championship programme in July, the Leicestershire side made a short tour of Northern Scotland, playing four one-day matches at Inverness, Nairn, Elgin and Aberdeen – Geary helped himself to 21 wickets. A Leicester side also went to Denmark on a short tour and the team included two first-class players, Dowen and Parkinson.

The Committee in the winter of 1923–24 had decided that some new schemes were required to bring fresh talent into the First Eleven. E. G. Hayes, the former Surrey cricketer was appointed coach and for the first time the Club entered a team in the Minor Counties Competition.

The batting showed little improvement in 1924 – 14 times the County were dismissed for less than 100 in the Championship. The weather was partially to blame, rain causing many delays as well as difficult wickets. The match at home against Surrey failed even to start.

The bowling however remained strong and seven victories were hoisted which moved the team up into 11th place. A quite remarkable statistic was that only one individual hundred was made all summer for the County. C. H. Taylor played a flawless innings of 123 at Southampton, enabling Leicestershire to reach 425 for nine declared and victory was gained by ten wickets. Another convincing win came against Warwickshire when that county could only muster 188 and 157 against 401 for nine, giving Leicestershire an innings victory.

The other victories were against Gloucestershire and Derbyshire, a second against Hampshire and the double over Essex. Skelding returned as a regular member of the attack and took 86 wickets at 20 runs each; Geary was the only bowler to reach 100 wickets, but Astill with 96 narrowly missed and Shipman finished with 62 wickets at 19 runs each. Astill, however, continued his run by completing the 'double' in all matches for the fourth successive year. Both Astill and Geary played in the Test Trial and Geary went on to play in the fourth Test at Old Trafford; the game unfortunately was almost completely washed out.

Little can be said about the batting. Only Astill completed 1,000 runs and none of the regular eleven averaged 30. Taylor, as noted, made a hundred, but in his other 11 innings combined was unable to compile another hundred runs. Dawson, the other promising university batsman, was marginally more consistent.

Apart from Astill and Geary only the veteran King could be relied upon, his watchful back play being of great value on the slow wickets. H. C. Snary was the star of the Second Eleven, his 38 wickets costing 11 runs each, but in his late 20s he was scarcely a colt. W. L. Everard headed the batting, but Les Berry in second place caught the eye and was given a trial in the first team. Berry, a source of some slight confusion because he used his second Christian name and therefore his initials were given as L.G. instead of the G.L. with which his birth was registered, was to play for the County for more than two decades, making 605 appearances and not retiring until 1951. He had been born in Dorking, but moved to Market Harborough at the age of eight and was 18 when he made his first appearance in county cricket.

W. L. Everard, a member of the local brewing family, made a single appearance in first-class cricket in 1924, turning out against Cambridge University. He was long connected with Leicestershire Gentlemen and resided at Ratcliffe Hall. In 1924 he was elected Unionist MP for Melton Mowbray and in 1939 knighted.

Season 1925 started relatively well, an innings victory coming against Glamorgan at Aylestone Road with Geary and Astill bowling unchanged through both innings as the Welsh side collapsed for 60 and 36 – Geary took eleven for 61 and Astill eight for 35. Two more wins by the middle of June kept the County comfortably in mid-table, but 13 matches in succession then came and went with only one more victory. With three away games in the south to finish the campaign Leicestershire seemed destined

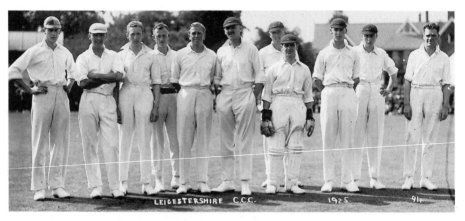

The Leicestershire team in 1925. From left: C. H. Taylor, E. W. Dawson, N. T. Dowen, A. Skelding, W. E. Astill, G. H. S. Fowke (Captain), G. Geary, T. E. Sidwell, A. W. Shipman, G. L. Berry, F. Bale. (NCCC)

for a very modest final place. Much to the surprise of most pundits all three matches were won.

Geary again dealt with Glamorgan, his 13 wickets costing 98 runs. Geary picked up another ten wickets at Gloucester to provide Leicestershire with an innings victory and finally Essex were beaten at Leyton by ten wickets, Astill removing nine batsmen, whilst Shipman, who had suddenly blossomed as a batsman, hit his maiden first-class century. Therefore, as in 1924, seven wins were recorded and the County fell only one place in the table.

Apart from Shipman, the other player to enhance the batting line-up was Berry. He completed 1,000 runs in his first full summer batting mainly at number three and scoring runs in a compact, unruffled manner which augured well for the future. The veteran King began with the first hundred of the season, but his form gradually faded and at the end of the year he decided to transfer to the umpiring profession – he was now aged 54.

Geary and Astill formed the best pair of all-rounders in county cricket. Astill, who also had the highest aggregate – 1,515 runs – for the County, completed the 'double' for the fifth consecutive summer. Geary just missed both 1,000 runs and 100 wickets. His bowling was handicapped by a strain which occurred in South Africa during the 1924–25 winter, when he toured with Tennyson's side – he topped the bowling averages in the unofficial Test series. Astill, who was coaching in South Africa, played in two of the Tests.

The left-arm spin of Frank Bale, who was now in his sixth season at Aylestone Road, at last captured a significant number of wickets at a reasonable cost – 61 at 21 runs each. H. A. Smith, a 24-year-old from Groby, played in 18 Championship matches. Very tall, and with a powerful physique, he was a fast bowler of great promise and he was also a hard-hitting lower-order batsman. In the 1930s he was to prove very effective and it was unfortunate that the Second World War brought his career to a premature close. The amateur N. T. Dowen played in a handful of matches in 1925 as a middle-order left-hand batsman. He was, however, unable to spare the time for regular county cricket, though he later became the Honorary Secretary to the County Club. The death occurred in 1925 of one of the earliest Honorary Secretaries, Thomas Burdett. He had been President in 1911 and 1912 and was a regular visitor to Aylestone Road up to the end.

Leicester City FC gave the Cricket Club a boost financially, handing over £1,000 from the receipts of their match with Airdrieonians. This was much appreciated because the financial situation was once more giving cause for alarm. One positive note was struck by the progress of the Second Eleven in the Minor Counties Competition. Leicestershire finished in fifth place, winning five out of eight matches. J. C. Bradshaw had a batting average of 58 and H. C. Snary took most wickets.

The highlight of 1926 was the defeat of the Champions, Lancashire, at Ashby-de-la-Zouch. Leicestershire gained a first innings lead of 91, but rain washed out most of the second day and Rudd, captaining the side in the absence of Fowke, had to gamble by declaring on the last afternoon and setting Lancashire 217 in 150 minutes. Geary proceeded to record the best analysis of his career to date, namely 17.4-4-33-9, and the famous Lancashire batting line-up was removed for 72 runs, five wickets falling in one spell for nine runs. Apart from Geary, Astill also had a splendid match, scoring 114 runs and taking six wickets.

This great performance was scarcely ever repeated during 1926 and only four other wins came, one each over Derbyshire, Essex, Glamorgan and Worcestershire. As in most other recent summers the batting was woefully inconsistent – a fact made clear in the averages. Eight batsmen made individual hundreds, but only Astill reached 1,000 runs, and this in a season when 65 batsmen reached the target. It was a sign of the batting problems that Hayes, the coach, in his 50th year, turned out in several matches. Nominally he topped the batting averages and made a splendid 99 against Notts before his partner foolishly ran him out. *The Cricketer* magazine in its review was rather unkind and accused the County Club of 'at present engaged in floating complacently down the stream of Time.'

Although Geary averaged only 21 with the bat for Leicestershire, when he was picked for England in the third Test at Headingley he saved the side with his batting, being at the wicket 150 minutes and helping to add over 100 for the ninth wicket.

Geary's bowling record placed him in the top ten English bowlers and he had the best figures for the County – 104 wickets at 18 runs each. Astill took 98 wickets, but Skelding, troubled by injury, captured only 45. Bale, following his success the previous year, played in every match, but his 49 wickets were rather expensive, at 28 runs each. Haydon Smith did not make the expected progress as a bowler and was played more for his batting.

C. A. R. 'Dick' Coleman made his debut during the summer. A fast-medium bowler and hard-hitting batsman, he played intermittently until 1935. After the Second World War he became a first-class umpire and officiated in two Test matches in 1947.

Despite the General Strike and the fact that nine complete days, including the first day against the Australians, were lost to rain, Leicestershire made a profit of £555 in 1926; the membership exceeded 3,000, which compared very favourably with the rest of the weaker counties. Sidwell received £576 from his benefit year.

The weather in 1927 was even more unfavourable than its predecessor. Six of Leicestershire's matches were excluded from the Championship table on the grounds that less than six hours play occurred. However the County made its best start to the season for many years. On 8 June, they were second in the table, with only the Champions, Lancashire, above them.

The Cricketer commented on June 11:

> Leicestershire's cricket this season has been uniformly good and of a consistently high standard, and it would, perhaps, be no exaggeration to say that the county is stronger now than ever before. As a match-winning force the side is entitled to great respect, and it seems safe to predict that a high place is assured it among the counties when the present campaign ends.

Up to that date eight matches had been played producing four wins and four draws. The summer had opened with a two-day victory over Worcestershire, Skelding and Astill being the dominant bowlers in a low-scoring affair. Two draws were followed by victory over Oxford University and then the second Championship success, over Gloucestershire. Skelding and Geary bowled unchanged to dismiss the opposition for 87 and when the western county collapsed a second time to the same bowlers, the margin of victory was 279 runs. Leicestershire came from behind to beat Sussex at Aylestone Road; Astill and J. C. Bradshaw formed a vital partnership in the final innings, adding 95 as Leicestershire won by three wickets. A drawn game at Leyton saw Shipman score 108 to give Leicestershire a first innings lead of 197, but rain and the inability of Geary to bowl due to injury allowed Essex to bat out time on the final day. The County then travelled from London to South Wales where they beat Glamorgan in two days, Astill hitting an unbeaten 164 in 225 minutes without a chance. All five bowlers shared the wickets.

The eight matches which followed produced seven draws, mainly on account of rain, and a defeat at the hands of Surrey. The middle section of July saw a return to happy times and victories were recorded against Derbyshire, with Geary taking six for 18, Sussex, a fine team effort, and Essex, despite the absence of Geary playing in the Test Trial.

The rain came back in torrents during August and the last eight matches of the season were all drawn. The one black spot came at the start of the month when Northants won at Aylestone Road, despite Leicestershire obtaining a first-innings lead.

Although therefore the County did not maintain their early season form, they still finished in seventh place, a great improvement on the last few years. This success was attributed to the coaching of Ernest Hayes, which provided the County with batsmen capable of producing runs more consistently. Astill headed the averages with 1,425 runs at just under 40 per innings. Shipman completed 1,000 runs for the first time and his aggregate was almost double his previous best. His defence remained sound, but to this had been added some more strokes of an attacking nature. His best innings came in the final match when he hit 120 off the Lancashire bowling, despite being hit several times by McDonald's deliveries. Armstrong also reached 1,000 runs for the first time, whilst Berry made 960. Bradshaw, in his second season as a professional, batted well and after the University match, E. W. Dawson gave a further boost to the run-getting powers of the side.

Geary seemed affected by his winter of hard work with MCC in India and took only 78 wickets, but Skelding, in his benefit year, bowled better than ever and exceeded 100 victims for the only time in his career. Shipman and Astill were the other two main bowlers. Bale had a poor summer and was eventually dropped from the side, giving way to the off-breaks of Snary, who proved very economical.

When the season closed, Major Fowke announced his retirement from the captaincy. He had seen the transition from the pre-war professionals to a largely young side and therefore left the team in a most promising position. Dawson, having completed his studies at Cambridge, was appointed the captain for 1928. The wet summer meant that spectators through the turnstiles were scarce, but membership subscriptions kept the balance sheet out of the red. One oddity about 1927 was that not a single new player made his debut for the County.

Dawson, Geary and Astill were all selected by MCC to tour South Africa in the winter of 1927–28. Astill played in all five Tests; Dawson appeared in the fifth Test; Geary took 12 wickets in the first Test, but injured his elbow in the second and missed the rest of the series.

This injury had a serious effect on Leicestershire during 1928. Geary played in only 14 matches and was hardly able to bowl. Late in the season he was operated on and this put right the injury in time for the MCC tour to Australia, but too late to help his County.

In addition Skelding suffered a strain, missed half the matches and was much more expensive when he did play. In comparison with 1927, when Leicestershire had three bowlers in the top 20 in the averages, Geary, Skelding and Shipman, in 1928 only Astill was among the leaders.

If the bowling therefore showed a decline, the same could not be said for the batting. For the first time in the history of the Club, six batsmen exceeded 1,000 runs. The consistency and depth in run-getting was a feature of the season. The new captain Eddie Dawson hit 1,632 runs at an average of 35.48 and scored five hundreds; he also carried his bat through the innings against Essex at Leyton. Opening the batting with Dawson was Alan Shipman, who also exceeded 1,500 runs and recorded the highest score of his career: 226 in seven hours against Kent at Tonbridge. Norman Armstrong was moved up the order to number three and was another batsman to score more than 1,500 runs, his average being marginally higher than the captain's. The fourth batsman to average over 30 was Les Berry who came in second wicket down.

Leicestershire in 1928, a season when the batsmen did better than the bowlers. Left to right, back: J. C. Bradshaw, G. L. Berry, H. A. Smith, H. C. Snary, N. F. Armstrong, T. E. Sidwell, S. C. Packer (Secretary). Front: A. Skelding, G. Geary, E. W. Dawson, W. E. Astill, A. W. Shipman.

Numbers five and six in the order were Bradshaw and Astill. Astill made over 1,000 runs and Bradshaw missed the milestone by just 33 due to being absent from several matches. The wicketkeeper, Sidwell, came in at number seven and completed 1,000 runs for the only time in his career. Not once during the summer were the County dismissed for under 100 and against the great Yorkshire side Leicestershire made 390 and actually enforced the follow-on. For so long the Leicestershire batting had let the County down, now the coaching scheme of Hayes had had time to work through and the results were plain to see.

Six Championship matches were won, but the season began with many drawn games – 11 of the first 15 fixtures were undecided. In July came five successive victories. Warwickshire were beaten by nine wickets; Gloucestershire by six wickets; Hampshire by 205 runs; Worcestershire by an innings at Ashby and then by eight wickets at New Road. The remaining Championship games produced seven draws and one defeat.

The College Ground at Loughborough was used for the first time, displacing Hinckley as one of the County's out-grounds. Ashby was the only other still in use. The College Ground is now the site of the Students' Union Building of Loughborough University.

In July the small stand at Aylestone Road was severely damaged by fire. The replacement, a more substantial structure, was built in the winter and ready for use in 1929.

Three new players were tried during the summer. D. S. Oscroft had been in the Uppingham XI in 1927. He went up to Cambridge and, opening the batting in the Freshmen's Match, hit 95. Leicestershire played the University on the following day and Oscroft was included in the County side and scored 50 off his fellow undergraduates. He appeared in one or two Championship games in the vacation, but joined the teaching profession after leaving Cambridge and did not continue in county cricket. The second 1928 debutant was E. A. Broughton, a hard-hitting batsman who made 25 first-class appearances spread over six years without much success, but who captained the Second Eleven and Club and Ground teams, joined the County Committee and later was Honorary Treasurer to the Club until his death in 1982.

The third fresh face was Harold Riley, whose father Edwin had played in the 1890s. A middle-order batsman he came from Stoney Stanton and was aged 25. He batted well in 1929 but never developed into a regular county cricketer and went up to Scotland as a professional.

No Leicestershire players were selected for the three Tests of 1928, but the resuscitated Geary topped the Test bowling averages on the 1928–29 MCC tour to Australia. Making the ball go with his arm he was particularly effective at Sydney in the fifth Test. Astill went to the Caribbean with Julien Cahn's side and like his colleague Geary he also topped the bowling averages; Dawson, who also went to the West Indies, had a moderate time with the bat.

With Geary back in fighting form it was to be hoped that 1929 would see the County move further up the table, but in the event they remained anchored at ninth. Geary himself had a very good year and this is reflected in the win total increasing by two, but Shipman suffered a strain and could not bowl effectively in many matches and Skelding faded away, to be appointed the County scorer. Geary's support thus came from Astill, who bowled as well as ever. Bowling for long periods round the wicket, Astill kept a nagging length and was suitably rewarded. Apart from Geary and Astill the only other bowler to deliver more than 500 Championship overs was Smith, whose wickets were relatively expensive at 26 runs each.

The batting remained very much the same as in 1928, except that Bradshaw reached 1,000 runs whereas Sidwell dropped below four figures. Coleman became a regular member of the side for the first time, batting at number seven and being used as a fast-medium bowler. Whilst not producing any outstanding figures he was a useful all-rounder.

July again proved a fruitful month with four of the nine victories. Somerset and Glamorgan were beaten by an innings, Astill taking seven for 34 to remove the former for 94 and Geary and Astill both took ten wickets at Loughborough to dismiss Glamorgan for 116 and 98. There followed another innings win at Chesterfield, where Armstrong hit 128 and Geary took six for 27. The fourth July win was over Middlesex at Aylestone Road when Shipman and Astill both hit hundreds.

Two wins came in August, the first against Worcestershire at Kidderminster, when Shipman made 183 and Dawson closed the innings at 551 for seven, and the second at Pontypridd when Geary's second innings figures of 16.2-8-18-10 constituted a new Leicestershire record. It was altogether a memorable match. Leicestershire collapsed on the first morning, all out 102. Glamorgan, due to 70 from their opener, Bates, made 160 and Leicestershire struggled a second time, unable to cope with the bowling of J. C. Clay. Glamorgan needed just 84 to win in the fourth innings. Geary proceeded to dismiss every Welsh batsman and victory was by 15 runs.

GLAMORGAN *v* LEICESTERSHIRE

Played at Pontypridd, 14, 15 and 16 August 1929

LEICESTERSHIRE WON BY 15 RUNS

LEICESTERSHIRE	FIRST INNINGS		SECOND INNINGS	
*Mr E. W. Dawson	b Arnott	1	run out	13
A. W. Shipman	lbw b Ryan	23	b Arnott	4
G. L. Berry	b Clay	9	c Davies (D.) b Clay	26
N. F. Armstrong	b Ryan	0	st Every b Ryan	18
H. Riley	c Rhys b Ryan	15	c Turnbull b Clay	24
Bradshaw (J. G.)	st Every b Ryan	0	lbw b Clay	6
W. E. Astill	c Hills b Clay	6	not out	26
G. Geary	not out	8	c Bates b Clay	1
†T. E. Sidwell	c Turnbull b Clay	4	b Clay	8
C. A. R. Coleman	b Clay	8	c Hills b Ryan	9
H. A. Smith	c Clay b Ryan	22	c Every b Ryan	4
Extras		6		2
Total		102		141

BOWLING	O	M	R	W	O	M	R	W
Arnott	6	1	15	1	12	3	27	1
Davies (D.)	2	0	13	0				
Ryan	20.2	10	38	5	28.2	13	49	3
Clay	17	7	30	4	24	7	63	5

GLAMORGAN	FIRST INNINGS		SECOND INNINGS	
W. E. Bates	c Armstrong b Astill	70	c Bradshaw b Geary	4
A. H. Dyson	c Astill b Geary	7	lbw b Geary	0
D. Davies	c Coleman b Geary	5	c Bradshaw b Geary	2
*Mr M. J. Turnbull	c Coleman b Astill	9	b Geary	20
D. E. Davies	c Astill b Geary	13	c Shipman b Geary	0
J. J. Hills	lbw b Geary	26	b Geary	0
Mr H. R. J. Rhys	c Armstrong b Astill	9	not out	6
Mr T. Arnott	c Shipman b Geary	0	lbw b Geary	0
Mr J. C. Clay	c Astill b Geary	10	c Berry b Geary	15
F. P. Ryan	st Sidwell b Astill	1	b Geary	2
†T. Every	not out	0	b Geary	0
Extras		10		19
Total		160		68

BOWLING	O	M	R	W	O	M	R	W
Shipman	2	0	14	0				
Geary	34.3	12	78	6	16.2	8	18	10
Astill	33	11	56	4	16	6	31	0
Smith	1	0	2	0				

Umpires: Parris and Oates

*Captain; †Wicketkeeper

The two other wins, both in the first half of the summer were at Aylestone Road against Gloucestershire and Somerset. The Somerset game was played on a tricky wicket after rain restricted the first two days' play to three hours. Astill produced the outstanding analysis of 14-7-23-8 in the second innings which left Leicestershire needing only 41 in the final innings. Dawson decided that the best solution was to hit out whilst the effects of the roller were still to be enjoyed. J. C. White however, opening the bowling with Wellard, took three wickets without a run being scored off him and Leicestershire lost six wickets before reaching the target.

The victory over Gloucestershire was due to a century by Berry, but the visitors were handicapped through an injury to Parker, hit on the knee whilst batting on the first day and unable to bowl. Leicestershire won by eight wickets.

One splendid feature of Leicestershire's cricket was the fielding. Berry excelled at cover-point and Riley was quite exceptional in the outfield. In August Dawson announced that, due to business commitments, he would have to retire from the captaincy and his resignation was accepted with much regret.

SEVEN CAPTAINS IN TEN SUMMERS

DAWSON HAVING RESIGNED, THE County Committee, faced with a complete absence of amateurs playing regularly in the side, save Dawson himself, took a chance and appointed John de Lisle. De Lisle's first-class cricket was limited to three matches for the County including his sensational debut against Kent in 1921, when he batted quite brilliantly for innings of 72 and 88. He was however now aged 38 and had spent most of his working life as a jute planter in India.

Dawson in fact spent most of the 1929–30 winter with the MCC team in Australia and New Zealand and played in all the Test matches. The MCC also sent a side out to the West Indies, the Leicestershire representative being Astill, who also played in all the Test matches: for the first and last time 'England' played two sets of Tests overseas more or less simultaneously.

The Leicestershire side for the first matches of 1930 was, captains apart, identical to that of the previous year. Berry was promoted in the order and opened the batting in place of Dawson, whilst the new captain went in at number eight. The whole of May went by without a single victory – three losses and six draws including three draws in friendly first-class matches – and the County languished in 16th place, having picked up a few points for first-innings lead. The first victory came on 10 June when Geary captured 12 Northants wickets at six runs each, taking advantage of a drying pitch. In the next match it was Astill's turn to produce a set of winning bowling figures, 52.4-23-80-11, and Surrey lost by 102 runs. This victory, however, was equally the work of Armstrong who batted five hours for 147, easily the best innings. A third success at the end of June, against Hampshire, when Astill picked up another ten-wicket haul, pushed Leicestershire up to 11th place and the following match produced the fourth win of the summer, Middlesex being beaten by 30 runs. Dawson had been persuaded back into the side for this match and made 58 and 23.

The County were unable to produce another win for the rest of the year but a number of games were badly affected by rain and their final place in the Championship table was 12th.

Both the batting and bowling powers of the County declined. In Championship matches only Astill and Berry exceeded 1,000 runs, but in the latter's case he owed much to a single innings of

232 against Sussex at Aylestone Road, when he occupied the crease for seven hours and hit one six and 34 fours. Shipman and Armstrong just crept over the 1,000 mark in all first-class games, but Riley, probably due to eye trouble, did not bat as well as in 1929 and though Coleman hit 114 against Gloucestershire (his only first-class hundred) he was very inconsistent. Bradshaw averaged just 13 compared with 25 in 1929; the new captain was little more than a passenger, his batting average being 8. At the top stood Dawson, who made nine appearances and averaged 40.

The bowling was more expensive. Astill once more accomplished the 'double'. Geary took 95 wickets at 19.56 runs each and played in one Test against the Australians. Snary found the soft wickets to his liking and was the main support for Astill and Geary. The others – Shipman, Smith, Coleman and Armstrong – all proved rather expensive.

Outside the Championship, Leicestershire played both universities and the tourists. Bradman, on his first tour of England, had made 236 in the first match at Worcester and then hit 185 not out at Aylestone Road, before rain ended the game.

Of the debutants of 1930 the best known was Percy Corrall. He made his first appearance at Fenner's when he batted two hours for four runs and remained scoreless at one stage for 80 minutes. He helped Geary add 112 for the eighth wicket. Corrall was acting as stand-in for Sidwell and had been on the Leicestershire staff since 1924. His career was rather curious in that he was the County's regular wicketkeeper from 1932 to 1936, then lost his place to George Dawkes, but when Dawkes went to Derbyshire, Corrall resumed behind the stumps in 1946 and carried on until 1951. In the immediate post-war period he stumped over a hundred batsmen off the bowling of Walsh.

A second newcomer was the Hon Arthur Hazlerigg, the son of the former captain. He had captained Eton v Harrow at Lord's in 1929, when he opened the batting. Going up to Cambridge in the autumn he gained a blue in 1930 mainly on account of his bowling; his slow spin picked up ten wickets in the Perambulators v Etceteras trial and against Oxford he took seven wickets at a very reasonable cost. After the University game he appeared in a few County games but with little success; his father was President of the County Club during 1930.

S. H. Wigginton, a promising opening batsman, played once in 1930 and later joined the ground staff. He took a professional engagement in Scotland in 1935 and thus ended his County career. In 1947 he emigrated to Rhodesia and became coach to the Rhodesian Cricket Association.

The County secured the services of Dawson for the whole of
1931 and he resumed the captaincy. It was to be assumed therefore
that the County's upward progress would be in evidence once
more, but nothing seemed to go right. The reviewer in *The
Cricketer* was quite bemused: 'The side is generally the same,
which is supposed to be almost a necessity for genuine achievement, the fielding is much improved, the bowling excellent, and
the batting would seem adequate.'

On paper Astill and Geary were the talented all-rounders they
always had been, but now Astill was 43 and Geary 38, both not as
vital as before, and Dawson's batting failed. It was as if pressure
had been brought to bear to bring him back into county cricket
and his heart was not really in it. His one great innings came
during Astill's benefit match against Gloucestershire when he hit
123, saving the side from almost certain defeat by an innings.

In all first-class matches Astill headed the batting, but there
were 39 batsmen from other sides making more than 1,000 runs
with a better average. The County possessed no batsmen capable
of really attacking the opposition bowlers. Only two Championship matches were won. One of these victories was against
Hampshire at Aylestone Road when Dawson declared behind on
first innings, rain having cut down the playing time. Hampshire
later made a sporting declaration, setting Leicestershire 223 in 150
minutes. Everyone responded to the challenge and the game was
won by three wickets in the last possible over. Dawson was
amazed commenting: 'I never thought the team had it in them to
do it.' The other victory was against Worcestershire whom Geary
bowled out for 68, taking eight for 20 on a drying pitch.

At Edgbaston Dawson and Wyatt, the opposing captains, were
involved in one of the 'freak' declarations that became fashionable
in 1931. There being no play on the first two days, the captains
agreed to declare each first innings closed after one ball and then
play for full points in the second innings. Berry and Hazlerigg hit
179 without being parted then Dawson declared leaving Warwickshire in the odd position of wanting 180 in 70 minutes. The
match was drawn, but each side obtained four points for a tie on
first innings.

With seven losses against two wins, Leicestershire occupied
16th place. Apart from Dawson the batsmen had similar records
to 1930, though Berry's figures showed some improvement.
Geary's bowling was marginally more effective, but his old
colleague, Astill, was more expensive. Snary had his best season
to date, 101 wickets at 18 runs each. Shipman did not bowl as fast
as in previous seasons and lost much of his effectiveness. Smith's

style was too similar to Geary's for the County to make the most of his ability. F. J. Bowley, a slow left-hander, who had played a few matches in 1930, was given more opportunity and looked very promising. Both he and Smith did very well in the Minor Counties Championship. The County had not competed in 1930, but rejoined in 1931 and won the title. Six out of eight games were won. The challenge match against Surrey, who were in second place, was washed out. A. T. Sharp, the 1921 first team captain, led the Seconds and topped the batting.

Anthony Riddington, a left-handed all-rounder, was seen for the first time in 1931. He was tried in only three games, but was given an extended run in 1933 and 1934. Achieving little he took a professional engagement with Stenhousemuir in 1935. After the Second World War he returned to county cricket and remained in the side until 1950.

Like several counties, Leicestershire were beginning to struggle financially and their representatives presented several ideas at the Advisory County Cricket Committee in November. They proposed that the season should run from mid-May to mid-September and that matches should be of two days duration, each day lasting seven hours. These proposals met with little support; another Leicestershire proposal to ignore drawn games in the Championship and count wins only did not find a seconder and was withdrawn.

In the spring it was announced that Dawson had declined to continue as captain. The Committee hoped to persuade A. T. Sharp to take over, but although he was happy to continue with the Second Eleven, he did not wish to play regular first-class cricket. No official captain was therefore appointed, but having failed to beguile Dawson and Sharp back, the club hoped that Lieutenant C. W. C. Packe would take charge for as many matches as possible. The eldest son of Lt-Col E. C. Packe of Great Glenn Hall, Charles had been in the Eton side of 1927 and opened the batting against Harrow. He then went to Sandhurst and played against Woolwich in 1928 and 1929. It was in the latter season that Packe made his debut for Leicestershire, but his experience of county cricket was, by the start of 1932, limited to a single match. An attacking batsman, he fared moderately in the 15 Championship games he played in 1932, but in Army cricket in the years up to the War he proved capable of scoring many runs. He was killed in action in Normandy in the summer of 1944.

Not for the first time Leicestershire's results in 1932 confounded the critics. With no proper captain and the side little changed from 1931, it was hardly to be expected that an improvement could be made. In fact the number of victories rose from two to six, plus one over the South Africans, and they moved four places up the table. The lack of a firm hand at the top showed itself in the losses column, eleven defeats being experienced and on some of these occasions the team seemed to simply lie down and let itself be trampled over. The Yorkshire, Sussex, Notts and Kent matches were examples of this.

Of the wins, Northants were twice put in disarray by Geary. At Leicester he took eleven for 74 and at Northampton eleven for 97: Leicestershire won twice by an innings. At Worcester, another innings victory, Snary took five for 16 in the first innings. Against Middlesex the batsmen nearly threw the match away. Requiring 89 in the final innings they limped home by three wickets and would have probably lost had the Middlesex captain had the courage to bring Peebles on earlier – he started to bowl with the total at 54 for two and took four for 15 in seven overs.

The most exciting match was at home against Notts. In reply to Notts' 211, Berry and Wigginton opened with a stand of 104, but Leicestershire failed to obtain a first-innings lead by five runs. In the final innings Leicestershire required 176 for victory. Berry remained steadfast as wickets fell at the other end, but when the last man Corrall arrived 22 were still needed. Facing Larwood and

The Leicestershire team in 1933. Left to right, back: S. C. Packer (Secretary), S. Coe (Scorer), W. H. Marlow, H. C. Snary, H. A. Smith, S. H. Wigginton, N. F. Armstrong, P. Corrall. Front: G. L. Berry, G. Geary, E. W. Dawson (Captain), W. E. Astill, A. W. Shipman. (NCCC)

Voce this was no easy task, but Corrall made three singles, whilst Berry took Leicestershire to success. The press commented: 'The ground was besieged by hundreds of people half mad with excitement and Berry had to submit to being carried shoulder high to the pavilion.'

All in all it was a summer of fluctuating fortunes for the County. *The Cricketer Annual* reviewed the leadership problem at the close of the year: 'Without specifying or being unjust, it may be truly said that some of the septet who exercised temporary authority knew far less about the niceties of cricket than several of the players under them.'

Of those players, Geary topped the bowling with 109 wickets at 18.33 runs each; Astill took 78 at 26.54 each; Haydon Smith had his best season to date with 83 wickets for just under 26 and Snary managed 68 wickets. Marlow took ten wickets in the final match against Derbyshire at Ashby which made his season's figures quite presentable.

Berry easily led the batsmen, passing fifty 15 times and hundred only twice, but managing to average 40. Armstrong had a good summer with five hundreds, but was not so consistent as Berry. Snary surprised everyone by hitting a century off the Indian attack, he never having reached fifty before. Bradshaw faded right away and nothing was seen of Sidwell, Corrall keeping in every match.

The Second Eleven, Minor County Champions of 1931, could only win twice and dropped well down the table. At the end of the year it was decided to withdraw from the competition.

The leadership question was resolved for 1933 by cajoling Dawson back but the move was not a success. Dawson himself failed to reproduce his batting form and only averaged a little over 20; the team was hampered by an injury to Geary – he never felt fully fit during the summer and played in only 16 of the 26 Championship matches with his wickets costing about 30 runs each. In a year when batsmen generally enjoyed themselves, the County had too many bad days – on 15 occasions the team were dismissed for under 150. There was justified criticism of the fielding. Supporters pointed to the serious injury which deprived the eleven of Corrall. Corrall was standing up to the bowling of Astill, with Washbrook at the crease. The Lancashire batsman attempted to hook a lifter, but his bat struck Corrall on the left ear. The injury was so serious that it was thought he might never play again. Happily he recovered and was fully fit in time for the 1934 season. Sidwell was brought out of retirement and played so well, both as a wicketkeeper and a batsman, finishing fourth in the averages, that perhaps he had been shunted aside too early.

The end of the season found Leicestershire at the bottom of the Championship. The County had been at the wrong end twice before, but each time – in 1898 and 1903 – they had shared the indignity. This time they were alone. Fifteen matches were lost, three wins recorded, the first of which did not occur until 21 July and then against Glamorgan, who occupied 16th place. A second victory was over Northants when Jupp made a sporting declaration and Leicestershire hit off the 283 runs required due to a splendid opening stand by Shipman and Berry worth 141. The great match of the year however was the win over Sussex.

At the time of the match, in early August, Leicestershire were anchored at the foot whilst Sussex were challenging Yorkshire for the title and stood second – Sussex had won 13 matches to Leicestershire's one. The venue was Ashby-de-la-Zouch. On the opening day 26 wickets fell for 287 runs and Sussex, having decided to bat first, were all out shortly after lunch for 106, Geary taking four for 20. Leicestershire made 145, then, in the late afternoon Geary took another four wickets for six runs and half the Sussex second innings had gone for just 17. The southern county improved slightly on the second morning and Leicestershire began the final innings needing 34. This light task took 40 minutes and cost four wickets. The review of Sussex after the season noted this as 'one of the most surprising results of the whole season, and in view of the well-known weakness of Leicestershire, one of the most humiliating.'

Aside from this, the satisfactory points of Leicestershire's cricket were the runs scored by Berry and Armstrong. The latter became the first batsman to reach 2,000 runs in a season for the County: 2,113 at 43.12 with four centuries. Berry hit 1,971 at an average of 37.19. No one else averaged above 25, though Shipman and Dawson did reach 1,000 runs. The bowling was terribly expensive. Haydon Smith topped the table with 118 wickets, but they cost 25 runs each. The other two leading wicket-takers were Marlow and Astill, both more expensive than Smith and with fewer wickets. No one else claimed more than fifty victims.

One major change in 1933 was the retirement of S. C. Packer as Secretary. He was replaced by Commander A. G. G. Webb, RN. A middle-order left-hand batsman, Webb had made his first-class debut for the Royal Navy in 1919. A native of Kent, he had appeared for that county's Second XI and was now aged 36. He was not yet qualified for Leicestershire, but did play in the match against West Indies and later captained the Second XI. Apart from Webb, seven other players made their debut in 1933. C. L.

Edgson had had a brilliant cricket career at Stamford School and was only 17, but on going up to Oxford he failed to make any first-class appearances for the University. A useful batsman, he played occasionally for the County until the outbreak of war. Fred Bowley's younger brother, Herrick, aged 22, batted well for the Second XI, but failed in Championship cricket and took a professional engagement in Scotland. George Ball was a 19-year-old amateur from Barwell, who turned out in 11 matches over four seasons as a batsman, but did little. P. H. C. Badham, the Winchester schoolboy, who was in his first year at Oxford, appeared for the County under birth qualification against the University. It was to be his only match for Leicestershire. He also played for Buckinghamshire and Dorset, but failed to obtain a blue. A. G. Weston, the Ivanhoe batsman, was yet another given a trial who failed to make an impression, though he scored well for the Second XI. J. E. Dickinson, an all-rounder with Ashby Hastings CC, appeared in two matches, but his left-arm spin failed to take a wicket. He later moved to Torquay and represented Devon. Finally, C. W. C. Packe's brother, R.J., who had captained Stowe in 1932 and was now at Sandhurst, was tried –

The Packe family. The members from left are: Robert Julian, who played for Leicestershire in 1933, Michael St John (1936–39, captain in 1939), E. C., Honorary Secretary 1933–35, Miss M. O. Packe and Charles William Christopher (1929–34, captain in 1932).

like Dickinson he was a slow left-arm bowler. He went out to India in 1935 and died there the same year of dysentery.

The Double International, H. T. W. Hardinge, was appointed county coach at the beginning of 1934. He had retired from county cricket after the 1933 season having had a career with Kent spanning more than 30 years and he had scored over 33,000 first-class runs with 75 hundreds. He brought with him from Kent G. S. Watson, a sound middle-order batsman, who had played county cricket as an amateur for his native county, but now joined the Leicestershire staff and would qualify in 1935. Another sign-ing for 1934 was F. T. Prentice from Knaresborough. Aged 22, he would also qualify in 1935.

The problem of the captaincy resurfaced once again, Dawson being unable to spare the time for regular county cricket. The Committee appointed A. G. Hazlerigg, who had captained Cambridge in 1932 and had now come down – he only played in one or two county games in 1933.

Whilst the County on paper had no greater strength in 1934 than in 1933, there was one vital factor which might bring better results, the return to full health of Geary. In the event he missed seven matches in mid-season, but his presence and the effective-ness of his bowling in the other games doubled the number of victories and pushed Leicestershire up into 12th place – if Geary had played all summer they might well have ended in the top half of the Championship.

The two outstanding victories came in August. On 10 August at Aylestone Road, Leicestershire beat Yorkshire for the first time in 23 years. Yorkshire began the game by bowling out the home side for 94, Bowes and Smailes being unplayable on a treacherous pitch. Yorkshire knocked up 196 for five, and con-fident of an easy win, Sellers declared 102 ahead. A sound innings of 98 not out by Armstrong meant that Yorkshire required 149 in the final innings. Smith made the ball get up and Yorkshire collapsed – all out 90, with Smith 25-8-39-6. The crowd cheered the Leicestershire players back to the pavilion and the cheering continued until they appeared on the balcony. The Leicestershire captain was not A. G. Hazlerigg, who had informed the Commit-tee that he was not available during August, but Flight Lieutenant W. K. Beisiegel. Beisiegel was the outstanding batsman at Up-pingham in 1925. He had joined the RAF and made his first-class debut for the service in 1928. Until 1934 he had never appeared in Championship cricket; after one or two games earlier in the year, he was now appointed captain for the rest of the summer, the Yorkshire match being the first of his stint.

Two matches later Beisiegel led the County at Trent Bridge and produced an even more dramatic victory, beating Notts by an innings and 106 runs. Again the County owed much to Armstrong. On the first day he batted in a very dogged fashion to reach 98 not out in over four hours and he eventually reached 117 out of 399. The press commented after the innings: 'However much the financial obligations of Leicestershire were increased by the appointment of Wally Hardinge as coach at the beginning of the season, if the batting displayed can be taken as a guide, it has been money wisely spent.'

Marlow, the slow left-arm spinner, then took six for 68 and Notts were dismissed for 158. Beisiegel enforced the follow-on, Marlow took another three wickets, and with the help of the extra half-hour, Leicestershire won inside two days.

Of the other four wins in 1934, Northants were beaten twice. Geary took ten wickets to defeat Gloucestershire by nine wickets, though the western county were without Hammond, and the other success was over Glamorgan at Hinckley, where Smith took nine wickets and Geary eight – Armstrong made the highest score.

As can be guessed, Armstrong was the most successful batsman of the summer. He hit 1,701 runs at an average of 42.52. In second place was Berry with 1,464, but at eight runs less per innings. Shipman, in his benefit year, was the third to top 1,000 runs. His benefit itself proved, like the County's finances, to be unhappy – he actually finished the match, *v* Derbyshire, £60 out of pocket. A special additional game was played for him and the proceeds of this, plus subscriptions, did bring him some recompense.

Of the other batsmen, Wigginton hit his maiden – and only – century, 120 not out against Worcestershire. He left the County at the end of the season. Hazlerigg made 805, his best innings being an undefeated 46 when the County were dismissed by Larwood for 103 in the home Notts match: truly a captain's innings. Geary and Astill made useful contributions.

Geary came eighth in the overall first-class bowling table, his 67 wickets costing 19.29 runs each, but this included expensive analyses in the first two Tests, and for Leicestershire his victims cost nearer 16 runs each. Smith was the only bowler to capture 100 wickets and had a very good summer. Astill took 78 wickets and after these three came Marlow with 44 wickets.

The two major debutants of 1934 were, as previously mentioned, Prentice, recommended by Herbert Sutcliffe, and Watson. Educated at Shrewsbury, Watson was one of a very few

Public School players to become a professional in the inter-war period. In addition to his cricket he was a talented soccer player, gaining an amateur international cap and appearing for the Casuals (not then amalgamated with the Corinthians). In 1930 he turned professional with Crystal Palace, having previously played as an amateur for Charlton Athletic. He was an exhilarating right-hand batsman and a superb field. His career continued until 1950. Prentice went on to 1951, his gritty style notching more than 10,000 runs.

Beisiegel was the only debutant to play at all frequently in 1934, but it turned out to be his only season in county cricket. He continued his career in the RAF and had reached the rank of Air Commodore when he died in 1973. Of the others who were tried during the year, W. H. Flamson was a medium-pace bowler in the style of Geary. He was already aged 29, but played regularly for the First XI in the three years immediately prior to the war – he died in 1945 aged 41. His local cricket was mainly for Ibstock Town. J. P. Hings was a product of Leicester Ivanhoe and whilst batting attractively for that club, did little during his two County games, both in 1934.

As the 1934 season wore on the financial plight of the County Club became increasingly desperate. One wild scheme which got as far as the press was that the County should join forces with Lincolnshire, field a combined eleven and play some matches at Skegness. It was Lincolnshire who rejected the idea. The attendances at home matches were poor. The gross gate and stand receipts for the year were £2,150 and the deficit on staging first-class matches over £4,000. The Club owed over £5,000. In January a few supporters clubbed together and paid off the deficit and it was hoped that this act of generosity would encourage more people to join the County Club. Matters however were very serious and at one stage there was talk of the Club folding up.

The leadership problem once more came to the surface. Hazlerigg, after being the official 1934 captain, but missing the final quarter of the summer, declined to continue. Beisiegel had returned to the RAF. A. T. Sharp had captained the side once or twice in 1934, but was now 46 and did not wish to be considered.

Sir Julien Cahn was beginning to play an increasing part behind the scenes in 1935. Cahn, who resided at Stanford Hall on the Notts–Leics border, had made a fortune from the family furniture business, both as a manufacturer and the owner of a chain of retail outlets. He was a great cricket enthusiast and ran his own team, having private grounds both at Stanford Hall and near Trent Bridge. The side he organised was up to the standard of the

GEORGE GEARY

The deadliest weapon in the armoury of George Geary was the leg-cutter pitched on or about the off stump, but he could also bowl a deceptive off-break, which caused the downfall of the unwary. Geary has been compared with both Barnes of Staffordshire and with his contemporary in the England side, Maurice Tate. He played 14 times for England but his most famous achievement was not with the ball, but was his innings of 35 not out at Headingley in 1926 when he saved England from defeat.

Though he never hit 1,000 runs in a season, his first-class total was 13,504 and he hit eight hundreds. A brilliant fielder in the slips, his large hands rarely missed a catch, as his total of 451 testifies.

He went overseas on three successive MCC tours, to India in 1926–27, to South Africa in 1927–28 and to Australia in 1928–29. The most successful of these was the trip to South Africa, where he bowled brilliantly on the matting wickets then in use.

The eldest of a family of 16 from Barwell, he joined the Leicestershire staff as a teenager and thought nothing of cycling each day the 15 miles to the county town and back again each evening. He retired in 1938 and became coach at Charterhouse for 21 years, then took a similar position at Rugby for the next eleven. He died in 1981 aged 87.

lesser first-class Championship teams and he employed a number of overseas professionals as well as good class 'amateurs'.

His main county interest had first been with Nottinghamshire and he had been a member of that county's committee since 1925. In 1933 he was elected Leicestershire's representative on the Advisory County Cricket Committee at Lord's and in that year gave Leicestershire a donation of £500. In 1934 he donated £1,000 and in 1935 appointed C. S. Dempster, the New Zealand Test batsman, as manager of one of his furniture stores in Leicester. Dempster moved into the County with the intention of qualifying to play for Leicestershire. Now aged 31 he had played so brilliantly for New Zealand on their 1931 tour to England – 1,778 runs, average 59.26 – that he would be a great asset to any county. Unfortunately he would not be qualified for the Championship until 1936. Leicestershire therefore required a captain for one year, pending Dempster's availability.

The season opened on the Bat and Ball Ground, Gravesend, and the Secretary, Commander Webb turned out as captain, batting at number ten. Leicestershire were spun out by Freeman, who took eight for 40 in the second innings and twelve wickets in the match. Kent won by 198 runs. The second fixture saw the tourists, South Africa, at Aylestone Road. Dempster made his County debut, but the visitors won early on the third day by 170 runs.

For the third match, Leicestershire fielded an all-professional side led by Astill. Some remarkable bowling by Smith and Geary – Smith eight for 83, Geary eleven for 40 – removed Sussex for 66 and 74 bringing victory by an innings and 50 runs. Astill was appointed captain for the season and what followed was the most successful summer the County had ever recorded with first-class victories totalling 12 (ten in 1921 had been the previous best).

The second win came in the second home Championship game against the formidable Lancashire side. Leicestershire made 275, Prentice 93 and Shipman 92, and gained a first-innings lead of 133. The Lancastrians never recovered and were dismissed in their second innings for 73, Geary taking six for 34. Two of the weaker counties were swept aside in the first days of June. Both victories came inside two days; at Stourbridge Geary picked up another ten-wicket haul as Worcestershire crumbled for 111 and 77; at Northampton Geary took nine for 62 and Smith eleven for 91 as the pair bowled unchanged through both innings. Northants were all out for 85 and 79.

Leicestershire, with four wins out of seven matches, were fifth in the table. Unfortunately J. C. Clay came to Aylestone Road for the next match and found a pitch just right for his off-breaks – he took eight for 46 – and Glamorgan brought the County's run of success to a temporary halt, inflicting defeat by 136 runs. Two drawn matches followed, but Geary picked up another eleven wickets at the expense of Hampshire and only the broad bat of Mead prevented the match ending a day early.

Records fell when the County went to West Bridgford to oppose Sir Julien Cahn's team. The wicketkeeper for Cahn's side, C. R. N. Maxwell, came in at number eight and hit 268, the seventh wicket partnership of 336 being only eight short of a world record. Dempster played for Leicestershire and was almost as aggressive as Maxwell; the New Zealander hit 207 in 210 minutes. The match was drawn.

Hinckley was the scene of Leicestershire's sixth Championship victory, Smith taking eleven wickets. A holiday game against Sir Lindsay Parkinson's side at Blackpool produced further success when Berry and Armstrong completed the match by adding an unbroken 254 for the second wicket; both men reached three figures. Armstrong hit another hundred in the following game against Worcestershire at Aylestone Road and victory was achieved by ten wickets.

The final weeks of the season produced four more wins. The most emphatic was on the United Services Ground at Portsmouth. Berry and Shipman batted quite brilliantly in response to a Hampshire first-innings total of 305, 219 being put on for the first Leicestershire wicket in less than three hours. Five wickets then fell cheaply. Walter Smith, the Wyggeston Grammar School old boy, came in at number six and hit an undefeated 125. Smith had played a few matches for the County starting in 1930. An attractive batsman this proved to be his most outstanding innings – he became a dental surgeon and his appearances, which lasted until 1946, were thus very intermittent. Due to Smith's batting the Leicestershire total reached 501 for nine declared. His namesake, Haydon, bowled out Hampshire for 169 when they batted a second time and Leicestershire won by an innings.

The other end of season wins were over Northants, Sussex and Kent, the final one being played at Oakham, a venue being used by the County for the first time for a Championship game.

Although Astill, now aged 47, returned modest figures in comparison with his great years, he still took 59 wickets at 22 runs each and was a very useful man to have coming in at number eight. He won great praise however for his captaincy. There was a much more positive spirit to Leicestershire's cricket. He was the most experienced cricketer on the county circuit and had the confidence and trust of his fellow cricketers. Outgoing by nature, Astill mixed easily in any company.

Geary and Smith had excellent seasons with the ball. The England player, though not chosen for any of the 1935 tests, took 129 wickets at 15.33 runs each, double his 1934 tally – he came third behind Verity and J. C. Clay in the first-class table. Smith took 150 wickets at 19 runs each. He captured five or more wickets in an innings 15 times. Astill and Marlow were the other bowlers used regularly, Marlow taking 71 wickets.

Three batsmen topped the 1,000 run mark. Armstrong reached 1,623, Berry 1,596 and Shipman 1,060. Newcomers Prentice and Watson usually batted at numbers four and five. Whilst neither had particularly impressive figures, both looked most promising. Prentice had a solid defence and Watson in contrast displayed a delightful range of strokes. Coleman reappeared in the eleven, but with such little success that he left county cricket at the season's end.

Of the players to make their debut in 1935, Dempster was naturally the most outstanding. He had played in the first Tests

Charles Stewart Dempster, the great New Zealand Test player who captained Leicestershire from 1936 to 1938 with success. (NCCC)

which involved New Zealand in 1929–30 and averaged 85.25 in that series. Coming to England with the 1931 New Zealanders he had hit 53 and 120 in the Lord's Test and the following winter had captained New Zealand against South Africa. He also led New Zealand in the two Tests *v* England immediately following the Bodyline tour in Australia. A very hard-hitting batsman, who kept the ball on the ground, his off-drives were quite brilliant.

K. Holland played only against Cahn's side; he was a bowler with the Ivanhoe Club. The third newcomer was J. M. Bradshaw of Oakham, a left-hand batsman. He died suddenly in 1938 aged only 31.

To celebrate the success of Leicestershire in 1935, a public dinner was organised and a presentation made to Astill in recognition of his captaincy. The finances were still causing concern, though the balance on the year showed a loss of £1,400, an improvement on 1934. Another problem was the state of the ground. Jim Smith, the head groundsman, had been retired to save money and the ground had suffered in consequence. Halfway through 1935, Walter White, an assistant groundsman at Old Trafford, was appointed. A step to help fund raising was the creation of a Supporters' Club and this worked hard for Leicestershire cricket until the war.

Dempster was confirmed as the new captain for 1936. The prospects for the County seemed very bright; apart from Coleman, the same principal players who had accomplished so much in 1935 were available. After a draw in Surrey's favour at Aylestone Road in the initial match, Leicestershire outplayed Lancashire and if time had allowed would have won by a fair margin, having been over 100 runs ahead on first innings. The County then went down to Hove. Centuries by Shipman and Dempster, the captain hitting an undefeated 164 in 180 minutes, put Leicestershire nearly 200 up and victory was attained by ten wickets. Corrall had a great triumph behind the stumps, dismissing ten batsmen.

The Indian tourists came to Leicester; the County were set 271 on the final day, but rain prevented the possibility of an exciting finish. The fourth Championship game was Geary's benefit at Hinckley, Warwickshire being the opposition. Unfortunately for Geary only 80 minutes play took place on the Saturday, but the rain suited Geary's bowling if not his pocket. He took six for 36 in the first innings and a remarkable seven for seven in the second: Warwickshire were all out for 133 and 78. The home side found batting against Eric Hollies just as difficult, but Dempster pulled them through – just. Victory was by a single wicket. On 26 May therefore Leicestershire were second in the table, one of only four counties not yet defeated. Kent were top, Surrey third and Yorkshire fourth.

The weather then treated the County most cruelly. The next four Championship games: against Northants, Sussex, Worcester and Hampshire, were all rain-affected draws. Out of the 12 days of possible play nearly five were lost. The four counties were all amongst the weakest and with ordinary luck Leicestershire might have been predicted to win at least two out of the four.

At the Wagon Works Ground, Gloucester, on 23 June, Leicestershire met their first defeat. Set to make 291 in 255 minutes, Berry and Armstrong took the total to 99 before the second wicket fell. Reg Sinfield then took four wickets for five runs in five overs, including Dempster for a duck and Gloucestershire won by 61 runs. Leicestershire were now ninth in the table. Nothing went right for the side from that moment on. Not a single victory was notched and in turn all the other counties save Glamorgan and Northants rose above them.

Some critics immediately blamed the change of captaincy for the sudden collapse of the side, but Dempster was keen, and had a good deal of experience. As a batsman he easily topped the table and was generally considered one of the best in England. It was rather curious that, by agreement, Julien Cahn had a prior claim to his services and he missed several matches when required by Cahn. Astill captained the side in his absence but failed to bring success.

Turning to the individual performances, whilst Dempster batted well, the two stalwarts of the side, Armstrong and Berry fell away considerably. Both reached only 1,100 runs and averaged under 30. The two newer batsmen, Prentice and Watson, continued to show promise, without making any marked advance. Shipman, as noted, made a century early on, but did so little latterly that he retired at the end of the summer. All the other regulars averaged less than 20 with the bat.

Geary and Smith again achieved a hundred wickets each, but lesser in number and at greater cost than in 1935 – Geary's 102 cost 19.16 runs each, Smith's 100, 26.80. Astill's slows were still effective and he took 64 wickets; Marlow however was expensive.

Two new players were tried. M. St J. Packe had captained Wellington College in 1934. The third of the brotherhood to play for the County, he went up to Cambridge in the autumn of 1934 and in 1936 played in three first-class matches for the University but did not obtain his blue. An attractive, attacking batsman he turned out in six Championship matches for the County in 1936

SUSSEX *v* LEICESTERSHIRE

Played at Hove, 16, 18 and 19 May 1936

LEICESTERSHIRE WON BY TEN WICKETS

SUSSEX	FIRST INNINGS		SECOND INNINGS	
John Langridge	c Corrall b Geary	5	b Prentice	14
J. H. Parks	c Geary b H. A. Smith	30	st Corrall b Astill	48
Mr A. Melville	c Corrall b Shipman	34	c Corrall b Astill	49
T. Cook	lbw b H. A. Smith	29	st Corrall b Prentice	10
Jas. Langridge	c W. A. Smith b H. A. Smith	6	b Geary	21
H. W. Parks	c Corrall b Shipman	71	c Corrall b Prentice	12
*Ft-Lt. A. J. Holmes	lbw b Geary	4	c Corrall b Prentice	0
M. W. Tate	b H. A. Smith	69	not out	35
A. F. Wensley	st Corrall b Astill	24	lbw b H. A. Smith	13
†W. Cornford	b Astill	16	c Corrall b H. A. Smith	0
J. Cornford	not out	0	b Astill	3
Extras	b 5, lb 4	9	b 1, lb 2	3
Total		297		208

BOWLING	O	M	R	W	O	M	R	W
Shipman	16	1	51	2	6	0	29	0
H. A. Smith	29	4	117	4	23	4	56	2
Geary	20	5	42	2	24	10	40	1
Prentice	9	0	38	0	16	4	39	4
Astill	10.2	1	36	2	16.2	3	41	3
W. A. Smith	1	0	4	0				

LEICESTERSHIRE	FIRST INNINGS		SECOND INNINGS	
A. Shipman	c John Langridge b Cook	103	not out	4
G. L. Berry	c Tate b J. Cornford	7	not out	18
N. F. Armstrong	c Wensley b J. Cornford	2		
Mr W. A. Smith	lbw b J. Parks	20		
F. Prentice	lbw b J. Parks	73		
*Mr C. S. Dempster	not out	164		
G. Watson	c J. Parks b Tate	69		
G. Geary	lbw b J. Parks	25		
W. E. Astill	not out	6		
H. A. Smith				
†P. Corrall				
Extras	lb	14	lb	1
Total	(7 wkts dec)	483	(no wkt)	23

BOWLING	O	M	R	W	O	M	R	W
Tate	30	8	66	1				
J. Cornford	38	4	118	2	2	0	11	0
J. H. Parks	28	9	80	3	1	0	6	0
Jas. Langridge	16	4	30	0				
Wensley	35	8	99	0				
Melville	9	0	57	0				
Cook	5	0	19	1				
Holmes					1	0	1	0
John Langridge					0.5	0	4	0

Umpires: W. Reeves and D. Hendren

*Captain; †Wicketkeeper

125

and in late August hit 118 off the Glamorgan attack, after the early batsmen had failed. He was to captain the County in 1939. A Lieutenant-Colonel, Packe was involved both in the evacuation of Dunkirk in 1940 and the airborne landings at Arnhem in 1944. H. C. Graham was on the groundstaff following club cricket in Ulster. A very hard-hitting batsman, he was chosen for 11 Championship games and played several useful innings. However he quit county cricket after two seasons and moved into League cricket.

The financial situation did not improve. Other counties were in the same situation and the MCC appointed a Committee to examine the current financial viability of county cricket. Geary had received just £10 from his benefit game, but fortunately money came in from other sources.

Demspter went overseas with Sir Julien Cahn's side in 1936–37 and topped the touring team's batting averages. There were no Leicestershire players on the MCC tour to Australia.

The County's batsmen had a great summer in 1937. Thirteen innings totals exceeding 300 were made; 23 individual hundreds hit – a record which stood alone until equalled in 1984. Leslie Berry hit 2,446 first-class runs (average 52.04) an aggregate which remains the record for the County. He finished seventh in the first-class table and his total of seven centuries remains another record, though now equalled, by Willie Watson in 1959 and Brian Davison in 1982. Dempster could not play as often as in 1936, but averaged 58.19, making 1,222 runs. Armstrong's tally was 1,734, average 41.28 and five hundreds. Prentice now confirmed his promise: 1,506 runs and four hundreds. He was used as Berry's opening partner in place of Shipman. Watson also reached 1,000 runs for the first time. Graham did not advance and Riley, who had been re-engaged for 1937, failed to make much impact.

The bowling on the other hand showed a dramatic decline. So despite the runs being obtained in plenty, wickets were much more expensive. So much so that only one match ended in victory – against Hampshire at Basingstoke on 9 August. This success was due to the bowling of Flamson, who had played a couple of matches in 1934. A right-arm medium-fast bowler he was powerfully built and took nine wickets in the match, Hampshire being dismissed for 180 and 254. During the season he totalled 60 victims, but they cost just under 34 runs each. The veteran Astill headed the bowling table with 53 wickets at 28 runs each; he was marginally ahead of Haydon Smith, who took 110 wickets. Geary's 68 wickets cost 31.18 each. H. B. Bowley, the spin bowler, was brought back for 11 matches, but it proved a costly experiment in terms of runs per wicket. Prentice was used twice as often as in 1936 but caused batsmen few worries.

Derbyshire, Glamorgan and Kent all achieved the double over the County and in all 12 matches were lost. A glance at the ages of the four bowlers – Astill 49, Geary 44, Smith 36 and Flamson 33 – reveals the stark reality. The two bowlers in their 20s who bowled more than 100 overs were Prentice and Bowley, both with averages in the middle fifties.

New bowlers were required desperately. Jim Sperry, a miner from Thornton, who bowled left-arm fast-medium was tried in one game, but failed to take a wicket; he was however to become a major part of the attack in the immediate post-war period. Gerry Lester, a leg-break bowler from Long Whatton, was a second debutant. He was to become much better known as a batsman after the war and played until 1958 scoring well over 10,000 runs. Two other new faces were Jack Walsh and Harold Mudge. Both were Australians from New South Wales who were employed by Sir Julien Cahn and played for his side. They were qualifying for the County by residence and in 1937 played only against Oxford University in The Parks.

Walsh was a slow left-arm bowler who baffled batsmen with his 'chinaman'. He played as an amateur until the outbreak of war. In the 1939–40 season he turned out for New South Wales, but joined Leicestershire as a full-time professional in 1946 and by the time he finished eleven seasons later he had taken over 1,000 wickets. No mean batsman, Walsh performed the 'double' in 1952. Mudge, in contrast, never appeared for the County after his debut. He was due to qualify in 1940, but most of his limited appearances in first-class cricket were for New South Wales. A good all-rounder, he bowled leg-breaks and usually opened the batting.

Two amateurs were given trials as batsmen. A. P. Thompson, the left-hand Shrewsbury old boy, who played for Ivanhoe, appeared in just two games; J. A. T. Sharp, the son of A. T. Sharp, who later became General Sir John Sharp, had been in the Repton side in 1936 and was up at Cambridge. A middle-order right-hand batsman he played four times for the County but with little success.

One player who was to become a familiar figure in post-war cricket made his debut during 1937 literally by accident. Paddy Corrall, the County's wicketkeeper, was injured during the Warwickshire game at Edgbaston. The next match was against Notts at Worksop and the initial paragraph of the first day's report ran:

WILLIAM EWART ASTILL

One of the select nine to score 20,000 runs and take 2,000 wickets in first-class cricket, Ewart Astill alone of that distinguished band did not enjoy a long and successful Test career. Indeed he never represented England at home, his international matches consisting of five in South Africa in 1927–28 and four in West Indies in 1929–30. It was said that his off-breaks lacked that little bit of devil which transforms county bowling into Test status and as a batsman he acquired runs by knowing the foibles of bowlers on the county circuit. The truth perhaps was that he was too nice a man for the matches against Australia. Home Gordon in his obituary note comments: 'He never had an enemy, and when Leicestershire did not do well, he took it as a matter of course and never lost his smiling equanimity.'

Astill joined the Leicestershire staff at the age of 15, his talent being encouraged by his uncle, Thomas Jayes, who was then playing for the County. Making his first-class debut in 1906, his career continued until 1939. He accomplished the 'double' nine times and his full career record was 22,731 runs, average 22.55 and 2,431 wickets, average 23.76.

Away from the cricket field he was an accomplished billiards player and a noted vocalist, singing to his own piano accompaniment. Born at Ratby in 1888, he died after a long illness in Leicester in 1948.

A 16-year-old boy cricketer, Dawkes, probably the youngest wicketkeeper ever to play in a first-class match, and a player who is not considered good enough to be allowed a place on his club's ground staff, was one of the personalities of the match at Worksop.

George Dawkes was 16 years and 328 days old. He was the youngest, to date, to represent Leicestershire, though Roy Julian, Rodney Pratt and Nigel Briers have now successively improved on that record. So well did Dawkes keep that he was retained for ten further matches during the summer and held his place through 1938 and 1939. After the war he decided to move to Derbyshire and Corrall resumed his place.

The 1938 season was almost a repeat of that of 1936. The County won four matches by the end of June and were still undefeated in the Championship (they had been trounced by the Australians in the first game of the season). Warwickshire were

George Dawkes was the youngest Leicestershire debutant when he appeared as a 16-year-old in 1937. An outstanding wicketkeeper, he switched to Derbyshire after the Second World War. (NCCC)

beaten at Aylestone Road. Geary hit his first hundred in the Championship for nine seasons and provided Leicestershire with a lead on first innings of more than 200. Warwickshire were rallied by Dollery, but Leicestershire won by four wickets. The match at Old Trafford was almost entirely washed out, then back at Aylestone Road, Leicestershire brushed Northants aside, Walsh taking ten wickets and Prentice making 154. Unfortunately Prentice damaged a cartilage whilst batting and was out of cricket for over a month as a result. Over at Ashby, Leicestershire had the better of a draw with Glamorgan, before returning to Leicester where Gloucestershire, without their Test stars, were beaten by five wickets. Geary surprised his fans by hitting another century and Walsh took another ten wickets. The Hampshire game at home was a tall-scoring draw – Geary hitting yet another century and Armstrong emulating him. Smith had one of the best bowling analyses of his career at Tunbridge Wells; Kent were dismissed for 58 and 87 with Smith having figures of 12 for 69. Dempster hit a brilliant hundred using his hook stroke to devastating effect and Leicestershire won by 387 runs. Leicestershire, with almost half the season over, stood fourth in the Championship. During July and August they failed to win another match and lost no fewer than nine. One obvious reason for the sudden change of fortune was that Dempster was unavailable for quite a number of matches and Sir Julien Cahn also required the services of Walsh. Despite the revival in Geary's batting, age was now beginning to tell so far as his bowling was concerned. He delivered less than half the number of overs compared with 1937 and this made a considerable difference to the County's attack, since they possessed no effective replacement. In fact Geary was left out of the last few matches and retired at the end of the summer to take a coaching position at Charterhouse. Very little was seen of that other veteran, Astill. He was put in charge of coaching and sent down only 87 overs in the Championship, his four wickets costing 52 runs each. With Flamson away injured for 11 matches, almost everything depended on Smith. He was over-bowled and thus lost much of his edge. His 92 wickets cost 26 runs each. Sperry was given a long trial, but was rather raw.

Dempster was in a class of his own as a batsman, scoring 1,262 runs with six centuries. Geary's three centuries put him in second place. Berry, Armstrong and Watson completed 1,000 runs each, while Prentice totalled only 850, due to his absence through injury.

The most interesting debutant was 19-year-old Maurice

Tompkin from Countesthorpe. He made his debut against Glamorgan at Ashby and in the second innings was unlucky to be run out nine short of a maiden century. One of the most popular cricketers in the first-class game, he gained a regular place in the side in 1939 and after the war his career continued until 1956. Victor Jackson, who was also to feature prominently in post-war cricket, also made his first appearance – in the Australian match. Like Walsh and Mudge, Jackson was a New South Wales player, who was employed by Sir Julien Cahn. He had made his first-class debut for his native state in 1936–37, and was a very useful middle-order batsman and medium-pace off-break bowler. He had narrowly missed selection for the 1938 Australian touring team. A third newcomer was L. D. Thursting, a Londoner who had been on the MCC staff. He came to Leicestershire as a slow left-arm bowler, but his 10 wickets cost 45 runs each and instead he scored some valuable runs, including 94 off the Warwickshire attack at Edgbaston. He was given a further trial in 1939, playing in eight matches, but after the war he took engagements in the Leagues and made just one further appearance, in 1947.

The former Wellingborough schoolboy, Peter Cherrington, was taken on the staff and tried in ten matches, but the form he showed in Leicester club cricket deserted him at county level. Two amateurs were tried in the match against Oxford in The Parks. Patrick Sherrard was an undergraduate at Cambridge, having captained Stowe in 1937. He played one first-class match for the University and was later seen in the Berkshire side. J. Brankin Frisby deputised for Dawkes in the Oxford game. He was Honorary Secretary both of the County Club and Gents of Leicestershire. The Coalville amateur, G. H. Palmer, whose father had played as a professional in 1906, played once or twice, but his medium-pace bowling was not of county standard. Another trialist was Alfred Adcock, the Ibstock professional, who played in five matches as a batsman. He moved to Grantham as professional to the local club and qualified for Lincolnshire.

A. G. G. Webb retired as Secretary to the County Club during the winter of 1938–39 and took a post with the British Sailors' Society. Webb had made his third and final appearance in the County side in 1938. Captain J. E. M. Skinner was appointed as Webb's successor and the former captain C. J. B. Wood was made Assistant Secretary. Another change was the resignation of Dempster as captain. He would be available for only a limited number of matches in 1939; M. St J. Packe, who had played first in 1936, was chosen as the new leader.

There were no Leicestershire cricketers on the winter tour to

Norman Foster Armstrong was called 'Valiant' Armstrong because he so often valiantly saved the side from collapse between 1919 and 1939. He made 1,000 runs in 1939, but being then 46, he did not re-appear after the Second World War. (NCCC)

South Africa, but Sir Julien Cahn took his side to New Zealand and included in his squad Dempster, Jackson, Walsh and Mudge, as well as Ewart Astill acting as scorer. Walsh had a very successful time with the ball, and Dempster hit a double hundred against Otago, in a match not ranked first-class.

Although the County had a new captain and a new Secretary, the biggest change for followers of the County in 1939 was the absence of Astill and Geary in Championship cricket. Astill had first appeared in 1906 and Geary in 1912. Leicestershire no longer possessed any pre–First World War members in the side. The average age of the eleven dropped quite considerably and on several occasions through 1939 their average age was the lowest in the country.

Unlike 1938 the season did not begin promisingly – in fact the reverse was the case. Of the first six Championship games, four were lost and two drawn – even Northants defeated Leicestershire and by the embarrassingly large margin of an innings and 193 runs. It was the first time Northants had won a match since May 1935. The new captain could not be blamed for this upset, since he did not play and in fact both Dempster and Walsh did.

It was moving towards the end of July when victory was finally achieved, on a damp wicket at Aylestone Road against Hampshire. Sperry took ten wickets and Armstrong's unbeaten 71 was the highest score in the game.

The Hampshire win was the only one of the summer and in general the Leicestershire batting was so moderate that only once were first innings points obtained, so the points total for the year was 16: Yorkshire at the top had 260.

Leicestershire finished bottom of the table and in other circumstances it would have been a relief to the players when the political situation caused the cancellation of the last Championship match.

The batting throughout the summer was inconsistent, only Armstrong being reliable. For some reason he abandoned his cautious approach and, laying bat to ball very positively, he made 1,394 runs to head the averages with 36.68. Berry was a mere shadow of his former self. He failed to hit a single century and only just crept over the 1,000-run mark. Neither Prentice nor Watson even reached that milestone and Tompkin made no progress at all. The new captain was rather out of his depth and his highest score was just 56. Dempster played in 11 matches, but for the first time since he joined the County failed. His average and aggregate were boosted by one exhilarating innings of 165 not out against Yorkshire at Hull.

Sperry topped the bowling table with 78 wickets at 23.88 runs each. Haydon Smith's wicket total fell to 77 and they cost four runs each more then Sperry's. Flamson was very expensive.

The one bright spot was the wicketkeeping of George Dawkes. The 19-year-old was marked down as a future England player and his batting also made a useful contribution to the side. The outcricket in general was not of a high standard.

The 1930s had been a difficult time for county cricket financially and the weaker counties suffered more than the old-established ones. Leicestershire survived mainly by putting out the begging bowl and were fortunate in possessing a rich patron, Sir Julien Cahn.

133

Leicestershire playing Nottinghamshire at Aylestone Road in 1939. The 'popular stand' on the far side was built in 1909. The ground was occupied by the United States Army Pioneer Corps and the National Fire Service during the Second World War and the County switched back to Grace Road after the war.

On the field the constant change of captaincy did nothing to improve the cricket and at times the professionals on the staff must have been frustrated by the system imposed upon them. When the decade began Astill and Geary were the dominant figures in the Club and they remained so almost until the end. It was a pity the three Australians, Mudge, Walsh and Jackson had not been available on a regular basis. The last two were, however, to take the places of Astill and Geary in the immediate post-war years.

PROSPERITY IN THE MIDST OF AUSTERITY

UNLIKE THE FIRST WORLD WAR, when many regarded the playing of cricket as unpatriotic, the game was to an extent encouraged in 1940 and during the five following summers whilst hostilities raged. Saturday cricket in the Northern Leagues continued unbroken with many of the county stars being engaged by clubs in the Bradford and Birmingham Leagues. Several of the first-class county clubs arranged programmes of one, and occasionally two-day matches. County cricketers of military age were either called up for the armed forces or employed in work of national importance, but many were available to turn out for Saturday matches.

It was unfortunate for Leicestershire that the Aylestone Road Ground was taken over by the National Fire Service almost as soon as war broke out. When the Fire Service left, the US Army Pioneer Corps moved in and remained for the duration. This put a major obstacle in the way of any Leicestershire County matches. The neighbouring counties of Northants and Notts were keen to arrange fixtures and with the travelling difficulties created by the war, it was natural that these two counties should seek fixtures with Leicestershire. In 1940 therefore Leicestershire played home and away with Northants and at Trent Bridge against Notts. Captain Skinner retired from the Secretaryship and C. J. B. Wood took over those duties.

The first of the three 1940 matches was a two-day game on the village pitch at Barwell. The Leicestershire side was almost up to first-class standard. Dempster scored well and C.H. Drake, who had played eight matches for the County in 1939 as a fast in-swing bowler, took six for 26 to dismiss Northants for 105. Drake was only 17 when he had made his first-class debut. Another youngster who had played a couple of games in 1939, A. R. West, took four cheap wickets in the second innings and Leicestershire won by eight wickets. In the return at Northampton, Leicestershire fielded a similar eleven and won by 68 runs. Dempster was unable to play at Trent Bridge. Notts hit up 263 for five, with Keeton making 108 and Leicestershire were set 294 in 165 minutes. They never approached the required scoring rate but Berry made an attractive 82 and the game was drawn.

Four fixtures were arranged in 1941, home and away with Northants and Notts, but as the Notts match at Leicester was rained off, only three games took place. Haydon Smith took six for 21 to dismiss Northants for 57 at Barwell and Dempster and Berry then knocked off the runs without being parted, producing a ten-wicket win in this one-innings game. Rain prevented Leicestershire attempting a reply to Northants' total of 165 for eight declared in the return at Northampton. Smith was again the best bowler. In the Notts match, Hardstaff and Simpson both made centuries – Hardstaff reached his 100 before lunch in 90 minutes. Rain once more frustrated Leicestershire's attempt at a substantial reply. As the 1941 season ended a long time supporter of Leicestershire cricket, Alderman John Parsons, died. He had held the office of Honorary Treasurer to the County Club for 45 years from 1888 to 1933.

Many members continued to pay their subscriptions to the Club and, as a result, the County were able to declare a profit of £161 in 1941, bringing their balance in hand to £1,000. The search for and training of young players was being continued and the Club hoped that when the Championship began again they would be well prepared. At the end of 1941 C. J. B. Wood resigned as Secretary, thus closing a 47-year association with the County Club.

For the third wartime season, the main matches were against Notts and Northants. Rain curtailed one fixture against each opponent. The other two were lost, both by a margin of five wickets. The Leicestershire sides in these matches were much weaker than in 1940 or 1941 and contained only a sprinkling of County players.

Three of the four 1943 matches were lost – two against Notts and one against Northants. The fourth game, against Northants at home, was drawn due to rain. G. B. F. Rudd and N. T. Dowen acted as joint Honorary Secretaries and E. W. King was the Honorary Treasurer. The financial position was sound with £2,000 in hand at the end of the season.

In 1944, with some prospect of an end to the war in sight, the County Club had discussions with the local Education Committee regarding the possibility of using the old County Ground at Grace Road for first-class matches. It was clear that Aylestone Road would not be in a fit state for several years and in the spring of 1944 it was announced that the Education Committee, who used the Grace Road ground as a sports field for the City of Leicester School, would agree to the County Club returning to the ground provided it did not interfere with its use for the School.

A. T. Sharp captained the County in the four matches of 1944. He was now aged 55 and had first played for the County in 1908.

His son J. A. T. Sharp won the MC in August 1942 for gallant and distinguished services in the Middle East.

Both home matches were won, Northants being beaten by one wicket and Notts by 40 runs. The Glamorgan opener, Emrys Davies, opened for Northants in the return and hit 101, which proved decisive in a Northants victory by 149 runs. At Trent Bridge R. T. Simpson made 133 for Notts and only stubborn batting by A. T. Sharp, who was 21 not out with Leicestershire 157 for nine, saved Leicestershire. Just after the close of the season, Sir Julien Cahn died aged 61. He had been a most generous patron to the County over the previous ten years. Major Charles Packe was killed in action shortly after D-Day in Normandy.

In the winter of 1944–45, the US Forces having left the Aylestone Road Ground, it was taken over by the Leicester Corporation for an extension to the adjoining electricity works. This effectively meant that the provisional plan of moving back to Grace Road whilst Aylestone Road was renovated had to be altered and the County Club needed to persuade the education authorities that Grace Road would become the permanent County headquarters for the foreseeable future. The authorities however wanted county cricket at Grace Road only during school holidays. Clearly there were going to be problems. The ground itself had scarcely altered since 1900 and a lot of work was required to bring it to first-class standard.

In 1945, Leicestershire increased their programme to include home and away games with Derbyshire. Four matches were lost and two drawn. The only individual innings of note for the County was 95 by Prentice against Notts. No Leicestershire players were called on to represent England in the 'Victory' Tests which were hastily arranged after VE Day against the Australian Forces side. Dempster played with some success for the New Zealand Services side, but did not appear in the only New Zealand first-class match.

In the autumn of 1945, with a full County Championship programme anticipated for the following summer, Leicestershire advertised for a full-time Secretary. There were 30 applicants from whom the Committee chose George O. J. Elliott. He had had a trial for his native Gloucestershire in 1934 as a bowler and played for Gloucester City CC. During the war he had been severely wounded in France early on, but had recovered sufficiently to found and run the West of England XI which had played many charity matches during the latter part of the war, and raised some £6,000.

Elliott's first positive step was to open negotiations with the Australians, Walsh and Jackson. Both agreed to terms and travelled back to England for the 1946 season. In the absence of a suitable amateur, Les Berry was appointed captain for the first few matches and performed so well that he remained in charge for the whole summer.

When the side turned out at Lord's for their first Championship game since 1939, the batting line-up, despite the six year gap, had a familiar look: Berry, Watson, Prentice and Tompkin were the first four, with only the 'Valiant Armstrong', as he became called, missing. Vic Jackson came in at number five and Riddington, who had played in the early 1930s, but had been a pro in Scotland from 1935 to 1939, came back to Leicestershire and held his place throughout the summer. Corrall came back as wicketkeeper, replacing Dawkes who was still doing military service. In fact Dawkes opted to move to Derbyshire and never returned to his original county. Sperry opened the bowling with a right-arm fast bowler, formerly of Middlesex, Geoffrey Udal. Udal played in only one other Championship game for Leicestershire. Walsh was the principal spin bowler, aided by Jackson. The 11th place in this first match went to Jack Howard, whose father had played for the County. Jack had been on the Leicestershire staff in 1938 and 1939 without appearing in the first team. A middle-order left-hand batsman, he was to play fairly often in the first three post-war years but with moderate success.

This first match was lost, but the second game, v Derbyshire at Derby, was won by seven wickets when Berry and Watson in the second innings added 190 before the first wicket fell. Berry made 121 not out and Watson 108 in 165 minutes. Vic Jackson finished the Derbyshire first innings off with a hat-trick and Eric Tilley, a fast-medium bowler taking the place of Udal, took a wicket, that of Alderman, with his first delivery in Championship cricket. Like Udal, however, he was not destined to play for the County after 1946.

The match against the Indian touring side on 18 May signalled the return of first-class cricket to Grace Road. Rain ruined the Saturday, but on Monday V. M. Merchant played a faultless innings of 111 not out before Pataudi declared. Merchant was also 57 not out when a second-innings declaration was made, but by then the match was heading for a draw.

The left-arm spin of Walsh, together with 94 from Prentice, brought Leicestershire their second win, Worcestershire being the opposition. Ashby was the scene of a third victory. Berry, who had made his debut on that ground 22 years before, hit 85 and 52, then Jackson did most damage with the ball. Five of the next six matches ended in defeat, but four wins in August – against Northants, Sussex, when Walsh took 14 wickets, Kent, when Walsh took another 14, and Notts, when Walsh seemed content with 11 – meant that Leicestershire finished in 11th place in the table. By coincidence this was the best position since 1935, the year in which Astill had been in command.

The individual figures, and the comments on the victories, reveal that Walsh was largely responsible for the position the County gained in the table. His use of the left-armer's googly was at times devastating and he was the only bowler in England to employ it regularly with any degree of accuracy. He took in all 148 wickets at 20.35 runs each. Most of his support came from Jackson, who missed the 'double' by just six wickets. Both the Australians could bat. Jackson's highest score was 77, but he rarely failed to make a worthwhile contribution and in all scored 1,063 runs. Walsh was a very useful man to come in at number eight or nine and hit 724 runs – he seemed particularly partial to the Essex bowlers and in both games against that county made the highest score, his contributions clinching first-innings points.

Apart from Jackson three other batsmen completed 1,000 runs. Berry headed the list with 1,572 at 34.17. Tompkin looked much more certain than he had in the pre-war seasons and came second to Berry. Prentice came third. Gerry Lester's batting powers were developing. Riddington played some good innings, but Watson, after his century in the second game of the summer, did very little.

Corrall proved to be Walsh's ideal partner. It is difficult today in an era of 'seam-up, wait for the batsman to make a mistake' to recall days when stumping dismissals were a feature of county cricket. Corrall stumped 32 batsmen during 1946 and a similar number in 1948. In the five seasons he played until 1950, he made a total of 128 stumpings, 83 off the wiles of Walsh.

Apart from Jack Howard, T. A. Chapman was the only 1946 debutant to play more than the odd game. Born in Barwell he was a right-hand batsman and occasional wicketkeeper. His highest score for the County during his five seasons at Grace Road was 74. After 1950 he emigrated to Rhodesia and played for that country in the Currie Cup. The present (1991) chairman of the County Club, J. M. Josephs, made the first of nine appearances during the season. He had topped the Clifton College bowling averages in both 1941 and 1942 and in the first year turned out for the wartime County side, aged 17. A slow left-arm bowler, he was also a useful batsman. The Jamaica-born A. L. 'Fred' Gibson was a hard-hitting batsman who had made many runs in local cricket. He played twice for the County but was not successful. An 18-year-old left-handed all-rounder, V. S. Munden, was another who appeared once or twice. He joined the full-time staff in 1948, and in 1951 at last gained a regular place in the County side and was ever-present until 1956.

With the restrictions placed on Grace Road, Leicestershire took first-class cricket to two new venues during 1946. Egerton Park, Melton, had a long history of country house cricket, being owned formerly by the Earl and later by the Countess of Wilton, both noted for their lavish hospitality. One match was played in the Park in each of the first three post-war seasons. Kirkby Road, Barwell, had been used for some wartime County games. Two matches took place there in 1946 and one in 1947. Neither venue however was really up to Championship standard. The County also played two games at Ashby in 1946.

Despite the rather primitive conditions for both spectators and players at the County's home venues and despite generally poor weather, the crowds flocked to the matches and gate receipts for the year were a record £4,397.

A. L. Gibson and Udal were released from the playing staff at the close of 1946 and during the winter Emmott Robinson, the Yorkshire all-rounder of the 1920s, now aged 63, was appointed coach, with the additional task of combing the county for new talent.

Leicestershire fielded an almost unchanged eleven through 1947. Berry, Tompkin, Jackson, Watson, Lester, Corrall and Sperry all played in every Championship game, while Walsh missed only two games, one of which was due to his selection for Players v Gentlemen at Lord's. Prentice also missed two matches and Riddington three. Chapman and Howard virtually divided the eleventh place in the team between them.

Three early matches – against Notts at Loughborough, when Walsh took ten wickets, against Northants at Northampton, when Walsh took eleven wickets and against Hampshire at Leicester – were won by convincing margins – two of the games were over with a day to spare. From then on until the end of July little went right. Only one further win was obtained – against Worcestershire at Barwell when Walsh and Jackson bowled the opposition out for 80 in the second innings when Worcestershire needed only 123 to win – and eight losses were suffered. It was a glorious summer, memorable for Compton and Edrich's run spree, but the Leicestershire batting failed time after time. In this middle period of the season, in successive home games, the

County were bowled out for 156 and 100, 196 and 171, 160 and 199 and away from home fell at Ilkeston for 104 and 118 and at Bath for 176 and 145.

At the beginning of August, playing at Grace Road, Leicestershire were set 391 in the final innings by Derbyshire. The visitors seemed to be moving towards a comfortable win until Pickering at number eight joined Jackson and the pair hit 140 in 90 minutes, with Jackson going on to an undefeated 120. The Australian hit a mighty straight drive to win the game with three wickets in hand. Harry Pickering had played three games for Essex in 1938 and had moved to Leicester, working in the Customs and Excise Office. A very useful right-hand batsman he played only five games for his new county, all in 1947, hitting three fifties, including one in the Derby match.

The only other success was in the penultimate game against Warwickshire when another brilliant innings by Jackson after the six other main batsmen were all out for single figures provided Leicestershire and Walsh in particular with sufficient runs to bowl Warwickshire out in the fourth innings: Walsh took 12 for 165 in the match.

Thus at the close of the year Leicestershire found themselves three places lower than in 1946 with six wins and 14 losses. Six players completed 1,000 runs. Berry with 1,840 headed the batting and had his best season since 1937. Tompkin's class was

Leicestershire in 1947. Left to right, back: J. Howard, G. Lester, J. Sperry, S. Coe (Scorer), M. Tompkin, A. Riddington, V. E. Jackson. Front: J. E. Walsh, F. T. Prentice, G. L. Berry (Captain), G S. Watson, P. Corrall. (NCCC)

now evident and he was not far behind Berry with 1,736 runs. Jackson, Watson, Prentice and Lester were the others with four-figure aggregates. In isolation their figures appear very impressive, but the opposing batsmen tended to score even more heavily and Berry was the only Leicestershire player in the top 40 in the first-class averages and he was 28th. All bowlers suffered in 1947. Walsh with 147 wickets at 22.64 runs each was easily the most impressive bowler. Jackson's 80 wickets cost 31 runs each and Leicestershire's only pace bowler, Sperry, now 37 years old, captured 76 wickets at 30 runs each. The rest of the attack, mainly Riddington, Lester and Prentice, were even more expensive, their wickets costing at least 40 runs each.

With sunshine and plenty of runs, even if mainly from the opposition, the crowds flocked to cricket. The first day of the Middlesex match at Grace Road drew a crowd in excess of 10,000 for the first time since the Australian visit of 1921. Leicestershire made 309, Jackson hitting 117, but Middlesex replied with 637 for four declared off 136 overs. Bill Edrich scored 257, Denis Compton 151 and their partnership for the third wicket added 277 in 130 minutes. A patient 154 from Leslie Berry meant Leicestershire avoided the innings defeat and Middlesex needed 66 in 25 minutes. The 'Terrible Twins' went in and hit these from seven overs. On the second day no less than 663 runs were made for the loss of six wickets.

Leicestershire's highest total of the year came at Hastings when Tompkin made 163 out of 547, but as Sussex had reached 422 the game was little more than a battle for first-innings points.

Despite the disappointing results, Leicestershire had few changes of staff for the 1948 season. All of the 1947 men were re-engaged and two newcomers, M. W. Etherington and W. B. Cornock, added. Etherington was a fast bowler from Hammersmith who had played once or twice for Middlesex in 1946. He appeared in three first-class games for Leicestershire but for him the season was marred by ill-health and he was not seen after 1948. Cornock was Australian by birth, but had spent most of his life in England and made a name for himself as a batsman in League cricket. A brilliant fieldsman, Cornock hit 801 runs and played in all but two of the Championship matches. It seemed as if he might develop into a very valuable county player, but at the season's end he decided to return to Australia.

Fred Root, who had been briefly on the Leicestershire staff in 1906 and later found fame with Derbyshire and Worcestershire, was engaged as a coach for April 1948. Unlike 1947 when the early matches produced wins, 1948 found the County struggling through the first three months. By July 20 only one out of 15 matches had ended in victory, whilst eight had been defeats. The team was bottom of the table with the same number of points as Northants. The single success thus far had been entirely due to the spin of Walsh. The venue was at Hove and the Australian slow bowler had taken eight for 73 in the Sussex first innings; Leicestershire then gained a slender lead. In the second innings Walsh took seven for 27 and after rain arrived threatening to end the match, Leicestershire just managed to knock off the 82 required to win.

In the final week of July suddenly fortune changed. Glamorgan were beaten at Cardiff Arms Park by 21 runs. The Welsh side, who were to end the summer as County Champions, needed 195 in the fourth innings, but Walsh and Jackson dismissed them for 173. Back at Grace Road, Leicestershire played their return game with Sussex. After high scoring in both first innings – Watson made 101 for Leicestershire – Jackson and Walsh removed Sussex cheaply in their second innings and Leicestershire won by six wickets. A third win in successive matches came at Northampton. Rain produced an ideal pitch for Walsh on the last day and Northants, requiring 277, collapsed with Walsh collecting six for 42. A fourth consecutive win came in the next match and this was perhaps the highlight of Leicestershire's year, for they beat Yorkshire at Bramall Lane. Leicestershire gained a first innings lead of 96, and, with rain cutting down the playing time, Berry later set Yorkshire the difficult task of 267 in 180 minutes. Hutton played a quite outstanding knock, but all his colleagues were confused by Walsh and Jackson and Leicestershire won by 66 runs, Hutton carrying his bat through the completed innings for 99. With Leicestershire having hit a winning streak it was unfortunate that the next two games were ruined by rain, and not until the final match of the year did Leicestershire again taste victory. Curiously this final success was against Glamorgan, so lowly Leicestershire were the only county to perform the double against the Champions. Prentice scored 99, supplying the backbone to Leicestershire's total of 264, then Walsh simply brushed the Welshmen aside twice, claiming 14 for 86 in the process and finishing the match and season off a day early.

In the end Leicestershire had a similar record to 1947, again having six victories, but with three less defeats they moved up the table to 11th place.

It would be wrong to pass through the 1948 season without reference to the all-conquering Australians. Leicestershire were rudely brushed aside – by an innings and 171 runs – on 4 May,

143

with Keith Miller hitting a double hundred and Bradman a mere 81. Fingleton in his report of the match makes an interesting comment on Walsh:

> He is a left-handed twisty bowler after the Fleetwood-Smith style. His googly, which is a leg-break to the right-handed batsman, is the hardest I know to pick, and after I saw Bradman once play for an off-break and miss the ball by a good two feet as it spun the other way, I guessed he might agree too. I had never before seen Bradman so completely beaten. Walsh bowls his googly in three different ways. One is from his palm, the other is through his fingers, and the third in a different manner through his fingers. He makes one very obvious, to try to mislead you with the others. No wonder it is hard to pick.

No Leicestershire player was chosen for England, but Walsh was the leading first-class wicket-taker with 174 at 19 runs each; 170 of these were for the County, a record which still stands. Five times he took ten wickets or more in a match. As if this was not enough he also hit 745 runs and took 26 catches. His maiden first-class century came off the Essex attack at Park Road, Loughborough and took only 95 minutes and contained seven sixes. Jackson came very close to the 'double' – 1,396 runs and 97 wickets, plus 32 catches. Sperry had his best summer for the County with 81 wickets at 23 runs each, but the rest of the bowlers achieved little.

The batsmen, even though five topped 1,000 runs, had overall an unimpressive record. Prentice led the way with 1,328 runs, average 36.89, but no one else came in the top 40 in the first-class table. Jackson was the only other to average above 30. Berry failed to make a single hundred, and Tompkin owed his average of 25 very much to a single innings of 152.

The County's cricket attracted some large crowds, though conditions at Grace Road for spectators, as well as players, were rudimentary. A record 16,000 watched the first day against the Australians. For the Whitsun game against Northants, the three days brought crowds of 8,000, 11,000 and 8,000 and at Ashby the first day's gate against Derbyshire was about 7,500. The financial position of the Club was, in contrast to the pre-war days, quite healthy.

Following his temporary post in 1948, Fred Root was appointed full-time coach for 1949. A far more controversial appointment however was that of S. J. Symington to replace Berry as captain. Having experience of the confused captaincy situation which dominated the 1930s, it might have been thought that the

Committee would have known the pitfalls of appointing an inexperienced man, who would not be available for all matches, to the leadership. Symington was a regular in the army and had obtained leave in order to play county cricket. He had headed the Canford School batting averages in 1944 and in 1948 made his debut for Leicestershire, turning out in two Championship games. Leicestershire registered Gwynn Evans, the 1939 Oxford blue, who acted as captain in the matches when Symington was not available. Evans, from Merionethshire, was a medium-fast right-arm bowler, who had played a few matches for Glamorgan after coming down from Oxford in 1939.

Relieving Berry of the captaincy had the desired effect of improving his personal batting record quite substantially, but the County's overall performance was not something to linger over. With only three victories they finished at the foot of the table. The general consensus of opinion in the cricket press was that Leicestershire were a better side than their record indicated. Enthusiastic the two new captains may have been, but the situa-

F. T. Prentice made his highest score, 191, and made his biggest aggregate, 1,742, in 1949, when he ceased playing regularly to concentrate on his business interests. He played 241 matches for Leicestershire. (NCCC)

tion could hardly bring out the best in an otherwise all-professional team. Dropped catches clearly depressed the already rather fragile attack.

The first of the three wins came against Notts at Loughborough. Walsh took seven for 61, Notts being all out for 175. Prentice then hit the highest score of his career, 191 and with Jackson over 200 was realised for the fourth wicket and with Watson over 100 for the fifth. Leicestershire declared at 455 for eight. Walsh began his second innings bowling with the wicket of Keeton, and having removed Woodhead and Meads with the last two balls of the first innings, he accomplished a hat-trick. The left-arm spinner then continued his domination of events, ending the game with 15 wickets and Leicestershire had victory by an innings. Six weeks were to pass before the County tasted victory for a second time. Surrey were the visitors to Grace Road and the teams were separated by only ten runs on first innings. In the final innings on a dusty pitch, the southern county needed 254. Squires batted well, but the eighth wicket fell at 194. Surridge joined Laker, and the pair added 33. Extra time was now being played and the match was very finely balanced. Walsh, however, then dismissed both Surridge and Laker bringing a win by 24 runs with 15 minutes of extra time to spare.

The third win came in the last match by the decisive margin of an innings and 100 runs. Gwynn Evans led Leicestershire against his former county, Glamorgan. It proved to be his final appearance for his adopted shire and appropriately he had a second innings analysis of 8-4-17-3 which took the fight out of the Glamorgan middle order.

Against the three successes were 14 defeats in the Championship. The match against the touring New Zealanders saw Wallace and Donnelly add 299 for the visitors' fourth wicket in 190 minutes, after both openers had failed to score. Leicestershire collapsed, all out 119 and followed on, but Lester, 70 not out, and Prentice, 104 not out, were well dug in when a thunderstorm ended the game.

The weakness of the County's bowling is quickly apparent from the tables. Walsh took 132 wickets at 28 runs each while Jackson's 75 cost 30 each and Sperry's 72, 33 each. The batting was generally sound and entertaining. Berry led the averages with 1,853 runs at 43 per innings and four hundreds. Prentice had five centuries before the end of June, but then lost his touch somewhat. In scoring 1,742 runs he reached his best seasonal aggregate and as already noted made his highest score. Tompkin, Jackson and Lester were the other three to top 1,000 runs. Watson failed completely and was dropped from the side. Vic Munden was given much more opportunity but his figures were not yet impressive. One continuous cheerful note was the wicketkeeping of Corrall, who equalled his record of six dismissals in an innings during the match against Middlesex. This was also his benefit game and his reward was a sum of £2,333, a new high for the County.

Several new players were tried during the summer. E. L. Williams from Charterhouse was a fast-medium left-arm bowler; N. L. Dunham, a right-arm bowler, played in local club cricket; P. H. Jaques from Wyggeston School scored many runs for the Ivanhoe Club; G. S. Smith, another local batsman, had been in the Bedford school side; P. H. Konig had been taken on the staff as the reserve keeper – he was born in Vienna, but had lived in Leicester since childhood. None of these five made any mark in county cricket, but C. R. D. Wooler, the nephew of the old South African Test cricketer, S. J. Snooke, had been spotted by Vic Jackson playing in Rhodesia. He appeared only in a three-day friendly game with Northants in 1949, but in 1950 was given a regular place as an all-rounder.

The 1940s ended with the resignation of G. O. J. Elliott from his post as Secretary; Symington indicated that he was unable to play regular county cricket and he resigned as captain; and Fred Root gave up the coaching position. Season 1950 was clearly to be the start of a new era.

A SCHOOLMASTER IN CHARGE

HAVING LOST BOTH A SECRETARY and a captain, the County Committee decided to fill both posts with a slight, bespectacled master from Bromsgrove School, C. H. Palmer. Palmer had played 66 matches for Worcestershire spread over six seasons, commencing at the age of 19 in 1938. A graduate of Birmingham University he had come to public attention at the start of the 1948 season, when he played an excellent innings of 85 for Worcestershire in the opening tour match against the Australians. Largely on the strength of this innings he was selected for the Gentlemen *v* Players later in the summer and for the MCC party to South Africa the following winter. Palmer had batted with success for Worcestershire in the summer holidays of 1949 and had returned a first-class average over 40 in 18 completed innings. The appointment of Palmer as Secretary was announced in February 1950 and the club then applied to Lord's for a special registration so that Palmer did not have to await residential qualification before playing. The position of coach, vacated by Root, was not filled until the following spring when Ashdown, the former Kent cricketer, was appointed.

Leicestershire had moved from Aylestone Road mainly due to the erection of the electricity cooling towers which now dwarfed the playing area, but during the inter-war period the proximity of the power station, even without cooling towers, had caused problems with clouds of fine ash from the chimneys covering everything, including spectators' sandwiches, with layers of grit.

Grace Road was grit free, but difficult to find, being tucked away off the main road. Only two buildings stood on the site, both on the North side. The pavilion's best feature was the first floor dressing rooms, which gave a good view of the play, but were rather cramped. There was no Long Room or proper accommodation for members to view the cricket on the ground floor of the pavilion; the members sat in rows of seats directly in front of the building. The second building had been erected by Messrs Wolsey Ltd as a recreation room for the firm's employees, when they occupied the ground. It now served as a gymnasium for children from the school which normally used the ground as a sports field, and as a dining room for members and players on first-class match days. On the side of the ground opposite these two buildings was a derelict area used for car-parking. A contemporary comment states:

> At the moment there is an impression of improvisation, a sense of making-do with temporary expedients, a suggestion of apology for unavoidable discomforts. Grace Road looks, in fact, what it is, a ground loaned for a county cricket match, rather than an established home of county cricket.

Apart from Grace Road, Leicestershire played at Ashby, Loughborough and Coalville in 1950. The Loughborough venue was that of the Town Club ground in Park Road. The Coalville venue was a new departure, the Town ground in Broom Leys Road. The facilities were poor and the 1950 Warwickshire game turned out to be the only first-class match staged there.

The 1950 season opened at Old Trafford. Palmer captained the County on his debut and the eleven also included Wooler, now fully qualified, and K. D. Smith, a 28-year-old right-hand batsman, who had spent most of his working life in the RAF. He had

Paddy Corrall kept wicket for Leicestershire from 1930 to 1951, surviving a serious accident in 1933 when struck on the head by the batsman's follow-through. He claimed 563 victims, an average of two per match. (NCCC)

played a couple of games for Northumberland in 1949, having been educated at Heaton Grammar School in Newcastle. Accurate bowling by Bob Berry meant that Leicestershire struggled to avoid defeat – with the last pair together in the second innings they were just ten runs ahead when stumps were drawn.

From Manchester to Pontypridd, the Leicestershire team travelled to play Glamorgan. Runs were difficult to acquire on a green pitch. Walsh took seven for 24, as the Welsh side were all out for 75; Muncer replied with six for 19: Leicestershire 95 all out. Palmer returned figures of 17-10-13-4 in the Glamorgan second innings and finally Berry and Lester had an opening stand of 77 which brought victory by six wickets. Two more away games followed, against Worcestershire and Notts, in both of which Leicestershire failed badly on the first innings, but on their second attempt fought back for a draw. At Trent Bridge Tompkin made a second-innings century and this feat was emulated by Lester and Jackson at Worcester. The first defeat came in the fifth match, again away, Hampshire winning by six wickets at Portsmouth. The three remaining matches of May produced a win, a loss and a draw. Leicestershire, with the first quarter of the season gone, were comfortably placed in mid-table – nothing spectacular, but a welcome improvement on 1949. The rest of the summer was not so pleasant. Only one more victory was gained – against Hampshire in mid-August, when Tompkin hit a delightful hundred and Jackson took eleven for 62 – and this was set against 11 more defeats. No county in 1950 suffered more reverses than Leicestershire, but they managed to hand over the wooden spoon to Essex by four points.

One of the more humiliating defeats of the season came against the West Indian touring side in July. Only two of the famous three 'W's needed to bat – Worrell and Weekes each made double centuries after Roy Marshall had missed the target by 12. West Indies declared at 682 for two, 621 coming on the first day, and won by an innings and 249. Four Leicestershire bowlers conceded over 100 runs with only one wicket between them.

The continued moderate performance was in no way due to the new captain. He hit 1,894 runs, average 33.82, topping the batting table, and with 40 wickets at 24 runs each also led the bowlers. The one criticism levelled against him was that he did not do enough bowling. Tompkin was marginally behind Palmer both in terms of run aggregate and average. He made five centuries, as did Berry. Jackson totalled 1,451 runs and also took 83 wickets and 28 catches. The three other major batsmen, Lester, Watson and Prentice all disappointed. It proved to be Watson's

LEICESTERSHIRE *v* WEST INDIES

Played at Leicester, 12, 13 and 14 July 1950

WEST INDIES WON BY AN INNINGS AND 249 RUNS

WEST INDIES	FIRST INNINGS		SECOND INNINGS
A. F. Rae	b Jackson	26	
R. Marshall	c and b Sperry	188	
F. M. Worrell	not out	241	
E. Weekes	not out	200	
C. L. Walcott			
†R. J. Christiani			
G. E. Gomez			
*J. D. Goddard			
P. E. Jones			
S. Ramadhin			
A. L. Valentine			
Extras	b 18, lb 6, w 1, nb 2	27	
Total	(2 wkts dec)	682	

BOWLING	O	M	R	W
Sperry	34	0	171	1
Wooler	28	6	103	0
Walsh	21	1	133	0
Jackson	9	3	24	1
Palmer	16	1	79	0
Lester	20	0	122	0
K. Smith	3	0	23	0

LEICESTERSHIRE	FIRST INNINGS		SECOND INNINGS	
G. L. Berry	c and b Valentine	121	c Walcott b Jones	5
G. S. Watson	c Goddard b Jones	10	c Walcott b Valentine	6
M. Tompkin	c Rae b Marshall	74	c Marshall b Ramadhin	11
*C. H. Palmer	b Ramadhin	9	b Ramadhin	20
V. E. Jackson	b Valentine	56	c Jones b Ramadhin	1
G. Lester	b Ramadhin	27	b Ramadhin	6
K. D. Smith	not out	14	lbw b Ramadhin	2
†J. W. R. Smith	c Walcott b Valentine	1	b Ramadhin	0
J. E. Walsh	c Marshall b Valentine	0	not out	24
C. Wooler	b Ramadhin	0	st Christiani b Valentine	4
J. Sperry	b Ramadhin	16	c Ramadhin b Valentine	1
Extras	b 16, lb 8	24	lb 1	1
Total		352		81

BOWLING	O	M	R	W	O	M	R	W
Jones	21	3	55	1	7	2	13	1
Gomez	12	7	21	0	2	2	0	0
Ramadhin	40.3	14	90	4	15	7	27	6
Valentine	57	27	101	4	19.4	8	40	3
Worrell	10	2	25	0				
Marshall	12	4	36	1				

Umpires: F. Chester and A. Skelding

*Captain; †Wicketkeeper

final season and Prentice also left full time county cricket, re-appearing in 1951 as an amateur.

The continuing weakness of the bowling – in the list of bowlers taking 50 first-class wickets, Walsh came 51st – was Leicestershire's main problem. Walsh was the only Leicestershire bowler to take 100 wickets. Apart from Walsh and his fellow Australian, only Wooler managed above 50.

Among the 1950 debutants was T. J. Goodwin, a 21-year-old left-arm fast bowler from the Staffordshire League and a nephew of Aaron Lockett, the former Staffordshire all-rounder. He appeared in 10 matches and, still feeling his way in county cricket, took 23 wickets at 40 runs each. He was to remain with the County for ten seasons. A more notable young player was Maurice Hallam, who was given a trial as a batsman, but was not to become a regular member of the side until after he had completed his National Service. Hallam developed into the mainstay of the County's batting and his career was to extend over 21 seasons.

K. D. Smith has been mentioned already, and the other three trialists made little impact. Donald Goodson was a 17-year-old schoolboy from the Grammar School at Melton, who played a few games as an amateur and then emigrated to South Africa; the

Les Berry during the innings in which he made his 30,000th run in first-class cricket against Surrey at The Oval in 1951. Tony Lock, who later gave Leicestershire great service in 65 matches is the finest of the short legs, between 'keeper G. N. G. Kirby and skipper Stuart Surridge. (NCCC)

Old Reptonian, J. W. R. Smith, who kept wicket for the Ivanhoe Club played in three games, two in 1950 and one in 1955; another Ivanhoe player was W. R. Parkyns who was tried in a few games as a batsman.

The Club's financial situation was not as comfortable as it had been in the immediate post-war years. A deficit of £1,584 was realised on the year's figures, but the club received £5,754 in compensation for the loss of the Aylestone Road ground.

Before the 1951 campaign opened, Berry announced that it would be his last county season – he was 45 in April. The County specially registered the young England and Yorkshire left-hander, Gerry Smithson, in order to give an immediate boost to the batting; a second Yorkshireman, Jack Firth, was also signed on, as deputy to the wicketkeeper, Corrall – Corrall was the same age as Berry. To strengthen the attack two Australians were engaged, and both would qualify in 1952. M. A. J. Sargent was a leg-break bowler and P. F. Saunders, a right-arm fast bowler. Both came from Adelaide; they made their debut for the County in first-class friendlies in 1951, played a few Championship games in 1952 and then decided to go back to Australia.

W. H. Ashdown was now established as the County coach and a number of local youngsters were engaged for the season. The downturn in the finances and the continued problems with the temporary tenure of Grace Road led to some speculation concerning the very existence of the County Club. The rumours reached a stage when Palmer, with his Secretary's hat on, was obliged to issue a statement to the press. He made it plain that the future of the Club was not in jeopardy and went on:

> We are spending heavily, not to avoid liquidation, but with the policy of developing so that we can hold our own with other counties in all respects. There is a firm intention to give Leicestershire a stronger foundation and the emphasis is on expansion. We have a large staff, a nursery with a coach and have spent a great deal on improving the ground. Within the Club it is felt that for too long Leicestershire has just kept its head above water and now is the time to gamble its resources and make it flourish as never before.

The Leicestershire first-class season began at Lord's. Smithson made his debut, batting at number seven, and Firth also made his first appearance – and in fact took over as the regular keeper, Corrall, played in only one match. Both debutants were dismissed without scoring in a drawn game ruined by the weather. After two more draws, victory was gained at the expense of

Somerset. Palmer made 144 and Firth hit freely for 71; in the fourth and final innings the western county collapsed before the spin of Munden and Jackson, the former taking five for 33.

It was not until early in July that Leicestershire tasted victory for a second time. After an even first innings, Worcestershire declared in their second, setting Leicestershire 292 in 230 minutes. Palmer batted in fine form against his old colleagues, making 118, but the support he received was erratic and when Sperry, the last man, came to the crease one run was needed and two minutes remained. Sperry hit the first delivery for three and victory.

By mid-August Leicestershire were vying with Notts for the wooden spoon, but a win at Ashby over Surrey – Jackson took six for 23 – and eight days later a second success over Kent, when Smithson hit 105 in 90 minutes, meant that Leicestershire finished in 15th place with four wins and seven losses, no less than 16 matches being drawn and another abandoned.

In its report at the close of the season *The Cricketer* suggested that: 'it was felt that the team played noticeably improved cricket and that there was a much better approach to the game.'

The reason why this did not produce better results was the absence of key players due to injury. Walsh missed half the season through illness, Wooler was absent due to injury and the promising Goodwin missed most of the summer. The bowling was therefore seldom at its strongest. Walsh's tally of wickets fell to 33 and the main burden of the attack was on Jackson's shoulders – he took 98 wickets at 23 runs each; Munden took 51 at 22 and Wooler 50 at 28. The veteran, in terms of fast bowlers, Sperry, took 62 at 22 runs each. Palmer was nothing like as effective as in his first summer, but he remained the principal batsman with 1,694 runs at an average of 40. Not far behind came Tompkin with 1,715 runs and an average of 37. Jackson was the only other player to exceed 1,000 runs. Smithson took time to settle down. He had made his Yorkshire debut in 1946 at the age of 19 and some good batting the following year had led to his selection for the MCC team to West Indies. At this time he was a 'Bevin Boy' – being employed as a miner instead of called up into the Services. Before he obtained release from the mines to tour, questions were asked in the House of Commons and his case became briefly headline news. He never really fulfilled his early promise, though he remained on the Leicestershire staff for six seasons. He died in 1970 at the age of 43. Firth, having taken Corrall's place, kept wicket for eight full seasons. He had played eight games for his native Yorkshire in the summers of 1949 and 1950, but the presence of D. V. Brennan meant he was unable to hold a regular

GEORGE LESLIE BERRY

Although he scored a total of 30,225 runs in a career which spanned 28 years, Les Berry played in only four first-class matches not involving Leicestershire. An opening batsman with an attractive range of strokes, he could be regarded as a County man pure and simple. Eighteen times he reached 1,000 runs in a season, but only once, in 1937, did the total exceed 2,000.

Born in Surrey, he moved with his family to Market Harborough when he was eight years old. After making some useful scores for the local club, he joined the County staff, but it was several years before he gained a regular place in the eleven. During the war he captained the RAF in the Middle East and on his return found himself appointed captain of the County – not a unique appointment, since Astill had led the side before the war, but in 1946 Berry was the only regular professional captain in the Championship. He remained in office for three seasons and finally retired in 1951. He coached at Uppingham School until 1979 and died in 1985 aged 78.

On contemporary scorecards he was always shown as L. G. Berry, since he was commonly known as 'Les', but in fact this was his second Christian name and his correct initials are G. L.

(NCCC)

first team place with that county. Coming in at number eight he made a useful contribution to the batting strength of Leicestershire.

Of the old hands, Berry had a poor summer. For the first time since 1928 he failed to reach 1,000 runs, though he played in every Championship game. Prentice managed only 86 runs in seven innings. Berry went to Uppingham School as coach; Corrall moved to the first-class umpires' list. Another retirement was that of Wooler, who returned to Rhodesia.

Apart from Smithson and Firth another notable debutant of 1951 was M. J. K. Smith. Captain of Stamford School he topped the school's batting averages for the second successive summer and in August played for the Public Schools at Lord's. He was away on National Service in 1952 and 1953; the next year he was up at Oxford, and he played in three University matches, scoring centuries in each one. In the vacation of 1954 and 1955 he re-appeared for Leicestershire, gaining his County cap in the latter year, but in 1956 threw his lot in with Warwickshire, captaining that county from 1957 to 1967 and leading England in 25 Tests. He also played fly-half for England on the rugby field and thus was one of the most talented sportsman born in the county – the county town being his birthplace.

D. G. Harron, an attacking batsman from County Durham, joined Leicestershire and played in ten matches, but in 14 innings only made one fifty. He left the County after the one season. The two Australians who made fleeting appearances have been noted previously.

The number of paying spectators at Leicestershire matches dropped in 1951, even compared with the poor total recorded the previous year. Seven days play were however washed out by rain. Berry received nearly £2,000 from his Testimonial Fund.

Palmer's answer to the deteriorating financial situation was the introduction of a football pool run by the County Club. Worcestershire had successfully organised such a venture for two years. In December 1951, a County Supporters' Association was formed to run the pool and it began in January 1952 with 1,647 members, and within six months £2,000 had been raised and presented to the County Club. The main organiser of the Association was Billy Butler and over the next ten years the scheme was to contribute over £20,000 to the Club.

In 1951 ill-luck in the shape of injury and illness as well as bad weather had caused poor results; in 1952 nearly everything went right. Walsh and Goodwin, the two most affected the previous year, played throughout the summer. Smithson regained his

The future England captain, M. J. K. Smith, made his debut for Leicestershire in 1951. Although born in Leicester, he decided in 1956 to switch to Warwickshire. (NCCC)

Yorkshire confidence and though the years finally brought Sperry to a standstill, Spencer developed into a very adequate replacement.

Not that everything clicked from the first match; on 24 June, Leicestershire were 15th equal in the table, only four points separating them from bottom-placed Sussex. Nine matches had been played, four lost, four drawn and one won. The single success was a quite brilliant match against, on paper, one of the strongest sides, Middlesex – the Middlesex of Compton, Edrich, Robertson, Young, Sims and Moss. Batting first Middlesex hit 407 before declaring with five wickets down, Compton and Robertson scoring hundreds. Not overawed, Leicestershire matched that total, Tompkin knocking up a hundred in two hours. Walsh and Jackson combined to bowl out the opposition for 215 and this left Leicestershire requiring 211 in 210 minutes. Tompkin batted quite splendidly, reached his second hundred of the match and victory was gained by seven wickets with 45 minutes in hand.

In late June the winning ways returned. Between 25 June and 18 July, the County played seven matches and won five. Walsh and Jackson disposed of Sussex at Worthing, Walsh taking eleven wickets, Jackson nine. The team crossed the south of England to Bath, where Walsh was again in excellent form – he hit the highest score of the game, 84, and in Somerset's first innings took six wickets; Leicestershire gained a reasonable first-innings lead, but nearly threw it all away by a feeble second innings batting display – 127 for nine, of which Lester made 65 not out. Good bowling by everyone saved the day and the margin of victory was 25 runs.

The next victory came at Grace Road against Hampshire, where for once Walsh did not play a major part. Spencer took five for 67 and Palmer five for 13, as Hampshire were tumbled out for 151. Smithson, Tompkin, Palmer, Jackson and Munden all made fifties as Leicestershire gained a first innings lead of 302 and went on to win by an innings. Back to the south coast, and victories were achieved at Southampton, by ten wickets, and at Folkestone, by seven wickets. In the latter fixture, Walsh took another eleven wickets and Munden completed a maiden hundred. Leicestershire had moved rapidly up the table and were now in eighth place.

Trevor Bailey writing in *The Cricketer* in mid-season reinforces the comments made by Fingleton in 1948 regarding Walsh and also gives an insight into Jackson's skill:

> Walsh is undoubtedly one of the most fascinating bowlers in the game. He spins his googlies and chinamen so much that they will turn on any wicket and what makes this even more interesting is that few batsmen have any idea which way the ball is going to break. I shall never forget a certain Essex player who became so confused by this, that he was eventually stumped flat on his face down the wicket. Walsh is also a more than useful hitter. Due to a habit of slipping his right hand down to the bottom of the handle before making a stroke, Jackson favours the cross bat and is particularly adept at playing the cut and the pull. His accurate slow off-breaks have brought him many victims. A purist might complain that his arm is rather low and at times he does produce the roundest of round-arm deliveries that must be a very close relation of a genuine lob.

At Liverpool, Munden hit a second hundred, Walsh took another nine wickets and Lancashire were comprehensively beaten, dismissed for 208 and 129, whilst Leicestershire could afford the luxury of declaring both their innings closed. Kent were overcome by Jackson at Park Road, Loughborough – all out 132 and 102, Jackson ten for 85 – and victory was by nine wickets. The ninth and final win of the season was against Somerset at Grace Road, Palmer and Munden bowling the visitors out for 91 and producing an unexpected innings win. There were nine defeats and ten draws. These figures placed the County in sixth position. *Wisden* described Leicestershire as 'the most improved side in the country'.

The enthusiasm and spirit of Charles Palmer was beginning to win through. The captain exceeded 2,000 runs in all first-class matches. These included an excellent innings of 127 for the Gentlemen against Players at Lord's. For the County he was supremely consistent; three hundreds and 15 fifties. The captain also took 35 wickets and held 14 catches. Five other batsmen reached 1,000 runs, headed by Tompkin with 1,638, then Jackson, Munden, Smithson and Walsh, the last three accomplishing the feat for the first time. As Walsh also took 116 wickets he became the second player ever to achieve the 'double' for the County, the last occasion being Astill's fifth 'double' in 1930.

Jackson took 82 wickets. He missed a couple of Championship games and thus was not quite as close to the 'double' as in previous years. Munden not only made his mark as a left-hand attacking batsman, but his left-arm slows took 38 wickets at less than 30 runs apiece, so the County possessed three effective all-rounders. Goodwin, the left-arm fast bowler, who had made his debut in 1950, now confirmed his promise, as he took 67 wickets. C. T. 'Terry' Spencer, a 20-year-old right-arm seam bowler from the county town, made his debut in the opening first-class friendly game with Cambridge and then in the second match, another first-class friendly against the Indian tourists, bowled so well that he subsequently appeared in every Championship match and ended the summer with 80 wickets. In addition to his bowling he was a brilliant close fielder and developed into a useful hard hitting late-order batsman. By the time of his retirement in 1974 he had captured well over 1,000 wickets for the County.

The wicketkeeping of Firth should not be forgotten. With 85 victims (60 caught, 25 stumped) he easily broke the existing Leicestershire record and his total remains the highest.

Apart from Spencer, two other youngsters made their debuts. L. A. Spence, a right-hand batsman from Blaby, played occasionally over three summers, but nearly 20 years later returned to Grace Road as first assistant and then head groundsman. F. G. Foulds was just 17. He played in the match against Cambridge, in the two following seasons he was on National Service, then in 1956 he made a second and final appearance for the County.

The experiment of organising a 'cricket week' on the Coventry Road Ground at Hinckley was tried for the first time, the visitors being Essex and Notts. The idea was relatively successful, and was to be repeated several times, but the County have not played at Coventry Road since 1964.

The *Playfair Annual* ended its review of the County's season with: 'The short term prospects are quite encouraging, the long-term very exciting.' The results for 1953 certainly confirmed the comment, for the County finished in joint third place – the best ever – and for several days in August were actually at the top of the table. Unfortunately Surrey had games in hand and therefore overhauled Leicestershire. Lancashire ended level with Leicestershire, while Sussex finished second.

Ten matches were won, but the start of the summer was not propitious. The County were beaten by an innings in two days by the Australians, Neil Harvey making an unbeaten 202 with 27 fours. Going to Bristol, the County dominated the match for two days, then on the last morning declared, giving Gloucestershire 260 minutes to make 302. Tom Graveney hit an unbeaten 126 and Leicestershire lost by six wickets. Matters went totally awry against Hampshire at Loughborough – on the Brush Sports Ground for the first time. Leicestershire made 179, and Hampshire were destroyed by Jackson, all out 68. Shackleton and Cannings responded by dismissing the home side for 84 in their second innings. The batsmen then took charge and Hampshire strolled to a nine-wicket victory, an opening partnership by Rogers and Gray being worth 160. Two drawn matches followed. At Portsmouth a second innings revival saved a match apparently lost and at Northampton the bowlers made no impression. Palmer hit a maiden double century in 285 minutes and Smithson, who helped the captain add 209 for the third wicket, also reached three figures.

Leicestershire's last Championship match of May produced their first victory. With rain having reduced the playing time, Gloucestershire, on the last day, declared setting a target of 189 in 135 minutes – Hallam hit the top score and the margin of success was four wickets. This upturn did not immediately herald a massive revival, since the eight Championship games in June produced only two further wins. On a newly laid pitch at Bath, none of the four innings mustered 200 runs, but with Munden taking ten for 42, Leicestershire won by 144 runs.

The first match of the week at Hinckley provided a second June victory. The visitors Worcestershire had great difficulty scoring runs – more than half the Leicestershire overs were maidens and R. E. Bird spent four hours making 55. Jackson took six for 54. Leicestershire's innings was a bit of an oddity. Six wickets went down for 55; Jackson and Walsh then almost doubled the total; Hallam arrived at number nine and proceeded to hit 98. The left-arm spin of Walsh and Munden prevented Worcestershire being resuscitated and the victory was by six wickets.

Like June, July provided two victories. By the end of the month Leicestershire were fifth in the table, but they had played more matches than the four teams ahead of them, save for Middlesex who led the field. August produced four more wins. Northants were beaten at Grace Road and Yorkshire on the following days at the same venue. At Loughborough Kent lost by seven wickets and back at Grace Road Essex lost by two wickets, when Jackson produced some excellent all-round figures. In the third innings he took six for 40 and in the final innings, with Leicestershire struggling to make 243, he was undefeated with 65. The County briefly held first place in the table, but in the end, with their last two games being a loss and a draw, had to settle for joint third with Lancashire.

The reason for the success was teamwork welded together by Palmer, rather than outstanding figures by one or two stars. The side had the advantage of four genuine all-rounders – Palmer (1,566 runs and 26 wickets); Jackson (1,408 and 73); Walsh (786 and 102); and Munden (732 and 62). Tompkin headed the batting with 1,919 runs at 36.90. Lester topped the thousand, while Smithson fell just short. Hallam was now back from National Service and played a full season. He scored only 898 runs, average 18.71. Midway through the season he was promoted to open with Lester, with Smithson dropping down the order.

The bowling attack was hampered by the fact that Spencer was doing his National Service and could get away for only 14 Championship games. The major surprise when the Test selectors chose 22 names for a Test Trial at Edgbaston in May was the inclusion of Spencer. Although he did not obtain a place in the subsequent matches against Australia, the report on the Trial was very favourable:

Spencer bowled extremely well at just over medium pace. With a high, easy action, he made the ball move off the seam and extracted more life from the slow turf than some of the other faster bowlers. He bowled Bailey and Compton with sharp break-backs and, by dismissing May and Simpson as well, enjoyed a thoroughly satisfactory first appearance in representative cricket.

With Spencer often absent Goodwin was the main seam bowler for the County. In a total of 86 wickets, his best return was seven for 73 against Lancashire at Grace Road and he was awarded his County cap.

Late in the season Brian Boshier, a 21-year-old, 6ft 5in giant from Leicester, was brought into the side. A fast-medium right-arm bowler he took 11 wickets at 24 runs each and earned favourable comments. As has been noted, Jackson, Walsh and Munden all returned good figures with their spin bowling.

The two other debutants were J. S. Savage, an off-break bowler from Lancashire who was qualifying by residence and played only against Oxford University, though he was to become a valued member of the side, and Raymond Julian, a 16-year-old wicketkeeper from Cosby, who later took over as the principal stumper.

Efforts were being made to improve the amenities at Grace Road and some additional terracing and seating to accommodate 800 spectators was erected at a cost of £10,000. The ground was still owned by the City Education Department and the County Club were therefore allowed only restricted access. The success on the field produced improved attendances both through increased membership and via the turnstiles.

Palmer's reward for his season was the appointment as player-manager to the MCC side touring West Indies in 1953–54. On this tour he gained selection for England and thus became the first Leicestershire cricketer to represent the county since George Geary.

With their renowned sense of perversity, Leicestershire slumped to 16th place in 1954. The reasons were not hard to find. The summer was wet and dismal all through, and, according to *Wisden*, the wettest since 1903. Unfortunately for Leicestershire the rain did not fall evenly over the 17 first-class counties and in the table of worst-hit counties, only Lancashire managed to exceed them. On twelve days the Leicestershire team sat in the dressing room without bowling a ball and of the other days, half were interrupted by rain or its effects. Two matches at Grace Road in August were totally abandoned, the first of which, against Lancashire, had been chosen by Tompkin for his benefit.

The second should have been against Gloucestershire. Despite Tompkin's misfortune, his popularity was such that through other avenues he received a total of £3,057, a new record for the County.

In the first half of the season only one win was notched; this took place at Gillingham on 25 May and was the result of some brilliant all-round cricket by Jackson. On the first day he batted about three hours to hit 108 out of Leicestershire's total of 290. He then captured six for 46, dismissing Kent for 178, and when Kent appeared to be getting on top in this final innings, needing a total of 264 and reaching 162 for four, Jackson ran through the later batsmen, picking up four of the remaining six wickets and bringing victory by 57 runs.

The one match in June worthy of note was the game at Huddersfield, which provided the County with the second tied game in its history. Yorkshire's two left-handers, Wilson and Watson, found the Leicestershire attack uncomplicated and added 168 in under two hours, so that Yardley declared with 351 on the board for the loss of four wickets. Tompkin retaliated with 149 and if the Leicestershire tail hadn't collapsed a first innings lead would have been achieved; as it was Yorkshire were 23 ahead. Spencer then produced the best bowling figures of his career – he was still on National Service and not available for every match. His final analysis was 23-3-63-9 and Yorkshire were 113 all out. Leicestershire therefore required 137. Trueman, Wardle and Appleyard made the batsmen fight hard. When the last over of extra time, bowled by Wardle, began, the final pair, Spencer and Boshier were in with seven required. Spencer drove the ball for a magnificent six over the sightscreen, levelling the scores, but a single was still required off the final ball. Spencer played back down the pitch, the batsmen ran, but Wardle threw down the wicket at the bowler's end and the game was tied.

July produced the second win. On a difficult wicket at Chelmsford the only batsman on either side to look comfortable for long – Brian Taylor swung his bat to the tune of 56 – was Palmer, who lasted over four hours and made 107. Leicestershire required 144 in the final innings, reaching their objective with five wickets in hand. Munden and Jackson were the bowlers benefiting most from the conditions. The former took seven wickets and the latter nine.

It was not until the 28th and final Championship match of the soggy summer that Leicestershire won at home. For once the sun shone. The match was comparatively even and Kent, batting last, needed 195, Leicestershire having made 224 in their second

JOHN EDWARD WALSH

A slow left-arm bowler he bowled both googlies and the chinaman, being regarded as the foremost exponent of this type of bowling in the immediate post-war era. He was compared favourably with Fleetwood-Smith, the Australian Test bowler of the 1930s, and he developed his bowling on the hard Australian wickets before the war, being born in Sydney, New South Wales, in 1912. In 1936–37 he topped the bowling averages for the Glebe District Club and in March 1937 began his association with Sir Julien Cahn's team, meeting the side in Colombo, when Cahn organised a short tour of Ceylon and Malaya.

Returning to England with Cahn's side, Walsh took 100 wickets in 1937 for that team and the following summer qualified for Leicestershire. He played a handful of county games before the war, at the same time being the principal bowler in Cahn's XI in both 1938 and 1939. Walsh returned to Australia and played two matches for New South Wales in 1939–40.

In 1946 he resumed his career in county cricket and between then and 1953 captured 100 first-class wickets in a season seven times. His best summer was 1948 when he took 174 wickets, average 19.56. As a batsman he seemed to improve with age, his most telling shot being the straight drive, and in 1952 he completed 1,000 runs for the first and only time in his career. He retired after the 1956 season and then for a short while acted as Second Eleven captain and coach. Later he coached both in Tasmania and Scotland, before finally settling down back in New South Wales. He died in 1980 aged 67.

(NCCC)

innings. The visitors progressed to 120 for five, then Jackson brought the match to a sudden end, the last five wickets mustering just 15 runs and Jackson finishing with six for 26.

Jackson was the player of the year. He was the only bowler to average below 20 runs per wicket and his total of 78 was the highest; he also hit 1,215 runs, coming third in the batting table.

Three other players completed 1,000 runs with Tompkin a clear leader – 1,592 runs, average 35.38. Hallam, who was awarded his county cap, reached 1,000 for the first time, but had yet to hit a century. Palmer was the fourth player to complete 1,000. Although not as successful as in 1953 he was very reliable. The other two regular players who were specialist batsmen, Lester and Smithson, had disappointing returns. Munden also failed to give much support and averaged only 13, with a highest score of 43.

After Jackson, Walsh took most wickets, but he was nothing like as effective on the damp pitches. Goodwin, who had looked so promising, played in 15 Championship games but performed so poorly that he eventually lost his place in the side. Boshier had somewhat better figures, though he was hardly a match winner.

Of the new players the most outstanding in retrospect was F. M. Turner, a 19-year-old local cricketer who had joined the staff on leaving school, but was now on National Service. A leg-break and googly bowler he played in the final match of the season. He was to play in nine more first-class matches finishing in 1959. By this time he was, initially, the club's cashier, then assistant secretary. In August 1961 he was appointed Secretary and in 1969 took the additional title of Manager. 'Mike' Turner has been the County's Chief Executive since 1988. He is a member of the TCCB, being their representative on the Cricket Council and serving on their Executive, Public Relations and Marketing, Finance and Registrations Committees. Commencing his administrative career at a time when county cricket very badly needed innovative thought and professisonal management, Turner must be considered as the most successful and influential administrator over the last 30 years.

Turner had joined the staff in 1951, the same year as L. R. Gardner, who also made his debut. Gardner, a middle-order right-hand batsman, was at his best in 1959 when he completed 1,000 runs but he never really made a name for himself in first-class cricket. The two other newcomers were M. F. Hickman from Market Harborough and an amateur fast bowler, A. S. Rice. The latter played just three first-class games, all in 1954, whilst Hickman made a dozen appearances spread over several seasons.

YORKSHIRE *v* LEICESTERSHIRE

Played at Huddersfield, 16, 17 and 18 June 1954

MATCH TIED

YORKSHIRE	FIRST INNINGS		SECOND INNINGS	
L. Hutton	c Firth b Munden	60	c Firth b Spencer	6
F. A. Lowson	b Walsh	38	b Spencer	8
J. V. Wilson	c Palmer b Walsh	138	b Spencer	18
E. Lester	c Boshier b Palmer	33	b Spencer	34
W. Watson	not out	80	b Spencer	0
*N. W. D. Yardley			b Spencer	22
D. B. Close			c Firth b Palmer	1
J. H. Wardle			b Spencer	0
†R. Booth			c Smithson b Spencer	8
F. S. Trueman			b Spencer	8
R. Appleyard			not out	1
Extras	lb 1, nb 1	2	b 4, lb 1, nb 2	7
Total (4 wkts dec)		351		113

1st inns: 1-82, 2-123, 3-183, 4-351
2nd inns: 1-13, 2-18, 3-43, 4-43, 5-82, 6-85, 7-87, 8-97, 9-108

BOWLING	O	M	R	W	O	M	R	W
Spencer	25	3	70	0	23	3	63	9
Boshier	17	3	51	0				
Palmer	12	4	33	1	12	6	18	1
Walsh	20.5	0	77	2				
Jackson	14	3	52	0	10	2	25	0
Munden	23	4	66	1				

LEICESTERSHIRE	FIRST INNINGS		SECOND INNINGS	
G. Lester	b Close	74	b Trueman	4
M. R. Hallam	b Trueman	24	b Trueman	2
M. Tompkin	st Booth b Wardle	149	c and b Appleyard	6
*C. H. Palmer	c Hutton b Wardle	15	b Wardle	31
V. E. Jackson	c Booth b Trueman	1	c Lester b Trueman	4
G. A. Smithson	c and b Close	25	c Lowson b Trueman	0
V. S. Munden	b Appleyard	19	run out	31
J. E. Walsh	b Wardle	0	c Hutton b Wardle	28
†J. Firth	not out	8	st Booth b Wardle	3
C. T. Spencer	st Booth b Appleyard	0	run out	8
B. Boshier	c Watson b Wardle	1	not out	1
Extras	b 8, lb 4	12	b 6, lb 11, nb 1	18
Total		328		136

1st inns: 1-58, 2-183, 3-216, 4-223, 5-281, 6-315, 7-315, 8-327, 9-327
2nd inns: 1-8, 2-15, 3-19, 4-21, 5-29, 6-72, 7-123, 8-123, 9-127

BOWLING	O	M	R	W	O	M	R	W
Trueman	22	1	83	2	18	2	44	4
Appleyard	31	11	62	2	20	8	38	1
Yardley	6	1	22	0				
Wardle	44.4	18	82	4	13	4	36	3
Close	21	3	67	2				

Umpires: E. Cooke and Harry Elliott (Derbyshire)

*Captain; †Wicketkeeper

Not surprisingly, the combination of wet weather and poor playing results was reflected in the balance sheet and a loss of £3,402 was made on the year. The administrative staff was strengthened with the appointment of the Gloucestershire amateur batsman, R. A. Diment, as assistant secretary to Palmer. A decision was also made during 1954 to re-enter the Minor Counties Competition – Ashdown continued as coach. The County had last entered its Second Eleven in the Competition in 1932.

A much better start was made to the 1955 season; after three Championship games, there had been two wins and one draw. Kent had been beaten at Gravesend by the spin of Walsh and Jackson; Gloucestershire also succumbed to Jackson, this time with Munden's assistance. Surrey then came to Grace Road for the match in aid of Walsh's benefit. The reigning Champions at this stage had won all their matches. Lock spun out Leicestershire for 114, despite an opening stand of 68 by Lester and Hallam. Palmer had a surprise for the all-conquering southerners. The Leicestershire captain, coming on as third change, produced figures of 14-12-7-8 and Surrey were all out for 77. Palmer had in fact decided to put himself on only in order to allow the two bowlers to change ends, but having clean bowled Peter May, decided to have a second over. Laker, coming in at number eight hit five runs off Palmer, otherwise the latter would have equalled Laker's incredible eight wickets for two runs in the 1950 Test Trial.

The Leicestershire team in 1955. Left to right, back: G. A. Smithson, C. T. Spencer, B. Boshier, M. Hallam, V. Munden, J. Firth. Front: G. Lester, J. E. Walsh, C. H. Palmer (Captain), M. Tompkin, V. Jackson. (NCCC)

When Leicestershire batted a second time, Palmer made 64 and the total was 165 so that Surrey required 203. This time the visiting batsmen treated Palmer's bowling with extreme respect – he returned figures of 13-12-1-0 – but they were not so frugal with the rest of the attack and won by seven wickets.

The month of May was rounded off with two more drawn games; June began with a three-wicket win over Notts at Grace Road. There followed a barren patch. Warwickshire, Lancashire and Notts each gained victories, the defeat by Lancashire being particularly brutal. Leicestershire were bowled out for 42 and 81 at Hinckley, the England trio of Statham, Tattersall and Hilton being the destroyers.

The schoolmaster Charles Palmer, who took over the Leicestershire captaincy in 1950 and so galvanised the County that they finished third equal in the Championship in 1953. In 1955 he took eight wickets for seven runs against the Champions, Surrey. (NCCC)

Leicestershire bounced back with a win at Grace Road against Middlesex – thanks to good batting by Hallam, Tompkin and Palmer – and a win on the Brush Ground at Loughborough over Glamorgan. The County were now in eighth place with half the matches played; the Championship race however was a two-horse affair, since Surrey and Yorkshire were way out in front.

The second half of 1955 was similar in pattern to the first. Lancashire annihilated Leicestershire for a second time – the margin being an innings and 59 runs, but this reverse was followed directly by wins over Hampshire, Jackson picking up nine wickets, and Essex, when Munden and Lester turned round a game heading for disaster by taking nine second-innings wickets in an hour for 47 hours – the victory was by 18 runs with extra time being played. There were then three successive defeats – Hampshire at Bournemouth, Northants at Grace Road and Yorkshire, also at headquarters. The last was of most importance, due first to Yorkshire's position in the table and second to the way Leicestershire fought. Each county made just over 300 in the first innings. Batting a second time Leicestershire could acquire only 176, of which Tompkin made 68 and Diment, who combined the assistant secretaryship with captaining the Second Eleven, made a stubborn 47. Palmer did not employ Spencer to open the bowling but brought on his faithful warhorses, Jackson and Walsh, when Yorkshire set about making 164. Walsh took five for 51 and the White Rose county won by just two wickets.

The rest of August was quite prosperous with wins over Sussex – Jackson took 13 for 152, Essex, when Palmer set them 201 in 115 minutes and victory was by 59 runs, Glamorgan, beaten by ten wickets, Jackson hitting 105, and Worcestershire, when the ubiquitous Jackson made 114.

The total of 11 Championship wins equalled Leicestershire's best-ever tally, made in 1935, and the sixth position in the table was a complete contrast to the previous year.

Tompkin had the best season of his career; in all first-class matches he hit 2,190 runs and came 15th in the overall averages. His greatest day came at Lord's in the Gentlemen v Players match, when he scored 115, the highest innings for his side and the first century for the professionals by a Leicestershire batsman since J. H. King in 1904. A curiosity was that Palmer made the only hundred for the amateurs in the same match. Tompkin was chosen to go with MCC to Pakistan in the winter. Tompkin's run aggregate for the County was 1,928, average 36.38. Behind Tompkin came Jackson and Palmer. The Australian also captured 109 wickets as well as making 1,480 runs. For the only time the

Maurice Tompkin (right), seen opening in a representative match with Hutton, had his best season in 1955, topping 2,000 runs. Sadly, this popular player died after an operation the following year. (NCCC)

'double' did not elude him. Palmer, bowling 'my own brand of occasionally effective economical nonsense', picked up 46 wickets at 18.85 each and was just ahead of Jackson in the averages.

Hallam and Lester both hit over 1,000 runs, Hallam again failing to make a century. An excellent slip fielder he pocketed 41 catches, a County record, but one which he was later to beat.

M. J. K. Smith had had a very successful year opening the

VICTOR EDWARD JACKSON

On the fringe of selection for the 1938 Australian team to England, Jackson, having found himself omitted, decided to come over under his own steam and obtained a position in Julien Cahn's side. He hit 1,831 runs for Cahn's XI in the 1938 season, including six hundreds, and also made his Leicestershire debut that summer, playing against the Australian tourists. His career proper with the County commenced in 1946 and lasted eleven seasons.

Vic Jackson was a hard-hitting middle-order right-hand batsman and a very useful medium-pace off-break bowler. His first-class career had begun at the age of 20 in 1936–37 with New South Wales, and he appeared for that state until 1940–41.

His best season in English cricket was 1955 when he achieved the 'double', with 1,582 runs and 112 wickets. This was in fact the only time he captured more than a hundred wickets, but on several other occasions he was very close to the target. In all eleven of his regular seasons with Leicestershire, Jackson completed 1,000 runs. In many post-war English winters, he went to coach in South Africa. In 1957 and 1958, having left county cricket, he played as professional for Rawtenstall in the Lancashire League. In the first year in the League he was the outstanding all-rounder with 618 runs and 72 wickets and was almost as successful in the second season.

Jackson was killed in a motor accident at a level-crossing near Manildra, New South Wales, in January 1965, aged 48.

(NCCC)

batting for Oxford and joined the County side in the vacation, initially at number four, but when Hallam missed several games through injury, Smith went in first with Lester. Munden and Walsh played occasionally useful innings, but Smithson was completely out of sorts and lost his place in the side, R. A. Diment being preferred.

Apart from Palmer and Jackson, Munden had the best bowling record. Walsh missed eight Championship games and in the 20 he had, took only 43 wickets, a long way below his totals in the early post-war years. At the age of 42 his career was drawing to its close.

The seam attack was unsatisfactory. Spencer, now released from the Army, played throughout the summer but his 67 Championship wickets cost 33 runs each; Boshier's 10 cost 53 runs each; Goodwin had a better record but was often injured.

R. L. Pratt, a 16-year-old fast bowler from Stoney Stanton was given a few matches; he was destined to hold a regular place in the side for several seasons, but was very much a raw recruit. He was one of a number of youngsters who appeared in the Second Eleven – the side failed to win a single match in the Minor Counties Competition.

The only changes at first-class level to the players available for 1956 concerned the move of M. J. K. Smith to Warwickshire, for which county he had been appointed assistant secretary, and the signing of a young Yorkshireman of Dutch extraction, John van Geloven. The 22-year-old middle-order batsman had played three games in 1955 for his native county, but with little hope of a regular position had decided to try elsewhere. He made his Leicestershire debut in the opening match, against the touring Australians, and hit an attractive 43, using his feet to get to the ball and driving through the covers. The County made 298, but the Australians, much to the annoyance of the crowd, batted out the rest of the match, hitting 694 for six, with Miller making 281, not only the highest score ever made by Miller, but the highest ever at Grace Road. The Australian total was a second Grace Road record.

In their first Championship game, Leicestershire picked up first innings points at Taunton, rain causing much delay; across at Ilford for the second match, Leicestershire came back after being 133 behind on first innings to win by four wickets, Palmer making 120 in 150 minutes and Smithson a fast fifty. The County were then surprisingly beaten by Cambridge University, the only success the students achieved against a county during the summer. Set to make 206 in 145 minutes, Leicestershire were bowled out for 111. This defeat seemed to unbalance the side and the next nine matches produced five defeats and four draws. The County, approaching the end of June, were sitting at the foot of the table. Walsh had dropped out of the eleven and Tompkin was totally out of sorts – the reason was to be revealed in the autumn. A second win did occur on 29 June, when Goodwin took eight for 81 and Sussex were overcome by eight wickets. The third and final victory was at Grace Road in mid-July when Pratt exploited a seamer's pitch and returned two very credible sets of figures, 18-6-33-5 and 9-1-27-5. The victims came from Somerset and the margin was an innings and 26 runs.

The weather affected quite a number of games, but the County had 12 defeats to stand beside the three victories. The reasons were easily found in the batting averages; three of the principal run-getters, Smithson, van Geloven and Tompkin, each had an average of 16. Only Hallam averaged above 30 – in his 182nd first-class innings he finally completed a maiden century, 126 *v* Kent at Grace Road. Palmer hit two centuries, but in all matches could score no more than 1,048 runs. Jackson was the other batsman to obtain a four-figure aggregate.

Palmer topped the bowling table with 50 wickets at 17 runs each; Spencer, Goodwin and Jackson took 59, 63 and 58 wickets respectively. Munden had a poor summer with both bat and ball.

Apart from van Geloven, there were two other debutants. P. T. Smith, who came from Leicester and had been on the staff since 1951, scored many runs for the Second XI but never succeeded at the top level. R. C. Smith, who had headed the batting at Stamford School in 1952, was a useful all-rounder. He played in the County side on and off for nine years, but aside from two or three favourable bowling figures, made little impact.

The records were all against the County in 1956; the two batting ones in the Australian match have been noted. Another was the unique (up to that date) feat of Lancashire in winning the game at Old Trafford without losing a wicket in either innings: Leicestershire all out 108 and 122; Lancashire 166 for no wicket declared and 66, again without loss. For Notts A. K. Walker took a wicket with his final delivery in the first innings and then performed the hat-trick with his first three deliveries in the second (Leics were thus 0 runs for three wickets).

After the season ended came the tragic death of Tompkin. He had complained of pains in the back and abdomen during his tour to Pakistan the previous winter, but had played in most of the matches of 1956. In early September he underwent an internal operation and died in a Leicester hospital on 27 September.

The season also saw the ends of the county careers of Smithson, Walsh and Jackson. Smithson's contract was not renewed; Walsh was appointed captain of the Second Eleven; Jackson, who was 40 in October, signed a contract to play for Rawtenstall in the Lancashire League. He later returned to Australia and was killed in a motor accident in January 1965 at the age of 48.

Despite the loss of Jackson and Tompkin, the County did not seek any ready-made replacements from outside. Instead, for 1957, they hoped that the large groundstaff of young hopefuls would produce the talent to fill the gaps. In addition to Jackson and Tompkin, there were the places of Walsh and Smithson to fill, for which adequate substitutes had not been discovered in the course of 1956. Gardner, R. C. Smith and Savage obtained more or less regular places in the eleven. The off-spin of Savage proved very effective. He took 80 wickets at 19 runs each and thus filled Jackson's bowling role, but Jackson also generally averaged near 30 with the bat; Savage managed 7 runs per innings. R. C. Smith took 35 wickets with his left-arm slows and went a little way towards filling Walsh's bowling role, but, again, Walsh averaged 17 or 18 with the bat, while R. C. Smith managed 7. The new

Gerry Lester's career spread over 22 seasons interrupted by the war, and took in 373 first-class matches. An excellent all-rounder, he was appointed coach on his retirement in 1958 and held the post till 1966. (NCCC)

specialist batsman, Gardner, scored 901 runs with a highest innings of 82.

These three were the main replacements for those retired, but the County's strength was further eaten away by the fact that Vic Munden performed so moderately that he had to be dropped from the side – he was not re-engaged at the season's end. Goodwin also was seen infrequently, but Boshier came back and usually opened the attack with Spencer.

Only Hallam and Palmer reached 1,000 runs, though van Geloven improved a little on his first year and hit 895 at 20.34. Diment was drafted into the side and made some runs.

To augment the bowling quartet of Savage, Boshier, Smith and Spencer, the captain tried his hand at strange high-tossed donkey drops. These hit the headlines when the West Indian tourists visited Grace Road. The expertise of such renowned batsmen as Rohan Kanhai and Frank Worrell was defeated by Palmer's aerial bombardment and as Bruce Harris noted in reporting the match: 'There is no ball so innocuous that sometimes it may not take a wicket.' Palmer's analysis in a West Indies total of 361 for seven was 25.1–12–40–4.

All good fun, but not the way to win the Championship. Leicestershire came bottom for the second successive season. Only two County games were victories; Sussex were defeated at Hove, Hallam making 146 and Lancashire, without Statham, defeated at Grace Road, Boshier taking eight wickets, in a match in which not a single batsman reached 50.

Against this were 16 losses and the argument used in 1954 and 1956 that the weather caused most of Leicestershire's problems did not carry much conviction for 1957. Two years of poor results affected the balance sheet and there was a deficit of £649 on the year – this despite the large financial aid provided by the Supporters' Association.

A sentimental touch to the season was the return of the County side to their old stamping ground at Aylestone Road. The pavilion remained much as it had been left in 1939, but the accommodation for spectators was poor and the cooling towers overbearing. The first game there was an utter rout – Derbyshire 244, Leicestershire 57 and 55, Edwin Smith taking nine for 36. The second and final County game was not much better with Hampshire winning by nine wickets, Shackleton having a second innings analysis of 30–19–20–7. The county also tried a new ground, that of the Snibston Colliery at Coalville. Glamorgan were the visitors and they inflicted an innings defeat. The adequate playing area and pleasant modern pavilion were spoilt by unsightly slag heaps along one side of the ground. One County match was played at this new venue until 1961. In 1966 the North Leicestershire Miners Welfare Community centre was opened adjacent to the ground and the slag heaps removed. A County Cricket Week was staged to celebrate the new surroundings, but the following season a change of policy concerning 'out' matches saw the ground dropped from the schedules and only two matches have been staged there in more recent times, a Sunday game in 1970 and a Championship match in 1982.

Palmer had announced in the spring of 1957 that he would be resigning as captain and Secretary of the County Club in September and thus the Palmer 'era' ended at Grace Road with the Essex match on 21, 22, 23 August. The captain began by winning the toss and then batted 270 minutes for 103, a fitting farewell to his eight years at the helm. It had been a time of dramatic changes of fortune, though apart from the last year the side had been composed largely of the same players. In acknowledgement of the contribution the bespectacled schoolmaster had made to his adopted County's cricket, a testimonial fund was launched. Palmer did in fact turn out in a few matches in both 1958 and 1959 and later became Chairman of the Club and in 1978–79 President of MCC.

A QUIET YORKSHIREMAN

'STANDING VERY UPRIGHT AND moving with a calm deliberation, he seemed, as the day passed, to change cricket history, yet to do so impersonally, as if he had been sent by the cricketing deities to demonstrate that perfect batsmanship is invulnerable.'

That was John Arlott's description of Willie Watson's innings which saved England from defeat at Lord's in the 1953 Test against Australia. To replace Palmer as captain and major batsman, the Leicestershire Committee were fortunate to find the 38-year-old left-handed Yorkshire player anxious to leave the maelstrom of Leeds. Making his Yorkshire debut in 1939, Watson had first played for England in 1951, and although regarded by some critics as the best left-hander in the country, had had a very in and out career in Test cricket, appearing in only 17 of the 55 England Tests played between 1951 and his Leicestershire move.

Leicestershire further strengthened their staff by signing a second seasoned county cricketer, Alan Revill. Revill, a middle-order batsman who had played 321 matches for Derbyshire since 1946, was three years younger than Watson. At the same time, Vic Munden, P. T. Smith and M. F. Hickman had been released. Walsh remained as Second Eleven captain and assistant coach to Ashdown. Palmer became joint honorary secretary with the County's historian, E. E. Snow. Diment took over Palmer's post as Secretary.

The first month under the new leader did not reverse the pattern of the two previous summers. Seven first-class games were played, resulting in four losses, two draws and a solitary victory. The success came at Queen's Park, Chesterfield. After a tie on first innings, Savage and Boshier dismissed Derbyshire for 144 and a sound innings by van Geloven meant a five-wicket win. June provided two further victories at the expense of Glamorgan at Newport, where Savage took five for 28 and at Worcester, when an all-round performance saw off the home side with an innings to spare. These successes took Leicestershire into the middle of the table. Watson was in splendid form; he was the third batsman in the country to reach 1,000 runs and at the end of June was averaging over 60, only Peter May and Subba Row (due to his triple hundred) being ahead of him.

Unfortunately for Leicestershire, Watson's batting caught the eye of the selectors and he was returned to the England side for the fourth and fifth Tests. Without him, the County managed a good win against Essex at Snibston Colliery, Hallam hitting 134 and Firth 90, the highest of his career. There were two further successes in August, against Northants away from home and Glamorgan at the Brush Ground in Loughborough. In the latter game Hallam and Watson opened the batting with a partnership of 176, both players making 95, then the spin of Savage and Ray Smith caused the Welsh side to collapse – the victory was by an innings.

The 1958 season produced therefore seven wins and thirteen Championship defeats which put Leicestershire in 12th place. The weather was poor for much of the season and was the reason for many of the drawn matches. Watson's batting figures of 1,521 runs, average 47.53 were better than they seemed on paper because for much of the time the damp pitches assisted the bowlers – he finished the season second to Peter May, who was the only player to average more than 50 runs per innings. It was in this season that Les Jackson headed the bowling table with 143 wickets at 10 runs each. Watson gained himself a place in the 1958–59 MCC team to Australia. Hallam and Revill both exceeded 1,000 with an average around 25. Revill's other asset was his brilliant close to the wicket fielding, usually on the leg side. The other three regulars in the batting line-up, Gardner, van Geloven and Diment had moderate returns. Lester dropped out of the side, having an average of 11 from 19 Championship innings and not taking a wicket.

The surprise of the year was the blossoming of Boshier. Taking 108 wickets, virtually double his previous best, he topped the table with an average of 18.78. He and Spencer played in every match, Spencer taking 85 wickets, and therefore Goodwin found himself more often than not redundant. The spinners, Savage and van Geloven, also had good returns, their wickets costing less than 20 runs each. Pratt was doing his National Service and played in just one Championship game.

E. F. Phillips, a right-hand batsman from Shropshire, who had done well in the Second Eleven in 1957 and had played one match that summer for the senior side, was given an extended run in the 1958 First Eleven, but was out of his depth. G. W. Burch from Leicester was tried in seven Championship games, keeping wicket when Firth was absent. He played for the County until 1964, only playing regularly in 1959.

The weather did not help the financial situation and the loss on the season was nearly £3,500.

H. J. White returned to Grace Road as Head Groundsman after

*Willie Watson was the first Test player to move from Yorkshire to captain
Leicestershire. He brought backbone to the batting between 1958 and 1964.
(Leicester Mercury)*

a break of ten years. In contrast a familiar face left during the year, Walsh taking up a post as coach in Tasmania. Lester took over as Second Eleven captain and assistant to Ashdown.

Apart from the preference for Julien instead of Firth behind the wicket, the 1959 side did not show any substantial change over its immediate predecessor. Up to mid-July the results compared favourably with Watson's first summer, with five matches won, the last at Ashby against Middlesex on 14 July. Boshier dismissed the opposition for 178, taking six for 51 and Watson made 109 and 74 not out – two exceptionally fine innings. The victory was by eight wickets. Misfortune then struck – Boshier seriously damaged an Achilles' tendon and the injury finished his cricket for the summer. Twelve Championship matches remained and Leicestershire plummeted ever downwards as they failed to gain one single extra point for the rest of the season. Van Geloven was given the task of opening the bowling with Spencer – clearly Goodwin, who was playing in the Second Eleven, was still too prone to injury. Goodwin made one Championship appearance all summer.

When the university term ended, David Kirby, the Cambridge blue, joined the side as an opening batsman. Kirby had gained a brilliant reputation as a schoolboy cricketer. He had captained St Peter's, York, for two successive summers, 1957 and 1958, headed the batting averages in both and the school had been beaten only twice under his leadership. In 1958 he had captained one of the sides in the Public Schools game at Lord's and then led the Public Schools against the Combined Services. Now aged 20 he played in eight Championship games, opening the innings with either Watson or Hallam, his best performance coming against Warwickshire when he hit 70.

Watson had not had a happy time in Australia during the winter – England had lost the series four matches to nil – and thus he was not in the 1959 Tests against India. Available therefore without interruption for the County, he had an impressive record. For the second year he was runner-up in the first-class averages, the former Leicester boy, M. J. K. Smith, being at the summit. Watson was only the second batsman to hit 2,000 runs in a season for the County, his total being 2,212 with seven centuries. The first batsman had been Les Berry in 1937. Watson's seven three figure innings equalled the record held by Berry.

Behind Watson in the batting table came Hallam. His Championship figures of 1,750 runs, average 33.01, and in all first-class matches 2,070 runs, with a slightly higher average, look impressive, but are slightly misleading in that he scored almost 600 runs in two matches early on. Against Derbyshire he hit exactly 200 out of 337 for four declared at Grace Road – he and Watson added 207 for the fourth wicket. A fortnight later, also at Grace Road, Hallam scored 210 not out in the first innings and 157 in the second. In this match, in which the opponents were Glamorgan, he broke several records. His century in the second innings, when Leicestershire needed 269 in just under three hours, came in 71 minutes and was the fastest of the summer so far, and his 210 was the highest post-war innings thus far for the County. In the next match he became the first batsman to reach 1,000 runs in 1959, the date being 4 June.

In contrast to the days of Jackson, Walsh and others, the County now possessed just one county-standard all-rounder, van Geloven. He was awarded his county cap, having scored 1,324 runs and taken 72 wickets. The fourth player to reach 1,000 was Revill, whilst Gardner made the magic number with his final scoring shot of the summer, finishing with exactly 1,000.

The loss of Boshier midway through the summer meant that Spencer was overbowled. Both he and Savage delivered more than 1,000 overs – missed catches did nothing to encourage those two toilers. The other principal bowler was Smith, whose wickets proved rather expensive.

So Leicestershire ended the year in 16th place, with 16 losses balancing the five early victories.

The County fared almost as badly in the Minor Counties Championship and at the season's end withdrew from that competition. The First-Class Counties Second Eleven competition was now operating and as players did not have to be qualified to appear in the latter it was felt that Leicestershire should just continue in that; it provided more opportunity to try out players from outside the county boundaries.

On medical advice S. H. B. Livingston retired as President of the Club, having held office for 19 years. A member since 1901, he was also one of Leicestershire's greatest benefactors and came to its aid in the difficult financial years between the wars. He was to die after a long illness in 1963, but his name lives on in the Livingston Cup and the Livingston Doughty awards. Livingston was replaced as President by William Bentley, who was destined to serve even longer than his predecessor.

Although the fine weather improved attendances and boosted gate receipts, the Club had a deficit of almost £5,000 on the year's workings.

Apart from Kirby, three others made their first-class debuts in 1959, but none made any major impact. Bernard Cromack, a 22-

year-old Yorkshireman played for three seasons with limited chances and then turned out once in 1968. J. W. Carter, the Oxfordshire batsman, appeared in seven matches, all in 1959, and G. A. Hickinbottom played five times as a wicketkeeper.

Firth retired at the end of the season; Goodwin left the staff due to his continued leg injury; and Burch left to go to a teacher training college.

Just before the 1960 season began, Diment resigned as Secretary and the post was divided into two, F. M. Turner taking over the administrative side and Kirby the cricket. Two Yorkshiremen were signed on the staff, H. D. Bird and P. N. Broughton. The former had played 14 matches for his native county spread over four seasons, the latter six matches all in 1956. Bird is now much better known as a distinguished Test match umpire.

Bird was immediately drafted into the County side as an opening partner for Hallam; Watson and van Geloven mainly came in at numbers three and five with Gardner at number four. When the university team ended Kirby came in first wicket down, but the batting, with both Watson and Hallam having moderate seasons, was depressingly weak. Gardner averaged 20.36, Bird 19.58 and Kirby 15.80, all for Championship matches only. Hallam and van Geloven had averages in the mid-20s and Watson alone exceeded 30. The other experienced batsman, Revill, fared so poorly that he was left out of the side, appearing in only seven Championship games. *Wisden's Almanack* review noted: 'In almost every match Leicestershire's batting seemed quite good while Watson and possibly Hallam and van Geloven were at the crease, but once the opposing bowlers achieved success there was nothing to stop them sweeping through the tail.'

It was not surprising therefore that the first victory did not come until the eighth Championship game – including 1959, the side had played 20 county matches without a win. Somerset were beaten at Grace Road due to the batting of van Geloven and Gardner, both hitting hundreds and adding an unbroken 218 for the third wicket. Somerset then had to bat on a rain-affected wicket and Pratt and Spencer bowled them out for 106 and 185.

Languishing at the foot of the table, Leicestershire limped on and a second and final victory did not occur until the last match, when Kent were beaten at Dover. Two declarations left Kent with 185 needed at about 75 runs an hour and despite collapsing to 88 for five, Kent continued to hit out, losing by 50 runs.

Had Leicestershire not won this match they would have ended

the summer with fewer points that any other side in the Champion-ship in post-war years. As it was their total amounted to no more than 46. Seven matches ended in defeats by an innings and seven matches also finished inside two days. Lancashire dismissed the County for 37 at Grace Road in May, Statham taking seven for 17 – he took another seven in the second innings.

The most memorable match of the year took place at Snibston Colliery. Leicestershire made 285, Watson scoring 110, in the course of which he suffered a cracked rib. Hampshire made 367 for four declared and Leicestershire disintegrated, the score falling to 52 for eight. Watson then came to the wicket, with 30 runs needed simply to avoid the innings defeat and a whole day to play. He and Gardner added 125 for the ninth wicket and batted so long that when the final wicket fell, Hampshire had 110 to make in 40 minutes. Hitting out they were 31 for four when the chase was abandoned.

Details of the batting figures for 1960 have been already noted; Boshier headed the bowling, but injury forced him out of over half the matches. Broughton was used as Spencer's opening partner when Boshier was unavailable but the Yorkshireman had only moderate success, Pratt being more effective. Cromack and Savage provided the spin attack, and both had averages of 27.

Apart from Bird and Broughton, one other player made his County debut during the summer, Donald Munden, the youngest of the three Munden brothers. Aged 25, he was a useful all-rounder, but failed to gain a regular place in the First Eleven, though flourishing in the Second Eleven Competition. Paul Munden played in nine Championship games during the year, but his highest innings was only 59.

To produce any improvement, the County had to reinforce its staff with some more experienced players, since the youngsters developed through the various coaching schemes in the county were not in the short term likely to make any major contribu-tions. The County therefore signed four cricketers from outside. Of these only two could qualify immediately for Championship matches. These were Alan Wharton and Jack Birkenshaw.

A 38-year-old Lancastrian, Wharton had played nearly 400 matches for his native county. He had played once for England, in 1949, and in 1959 had hit over 2,000 runs. Regarded as one of the most attacking left-handers in county cricket, he was particularly severe on anything on the leg side. Although playing as a profes-sional, Wharton was a qualified schoolteacher and had for several years been a JP; in his younger days he had played rugby league at a high level, mainly for Salford.

Jack Birkenshaw came from Rothwell, Leeds, and had played for Yorkshire for three seasons. He had played in 12 Championship matches for Yorkshire in 1960, but as an off-spin bowler he had to play second fiddle to Illingworth and the county had an excellent slow left-armer in Don Wilson. Birkenshaw thought he had little prospect of county cricket with Yorkshire. He was specially registered by Leicestershire and made an impressive debut for his new club in June with a second-innings analysis of 12.1-4-14-4 against Northants.

The two other mature players were Stanley Jayasinghe, a 30-year-old middle-order batsman and Clive Inman, a 25-year-old left-hander. Both came from Ceylon and had played representative cricket for their country for several years. Jayasinghe was a professional for Colne in the Lancashire League, whilst Inman had been a professional in Penzance.

The two Sinhalese played in only friendly first-class games for Leicestershire in 1961, but their presence in the Second Eleven was very evident; Jayasinghe's run total of 1,485, average 57.11, was easily the highest in the Second Eleven Competition in 1961 and Inman hit 922 runs; Leicestershire finished runners-up to Kent in the table.

Although the County won two early friendly first-class matches – against Cambridge University and Ireland – they won only one Championship game in the first month and this was a nerve-racking occasion. Glamorgan came to Grace Road and the bowlers were in complete control. The visitors made 118, Leicestershire 127, then Glamorgan in their second innings 115. Thus the home side needed 107 in the final innings, but the ninth wicket fell with the total at 101. Savage joined Spencer and the latter struck out to bring victory. The second Championship win was equally low scoring, though on this occasion it was the opposition who batted last and needed 208 in the fourth innings – they, Worcestershire, were all out for 65, Spencer finishing with five for 29 and eleven wickets in the match. That game was at Snibston Colliery. A third win was hoisted in the following fixture at Kettering, where Savage took ten for 113.

There followed a barren patch, when the County were even beaten by Cambridge University, the latter captained by Kirby. The game was remarkable for the bowling feat of an unknown undergraduate, Tony Pearson, in his first year. His second innings analysis read: 30.3-8-78-10. After this humiliation, Leicestershire picked themselves up and beat Somerset on the Brush Ground at Loughborough. Needing exactly 200 in the last innings, Somerset appeared to be in control, being 140 for five, but Savage brought them hurriedly to ground with a hat-trick and victory was by 41 runs. Leaving Loughborough for The Oval, Leicestershire put Surrey in precisely the same position. The home side needed 203 in the last innings and Peter May and Bernard Constable looked set to knock off the arrears, producing a fourth wicket stand of 108 to take the total to 144 for three; at this point May was dismissed by van Geloven. Constable batted on and when he was caught and bowled by the same bowler, four wickets remained with 21 required. Spencer and Boshier then finished Surrey off and Leicestershire won by a single run.

This was not the end of tight finishes for 1961. A fortnight later at Stourbridge, Worcestershire on a wearing pitch had to battle their way to victory when needing 135 – they won by two wickets. Batting was difficult from the very first ball and a young Leicestershire player, in just his third Championship game, won some fulsome press praise with an unbeaten 55, using his feet to the spin of Norman Gifford. The tyro was Graham Cross, a 17-year-old, from Leicester. His County career was to last 16 years, but in that time he played in only 83 matches and became much better known on the soccer field, appearing originally for Leicester City, but later for Brighton, Chesterfield, Preston and Lincoln.

Yorkshire came to Grace Road directly after the Stourbridge game and were comprehensively outplayed. Bowled out for 101, Boshier six for 46, in reply to Leicestershire's 255, Yorkshire found themselves needing 383 in the fourth innings with nine playing hours in hand. They were removed for 233 and Leicestershire recorded their best post-war win over the White Rose county.

Although not in a position to challenge the front runners, Hampshire, Yorkshire and Middlesex, in the title race, Leicestershire, following their success against Yorkshire seemed capable of fifth or sixth place. However they were on the losing end of yet two more exciting finishes at the start of August. Middlesex won at Grace Road by 28 runs, despite a century in each innings by Wharton – in the second innings the Lancastrian seemed to be taking Leicestershire to victory, when he collided with Savage in attempting a second run and was run out. Wharton had scored 108, the next highest score was 32. Then at Edgbaston Leicestershire lost by two wickets. Warwickshire were set 222 in 150 minutes and Stewart and Kennedy added 90 in an hour for the second wicket. Van Geloven brought Leicestershire back into the game – he took six for 85 – but the home side won with just two minutes to spare.

SURREY *v* LEICESTERSHIRE

Played at The Oval, 12, 13 and 14 July 1961

LEICESTERSHIRE WON BY ONE RUN

LEICESTERSHIRE	FIRST INNINGS		SECOND INNINGS	
*M. R. Hallam	b Loader	20	lbw b Lock	68
A. Wharton	c Stewart b Gibson	6	c Stewart b Loader	39
J. van Geloven	b Gibson	0	b Lock	36
L. R. Gardner	b Gibson	0	c and b Lock	10
D. F. Munden	b Gibson	1	b Lock	2
J. Birkenshaw	c Barrington b Loader	31	b Gibson	5
R. L. Pratt	b Lock	21	c Stewart b Lock	6
†R. Julian	run out	9	c Barrington b Lock	3
C. T. Spencer	c May b Loader	0	c Willett b Gibson	1
J. S. Savage	c Swetman b Gibson	4	not out	4
B. S. Boshier	not out	0	b Gibson	2
Extras		0	b 4, lb 1	5
Total		92		181

1st inns: 1-22, 2-22, 3-26, 4-27, 5-30, 6-79, 7-79, 8-88, 9-92
2nd inns: 1-105, 2-117, 3-127, 4-129, 5-144, 6-151, 7-169, 8-170, 9-178

BOWLING	O	M	R	W	O	M	R	W
Loader	14.1	3	33	3	11	1	53	1
Gibson	13	2	32	5	21.4	3	57	3
Lock	8	1	27	1	23	6	54	6
Willett					4	0	11	0
Bedser					5	4	1	0

SURREY	FIRST INNINGS		SECOND INNINGS	
M. J. Stewart	c Julian b Boshier	1	b Boshier	1
A. B. D. Parsons	not out	30	c Julian b Spencer	13
K. F. Barrington	c Hallam b Boshier	6	c Wharton b Spencer	7
B. Constable	hit wkt b Spencer	9	c and b van Geloven	66
M. D. Willett	c Julian b Spencer	3	c van Geloven b Pratt	11
*P. B. H. May	c Hallam b Boshier	2	c Julian b van Geloven	73
†R. Swetman	c Julian b Spencer	1	c Hallam b van Geloven	5
G. A. R. Lock	b Spencer	0	run out	1
E. A. Bedser	lbw b Boshier	1	not out	6
D. Gibson	c Julian b Boshier	9	c Hallam b Boshier	6
P. J. Loader	b Pratt	7	b Spencer	0
Extras	nb 2	2	b 5, lb 5, nb 2	12
Total		71		201

1st inns: 1-1, 2-9, 3-22, 4-26, 5-29, 6-31, 7-31, 8-36, 9-59 (2.14 an over)
2nd inns: 1-3, 2-14, 3-36, 4-144, 5-164, 6-182, 7-188, 8-188, 9-189

BOWLING	O	M	R	W	O	M	R	W
Spencer	14	4	26	4	35	9	63	3
Boshier	14	3	28	5	28	9	45	2
Pratt	3.1	0	6	1	11	1	37	1
Van Geloven	2	0	9	0	11	3	22	3
Savage					6	3	22	0

Umpires: L. H. Gray and A. Jepson
*Captain; †Wicketkeeper

Three wins came later in August – against Kent and Notts at Grace Road and finally at Worthing where Hallam overshadowed all. He scored 203 in the first innings out of 376 for seven declared and 143 in the second out of 256 for two declared, both innings undefeated, and he was therefore on the field of play throughout the match. Hallam in fact had already scored 130 not out in the victory early in the month over Notts and in the match preceding the Sussex one, had hit 152 not out against Gloucestershire, carrying his bat through the completed innings. This final flurry of runs meant that he topped 2,000 runs – 2,096, average 39.55 – and to date he is the last batsman to reach this aggregate for Leicestershire.

The County ended the season in ninth place with nine Championship wins and the press, spectators and players all expressed their view that in terms of positive, exciting cricket, 1961 was equal to any previous season the County had played.

Apart from Hallam, who incidentally also created a new record with 56 catches, Watson and Wharton exceeded 1,000 runs. The captain missed 11 Championship games, but still finished in the top dozen in the first-class averages and totalled 1,302 runs. Wharton hit 1,588 with five hundreds. Kirby, playing in ten games, scored 599 at an average of 31.52, but the only other batsman averaging over 20 was Birkenshaw, who made more impact with his batting than his bowling. Van Geloven, Bird and Gardner had moderate batting returns.

The bowling figures were most impressive. Boshier, fit again, took 103 wickets at 17 runs each, closely followed by Spencer with 119 and Savage 108, both averaging 19 runs per wicket. Van Geloven took 84 wickets and Pratt 65. It was the first time three Leicestershire men had captured 100 wickets in the same season for the County. Only Worcestershire's bowlers had better figures in 1961.

Two young players not previously mentioned appeared in the County's ranks for the first time in 1961. Roy Barratt, a 19-year-old slow left-arm bowler, had joined the staff in 1958 but left after the 1962 season. He continued to play for the County on the odd occasion until 1970 and returned one or two good analyses. John Mitten, who was the son of the well-known Manchester United footballer, acted as substitute wicketkeeper in a few games spread over three summers, but like his father, was better known on the soccer field.

At the end of the season Watson announced his retirement as captain, since he was now a Test selector, which meant missing some matches, and he intended to give up county cricket at the

LEICESTERSHIRE *v* SUSSEX

Played at Worthing, 30, 31 August and 1 September, 1961

LEICESTERSHIRE WON BY 62 RUNS

LEICESTERSHIRE	FIRST INNINGS		SECOND INNINGS	
*M. R. Hallam	not out	203	not out	143
H. D. Bird	b N. Thomson	0	lbw b Doggart	65
A. Wharton	c Parks b N. Thomson	0	c and b Doggart	4
L. R. Gardner	c Langridge b Snow	18	not out	40
J. van Geloven	c Langridge b Pountain	8		
J. Birkenshaw	c Parks b N. Thomson	95		
R. L. Pratt	b Smith	7		
†R. Julian	b N. Thomson	2		
C. T. Spencer	not out	33		
J. S. Savage				
B. S. Boshier				
Extras	b 5, lb 4, w 1	10	b 3, lb 1	4
Total	(7 wkts, dec)	376	(2 wkts, dec)	256

1st inns: 1-3, 2-5, 3-51, 4-66, 5-241, 6-266, 7-309 (3.87 an over)
2nd inns: 1-136, 2-144

BOWLING	O	M	R	W	O	M	R	W
N. Thomson	23	5	79	4	8	2	16	0
Smith	22	5	76	1	18	1	71	0
Pountain	22	1	79	1				
Snow	16	1	76	1	4	0	19	0
Oakman	7	1	32	0	11	2	35	0
Suttle	7	1	24	0	11.3	1	36	0
Doggart					24	4	75	2

SUSSEX	FIRST INNINGS		SECOND INNINGS	
A. S. M. Oakman	c Julian b Boshier	10	c and b Pratt	20
R. J. Langridge	c Hallam b Savage	95	c van Geloven b Boshier	5
L. J. Lenham	b Boshier	17	st Julian b Birkenshaw	43
K. G. Suttle	c Hallam b Savage	65	c Julian b Birkenshaw	55
†J. M. Parks	c Julian b Pratt	32	c Julian b Birkenshaw	47
G. H. G. Doggart	c Wharton b Savage	37	lbw b Savage	6
*D. V. Smith	c Hallam b Savage	0	c Hallam b Savage	0
R. H. Thomson	b van Geloven	21	st Julian b Birkenshaw	1
N. I. Thomson	lbw b Savage	0	b Birkenshaw	20
F. R. Pountain	b Boshier	12	c Hallam b Savage	27
J. A. Snow	not out	15	not out	35
Extras	lb 2, nb 1	3	lb 4	4
Total		307		263

1st inns: 1-13, 2-65, 3-176, 4-201, 5-227, 6-234, 7-275, 8-275, 9-280 (2.98 an over)
2nd inns: 1-20, 2-28, 3-101, 4-154, 5-154, 6-166, 7-166, 8-197, 9-220

BOWLING	O	M	R	W	O	M	R	W
Spencer	15	3	54	0				
Boshier	16	1	64	3	6	0	20	1
Pratt	7	3	10	1	6	0	29	1
Savage	40	12	89	5	20	5	86	3
van Geloven	9	2	39	1				
Birkenshaw	16	2	48	0	19.5	0	124	5

Umpires: W. E. Phillipson and W. F. Price
*Captain; †Wicketkeeper

close of 1962. Kirby had now come down from Cambridge after three seasons as a blue and was invited to replace Watson for 1962.

Off the field the Committee made other changes. F. M. Turner was appointed as Secretary with overall control – previously the duties had been split with Kirby – and Ashdown was retired as coach, a position he had held since 1951. Ashdown was later to take over as scorer.

The changes when the players assembled for the 1962 pre-season practice were that Cromack and Donald Munden were no longer on the staff, but Jayasinghe was now qualified for county games – the rules regarding overseas players were in fact altered in 1962 and players from abroad now had to live for only two years in the county to complete a residential qualification, instead of the three years previously stipulated.

With the general financial state of county cricket having an unhealthy pallor, the MCC in 1960 set up yet another committee of inquiry, the fourth in 25 years, this time under Colonel R. S. Rait Kerr. This issued an interim report in 1961 and among other topics was the question of the introduction of limited-overs county cricket. Mike Turner, the Leicestershire Secretary, was an early advocate of one-day matches and in order to put the experiment into practice in the spring of 1962 he arranged a competition with Derbyshire, Notts, Northants and Leicestershire. The first two matches took place at Grace Road and Trent Bridge on 2 May. Leicestershire beat Derbyshire by seven runs; Northants beat Notts by 31 runs. A week later Northants beat Leicestershire in the 'Final' by five wickets. The innings were limited to 65 overs and play was from 11.00 to 7.30. Each bowler could bowl a maximum of 15 overs and fielders were limited to a maximum of six on the off side and five on the leg. Although 2 May proved to be a bitterly cold day, about 1,000 spectators came to Grace Road. The games were studied with interest and the rules adjusted for the inauguration of the Gillette Cup, involving all counties, in 1963. Turner can take much credit in promoting and pushing forward the development of limited-overs cricket at county level.

On paper the 1962 Leicestershire side should have improved on the results of the previous summer. Unfortunately the main strike bowler of 1961 broke down; Boshier only played in seven matches, taking 16 wickets, compared with over 100 at 10 runs less per victim in 1961. In addition Kirby failed to find his batting form, perhaps due to the cares of captaincy, and his average dropped from over 30 to under 20.

Only two wins were recorded; the one against Sussex was due

to the opposition declaring in both innings, which left just the victory over Northants as a thoroughly convincing success. In this game, played at Wellingborough School, van Geloven took six for 28, dismissing Northants in their second innings for 80, and the winning margin was 216 runs. The best batting came from Watson with a splendid knock of 91 in 150 minutes.

As in 1961 there were some very close finishes, but none ended in favour of Leicestershire – the County seemed to lack the knock-out punch they had possessed under Watson. Against Notts at Grace Road, Leicestershire needed 114 in the final innings in what turned out to be 56 overs. They finished at 112 for nine, two runs short of the target. Against Hampshire at Grace Road, Leicestershire needed 197 in 120 minutes and finished at 190 for four, seven runs short. At Lord's against Middlesex, following a washed-out first day and two declarations by the home side, Leicestershire were required to make 208 in 165 minutes, but were unable to cope with the spin of Titmus, who took seven for 59, and the match was lost by 25 runs.

On the other hand van Geloven recorded his first hundred in two years when he saved the side from defeat by Northants at Grace Road. Leicestershire required 295 in the final innings, but plummeted to 73 for five. Van Geloven made an unbeaten 102 in 150 minutes and with three wickets standing Leicestershire were only 32 from victory when time was called.

The season ended with Leicestershire at the foot of the table. Watson headed the batting averages, scoring 1,139 runs with three hundreds and an average of 42; Hallam hit 1,794 runs and Jayasinghe 1,499. Wharton and van Geloven just topped 1,000 runs and the latter also took 100 wickets, becoming the first Leicestershire player since Jackson in 1955 to complete the 'double'.

Van Geloven was alone in capturing 100 wickets; his main support came from Spencer with 89. The injury to Boshier has been noted, but Pratt also missed many matches due to a damaged ankle. Savage proved to be expensive as did Broughton, whose 25 wickets cost 38 runs each.

Broughton, Gardner and Barratt were not re-engaged for 1963, and Watson left the County, as did Kirby who took up a scholastic appointment at St Peter's, York. Another era in the County's history thus ended.

HALLAM AND THE EFFERVESCENT LOCK

THE COUNTY DECIDED TO APPOINT Hallam, the senior professional, as captain for 1963; although at the end of 1962 the division between amateur and professional was finally abolished in county cricket. The ploy had worked well in the past – Astill in 1935 had pushed the County six places up the table and Berry in 1946 had produced an equal improvement.

Hallam of course had the disadvantage of being without Watson, though to balance this Inman, the Sinhalese batsman, was now qualified. No one had made their first-class debut for the County in 1962, but it was hoped that the Durham-born Stephen Greensword, who had joined the staff in 1960 as a 16-year-old and had good figures in the Second Eleven in 1962 would break into the first team in the coming season.

Boshier was now recovered from his injury, but otherwise the attack was anticipated to be much as the previous summer.

After Mike Turner's enthusiasm for one-day cricket, it was unfortunate that Leicestershire were drawn against Lancashire at Old Trafford in a Preliminary Round of the first Gillette Cup and found themselves comprehensively beaten. Peter Marner hit 121 and won the first gold medal and £50, as Lancashire, batting first, reached 304 for nine off 65 overs. Leicestershire were dismissed for 203, but the new captain made a splendid 106 amid the wreckage. This first game was played on 1 and 2 May. Leicestershire then travelled to Cardiff for the three-day match against Glamorgan and were again outplayed, being bowled out for 87 in their second innings and losing by 213 runs.

Crumbs of comfort came in the form of victories against Cambridge University and Ireland (this was a two-day match) but it was not until 18 July that the first Championship success was achieved; on a difficult wicket at Loughborough Worcestershire were beaten by seven wickets. Savage's off-spin and Smith's slow left-armers proved just the recipe for the wicket. Savage took eight for 70 and Smith seven for 15, including figures of 4-4-0-3 in the second innings. Less than a fortnight later the same pair outwitted Essex at Grace Road. This time Savage took nine for 45 and Smith nine for 75. Essex were all out for 75 and 102. Smith and Savage had a third successful foray in early August when Northants were dismissed for 94 and 108. Smith took eight for 77 and Savage nine for 71, bringing victory by 126 runs.

These three wins moved the County up to 14th place in the table on 6 August. Nine Championship matches remained. Leicestershire failed to win any and lost six. Since the counties below them all managed some success, Leicestershire sank to 16th place, only Derbyshire having a poorer set of figures. Unlike 1962, when several matches could have gone Leicestershire's way, most of the defeats were by substantial margins.

Ray Smith topped the bowling table taking 47 wickets at 20 runs each and Savage took 105 at 22. The wet wickets did not suit the pace attack and Spencer and Boshier both had modest returns. Van Geloven was nothing like his 1962 self and his wickets cost 35 runs each.

Inman, who was regarded as a dashing player whose form would probably be variable, proved to be the model of consistency. He came in usually at number 4 or 5 and his highest Championship innings was 83, but he hit 1,482 Championship runs, averaging 38.00. Against Cambridge he made his only first-class hundred of the season. Hallam was the only player to reach a century against another county and the only other batsman to record 1,000 Championship runs, though in all first-class games Jayasinghe also topped 1,000. For the second successive summer, Wharton failed to live up to his reputation and at the end of the year retired to resume a full-time teaching career. Birkenshaw, Bird and van Geloven all averaged below 20 with the bat. Greensword played in 13 Championship games, but 53 was his best innings. He was to continue in the side intermittently until 1966 before retiring back to the North-East. His later career was most successful in Minor County cricket, and he regularly represented the Minor Counties.

Apart from Greensword, three players made their debuts for the County, but none made a name in county cricket. M. H. Rose, who obtained his blue at Cambridge in 1963, played in four matches for Leicestershire as a batsman; T. Thompson, who was educated at Loughborough College and had played for his native Cumberland since 1956, played nine matches for Leicestershire as an off-break bowler; and Geoff Coe from Earl Shilton, a 20-year-old left-arm fast bowler, played just one game.

The financial situation was still of grave concern. In 1962 the deficit had been £9,373, in 1963 this rose to £11,331.

In an effort to bring additional strength to the batting, the County signed Brian Booth, the Blackburn opening batsman, who had played for Lancashire since 1956. Booth had done very well in 1961, when he hit 1,752 runs, average 31.85, but in the two following seasons he had found difficulty keeping a place in the Lancashire side.

The start of the 1964 season was a depressing experience. Warwickshire won the first match by five wickets, Notts won the second by an innings, Warwickshire were then successful for a second time, by nine wickets, Sussex won by 174 runs and Worcestershire by 44 runs: five matches, five successive defeats, and this despite the re-appearance of Watson in all five games.

Rain saved Leicestershire at Bath in their sixth match, then going to The Oval they played with more determination; Booth batted four hours for 61 and Surrey had to fight to produce a draw.

With a record of seven matches, five defeats and two draws, it was not a confident eleven which opposed Northants in the Gillette Cup at Grace Road. The match was one of the shortest between two first-class counties ever played in the competition. Leicestershire's innings lasted 100 minutes and 26.2 overs, the total being 56. Northants made 59 without loss in 13.5 overs.

The rains came. The Yorkshire match at Grace Road came to an abrupt halt when the third day was washed out; Surrey came to Ashby and the entire match was abandoned; Derbyshire then followed Surrey to the same venue and spent the first two days in the pavilion. A match was started under one-day rules, but the weather prevented even that finishing. The season was now entering the middle of June; ten matches plus the Gillette game had come and gone without a win.

Gloucestershire visited Grace Road. Booth spent five hours over 95 as the total reached 241. Birkenshaw dismissed Gloucester for 131, then Leicestershire had difficulty with the spin of Mortimore and Allen. So in the final innings Gloucestershire required 268 in 225 minutes. In the earlier stages the visitors kept pace with the run-rate, but they then dropped behind as wickets fell. When the final over began – Hallam gambled by using the leg-breaks of Booth – two wickets remained. Off the third ball Booth had Etheridge caught. Ashenden the last man arrived and was bowled off his pads by the fifth delivery. Leicestershire had won their first match of 1964.

A fortnight later, Hampshire, on an easy pitch at Portsmouth challenged Leicestershire to hit 237 in 135 minutes and victory was gained with five minutes to spare, Inman finishing the match with a four; an appropriate blow, since the Sinhalese batsman had made an excellent 106 in the first innings.

It was a bright moment before the darkness descended – of the next 13 Championship matches 12 were lost and one drawn. At

After three matches for his native Yorkshire, John van Geloven joined Leicestershire in 1956 and remained a leading all-rounder for the County for ten years. (Leicester Mercury)

Grace Road near the end of August the third and final win of 1964 occurred. It was another run challenge, Leicestershire being set 187 in 135 minutes by Glamorgan. Booth and Inman put on an unbroken 123 for the third wicket and 15 minutes remained when the winning hit was made.

Leicestershire finished in 16th place with three wins – the same as in 1963. The continued modest form of the County was clearly affecting Hallam. For the first time since 1953 he failed to complete 1,000 runs and his only century came in the last match of the summer. Only Inman managed a batting average above 30. He was one of three players to hit 1,000 runs, the others being Booth, who was awarded his County cap, and Jayasinghe, who missed several games through illness. Watson's comeback was not a success – in 14 innings he averaged 16.84.

The fact that Cross topped the bowling table with 31 wickets at 27 runs each amply illustrates the weakness of the attack.

In contrast to the First Eleven, the Seconds came third in their Competition. Greensword, Constant, P. A. Munden and Bird all had batting averages above 30 whilst Boshier, Barratt, Thompson and Pratt could point to good bowling returns.

The finances were still shaky, the loss being £12,874, though Spencer received £3,500 from his benefit fund. One move designed to improve the viability of the club was the abandonment of cricket weeks at Ashby and Hinckley. The ground at Coventry Road, Hinckley, was sold in the following year. The money coming from the Gillette Cup and other sponsorship was beginning to assist the overall financial picture of county cricket.

Booth and a 20-year-old Cumberland fast bowler, Howard Jeffery, were the two newcomers of 1964. Jeffery seemed a very fine prospect, but after two matches comments were made concerning the legality of his bowling action and he was dropped.

During the 1964–65 close season vigorous efforts were made to persuade cricketers who had not been re-engaged by their own counties to join Leicestershire. Peter Marner from Oldham had played for Lancashire since 1952. In August 1964 there had been something of a hiatus at Old Trafford, the exact cause of which was never satisfactorily explained, but the Club issued a statement which included: 'A firm decision was taken not to re-engage P. Marner and G. Clayton on the grounds that their continued retention was not in the best interests of the playing staff or the Club.' Problems over the captaincy of the Lancashire side had led to players becoming disillusioned and Marner, who had been a very promising schoolboy cricketer – he was 16 when he made his Lancashire debut – had lost his way. In 1956 he had been stricken with meningitis and later a serious knee injury whilst playing rugby had lost him almost an entire summer. He was even now only 29 and Leicestershire signed him with every reason to hope that his best years were still ahead of him.

A second experienced cricketer came to boost the bowling. John Cotton had played for Notts in 138 matches, starting 1958 and was still only 24. A lively fast bowler he, like Marner, had been looked upon as a possible Test player of the future, but had not felt at home with his native county in the last year or two.

In addition Leicestershire signed two players from Minor Counties. Barry Dudleston from Cheshire was a 19-year-old right-hand batsman; Roger Tolchard came from Devon. He had played Minor Counties cricket in 1963 and 1964, but was still only 18, having played for the Public Schools at Lord's in 1964. He was a talented wicketkeeper at Malvern and a useful batsman. This was not the end of Leicestershire's new look. Riaz-ur-Rehman, a 25-year-old Pakistan batsman, who had played League cricket in England, was engaged and would need to qualify by residence. His efforts in 1965 were to be confined to the Second Eleven.

Having signed these five players, plus A. J. Matthews, an off-spinner, who though born in Scotland, had been playing local cricket, Leicestershire achieved an even bigger scoop, when in February 1965 they persuaded Tony Lock to return to county cricket.

Lock, born in Limpsfield in Surrey in 1929, had had a brilliant career with his native county as a slow or medium left-arm foil to the off-spin of Jim Laker. Through the 1950s they had had much to do with the long run of success by Surrey under Stuart Surridge. In 1955 Lock had taken 216 wickets at 14.39 runs each and his overall record for Surrey was 1,713 wickets at 17 runs each. He had had problems with the legality of his faster delivery and had been no-balled for throwing, but this had been resolved satisfactorily.

In the late summer of 1962 the England selectors caused something of a sensation by omitting Lock from the MCC side to tour Australia.

John Clarke commented in *Challenge Re-Newed*:

> The selectors met for four hours and at the appointed time their news was released – the astounding news that though they had picked seventeen to go to Australia, Lock was not among that number; and three off-spinners had been chosen. It was a situation of great poignancy as well as one that shook most people by its oddity. For Lock alone of the team playing at Nottingham (in the current Test) was not among the chosen.

According to rumour Lock was made all sorts of offers from League clubs and elsewhere. In the event he signed a contract to play for Western Australia. This had the approval of Surrey, but having come back to play for that county in 1963 after the winter in Australia, he then announced that he was emigrating to Australia. In 1964 he did not appear in county cricket. For 1965 he had already signed as professional for Ramsbottom and thus would only be available for Leicestershire in certain mid-week matches. It should be added here that apart from his bowling, Lock was considered the best close-to-the-wicket fielder in England and no mean batsman.

After two evenly balanced draws against Sussex and Somerset, Leicestershire entertained Lancashire at Grace Road, with Lock making his debut and also Marner and Cotton in the side. Lancashire were outplayed from the start. Having removed the opposition for 126, with all the home bowlers doing their bit, Leicestershire obtained a lead of 171 and then removed Lancashire cheaply a second time, winning by nine wickets. Lock took six wickets, hit 40 and held two superb catches. The victory inspired the side to beat Surrey in the following game, Cotton taking seven wickets at little cost, whilst Jayasinghe and Inman batted very well.

Not everything went Leicestershire's way through the remainder of the summer, but with victories over Middlesex, Hampshire, Notts and Oxford University to add to the other two wins, the County moved up to 14th and as the three teams above them also had the same number of wins, a little more good fortune would have seen them further up the ladder.

Booth, Inman, Jayasinghe, Hallam and Marner all completed 1,000 runs, but they too often all failed together – at Ebbw Vale the County were dismissed for 33, Don Shepherd having figures of 10-8-2-5, while at Grace Road, also against Glamorgan, the total was a paltry 40, I. J. Jones taking eight for 11. In all Leicestershire were dismissed for under 100 ten times in the season.

Hallam made a century in each innings, 107 and 149, both not out, *v* Worcestershire at Grace Road; Booth repeated the same feat against Middlesex; Inman was awarded the Man of the Match accolade in the Gillette match *v* Yorkshire. But for the third year Leicestershire lost their single match in the competition.

Lock topped the bowling table with 35 wickets at 19 runs each; Cotton took most wickets, 76 at 21.42 runs each and Marner took 63 wickets at a reasonable cost, so the new recruits made worthwhile contributions.

The year saw the last county match to be played on the Brush Sports Ground in Loughborough – Loughborough was the only venue for home matches, except for Grace Road. In 1966 the County were to return to the Snibston Colliery ground, which replaced Loughborough as the single out of town venue.

The financial situation, not helped by poor weather, continued to be unhealthy, nearly £16,000 being lost on the year's workings.

Apart from those previous mentioned D. J. Constant, having spent 1964 in the Second Eleven, was given a chance in the first team, and played one or two useful innings as an opening batsman.

At the end of the season Hallam asked to be relieved of the captaincy and the County were able to sign Lock on a full-time basis for 1966, appointing him the new leader. Two other changes were the decision of Jayasinghe to return to Ceylon and the signing of the Northants batsman, Michael Norman. Aged 33 he had played for his native county since 1952 and his best season was 1960 when he hit 1,964 runs. In 1965 however he had missed nearly half Northants' games and had a very ordinary set of figures.

The mass importation of players – there were now six 'special' registrations' on the staff – was not to the liking of the more conservative supporters of county cricket, but there was clearly no other way for Leicestershire to obtain a well-balanced team. Aside from the changes in the playing staff, the Club were now changing Grace Road. During the winter they bought the ground from the local education authorities for £24,500 and put into operation an £80,000 building improvement scheme. A new pavilion was built, designed by a local architect, S. Dudley. The ground floor contained the offices and second team changing rooms; the first floor was devoted to the main changing rooms, the Secretary's office and the committee room – up until now the Secretary's office and committee room had not been at Grace Road, but in separate premises in Leicester. The building of the new pavilion had been preceded by a transformation of the old Richards Stand, which was renamed 'The Meet' and when reno-vated contained the members' and public bars. The money to pay for all this came from the Club football pool, which in ten years had brought in about £100,000. As with the strengthening of the playing staff, much of the credit for the work went to Mike Turner.

The new surroundings, the new captain and what Henry Blofeld noted as 'a strong individual effort to put Leicestershire cricket back on the map' was rewarded by a place in the top half of the Championship table for the first time in ten years. Eight matches were won and the County moved from 14th place to eighth. It was the season when the strange regulation was intro-duced limiting the first innings of 12 matches per county to 65 overs. The early matches did not bring much happiness, though on 29 May, Sunday cricket took place in a Championship Match at Grace Road for the first time. As many as 5,000 spectators turned out and though it was illegal to charge an entrance fee, sales of programmes realised £420. The game was against neigh-bouring Northants and even though the first two innings were restricted to 65 overs and Northants declared their second innings closed, the match still ended in a draw. Leicestershire had 260 minutes to make 334 and were 279 for eight at the close. By the time of the second Sunday match on 26 June against Surrey, when the new pavilion was officially opened by the Bishop of Leicester, the County were languishing in 16th place, with only a single win – at Grace Road *v* Lancashire, when the three emigrants from the opposition, Marner, Booth and Savage, played a major part in the success.

The opening of the pavilion seemed a signal to change course and, though rain ruined that particular match, the following game was won – by one wicket against Notts. Two more victories came in July. Lock took ten wickets for 70 at Chesterfield to beat Derbyshire and Marner took eleven at Coalville to beat Glamorgan, both wins being by fair margins.

In August Worcestershire and Kent were overcome in successive matches. The Worcestershire game at New Road was a very low scoring affair. The home county were bowled out for 94 and 99, Spencer taking eleven for 65 and Leicestershire managed 90 and 163. Runs were not much more plentiful in the Kent game with the highest individual innings being 57 by Luckhurst and Leicestershire's winning margin being seven wickets.

The final two Championship games also produced victories, both away from home. Essex set Leicestershire 262 in 185 minutes and 74 in 48 minutes from Inman together with 63 in an hour by Marner meant victory by four wickets. Finally all-round cricket by Marner and a century by Inman beat Lancashire at Old Trafford.

One factor in the improved results was the settled nature of the side. Only 14 players appeared in the 28 Championship games, the 12 regulars being Hallam, Norman, Inman, Booth, Marner, Constant, Lock, Birkenshaw, Tolchard, Savage, Cotton and Spencer.

The major alteration, apart from Norman replacing Jayasinghe, was the switch of wicketkeepers. Tolchard played in all 28 matches, which meant that Julian's role was confined to Second Eleven cricket. Julian officially left the playing staff at the end of the summer, but remained employed at Grace Road, and captained the Second Eleven. He played for the County team in emergency until 1971 after which he joined the first-class umpires' list.

Tolchard's career was destined to last until 1983 and he captained the County in his final three summers. By the end of his career he had amassed a record number of wicketkeeping dis-

John Savage bowled his off-breaks for Leicestershire from 1953 to 1966 before ending his career in Lancashire, where he was born. (NCCC)

missals (794 catches and 109 stumpings) for the County. On retirement he took up a teaching post at Malvern.

Lock was undoubtedly the inspiration behind the team's improved showing. He took 109 wickets at 19.56 runs each, held 38 catches and hit 658 runs. Hallam, relieved of the captaincy, found his form again. He scored 1,502 runs topping the batting table. Booth, Inman, Marner and Norman also completed 1,000 runs. The main support to Lock in the bowling came from Spencer and Marner, though Cotton, when not injured, and Savage also made substantial contributions. Savage however asked to be released from his contract at the end of the summer and rejoined Lancashire, where he later became coach. The financial situation was still critical with a deficit of £11,500 and apart from Savage and Julian, Greensword and Barratt were released; Ashdown was no longer employed as chief scout, though he remained as scorer, and Gerry Lester was not offered re-engagement as coach. In appreciation of his long service (since 1936) he was elected an Honorary Life Member.

Norman was the only debutant to play any substantial role in the 1966 side, but two others made their first-class debuts. The first was Barry Dudleston, whose single game was against West

Indies; his opportunities were to come in the season which followed. The second was Riaz Rehman, who played against Oxford, but died in a road accident in July whilst on the way to a Second Eleven match.

Despite their success in 1966, the County's search for new players did not end and they signed Barry Knight, the Essex and England all-rounder, in the winter. The application for special registration however was rejected and Knight was forced to qualify by residence and was thus not able to play in 1967 – his efforts being largely confined to the Second Eleven.

The 1967 side showed only one change, the inclusion of Dudleston in place of Savage, but the influence of Lock was now thoroughly ingrained in the eleven. Not one of the 20 men chosen for England during the summer came from Leicestershire, yet the County won 10 matches and finished the season in third place, only ten points behind the winners, Yorkshire. It equalled Palmer's great summer of 1953 – in fact in 1967 they tied on points with Kent, but the latter had won more matches and therefore claimed second place.

The season opened with the first round of the Gillette Cup – against Somerset at Taunton. Lock's decision to put Somerset in misfired and Leicestershire were easily beaten – the fifth year in the competition and the fifth time the County had failed to win a match. The first Championship match gave no hint of future prosperity, Derbyshire winning at Derby by nine wickets. The first success came on the United Services ground at Portsmouth. Leicestershire bowled out Hampshire for 122 and 183. Lock achieved an unusual hat-trick, dismissing the last two batsmen in the first innings and Livingstone in the middle of the second. Inman made 65 not out, the highest innings in the match. Going back to Grace Road for the first home game of the season – the County played all their home games at this venue for the first time, another economy measure – Glamorgan were beaten by seven wickets. Rain then came to mar the rest of the month. The match against Yorkshire at Headingley was entirely washed away and large portions of the games with Sussex, Northants and Worcestershire suffered similarly. Fortunately for Leicestershire the rest of England was under water, so that as May ended, the County, with two wins from seven games, were in second place behind Hampshire.

Kent were at Grace Road in the first days of June and met Cotton at his best. He took six for 38, dismissing Kent for 72 to provide Leicestershire with a lead of 131. Underwood provided the home side with plenty to think about in their second innings, but Birkenshaw picked up six cheap wickets in the final innings when Kent failed to approach the 241 they needed and the game ended soon after lunch on the third day.

Going to Guildford to meet his former county colleagues, the captain's ploy to put the opposition in failed, Surrey achieving a first-innings lead of 157 and going on to win by ten wickets.

Two victories by comfortable margins against Essex and Gloucestershire were followed by an exciting two-wicket win over Somerset at Grace Road, where Leicestershire were set 296 in four hours. There were still 150 needed in the final 90 minutes, and after Birkenshaw and Tolchard had brought the target within reach, Lock appropriately hit the fifth ball of the last possible over for four, then threw his bat in the air as excited applause broke the tension.

These three wins placed Leicestershire at the head of the table, but Illingworth brought them down almost single-handed. He took six for 52 and five for 27, dismissing Leicestershire for 161 and 96, then hit 60 in Yorkshire's total of 380. No less than five drawn matches followed and it was not until 4 August that Leicestershire won another Championship game, Lock taking ten wickets at Derby's expense. There were three more draws, before the County ended the season in quite brilliant form. Gloucestershire were beaten at Cheltenham by six wickets, Birkenshaw taking ten wickets and Lock hitting 81, his highest in first-class cricket to date; Worcestershire were beaten in two days, Lock returning figures of ten for 41; finally Northants were confused by Lock whose analysis was 48.2-24-118-13 and Leicestershire won by 163 runs. Prideaux, the opposition captain, complained that the wicket was not fit for Championship cricket, but Hallam and Norman began Leicestershire's innings with a partnership worth 185.

Leicestershire called upon only 13 players for their 27 Championship games. Birkenshaw bowled better than in his previous seasons, taking 111 wickets at 21.41 runs each – his best until then was 27; he also made 840 runs. Norman headed the batting with 1,545 runs, average 35.93, the highest of his four three-figure innings being 221 not out against Cambridge at Fenner's; Booth also made four hundreds as well as his highest score of 171 not out against Notts at Newark; his aggregate was 1,423. Hallam, Inman and Marner were the others to top 1,000 runs and Dudleston did well in his first full year with 668 runs and a maiden hundred at Taunton. The opening bowlers, Spencer and Cotton, took 60 and 71 wickets respectively, but Birkenshaw, as noted, and Lock were the dominant bowlers. The captain claimed 128

CHARLES TERRANCE SPENCER

Terry Spencer made a lasting impression on the Leicestershire County captain when, in the pre-season friendly in 1952, he cleaned bowled Palmer, knocking out his off-stump. A few days later he made his first-class debut and by the time the 1952 summer was at an end, Spencer had become one of a very select few to appear in every Championship match of their debut season.

He took 80 first-class wickets and the press were quick to predict that he was an England cricketer in the making. Those however were the days of National Service and the two following summers found Spencer occupied elsewhere, with his cricket opportunities limited, though the English selectors were impressed enough to pick him for the 1953 Test Trial.

His best season in first-class cricket was 1961 when he took 123 wickets at an average of 19.56 and was short listed for the MCC tour to India the following winter. He did not in fact make the trip and thus lost any chance of playing for England.

Officially he announced his retirement from first-class cricket at the end of the 1969 season, when he was elected an Honorary Life member of the County Club, but it was not until 1974 that he made his final bow and by then he had played in 496 matches for the County and in all first-class cricket taken 1,367 wickets. Apart from his seam bowling, Spencer was an excellent fieldsman, who made difficult catches look easy, and a late order batsman who enlivened matches with some hard-hit sixes.

(NCCC)

wickets in all first-class matches, only two bowlers in England obtaining more – only three bowled more overs.

The County gave trials to two youngsters, Norman Briers and Ivan d'Oliveira, both related to other players who achieved fame. Ivan was the brother of the England cricketer and Norman a cousin of N. E. Briers.

During the winter of 1967–68 the MCC toured the West Indies, winning the Test series by one match to nil, with four drawn; it was the last time England have won a series in the Caribbean. Shortly before the third Test, Fred Titmus suffered the loss of four toes in a boating accident and was forced to return home. Tony Lock, having just led Western Australia to top place in the Sheffield Shield, was called out as a replacement. Playing in the last two Tests, he scored a robust 89 in the fifth, which was his highest score in first-class cricket, eclipsing the 81 he made for Leicestershire a few months before.

After the last Test Lock flew back to Australia and to the dismay of Leicestershire announced that owing to his wife's poor health and for other domestic reasons he would be unable to continue his contract with the County. The County Committee had no option but to accept this situation and Hallam was appointed as captain for the summer. Lock's captaincy had lasted just two seasons – he was 37 and Leicestershire might have hoped for two or three more years under his guidance. The ever-active Secretary, Mike Turner, was soon exploring how best to fill the gap left by Lock and his endeavours were not long in bearing fruit. In theory the inclusion of Barry Knight should have gone a considerable distance towards solving Lock's absence. Knight was now 30, he had achieved the 'double' no fewer than four times, 1962 to 1965 inclusive, played in 22 Tests and was considered likely to resume his Test career in 1968 (in fact he did play in the second and third Tests).

The Club had been very busy with further building work at Grace Road during the winter of 1967–68 and a large members' Long Room was constructed adjacent to the dining room. A folding partition between the two rooms meant that in the winter they could form a single entity to be used as two indoor nets. The Warwickshire Supporters Club provided an interest free loan to cover some of the cost of this work. The Long Room was officially opened by the Lord Mayor of Leicester on 11 May 1968 and the nets were in operation the following October, with Jack Birkenshaw in charge.

The 1968 season began with a victory over Cambridge University at Fenner's. Hallam made a hundred and Birkenshaw took nine wickets, but the interesting feature of the match was the operation, for the first time, of the rule requiring 20 overs to be bowled in the final hour.

The Championship season opened with rain at Cardiff, the whole of the first day and a large section of the third being washed out. The Australians then came to Grace Road; Knight took five for 77 on the first day with the tourists bowled out for 233, but rain caused havoc with the rest of the play. There followed three successive Championship defeats. Leicestershire met Somerset in the Gillette Cup on 25 and 26 May. At last Leicestershire recorded a win in the competition. Somerset were bowled out for 134, having decided to bat. Hallam and Norman replied with a first wicket stand of 71 and though Booth and Inman failed to score, the match was won by four wickets. In the next round the County went to Lord's and ought to have beaten Middlesex. With 11 overs remaining Leicestershire had lost only two wickets and needed just 40 runs. Booth was batting well, but he was involved in the run out of both Marner and Inman, then the remaining six wickets disappeared. Eight batsmen were out in the space of 45 balls while 21 runs were scored. C. J. Barnett, the former Gloucestershire and England batsman, gave the Man-of-the-Match Award to Price of Middlesex for his brilliant fielding on the boundary.

Between the two Gillette matches, Leicestershire managed two Championship wins. Worcestershire were beaten at Grace Road and Gloucestershire at Bristol; these successes were balanced by three defeats, including a remarkable game at Sheffield when Knight took eight for 82, dismissing Yorkshire for 297, Boycott having carried out his bat for 114. This bowling feat persuaded the Test selectors to pick Knight for the forthcoming Test at Lord's. Yorkshire in their second innings scored with ease, Illingworth making 100 and Hampshire 96, then Trueman took six for 20 and Yorkshire won by 143 runs.

There were to be four other victories in Championship matches, the best of which came late in August at Taunton. Leicestershire made 424 for nine with nearly everyone contributing, but the highest individual score only Hallam's 81. Somerset were dismissed for 131 and 240, John Pember taking five for 45 in the first innings. Pember had made his debut earlier in the season and was the County's only 1968 newcomer. Born in Creaton, Northants, he was a right-arm medium-pace bowler and attacking left-hand batsman. He did well for the Second Eleven, but his first-class career was to be limited to 24 matches spread over four seasons.

With six victories and ten defeats, Leicestershire finished the summer in ninth place and were never among the Championship leaders. Hallam's batting was affected by the captaincy and he failed to complete 1,000 runs. Inman was the most reliable batsman and remarkably consistent, completing 50 on 17 occasions but only once reaching three figures. His aggregate was 1,735, average 37. Booth, Marner and Norman also topped the thousand mark. Birkenshaw completed a maiden hundred and took 92 wickets – easily the highest – to prove he was now an accomplished all-rounder. There was little to choose between him and Knight, whose totals were 735 runs and 61 wickets, nothing like the figures he had achieved for Essex.

Spencer continued to bowl with accuracy, but Cotton lost his line and length. His 32 wickets cost almost 40 runs each. Dudleston also had a disappointing year and temporarily lost his place in the side.

Roy Barratt was re-engaged when Lock announced his retirement and his left-arm slow bowling was used in 17 matches, but he took only 30 wickets. The footballer, Cross, actually headed the bowling table, his 11 wickets costing 12 runs each, but he turned out in only two Championship matches. Constant, who, while scoring many runs for the Second Eleven, failed when selected for the first team, was not re-engaged at the end of 1968 and the following summer began his long career as an umpire. Matthews, who had appeared in six Championship games during the summer, gave up county cricket and emigrated to Australia. Willie Watson also emigrated – to South Africa.

ILLINGWORTH ARRIVES

THE SAGA OF YORKSHIRE's self-inflicted wounds during the past 30 years have filled the biographies of Boycott, Trueman, Close, Illingworth and quite a few other famous cricketers and commentators. To understand why Raymond Illingworth, the leading wicket-taker in England in 1968, had decided to resign from the Yorkshire County Club, it is necessary to study the history of that club over the previous decade or more. What brought Illingworth into conflict with Yorkshire in the middle of 1968 and sparked his resignation letter was the tradition that Yorkshire, unlike the other 16 counties, gave players only one-year contracts. Illingworth applied for a three-year contract, lit the blue touch paper and awaited the result. Brian Sellers, the autocratic ruler of the club, exploded and according to Bill Bowes, the former Yorkshire fast bowler who was then a journalist, Sellers announced that Illingworth could go and 'any bugger else that wants to could go with him'. The tradition set out many years before by Lord Hawke was not going to be altered by Illingworth or anyone else.

The practical Illingworth did not set off this reaction without making discreet enquiries first. He let it be known that he might need a new cricketing post for 1969 and the offers came flooding in. Five counties made overtures and several League clubs. Illingworth was keen to captain a county and when Mike Turner suggested that the Leicestershire captaincy might be available, Illingworth seized the opportunity.

Illingworth was now nearly 37, he had played for Yorkshire since 1951 and for England in 30 Tests, including the final three of 1968. He had completed the 'double' six times, but his experience as a captain was virtually non-existent. Leicestershire therefore were taking a slight gamble on this aspect of his cricket, though Illingworth in his autobiography states that he made it clear to Leicestershire that he would be willing to resign the captaincy and play under someone else if his style of leadership proved unacceptable.

The County signed a second well-known player for the 1969 season – Graham McKenzie, the Australian fast bowler, who had headed the Australian Test averages in the series v West Indies which finished just before the English season began. McKenzie was 27 and played for Western Australia. In 1968 the authorities had announced that counties could sign an overseas player without the need for residential qualification. Such well-known figures as Gary Sobers, Mike Procter, Barry Richards and Rohan Kanhai had immediately joined the County Championship, but Leicestershire waited for McKenzie, who, in 1968, was touring England with the Australians.

Mike Turner was now confident about the County prospects for the coming season and wrote:

> In every aspect of the game we look forward with confidence to the new season when once again every effort will be made to play positive and purposeful cricket . . . We believe that the inclusion of these two Test cricketers in the side will make Leicestershire one of the most powerful and attractive teams in the Championship and Players' League this summer.

The 1969 season was the first of the Sunday League sponsored by John Player.

The summer got off to a wet start, and the first five of Leicestershire's first-class matches, four in the Championship and one against Cambridge University, were drawn due to rain. Of the four Sunday League games in the same period, two were totally abandoned, but the other two produced victories. At the end of May came the first Championship victory, Hampshire being beaten by an innings at Grace Road. The match which followed, at Headingley, was washed out and as it ended came the announcement that Illingworth had been appointed captain of England. This ended some days of newspaper speculation. Colin Cowdrey had captained England on the 1968–69 tour to Pakistan but on 24 May, whilst playing for Kent in a Sunday League match, Cowdrey had snapped the Achilles' tendon in his left leg, putting himself out of cricket for the rest of the summer. The two main contenders for the England captaincy were Illingworth and Graveney: according to Illingworth's autobiography certain selectors were not in favour of Graveney and so it proved.

Illingworth celebrated his appointment by leading Leicestershire to victory over Sussex at Hove, but when Illingworth was leading England to victory over West Indies the following week, Leicestershire were being beaten by the narrow margin of five runs by Gloucestershire. The County were seventh in the Championship table with a third of their programme played.

They were destined to win only two more games – against Northants, when Birkenshaw took nine wickets, and against Derbyshire in a contrived declaration contest – and thus drifted gently down the table to end in 14th place. A sad finish to a season which began with such optimistic hopes. The results in the new Sunday League were scarcely better, with a final position of 11th

Raymond Illingworth, the Yorkshire all-rounder, arrived to captain Leicestershire in 1969 and led the County to the most successful decade in their history, including a Championship win in 1975. (Patrick Eagar)

from six wins. The Gillette Cup produced a three-wicket win against Kent, followed by a defeat at the hands of Sussex, when the batting failed.

The absence of Illingworth due to the six Test Matches meant that he missed nine of the 24 Championship games and an equal portion of Sunday matches. How much the County missed him can be gauged by the seasonal averages which show him top of both batting and bowling tables. In addition, Knight played in five Tests and missed seven matches.

McKenzie took most wickets – 77 at 22.14 runs each – but he failed to rank in the top 20 in the first-class averages and only in the Championship win against Sussex did his bowling provide the County with a first-class victory.

Cotton and Spencer were treated as yesterday's men. Spencer's 19 wickets in nine Championship matches cost 34 runs each; Cotton could only take eight wickets in seven games. The off-spin of Birkenshaw proved effective and he also averaged over 30 with the bat. Dudleston, who batted as an opener in several matches, but more usually in the middle order, completed 1,000 runs and came second to Illingworth in the averages. Inman just missed 1,000, but his average was only marginally below Dudleston's. Tolchard, usually coming in at number nine, averaged 28 with the aid of many incomplete innings. He was regarded as an England prospect and turned out for MCC in one or two games.

Apart from Illingworth and McKenzie, the one player to make his debut for the County in 1969 was Paul Haywood. A right-hand batsman who had learnt his cricket at Wyggeston School, he never really made his mark in county cricket, but was a brilliant fieldsman and was played as much for that aspect of his game as his batting.

Hallam, Cotton and Spencer left the County staff at the end of 1969 and Norman indicated that he would be available only in the school holidays. The County lost £3,105 on the year, though £20,136 was received from lotteries and competitions. Expenditure rose to a record £48,944. As the 1970 season was opening, Knight announced that he would be staying in Australia and was thus ending his five-year contract with the County, despite the fact that it had two years to run.

The 1970 season was dominated by the move to stop the South African tour. Anti-apartheid protestors visited Grace Road and painted slogans on various buildings and the Club was forced to employ night patrols in order to safeguard the playing area. When the tour was officially abandoned, five matches between England and a Rest of the World team were arranged to replace the Tests.

MAURICE RAYMOND HALLAM

In many ways, Maurice Hallam's career was an echo of Les Berry's. Hallam effectively succeeded Berry as Leicestershire's opening batsman and had a long and distinguished career without ever being chosen for England. Like Berry, Hallam was called upon to captain the County, and to continue the parallel, both had been useful soccer players in their younger days.

Unlike Berry however, Hallam was a native of the County, being born in Leicester in 1931. He first reached 1,000 runs in a season in 1954 and in 1957 made 2,068 runs. His best summer was 1961 when he hit 2,262 at an average of 39.68.

His most remarkable match was at Worthing in 1961 when he made 203 not out in the first innings and an unbeaten 143 in the second. In all he compiled 32 hundreds and completed 1,000 runs in 13 seasons.

He led the County in 1963 to 1965 and again in 1968. An excellent fielder close to the wicket, he held 453 catches.

Hallam's first-class career lasted 21 seasons until 1970, and for the four following years he captained the Second Eleven, grooming the young players of the future. A popular man both on and off the field, he has made many cricketing friends in Leicestershire and throughout the country.

(NCCC)

Leicestershire in 1969. Left to right, back: B. R. Knight, P. T. Marner, R. W. Tolchard, B. J. Booth, R. J. Barratt, J. Birkenshaw, B. Dudleston. Front: C. T. Spencer, G. D. McKenzie, R. Illingworth (Captain), M. R. Hallam, C. C. Inman. (NCCC)

Leicestershire found themselves deprived therefore not only of Illingworth, who remained England's captain, but also McKenzie, who was recruited for the opposition. With Knight leaving without notice, this meant the attack was weakened beyond expectations and it was thus no surprise that the County's fortunes fell, even below the modest record of 1969.

Three additions were made to the playing staff. Peter Stringer the 27-year-old Yorkshire fast bowler came in for Spencer; John Tolchard the elder brother of Roger, who had played for Devon since 1963, came to bolster the batting, and John Steele, of Staffordshire, brother of the Northants and future England batsman David, was a useful bowler. It was however too much to hope that these three would make an immediate difference to the overall playing strength.

The season began with a visit to Old Trafford, where the frailty of the new Leicestershire side was fully exposed. In the Championship match, Lancashire won in two days by six wickets and in the Sunday League game, the margin was 92 runs. A draw against Sussex at Grace Road was followed by a defeat at Chelmsford, where the leg-breaks of Hobbs and a century from Edmeades brought Essex victory in the Championship game, whilst accurate bowling gave them the edge in the Sunday League fixture. At the end of May the County stood in 15th place in the table, but June brought some comfort in the form of wins over Derbyshire at home and Warwickshire at Nuneaton. Dudleston hit 104 and Roger Tolchard 92 in the match against Derbyshire, with Illingworth taking five for 35 in the second innings. At Nuneaton Birkenshaw bowled out the home side for 90 and Marner, captaining the side in Illingworth's absence, made the highest scores in both innings, as Leicestershire won by eight wickets.

July started with some brilliant batting by Marner at Sheffield. Marner hit a hundred off 69 balls in 83 minutes with four sixes and 14 fours. Inman hit a hundred in the same innings off 95 balls and Leicestershire could afford the luxury of a declaration, setting Yorkshire 319, a target they did not attempt. Of Championship victories, however, the month added just one; McKenzie put in his best bowling of the summer taking 12 for 127 and with the aid of an unbeaten hundred by Illingworth Glamorgan were beaten by nine wickets. Some idea of Leicestershire's problems can be shown by the fact that in the next match, the return against Yorkshire, in mid-July, the County for the first time in the season reached a total over 300. This was due to an opening stand of 126 by Dudleston and Haywood; one of the major problems of the side was the inability to find a settled pair of opening batsmen. Norman did solve this difficulty when he finished his school term.

Two victories came at Grace Road in August, the first being Inman's benefit game against Notts and the second against Middlesex, making a total of five Championship wins, and the County finished in 15th place in the Championship, just seven points clear of Middlesex and Gloucestershire, who were equal 16th.

In the Player League seven wins were recorded and seventh place obtained, but the major limited-overs competition, the Gillette Cup, saw Leicestershire once more knocked out in their first match, when Notts beat them at Grace Road by 43 runs.

Marner, Inman and Dudleston completed 1,000 runs for the County; Tolchard missed the milestone by 27. Illingworth had a fine record for England and was appointed to captain the team to Australia, but his contributions to Championship cricket were very limited. McKenzie had a good summer, heading the bowling averages and in the overall season's figures only Shepherd of Glamorgan and Gifford of Worcestershire had better figures. Stringer, opening the attack with the Australian, did well in the early part of the campaign but faded, his wickets costing 30 runs each. Birkenshaw sent down 100 more overs than any other

Clive Inman played for Leicestershire in 11 seasons from 1961 to 1971 and scored 1,000 runs eight times. He hit the fastest 50 in first-class cricket, in eight minutes, for the County against Notts at Trent Bridge in 1965. (Neville Chadwick Photography)

bowler and was McKenzie's main support, but unfortunately his batting was not as effective as in 1969 and his average fell by almost ten runs.

Three of the four new players, Steele, Jeff Tolchard and Stringer have previously been noted. The fourth, though he achieved little in 1970, was destined to have a big impact on the County's cricket in later years. Brian Davison, born in Bulawayo

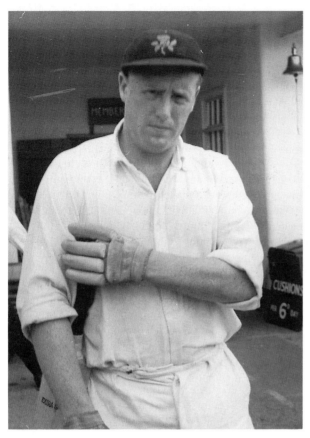

After a successful career with Lancashire, hard-hitting Peter Marner served Leicestershire for six seasons up to 1970. (NCCC)

in 1946, had played for Rhodesia for three seasons and for Leicestershire 2nd XI in 1969. A very hard-hitting batsman and one who liked to attack the bowling at almost every opportunity, he was a lithe fieldsman who was determined to attempt every catch and in the process made some miraculous dismissals. Apart from cricket he also played hockey for Rhodesia.

Season 1970 marked the founding of 'The Friends of Grace Road', with L. Wallace as chairman. The main object of the new association was to improve amenities on the County Ground and many of the small improvements over the last 20 years have been due to this organisation.

Soon after the 1970 season ended Marner announced that he was retiring from full-time county cricket to concentrate on a business career and that he would be playing for Todmorden, but if required would play for Leicestershire on Sundays. All the other players on the staff were offered terms for 1971 while the club was searching for another fast bowler, since McKenzie would probably be playing for Australia in 1972. The Leicestershire playing staff was, and had been for several years, the smallest in the country, numbering only 14 players, whereas most other counties had 18, 19 or 20. This made the running of the Second Eleven difficult, but in 1970 the side finished a creditable fifth in their Competition.

Illingworth, who had a very variable press on his appointment to lead England in Australia, came out of the tour triumphant. He welded the players into a determined team and won the Ashes. For Leicestershire the result was that he was required for six Tests in 1971, three each against Pakistan and India – he missed no less than ten Championship matches out of 24 – and in place of Marner, Roger Tolchard captained the County when Illingworth was needed elsewhere.

The 1971 season began on a down note with the County beaten by Cambridge University at Fenner's by seven wickets – a certain P. H. Edmonds, then unknown to cricketing fame, took nine for 98 and Majid Khan hit 112. The first four Championship matches were high-scoring draws; Inman hit hundreds against Somerset and Derbyshire, Booth reached 138 against Notts. Against Middlesex in the fifth match however, the batting collapsed, the England fast bowler, Price, taking six for 29, and the total being just 65. Leicestershire followed on and but for a seventh wicket stand of 92 by Roger Tolchard and Birkenshaw would have been defeated by an innings – as it was defeat came by ten wickets. There followed five more draws and one more reverse, then Leicestershire went to Northampton and won by an innings inside two days. Illingworth had the remarkable analyses of 19.3-11-15-4 and 16.5-6-17-5 with Northants dismissed for 104 and 102. In the following game another spinner dominated the proceedings, Chandrasekhar dismissing the County cheaply and giving the Indian tourists an innings victory.

It was the last first-class defeat the County suffered during the summer and wins over Sussex, Worcestershire and Glamorgan, all by innings margins, and one against Lancashire meant that Leicestershire finished the campaign in fifth place, a vast improvement on 1970. In the Sussex match at Hove, Dudleston and Steele opened with a stand of 152 and the total was 416 for eight when Illingworth declared; Sussex failed by one run to make Leicestershire bat a second time. Against Worcestershire at New Road, spectators witnessed the now unusual sight of the opening bowlers bowling unchanged through the completed Worcestershire innings – McKenzie took five for 16 and Matthews three for 21 – the home side were all out for 40. It should be pointed out though that Worcestershire had two men absent injured. If Worcestershire's total was low, then Glamorgan's a fortnight later was abysmal. This time McKenzie and Spencer bowled unchanged and the score was just 24, the lowest ever recorded in a first-class county match in Leicestershire. The game took place at Grace Road, as did all Leicestershire's First XI games in 1971. Glamorgan did little better in their second innings, being all out for 66 and McKenzie had match figures of 25.4-9-37-11. The Australian also hit the highest individual score in the game, 53 not out, and his ninth-wicket stand with Roger Tolchard raised Leicestershire's total from 123 for eight to 209. The other victory, over Lancashire by 75 runs, was also a low-scoring match and these two matches were in complete contrast to the rest of the season at Grace Road, where the bat ruled supreme – all the other Championship games being drawn.

Despite finishing fifth, Leicestershire never really challenged for the Championship title, the battle being between Warwickshire, Lancashire and, in the later stages, Surrey, who had a brilliant patch in August and overtook all rivals. It was a different story in the Sunday League. Leicestershire began with six successive victories and even though they then suffered three defeats, they were only one point behind the leaders when ten matches had been played. What proved to be the crucial match for the County was against Northants on 22 August. The Pakistan pace bowler, Sarfraz Nawaz, proved too much for Leicestershire, who were all out for 111 and Northants had little difficulty in reaching this target. So, though Leicestershire won their final game, the four points gained were only enough to keep them in fourth place.

In the Gillette Cup, Leicestershire nearly threw their first match away – four wickets went down gathering the last 19 runs needed for victory over Derbyshire and the margin of success was one wicket. In the next round, Kent came to Grace Road. The visitors made 231 for eight in the 60 overs. Leicestershire began their reply in promising fashion, Dudleston and Norman putting on 88 for the first wicket. Once that partnership was broken, however, the batting simply folded up and with eight players failing to reach double figures, the all out total was 153. Woolmer received the Man of The Match Award for his bowling, his figures being 12-1-37-4.

Four batsmen completed 1,000 first-class runs: Inman,

Davison, Steele and Dudleston. Inman had by far the best average, 42.54, with 1,404 runs. Booth made 920 runs and Roger Tolchard 833.

Birkenshaw (89) and McKenzie (82) took most wickets, at 23 and 20 runs each respectively. John Steele held 32 catches as well as taking 43 wickets. He was the side's leading all-rounder.

John Christopher Balderstone was signed from Yorkshire, having made his debut for that county in 1961. A professional footballer with Huddersfield Town, Carlisle United, Doncaster Rovers and Queen of the South, his allegiance to the soccer field meant that he had been unavailable for Yorkshire at the start and end of each season and the Yorkshire Committee therefore had tended to give preference to other young players. Getting more opportunities after joining Leicestershire, his right-hand batting soon developed to the extent that, in 1976, he gained two England caps against West Indies, His slow left-arm bowling was also very useful. By the time he retired, in 1986, he had hit 17,627 runs for his adopted county, with 32 centuries, taken 271 wickets and held 185 catches.

The two other 1971 debutants were R. B. Matthews, a 6ft 4in fast bowler, and N. E. Briers. Matthews was already aged 27 and had played Minor Counties cricket for Oxfordshire since 1964. He played intermittently for Leicestershire for three seasons before deciding to concentrate on a career in engineering.

Nigel Briers, a pupil at Lutterworth Grammar School, played against Cambridge University and, aged 16 years, 104 days, was the youngest cricketer to represent the County. In 1972 he appeared against Oxford University, but owing to his studies it was not until 1976 that his career in county cricket commenced on a regular basis. In the meantime, however, he played representative schools cricket for three seasons and latterly captained the English Schools side. A talented right-hand batsman, he was initially found in the middle order, but in later years opened the batting. In 1990 he was appointed County captain.

Improvements to the ground and facilities in general at Grace Road had been progressing steadily and during 1971 the new entrance gates at the Milligan Road entrance were officially opened. The President of the County Club, Mr William Bentley MBE, defrayed the cost and the gates were named after him.

Mindful that McKenzie would probably be selected for the 1972 Australian tour of England, the County's search for a replacement ended with the signing of Ken Higgs. A fast bowler who hailed from Staffordshire, Higgs had made his debut for Lancashire in 1958 and had quickly become a force in county cricket – in 1960 he took 132 wickets at 19 runs each – and in 1965 had made his debut for England. At the age of 32, during the winter of 1969–70, Higgs had suddenly announced that he was leaving county cricket and joining Rishton in the Lancashire League. He took 91 wickets at nine runs apiece for his new club in 1970. He was equally successful in 1971 and several counties were trying to entice him back to the first-class game. Leicestershire succeeded. Having obtained Higgs' services it was slightly em-barrassing to discover in the spring of 1972 that the Australian selectors, much to the surprise of the press, had decided to do without McKenzie, chosing instead an unknown fast bowler, Jeff Hammond.

With Higgs, McKenzie, a rejuvenated Spencer, and Davison, the County had an ideal seam attack for limited-overs cricket, which now had its third competition with the creation of the Benson & Hedges Cup. The new competition was in two parts: the first being a league, with five teams in each of four groups. The two top teams in each group then met in the second part: a knock-out competition. Three days were allowed for each match, commencing on a Saturday, and to accommodate the revised programme, the County Championship was cut from 24 to 20 matches.

Australian Test fast bowler Graham McKenzie was a great success when Leicestershire imported him in 1969, taking wickets for seven seasons. (NCCC)

Illingworth continued as England's captain – he was destined to appear in only eight Championship games – but Roger Tolchard proved an able deputy and the County were in fine form right from the season's start. They took the Benson & Hedges Cup by storm, and headed the Sunday League for much of the year, only to end in second place, and they were among the front runners in the Championship until the final few matches.

The B&H campaign began at Northampton. McKenzie took four for 19 dismissing the home side for 120 and Tolchard gained the Gold Award as he hit an unbeaten 63 with victory won by seven wickets, nearly 15 overs not required. In the second match, at Coventry, Leicestershire batted first. Davison played one of the most remarkable innings of his career. His fifty came in 38 minutes, a hundred in 65 minutes and 150 in 92 minutes. The Rhodesian reached 158, at that time the highest individual score in any limited-overs county competition. Leicestershire's total was 327 for four. Warwickshire were thoroughly demoralised and Higgs picked up four wickets as they crashed to defeat by 184 runs.

In this sort of form it was clear that Leicestershire's next opponents, Cambridge University, would not cause too much trouble: Leicestershire won by eight wickets with nearly 20 overs not required. The fourth match in the B&H League section was played at Worcester. Dudleston and Norman opened with a stand of 73 and the Worcestershire bowlers were therefore happy to contain their opponents to a total of 202 for eight. The Leicestershire attack then bowled with an accuracy that made runs very difficult to amass. McKenzie's figures were 7-4-12-4, Illingworth's 11-5-20-2 and the others were not much more expensive. Victory was by 56 runs; Leicestershire were the only side in the competition to win four out of four matches.

The quarter-finals brought Lancashire, regarded at the time as the most expert one-day county, to Grace Road. One of the largest gatherings for some years, 7,000, came to urge Leicestershire to success. Lancashire could make little headway against McKenzie, Higgs and Spencer, and only 19 runs were on the board with 14 overs bowled. When they tried to force the pace, Illingworth took three quick wickets and the all-out total amounted to just 135. Dudleston, with plenty of overs in hand, took his time and when the winning run had been hit, he was 65 not out, batting about three hours. The victory came with five overs in hand; Dudleston gained the Gold Award.

Leicestershire were lucky to obtain a home draw in the semi-final. This time the crowd swelled to 10,000 and Warwickshire provided the opposition. The match largely followed the pattern of its predecessor as the visitors found run–scoring impossible, and were dismissed for 96, all the bowlers proving effective. When Leicestershire batted Dudleston and Norman put on 51 before being parted and the win, with 18 overs in hand, was by seven wickets. Illingworth gained the Gold Award for his captaincy as much as his bowling.

On 22 July, Leicestershire went to Lord's for the first Benson & Hedges Final, against Yorkshire. Sharpe won the toss and rather surprisingly in view of Leicestershire's record, decided to bat. As John Arlott noted at the time in *The Guardian*: 'Leicestershire brought a side especially chosen, equipped and directed to win over–limit matches and they won it by the most effective tactical methods yet devised to do so in the humid conditions.'

It was a match in the best dour traditions of Yorkshire with no quarter given and each run hard fought, but the Tykes had no answer to the parsimonious Leicestershire bowlers and the total reached only 136 for nine off the 55 overs. Norman, and latterly Balderstone, replied effectively bringing off the victory with five

Three years after a long and successful career with Lancashire and England, Ken Higgs returned to first-class cricket in 1972 with Leicestershire and over the next decade played 167 first-class matches with them. (Patrick Eagar)

221

BENSON & HEDGES CUP FINAL
LEICESTERSHIRE _v_ YORKSHIRE

Played at Lord's, 22 July 1972

LEICESTERSHIRE WON BY FIVE WICKETS

YORKSHIRE

*P. J. Sharpe	c Tolchard b Higgs	14
R. G. Lumb	b McKenzie	7
B. Leadbeater	run out	32
J. H. Hampshire	lbw b McKenzie	14
R. A. Hutton	c Spencer b Steele	8
J. D. Woodford	c Spencer b Illingworth	1
C. Johnson	b Higgs	20
C. M. Old	lbw b Illingworth	6
†D. L. Bairstow	c Tolchard b McKenzie	13
H. P. Cooper	not out	7
A. G. Nicholson	not out	4
Extras	lb 9, nb 1	10
Total	(9 wkts, 55 overs)	136

Fall: 1-17, 2-21, 3-60, 4-65, 5-77, 6-83, 7-113, 8-122, 9-124

BOWLING	O	M	R	W
McKenzie	11	2	22	3
Higgs	11	1	33	2
Spencer	7	2	11	0
Davison	11	2	22	0
Illingworth	10	3	21	2
Steele	5	1	17	1

LEICESTERSHIRE

B. Dudleston	c Bairstow b Nicholson	6
M. E. Norman	c Sharpe b Woodford	38
†R. W. Tolchard	c Bairstow b Cooper	3
B. F. Davison	b Cooper	17
J. C. Balderstone	not out	41
*R. Illingworth	c Bairstow b Hutton	5
P. R. Haywood	not out	21
J. F. Steele		
G. D. McKenzie		
C. T. Spencer		
K. Higgs		
Extras	b 2, lb 2, w 4, nb 1	9
Total	(5 wkts, 46.5 overs)	140

Fall: 1-16, 2-24, 3-58, 4-84, 5-97

BOWLING	O	M	R	W
Old	9.5	1	35	0
Nicholson	9	2	17	1
Hutton	11	1	24	1
Cooper	9	0	27	2
Woodford	8	1	28	1

Umpires: D. J. Constant and T. W. Spencer
*Captain; †Wicketkeeper

wickets in hand and 8.1 overs unbowled. Balderstone took the Gold Award amid much cheering and singing from the Leicestershire supporters.

The County's performance in the Sunday League proved that the B&H success was not because the toss and the weather combined to favour Leicestershire in seven matches.

A batting failure led to Derbyshire beating Leicestershire, with just three deliveries unbowled in the very first John Player game; there followed seven consecutive wins. The best were against Worcestershire at New Road, Gloucestershire at Bristol and Northants at home. Worcestershire were totally humiliated, dismissed for 84 in 28 overs, Illingworth's figures 6-2-5-4, before Norman and Dudleston hit off the runs without being parted in 25.4 overs. Gloucestershire suffered at the hands of Davison, 68 out of 88 in 16 overs; victory came by seven wickets. Davison's hitting, 63 in almost as many minutes, also won the game with Northants.

Leicestershire, at the halfway stage, were clear leaders at the top of the Sunday table. At the same time they were in third position in the Championship and their prospects seemed so bright that the press commented: 'With the Gillette Cup still to come, can Leicestershire pull off the Grand Slam of British cricket by winning not just their first, but all four major titles?'

On 9 July however they met defeat in the Sunday League, beaten by one wicket at the hands of Lancashire at Old Trafford. The Leicestershire bowlers even in this match fought a forlorn cause to the bitter end. Leicestershire, batting first, were all out for 90: Lancashire won in the final over with one wicket left!

McKenzie performed the hat-trick the following Sunday as Essex were crushed by six wickets and the following Sunday game, played the day after the B&H Final, saw 7,000 at Grace Road cheering their County to a ten-wicket win over Glamorgan, with Dudleston and Norman putting on 137 for the unbroken first wicket. Despite an upset against Hampshire, when the South African Barry Richards hit 105, the end of July saw Leicestershire still in first place. With four matches to play they were six points ahead of Middlesex and seven ahead of Yorkshire, but the latter had a game in hand. Kent then beat Leicestershire at Gillingham. Matthews was left with the unenviable task of hitting six off the last ball if Leicestershire were to win; he failed to connect. This result pushed Kent up into third place.

Leicestershire's last Sunday match was at Headingley on 27 August. If they won the title was theirs, even though Kent, now in second place, had a game in hand. Leicestershire were without

Illingworth, Norman and Spencer, all injured, but Yorkshire lacked Boycott and Hampshire, playing for England in limited-over internationals. Tolchard put Yorkshire in. Lumb and Lead-beater added 85 for the first wicket, but the rest floundered and Leicestershire needed 177. The score reached 108 for one, but the light then became poor; the vital wicket of Davison fell to Richard Hutton and eight runs were required off the final over. Birkenshaw and Higgs could manage five. The people of Leicestershire had then to wait for a fortnight to see if Kent could win their last match and take the title – they beat Worcestershire by five wickets.

The other limited-over competition, the Gillette Cup, had so often proved Leicestershire's Achilles' heel and so it was in 1972. They were beaten in their first match, by Warwickshire at Edgbaston, though it was a close thing. Leicestershire required five off the final over with two wickets left. McKenzie hit a single off the first ball, Spencer was caught off the second and last man Higgs perished off the fourth.

The County warmed up for the County Championship with three-day matches against each university before tackling Middlesex at Lord's. For the first university game, at Fenner's, Leicestershire fielded their best side, but in The Parks several young hopefuls were tried. G. A. Knew, the son of the 1939 professional, was aged 18 and a middle-order right-hand batsman. He was yet another product of Wyggeston School, but he decided against a cricketing career and played in only four matches in this and the following season. The Lutterworth Grammar School wicketkeeper, D. J. Harrop, replaced Tolchard behind the stumps for this game – he had been taken on the groundstaff as the Second Eleven 'keeper, but left at the end of the summer, and this match proved to be his only first-class appearance. T. K. Stretton, a medium-pace bowler from Cosby, was another new recruit to the staff in 1972. He was to remain at Grace Road for four years, but made only six first-class appearances in that time. The fourth debutant against Oxford was Peter Booth, a 19-year-old fast bowler from Shipley. He had played for the MCC Schools at Lord's for the two preceding years, opening the bowling against Combined Services. In August 1972 he was chosen for the England Young Cricketers tour to West Indies, but an injury meant he played only in the early matches. He was regarded as having great potential, but, though his county career spanned ten years, his total number of wickets amounted to only 162 at 28 runs each.

Having given this clutch of youngsters a trial, the side returned to full strength for the Middlesex game, which saw high scoring on the first two days – Haywood hit a maiden hundred for the County – then rain kept everyone indoors on the third day. The next two games were drawn, but Notts were beaten at Trent Bridge, when the seam attack of McKenzie, Higgs and Spencer dismissed the opposition for 143 and 137. The next game produced another victory; this time the spinners Illingworth and Birkenshaw made Gloucestershire squirm, Birkenshaw's second innings figures being 14.2-6-30-7. Rain ruined the match at Cardiff, but when Surrey came to Grace Road, even though the Saturday was washed out, Leicestershire won by six wickets. It was no contrivance, as the visitors were bowled out for 159 and 120. Curiously the best bowling in each innings was not produced by the five mentioned in the previous wins, but by Haywood and Dudleston, the latter's left-arm resulting in figures of 4.4-2-6-4 in the second innings.

These victories moved Leicestershire to the top of the Championship on 13 June. Rain thwarted Leicestershire in their next two encounters, though the second, against Notts at Grace Road was one of the most exciting of 1972. Notts were dismissed for 176; the home side replied with 143. Birkenshaw then took five for 34 to remove Notts for 110, leaving 144 to get in the final innings for victory. Barry Stead, the Notts left-arm seamer, made Leicestershire's batsmen struggle and six wickets were down for 71. Booth and Birkenshaw then held firm and added 34 for the seventh wicket. The latter was bowled by Taylor, but McKenzie helped to push the total to 120 for seven at tea – 24 required. At this point the rain came.

Leicestershire did not wait for the rain when they travelled to Bournemouth for the next Championship game: victory was achieved by nine wickets in two days, Illingworth and Birkenshaw doing the damage after the seamers, in each innings, had taken care of the cavalier Barry Richards. On 12 July, Leicestershire had dropped to third place, 13 points behind the leaders; a month later they remained third, but 19 points in arrears, having gained only one more victory, that being against Somerset at Taunton. In that game Dudleston and Norman hit centuries and Birkenshaw returned the best figures of his career, eight for 94. The County could achieve only one win in the final seven matches of the summer, one of the main reasons for this being the absence of Illingworth through an injury received in the fifth Test; Norman and Spencer were also unavailable for several of these matches.

So the County ended in sixth place, one below 1971, but they were beaten in only two Championship games and could be well satisfied with their season in the three-day game.

The reduction in matches meant that Steele and Dudleston were the only batsmen to reach 1,000 runs, but Tolchard was close with 979. Birkenshaw took 87 wickets at 21.49 runs each, McKenzie's 63 wickets cost 25 runs apiece and Higgs' 50 cost 26. The fact that not a Leicestershire name appeared in the top 30 in the batting averages and, apart from Spencer and Illingworth, both of whom took less than 20 Championship wickets, there were no Leicestershire men in the top 20 bowlers, showed that the County achieved their good record by team work. The ground fielding and catching was regarded as the best in the country and Illingworth got the best out of the younger players.

Two Leicestershire players were chosen for the 1972–73 tour to India and Pakistan, Roger Tolchard and Birkenshaw. The former acted as reserve to Alan Knott and thus had few opportunities, while Birkenshaw played in two Tests against India and one against Pakistan.

When the Leicestershire Secretary-Manager, Mike Turner, came to preview 1973 he listed 23 players on the staff – the County had moved from being one which employed least groundstaff to almost the largest employer. Peter Stringer retired to coach in South Africa, but Martin Schepens from Quorn was engaged for the first time.

After the heady days of 1972 however, the following season was a great disappointment. Leicestershire fell to ninth place in the Championship, fifth in the John Player League, and progressed only as far as the third round of the Gillette. In the Benson & Hedges Cup they barely qualified from the regional league and then were eliminated in the quarter-final. Given that the playing squad was identical to 1972's, what was the cause of the decline? One could point to the absence of Illingworth due to Test match duties, but in fact he played in the same number of Championship games in both seasons. Of the regular first eleven the one new face was Chris Balderstone – in 1972 he had played in three Championship matches, this time he played in every one and replaced Brian Booth, who languished in the Second Eleven.

A comparison of the averages gives a clue to the problem. The batting remained very similar to 1972, but all the bowlers found wickets more expensive: in the *Wisden* first-class table the best-placed Leicestershire bowler was McKenzie in 38th position.

The inability to dismiss the opposition twice meant that not a single victory came in the first eight Championship matches, and when success eventually arrived it was because Derbyshire declared and set a target of 298 in 5 hours and 20 minutes. A fine innings of 90 by John Steele resulted in victory off the first ball of the last possible over by just two wickets. The County had to wait until 30 July for the kind of result which had seemed so common 12 months before. Essex were beaten by an innings in two days at Chelmsford. McKenzie took six for 40, removing the opposition for 91, whilst the left-arm spin of John Steele did the damage in the second innings. Trent Bridge in mid-August was the venue for the third Championship win. Dudleston and Davison enjoyed themselves at the expense of the moderate Notts bowlers. The former hit 108 in under three hours, then Davison reached 105 at a run-a-minute. Leicestershire declared with 316 for six. McKenzie dismissed Notts for 143 and the follow-on was enforced. Leicestershire proceeded to win by eight wickets. The fourth and final Championship win was at Derby, when the home side set Leicestershire 259 in three hours. As in the first match between the two sides, Steele was the architect of victory and Leicestershire won again in the last possible over.

The Sunday League programme began full of promise with a win by nine wickets over Glamorgan, Ken Higgs having the remarkable figures of 8-3-17-6. Further wins over Warwickshire, by five wickets, and Derbyshire by eight wickets, meant that the County were among the leaders after five matches had been played. But three successive defeats sank their aspirations and though a total of eight victories was recorded, the County could command only fifth place and were 16 points behind Kent, the Champions.

The most impressive of the three wins which took the County to the top of their section in the B&H preliminary matches was at Northampton. Davison hit 74 in 79 minutes and with Dudleston added 107 for the third wicket after the Northants batsmen had fought a grim battle for runs against the seam of McKenzie, Higgs and Spencer. Meeting Essex at Ilford in the quarter-finals, Leicestershire batted too slowly at the start – 50 off 20 overs – so that the failure of Davison meant a total of only 177. Essex had no difficulty in reaching the target.

There was an exciting second round match in the Gillette Cup, when Leicestershire went to Taunton. Requiring 213 to win, Leicestershire lost both openers without either scoring a run. Balderstone virtually batted on his own, scoring 119 not out, and took his side to victory by two wickets. No other Leicester batsman reached 20, the best being number ten, Ken Higgs, who made 16 and assisted Balderstone in a ninth wicket stand of 48. In the third round, Leicestershire were required to make 203,

Worcestershire having batted first. This time it was Davison on his own – he made an undefeated 61, but ran out of partners before the target was attained. Gifford, the spin bowler, caused most problems and returned figures of 12-7-13-3.

Davison, Balderstone, Dudleston and Steele all topped 1,000 first-class runs, but as an opening pair Dudleston and Steele were unreliable and too often the side lost an early wicket. Roger Tolchard's batting improved after he handed over the vice-captaincy to Higgs. At Headingley, Tolchard caught the first six Yorkshire batsmen in the first innings, but in terms of wicketkeeping statistics he was well down the county table.

Aubrey Sharp died on 15 February 1973, when he was knocked down by a car in Belvoir Street, Leicester. He was still a Vice-President of the County Club and had served the Club on and off the field for a total of 65 years.

Martin Schepens was the only player to make his first-class debut during the season. A sound middle-order batsman from Barrow-on-Soar, he played in 19 matches spread over eight years, but with little success.

The most important development so far as Leicestershire were concerned as the 1973 English season drew to a close, was the England selectors' decision to dispense with the services of Illingworth. England under Illingworth had been beaten by the West Indies two matches to nil, with one drawn, in the second half of 1973. The disastrous match for England had been the third Test played at Lord's commencing 23 August – West Indies won by an innings and 226 runs – and the team to tour West Indies the following winter was announced during the last Test. Denness was appointed captain. Illingworth, explaining the Lord's defeat, commented: 'Playing that Test had been rather like fighting a battle with half the army wounded and the other half playing a kamikaze role.'

In County terms the sacking meant that Illingworth would be, in all probability, for the first time available for Leicestershire all season. The County had one representative in the 1973–74 West Indian squad – by coincidence Birkenshaw took Illingworth's place as off-spinner-cum-batsman. It will be remembered that Tony Greig was the star of the tour, being the only bowler to take more than ten Test wickets and his outstanding performance won the fifth Test and thus drew the rubber. Birkenshaw was an also-ran. He played in two Tests, but the bowling was too fast for him as a batsman, and his two wickets cost 48 runs each.

When the players reported to Grace Road for the start of 1974, there were two newcomers replacing two old faces. Brian Booth and Paul Haywood had left the staff. Norman McVicker and David Humphries had joined. McVicker was 33. A fast bowler, originally from Lancashire, he had played for Lincolnshire from 1963 to 1968 and in 1966 had taken 71 wickets for that county enabling them to take the Minor Counties Championship; he had been almost as successful in 1967 and 1968. Warwickshire had persuaded him to sign for them for the 1969 season and apart from 1970, he had been the leading seam bowler for the county – in 1972 he had played a major part in Warwickshire winning the Championship. Leicestershire had brought him in to replace Spencer, who was now available only on a part-time basis. David Humphries was another Minor Counties product, having played for Shropshire. He was a wicketkeeper. His opportunities were limited and he later found a place in the Worcestershire side.

The 1974 season saw the experiment of limiting the first innings of Championship matches to a maximum of 100 overs for each side. This had the required effect for Leicestershire at least: 14 of the 20 matches produced a definite result, double the 1973 total. Seven matches were won and seven lost – nearly all the margins of victory or defeat were large, which might indicate a variable performance.

Interest in the early weeks of the season centred on the Benson & Hedges Cup. Leicestershire won three out of four zonal matches. An easy win over Northants at Grace Road was due to Steele and Dudleston's opening stand of 102 in 25 overs; at New Road, Worcester, the following week, the batting collapsed, unable to cope with d'Oliveira and Gifford. Worcester won by 65 runs. It was essential to win the other two zonal games to get a place in the finals. Steele was the principal architect of the win over Warwickshire; he hit 59 and had bowling figures of 11-1-29-3. Victory was by 20 runs. The final match was even closer. Leicestershire made 235 for five. Middlesex, the opponents, lost early wickets, but coming in at number five Brearley batted brilliantly. Leicestershire just nosed in front when Middlesex, needing 11 off the last over, only made five. This victory meant that Worcestershire, Leicestershire and Warwickshire all had nine points, but the run rate enabled the first two to go through to the quarter-finals.

Leicestershire went to Canterbury. Batting first they made 238 for eight with a fast 98-run partnership in 18 overs between Dudleston and Davison the main contribution. Kent had a terrible start. With eleven overs bowled the total was 12 for three. Luckhurst and Julien fought back, and the latter went on to 111 and was out off the penultimate ball, when ten runs were required. Leicestershire won a great game by eight runs, but Luckhurst deservedly gained the Gold Award. Leicestershire now were drawn against Somerset at Grace Road in the semi-final. The home side had little difficulty making 270 for eight, with Steele 91 and Davison 73. Rain meant the match went into a second day and the wicket broke up, just suiting Illingworth. The captain returned figures of 11-2-20-5 as Somerset fell to 130 all out. The Somerset captain, Brian Close, complained about the state of the wicket, which had bare patches from the start, but had been well covered against the rain.

So to the Final at Lord's. Surrey won the toss and decided to bat, but Illingworth's tactics, both in field placings and bowling changes, seemed to unnerve the Surrey batsmen and they were dismissed for 170, with Higgs performing a hat-trick to remove any danger from the tail.

Arnold struck back dismissing Dudleston with the first ball of the Leicestershire innings. Steele and Norman dug in taking the score to 46. Then calamity: Norman and Tolchard were lbw, Steele was stupidly run out and worst of all, Davison fell into a trap and was caught. The score tumbled to 65 for five. A lame Illingworth struggled on, but defeat was inevitable as Arnold and Pocock bowled at their meanest.

All was not however gloom and doom at Grace Road. The day after the defeat at Lord's, the team went to Cardiff for the Sunday League game against Glamorgan. Dudleston hit 95 in 93 minutes; Davison stormed to 50 out of 81 in 59 minutes and Glamorgan were overwhelmed by 83 runs. This success meant that Leicestershire had played eleven Sunday matches and won ten; they were eight points clear at the top of the table. The following week saw another win when Balderstone hit a six off the last possible ball to beat Yorkshire by four wickets. Rain washed out the 13th match at Leyton, so Leicestershire were eight points ahead of both Kent and Somerset, but Kent had two games in hand and Somerset one. In the next set of matches, on 11 August, Kent lost, but both Leicestershire and Somerset won. Leicestershire had no problems getting the better of Middlesex, Davison hitting a brilliant 68 not out and the win being by seven wickets with four overs to spare. The 15th match was at Hove. A crowd of 7,000 turned out to see Birkenshaw and Norman scramble a second run off the last ball and tie the match: Sussex 213 for seven (M. J. J. Faber 86), Leicester 213 for four (R. W. Tolchard 78, M. E. J. C. Norman 53 not out). In the meantime Somerset had won their match. The gap was now six points, but Somerset had a game in hand. The western county came to Grace

Road for Leicestershire's final match in the competition. Somerset scored 162 for nine off 39 overs, the 40th not being bowled because the last batsman to come in took over three minutes and thus time ran out. This caused a minor uproar, but during tea, rain arrived and washed out the rest of the match. Each team received two points and Leicestershire collected the title. Somerset, in fact, won their remaining game and thus only two points separated first and second places.

In the other limited-overs competition, Leicestershire beat Northants in the second round of the Gillette Cup, Steele scoring 85 not out in a total of 182 for eight; Northants then crashed to 62 all out. In the third round the Leicestershire bowlers suffered as Kent hit 295 for eight, Luckhurst reaching 125. Davison lashed out, making 82 in as many minutes, but defeat was by 66 runs. Kent went on to take the title.

The Championship programme did not begin very promisingly. Surrey won the opening match by an innings. Arnold took nine wickets, including a hat-trick, and Younis Ahmed hit a hundred. Rain then prevented Leicestershire beating Derbyshire, and the third match of the campaign, at Cardiff, was lost by 37 runs. Leicestershire, batting last, required 291 and reached 227 for three, then inexplicably collapsed. The first win came at the expense of Gloucestershire at Grace Road. It was still relatively early in the season, but Hampshire, Worcestershire and Surrey were setting a brisk pace at the head of the table and though Leicestershire improved steadily and indeed ended in forth place, they never threatened Worcestershire and Hampshire; Surrey fell by the wayside. The Championship season did however end with a flourish at Lord's. Leicestershire met Middlesex on a relaid section of the square. The only individual score over fifty was Davison's swashbuckling 109. Leicestershire made 269 and 214; Middlesex 204 and in the final innings only 41. McKenzie and McVicker bowled unchanged taking four for 22 and six for 19 and at one time Middlesex were 10 for six. This was Leicestershire's first win at Lord's in the Championship. Umpires and captains reported the pitch as unsuitable for first-class cricket.

Davison, with 1,670 runs, average 46.38, and Dudleston with 1,337, average 37.13, were the leading batsmen of the season. Both hit four hundreds. Steele made 953 runs and Tolchard 728. Balderstone could play in only 14 first-class games owing to his footballing engagement with Carlisle United, and this weakened the side during August. Norman, on the other hand, was available only in the school holidays and took Balderstone's place, but he achieved little. Illingworth's record of 57 wickets at 17.78

placed him eighth in the first-class averages and McKenzie was not far behind with 71 wickets at 18 runs each. McVicker was the next most successful bowler and was a very useful hard-hitting batsman late in the innings.

Birkenshaw was given the Yorkshire Sunday League match for his benefit and by the end of the year received the record sum of £14,000. Another 'record' was the fact that H. D. Bird and D. J. Constant, both ex-Leicestershire players, umpired together in the Test at Old Trafford.

THE DOUBLE

ON MONDAY, 15 SEPTEMBER 1975 LEICESTERSHIRE were proclaimed County Champions. The welcome sounds of success that had been increasing in tempo during the decade had reached their crescendo. The Benson & Hedges title had been gathered in July and thus, for the first time, a county won both the Championship and a limited-overs title in the same season.

It had been a long, sometimes frustrating, haul for all those, both players and administrators, who had kept county cricket alive in Leicestershire since the tentative beginnings in 1879 when Messrs Miles and Freer launched the club on its course. A course which proved to be strewn with obstacles, both financial and otherwise.

Before a description of the season's events, a recap on the players that achieved the 'double' reveals the team's strengths.

Raymond Illingworth, the captain, was now aged 42, generally batted at number five and normally did not bring himself on to bowl until second or third change. The County's opening batsmen were Brian Dudleston, in his 30th year; he had been capped in 1969, and 1970 had been his best season to date. Partnering Dudleston was John Steele, a year younger. Chris Balderstone occupied the first wicket down position. Having joined Leicestershire in 1971 after ten years with Yorkshire, he was capped by his adopted county in 1973. His slow left-arm spin was confined largely to first-class matches. Brian Davison came in at number four and was the dynamic personality of the side and the batsman most likely to change the course of a match in his side's favour. His fielding was brilliant. His medium-pace bowling was not frequently used, or indeed required. The wicketkeeper, Roger Tolchard, normally followed Illingworth, though sometimes he went in earlier. Aged 28, he was now in his 10th season as a capped player. He was to score 1,000 runs for the first time in 1975, but generally made about 900, his average being boosted by 'not outs'.

Jack Birkenshaw, now 34, had been playing for the County since 1961 and, discounting Spencer, was the senior capped player. He had never made 1,000 runs in a season, but had come very close and was a most useful player to be batting at number seven. His off-breaks as a rule came on directly after the opening seamers had completed their stint, but this was in three-day matches. He was not often picked for limited-overs games. The pace attack consisted of McVicker, McKenzie and Higgs. The first was in only his second season with the County; the Australian Test bowler was coming to the end of his career, now being in his mid-30s.

Those were the ten players who were the regulars of the 1975 side. There was keen competition for the 11th spot, not least by a young batsman, David Gower, about whom more later. The footballer, Cross, was still appearing when available; Jeff Tolchard appeared in eight Championship games; Norman was seen occasionally, and the first reserve as a seam bowler was Peter Booth. On the sidelines was the 21-year-old Rhodesian, Paddy Clift. He made his first-class debut for the County against the Australians, but was not available for Championship games.

The World Cup was inaugurated in 1975, and played in England during 14 days in mid-June, and the events leading up to this as well as the competition itself, which was played in perfect weather before large crowds, tended to dominate cricket and the cricketing press.

The first month of the County Championship was, for Leicestershire, rather mundane, except for their game at Chelmsford and that was extraordinary for the wrong reasons.

Leicestershire in 1975. The Benson & Hedges cup semi-final against Hampshire. The County Championship followed triumph in the B & H. Left to right, back: B. Dudleston, J. Steele, C. Balderstone, G. Cross, P. Booth, B. Davison, N. McVicker, J. Tolchard. Front: J. Birkenshaw, R. Tolchard, C. Palmer, R. Illingworth (Captain), F. M. Turner, K. Higgs, G. McKenzie. (Patrick Eagar)

The star of the Chelmsford match came from the opposition. Keith Boyce, the West Indian, came in at number five in the Essex first innings and proceeded to hit a century in 58 minutes. He scored eight sixes and seven fours, Illingworth and Balderstone being the bowlers to suffer. Essex made exactly 300. Boyce then opened the Essex attack and returned figures of 13.1-6-25-6, as Leicestershire were dismissed for 60. The first seven wickets went down for 20, but Illingworth managed 33 and saved total disgrace. The follow-on was enforced, Balderstone compiled a very determined 101 and Leicestershire managed to bat out time – rain having reduced the playing hours. Boyce had time to pick up another six wickets, making a total of twelve for 73 in the match.

The Leicestershire Championship season had begun the previous week at Bristol on a plumb wicket. Gloucestershire reached 303 and maximum batting points for the loss of three batsmen; Leicestershire did the same, but lost six men in the process, with Steele making 103. The Gloucestershire second innings produced another run glut and such was the state of the pitch that Brown, the home captain, did not dare declare until Leicestershire faced a target of 283 in 200 minutes. Davison hit 49 in an hour, but wickets fell and the game was drawn.

The first Championship home game produced a third draw. Sussex came to Grace Road. Neither side came to terms with the bowling, so after 100 overs, Leicestershire had pottered to 264. Sussex made 288. Time was again lost through rain and eventually Sussex were set 174 in 130 minutes. Birkenshaw bemused the visitors and when stumps were drawn the total was 64 for seven; Birkenshaw took five for 20.

The fourth Championship game produced the first win. Leicestershire batted and found the Pakistani, Sarfraz, in top form. Four wickets fell for 16; Tolchard then joined Illingworth in a stand of 90 in as many minutes. The captain was run out, but Birkenshaw arrived to keep the runs coming and both he and Tolchard completed hundreds, so that full batting bonus points were achieved. The Northants batting did not flourish and a good first innings lead allowed Illingworth to declare Leicestershire's second innings closed. The home side went on to victory by 143 runs.

Rain seriously affected Leicestershire's trip to Bradford and there was only just time to complete a first innings on each side. After five matches the County languished in tenth place in the Championship table. Hampshire were galloping ahead, having four wins from their five contests.

In between times the league section of the Benson & Hedges

Cup had been played. Leicestershire had little difficulty in beating Northants in their first match, the margin being five wickets and almost five overs. Davison gained the Man of the Match award for his robust innings of 76. The Combined Universities gave little trouble in the second game; this time Balderstone was the top scorer and Man of the Match. At Edgbaston, Leicestershire had to bat first; no one managed a decent score and the total was only 148 for nine off the 55 overs. It was a hopeless cause to defend, but the task took Warwickshire 51.3 overs. Warwickshire had won all four matches in the zone. To be certain of going through to the quarter-finals, Leicestershire had to win their last match, at Worcester. Worcestershire had been the great side of 1974, but only twelve months later the team seemed to be falling apart and there was trouble behind the scenes. This spilled onto the field. Worcestershire made 198 for eight, McKenzie being the best bowler. Dudleston went early when Leicestershire batted, then Steele and Balderstone took the total to 111. Steele was out, and disaster followed when Davison fell for a single. Illingworth came in and without further alarms the match was won.

Against Lancashire in the quarter-finals at home on 4 June, Illingworth won the toss and put the opposition in. The Leicestershire bowlers kept control – the only blemish was when Hayes was dropped early on, and went on to hit 67. Leicestershire had a target of 180 to beat. Dudleston, Steele, and Balderstone all went without making a worthwhile contribution. Davison struck out briefly, but the seventh wicket was down with 49 still needed. Tolchard and McVicker added a crucial 38 for the eighth wicket and the former took his team to victory with nine deliveries and two wickets to spare. He gained the Man of the Match award.

The Championship game which followed the Benson & Hedges quarter-final produced another draw for Leicestershire, again high scoring with maximum batting points to both sides. Balderstone hit 103 in Leicestershire's 331 for eight; Rodney Cass and Yardley each hit hundreds in Worcestershire's 322 for two. The runs continued in the second innings, when this time Davison was the centurion. His innings had an unfortunate end when he was struck in the face by a ball from Brain and retired hurt. In the final innings Worcestershire were set 361 in 255 minutes. At last the batting monopoly was broken and they fought their way to a draw against some good spin bowling.

The other three Championship games in June turned Leicestershire into serious title contenders. All three ended in wins and, almost as important, the County picked up 22 out of a possible 24 bonus points. This sent the County hurtling up the table and as the early front runners, Hampshire, were without their West Indian stars, Roberts and Greenidge, who were involved in the World Cup, the Hampshire bandwagon shuddered to a temporary halt. Leicestershire moved into fifth place and were only 14 points behind the joint leaders, Essex and Lancashire. All the top clubs had played nine matches.

Somerset came to Grace Road on 18 June. Dudleston hit his first hundred of the summer; Davison, recovered from his blow in the face, made a quick 81 and the total was 316 for five when the 100th over was complete. Leicestershire required 74.1 overs to dismiss Somerset, Higgs taking advantage of a rough patch on a length and picking up six wickets. This gave Leicestershire a lead of 119 and with the pitch continuing to assist the bowlers, Illingworth was able to declare and set a target in excess of 300. It took the bowlers 110 overs to take all ten wickets.

A crippled Barry Richards made a brilliant hundred, aided by a runner, when Hampshire came to Grace Road. This meant that after the first innings were complete the match was even, only 16 runs separating the teams. On the final day Illingworth set Hampshire 248 in 260 minutes. With the injured Richards unable to open, the visiting batsmen failed to get any impetus behind the run rate; the score however was 137 for four when the final 20 overs began. It looked increasingly like a stalemate until Balderstone broke through, picked up five for 15 off nine overs, and Leicestershire won with three balls to go.

A third consecutive Championship match was played at Grace Road, Glamorgan being the opposition. The Welsh county were in the midst of a very erratic summer, during which they seemed to perform brilliantly one day then disintegrate the next. They selected Leicester for one of their more inept efforts, managing to be nearly 200 runs in arrears on first innings. Dudleston and Steele put together the second highest opening partnership in Leicestershire's history, their 335 being exceeded only by Wood and Whitehead's 380 in 1906. Glamorgan just managed to avoid an innings defeat.

This victory put the side in the right mood for the following day, which had been allocated to the Benson & Hedges semi-finals. Drawn at home against Hampshire, Leicestershire made a confident start by dismissing Barry Richards for 2. However Gordon Greenidge had returned from the World Cup and was not overawed by the bowling. He hit 111 and the score was 216 all out. Andy Roberts countered by removing Dudleston for 2; it was Balderstone's turn to bring success. He reached his hundred in the penultimate over and victory came off the last ball of the final over from Roberts – the margin five wickets. So Leicestershire secured a place in the final.

Having had so many home matches, Leicestershire now travelled to The Oval for their Championship game with Surrey. Surrey had had a poor start to the summer, but two wins late in June had restored the team's faith in itself and this remarkable match was to bring them into possible contention for the title.

The first innings, in which Surrey made 259, was nothing out of the common. Leicestershire were initially put into disarray by Geoff Arnold, then Intikhab and Pocock mopped up the tail. The total was 68; Arnold five for 17. Following on, Dudleston and Steele added 85 before being parted and with a sensible innings from the captain, 283 runs were amassed. Still Surrey required less than a hundred to win. McKenzie had Butcher and Howarth out before a run was on the board. Illingworth accomplished the first hat-trick of his long career and the total slumped to 65 for nine. Pocock the last man joined Intikhab and the pair somehow managed the 28 required, giving Surrey a win by one wicket.

There was similar embarrassment for the Leicestershire bowlers in the next game. This time everything went right, until

Raymond Illingworth, having come straight from the pitch where he was batting when victory was won, holding up the Benson & Hedges Cup at Lord's in 1975. (Patrick Eagar)

the fall of Essex's eighth wicket in their second innings. Smith, the wicketkeeper and John Lever joined forces and the pair added 96 in 50 minutes. Fortunately the deficit was so great that when the stand was broken, Leicestershire still won by 130 runs. The Championship was developing into one of the most open races of all time – at the halfway stage only a handful of points separated the top seven counties.

Leicestershire broke off their campaign in order to go to Lord's, meeting Middlesex in the Benson & Hedges final. The morning skies were damp with drizzle and Lord's was only three-quarters full. Brearley, captain of the home side, decided to bat first, but his team failed to respond, apart from an excellent 83 from Mike Smith out of 146 all out; McVicker took four for 20. Leicestershire were rather slow in their reply and Steele in particular found runs difficult to acquire. Tolchard and Illingworth were together with the total 121 for five and soon put matters to right. Victory was by five wickets. McVicker was Man of the Match.

Capturing the Benson & Hedges title kept the enthusiasm going in the very tight battle for the Championship. The game at Coventry was not for the faint-hearted. Rohan Kanhai was at his best with an innings of 178 not out and Warwickshire, batting first, made 334 for nine. The best that can be said of the Leicestershire reply was that the follow-on was avoided, only Davison with 68 coming out with much credit. Warwickshire hit out in their second innings and then set Leicestershire 311 in 300 minutes. Four wickets went for 107. Davison and Tolchard put on 80, but three more wickets went for the addition of 40 and it seemed as if Tolchard would be left stranded. McVicker, however, made an invaluable 35 and the last wicket of Tolchard and Higgs added 37 to gain victory, no less than 18 coming off the penultimate over, leaving two required from the last six balls.

There was some high scoring when the Australians came to Grace Road. Davison reached the best of his career, 189, and McCosker hit 120 for the tourists. On the final day the Australians were asked to get 275 in 280 minutes. Illingworth and Balderstone exploited the wicket, which now took spin, and the County won by 31 runs.

High-scoring draws, against Lancashire at Blackpool and Derbyshire at Grace Road seemed to reduce Leicestershire's chances of the Championship, but these were the prelude to an astonishing run of success which left the other contenders gasping for breath. In brief summary, Notts were beaten twice, by an innings and then by eight wickets, Northants lost by nine wickets, Kent by 18 runs, Middlesex by eight wickets and Derbyshire by 135

BENSON & HEDGES CUP FINAL
LEICESTERSHIRE *v* MIDDLESEX

Played at Lord's, 19 July 1975

LEICESTERSHIRE WON BY FIVE WICKETS

MIDDLESEX

M. J. Smith	c Tolchard b Booth	83
P. H. Edmonds	c Illingworth b McVicker	11
C. T. Radley	c Higgs b McVicker	7
*J. M. Brearley	c Davison b McVicker	2
N. G. Featherstone	c Tolchard b McVicker	11
H. A. Gomes	b Higgs	3
G. D. Barlow	b Illingworth	7
†J. T. Murray	c Cross b Steele	1
F. J. Titmus	run out	0
M. W. W. Selvey	c Tolchard b Booth	6
J. S. E. Price	not out	2
Extras	lb 10, nb 3	13
Total	(52.4 overs)	146

Fall: 1-26, 2-37, 3-43, 4-87, 5-99, 6-110, 7-117, 8-119, 9-141

BOWLING	O	M	R	W
McKenzie	7	2	20	0
Higgs	10	3	18	1
McVicker	11	3	20	4
Booth	8.4	1	25	2
Cross	2	0	9	0
Illingworth	9	1	31	1
Steele	5	0	10	1

LEICESTERSHIRE

B. Dudleston	run out	17
J. F. Steele	c Selvey b Titmus	49
J. C. Balderstone	run out	12
B. F. Davison	c Murray b Gomes	0
†R. W. Tolchard	not out	47
G. F. Cross	lbw b Titmus	0
*R. Illingworth	not out	13
N. M. McVicker		
P. Booth		
G. D. McKenzie		
K. Higgs		
Extras	b 3, lb 9	12
Total	(5 wkts, 51.2 overs)	150

Fall: 1-32, 2-67, 3-67, 4-118, 5-121

BOWLING	O	M	R	W
Price	9	3	26	0
Selvey	9.2	2	33	0
Titmus	11	2	30	2
Gomes	11	4	22	1
Edmonds	11	2	27	0

Umpires: W. L. Budd and A. E. Fagg
*Captain; †Wicketkeeper

runs – six wins in the final six matches, and in the majority full bonus points were secured.

The first of these wins came against Notts at Grace Road, when the northern neighbours were annihilated. Balderstone, 168 not out, and Davison, 184, added 305 for the third wicket and the 100 overs produced 427 for three. Northants kept up with Leicestershire in a low-scoring game, until the final innings when Leicestershire hit off the 154 for victory losing only Gower in the process. An unbeaten 125 by Dudleston in the return fixture with Notts sealed that County's fate a second time.

The match at Tunbridge Wells was not so clear cut. A comfortable lead was gained on first innings, but Leicestershire then faced Jarvis, who was making the ball lift and turn. At the start of the last day, Kent required 113 with seven wickets in hand. They moved cautiously to 160 for four. Illingworth found a spot and the last six wickets went for 23 – victory by 18 runs.

With two matches to play Middlesex visited Grace Road. McVicker took six for 85, dismissing the visitors for 260. A century from Dudleston provided a lead of 54; Illingworth and Balderstone kept the batsmen in two minds, the captain ending with figures of 17.4-5-23-4, and Leicestershire needed 126 in the final innings with plenty of time in hand. Victory was by eight wickets.

With one match to play Leicestershire had 224 points, Yorkshire 207 and Surrey 198, but directly behind those three were Hampshire, 197, and Lancashire, 195, both these counties having an extra match to play. These extra matches were to be played commencing 10 September, whilst Leicestershire had to wait until 13 September for their last game.

The result was that Lancashire picked up 18 points by beating Gloucestershire, but Hampshire failed to beat Derbyshire, though they acquired 8 bonus points. Lancashire now had 213 points, still 11 behind Leicestershire, but if Leicestershire failed utterly in the final match, Lancashire could take the title. Yorkshire could reach the top only if they gained full points and the Leicestershire match was effectively washed out, so Yorkshire chances were practically non-existent.

Leicestershire's final match was at Queen's Park, Chesterfield. Leicestershire batted first and against Ward and Hendrick found life exceedingly difficult. The total crept to 77 for six. The tail attempted a recovery and eventually 226 was reached with two valuable batting points. Over at Eastbourne, where Lancashire were playing their last match with Sussex, the Lancastrians dismissed Sussex for 160 and thus picked up four bowling bonus points. On the second day at Chesterfield, Leicestershire dismissed the opposition for 211, so another valuable four points were picked up; at Hove, Lancashire could score only 222, so gaining two bonus points instead of four. This gave Leicestershire the title.

Leicestershire duly went on to beat Derbyshire by a very convincing margin – 135 runs – Balderstone's all-round cricket doing most towards the success. He hit 116 and took three for 28. His appearance also had the curiosity angle that on the second evening he left Chesterfield to play soccer for Doncaster Rovers. It was perhaps the first time a player has played Championship cricket and League football on the same day.

At Hove the rain came and prevented Lancashire beating Sussex, so the final table left Yorkshire in second place and Hampshire third while Lancashire had to be satisfied with fourth position.

The City and County Councils of Leicester gave a civic reception to the team in recognition of their Championship success and the players later went to Buckingham Palace to receive the trophy from Prince Charles, acting on behalf of the Duke of Edinburgh. The only sad note on a season of great triumph was that the Club's profit for the year was only £388.

Only one player made his Championship debut during the summer, but that cricketer was to become, in the opinion of many, the most talented English batsman of his generation. David Gower, an 18-year-old, had captained King's School, Canterbury, in 1974 and topped their batting averages. He played for Leicestershire in the Second Eleven competition that year – he was qualified for the County having resided there since 1964 when his father took up a post at Loughborough College. In 1975 he played in three Championship and six Sunday League games, earning the joint description with Clift, in *Wisden's* review of 1975, of 'an exciting prospect'. However, he received no mention in a two-page article on Leicestershire's great season, published in *The Cricketer* in November 1975. In 1978 he began his long Test career which was to bring him virtually every honour in the game, from the England captaincy downwards. He has been a typical amateur batsman in the mould of R. H. Spooner, but unfortunately in an era that lumps all county cricketers into one class.

The other debutant of 1975 was Paddy Clift, who, as pointed out earlier, could appear only in 'friendly' first-class matches. Clift gained a regular first team place in 1976. He had come to the County due to the recommendation of Davison, his fellow countryman. A hard-hitting batsman and accurate medium-pace bowler he was an ideal man for limited-overs cricket.

The statistics of the season were impressive; 19 centuries were scored in first-class matches, five each by Dudleston and Balderstone, three each by Davison and Steele, two by Tolchard and one by Birkenshaw. Davison topped the batting with 1,498 runs, average 53.50; Dudleston, Steele and Balderstone all exceeded the thousand. Illingworth was only three runs short, averaging 45, and Tolchard made 973. The bowling was very much a team effort. Illingworth took 51 wickets at just under 21 runs each, Higgs was next with 50, McVicker took 46, Birkenshaw 44, Balderstone 43, Steele 34 and McKenzie 32.

The Second Eleven, not to be outdone, finished in second place in their Championship and were unbeaten in 14 matches, while the Under-25 Competition was won for the first time.

When the season finished, 'Garth' McKenzie and Michael Norman announced their retirement from county cricket. McKenzie decided to return to Australia and Norman wished to concentrate on his teaching career. Norman received over £10,000 from his benefit year.

Prospects for the 1976 season looked bright. As well as McKenzie and Norman, Jeff Tolchard announced his retirement, but this made little difference to the balance of the team, especially as Clift would now be available and Peter Booth had obtained leave from his teaching post and could be selected for all matches.

The season did not, however, open with success. The principal reason seems to have been the unexpected failure of the opening batsmen. John Steele was retained to open the batting all summer, but his highest Championship innings was only 60 and that was made at the end of August. One reason for the retention of Steele was the problems at the other end. Dudleston broke his finger several times and was fit to play in only eight Championship games. His first injury occurred early in May and Clift, Cross, Briers and Gower were among those promoted to partner Steele, with varied results.

It was hoped that Booth would prove an adequate replacement for McKenzie. He played in virtually every match, but was only occasionally effective.

The first half of the Championship programme – 10 matches – resulted in two wins, against Warwickshire at Grace Road and against Derbyshire at Chesterfield. The Warwickshire game was one of great fluctuation. Rain made inroads on the first day and Illingworth declared with 251 for five. Higgs bowled Warwickshire out for 158, but Leicestershire were at sea against Rouse in their second innings, being all out for 84; Dudleston, suffering his second broken digit of the summer, came in at the end and made 6 not out. Warwickshire required 178 in the final innings, but McVicker exploited the helpful pitch and took four for 21, helping Leicestershire to win by 50 runs. At Chesterfield, Derbyshire were in disarray, not due to the expertise of the Leicestershire cricketers, but due to one of their captaincy crises, Bob Taylor resigning the post immediately the match ended. Higgs, as in the Warwickshire game, caused the opposition most trouble and Derbyshire managed 129 and 138, the match ending Leicestershire's favour before lunch on the third day.

At the mid-point of the Championship season therefore, Leicestershire the reigning Champions, were ninth in the table, a considerable distance from Middlesex and Northants in first and second places.

In the middle of July, Illingworth regrouped his forces and fortune began to smile once more. Seven out of the next eight matches ended in victory. The first was a crushing defeat of Notts at Trent Bridge. Everyone managed to take runs off the Notts attack, 324 for eight being made off 100 overs. Notts then capitulated for 73, with Illingworth returning the unusual figures of 13.2-9-5-4. The follow-on was enforced and victory obtained by an innings and 82 runs. Middlesex suffered a similar trouncing at Lord's, McVicker taking nine for 40 in the match as the London side were all out for 114 and 99. The match, won by 301 runs, was also notable for David Gower's first first-class hundred. He and Davison, who made 124 not out, added 236 in an unbroken third wicket stand. The third victory in succession was not so easy; Zaheer Abbas hit a brilliant 177 in under four hours for Gloucestershire and Leicestershire were nearly 100 runs in arrears on first innings – and that deficit would have been much greater had not Birkenshaw and Clift added 92 for the eighth wicket. Birkenshaw then bowled in tandem with Illingworth to remove Gloucestershire cheaply in their second innings, which left Leicestershire needing 226 in four hours. Unfortunately for Gloucestershire, Mike Procter lost control of line and length, giving Tolchard and Birkenshaw some easy runs, and victory was by four wickets, with Birkenshaw undefeated with 74 – it was a splendid match for him.

Following a drawn game with Worcestershire, Sussex were beaten at Eastbourne in a match which belonged to Balderstone. He hit 52 and 41 out of the Leicestershire totals of 246 for nine and 194 for seven, took four for 49 in the first Sussex innings and ended the match with a hat-trick, dismissing Snow, Cheatle and Spencer with successive deliveries, his second innings figures being 5.2-2-18-4.

This victory created an interesting situation at the top of the table, for though Middlesex kept a clear lead, Hampshire, Essex, Northants, Leicestershire and Gloucestershire were all within a few points of each other behind the leaders.

There was another Leicestershire hat-trick in the match which followed the Eastbourne game. This time Clift dismissed three principal Yorkshire batsmen, Hampshire, Squires and Lumb. Yorkshire were all out for 85, but the wily Illingworth did not enforce the follow-on, determined to let his former colleagues suffer. Davison hit a century in three hours and was 112 not out when Illingworth declared, leaving Yorkshire needing 380 to win. Leicestershire's victory was by 152 runs. Leicestershire had little difficulty beating a lacklustre Hampshire at Bournemouth and Kent were brushed aside at Grace Road.

With two matches to play, Leicestershire were now in second place. They now had to play Northants, who were in third place, whilst the leaders, Middlesex, played Worcestershire. It was August Bank Holiday. The rain poured down. Middlesex picked up one point, in a match where there was only half a day's play. Leicestershire managed slightly more play and received three points, while Northants obtained two.

The outcome was therefore that Middlesex had 217 points, Leicestershire 202 and Northants 200. All had one match to play. Unless the weather treated Middlesex shabbily they were bound to take the title. The fixtures in fact meant that Middlesex played their final match a week before Leicestershire and Northants were due to play theirs. Middlesex won and thus took the title. The following week Leicestershire were beaten by Somerset, when the batting collapsed in the final innings after Close set Leicestershire a difficult target. Northants beat Yorkshire and Gloucestershire beat Worcestershire, so Leicestershire had to be content with fourth place.

The battle for the Sunday League ended with some complicated mathematics. Kent, Essex, Leicestershire, Somerset and Sussex all ended with 40 points, all having ten wins. Before the final round of matches Somerset and Sussex had 40 points, the other three 36, and by a twist of fate the two front runners both lost, whilst the other three all won. Kent and Essex however had more away wins than their rivals and thus the run rate between these two counties decided the title. Kent took the title. Essex then argued they should be entitled to second place, but the rules stated that the run rate and away wins stipulation applied only to the title. Essex thus shared second place with Sussex, Somerset and Leicestershire.

In fact Leicestershire for much of the summer were not considered to be in the running for the John Player title at all – then five wins in the last six matches meant they were involved to the end.

Leicestershire lost their only match in the 1976 Gillette Cup, a three-run defeat at home against Hampshire, despite 101 from Birkenshaw, which earned him the Man of the Match award. Leicester went out in the quarter-finals of the Benson & Hedges Cup, losing to Worcestershire by six wickets.

Davison was the outstanding batsman of the season, scoring six centuries, and his season's work amounted to 1,818 runs at the magnificent average of 56.81 – only Zaheer, Boycott and Amiss had better records. Balderstone had now given up football to concentrate on his late-flowering cricket career. For Leicestershire he scored 1,334 runs at an average of 37.06, in addition to his hat-trick against Sussex. His perseverance was rewarded by selection for England in the fourth and fifth Tests. Batting at number four he made 35 and 4 on his debut, but recorded a pair in the final Test. He was not chosen again, but he gave Leicestershire staunch service for another ten seasons.

Steele had a wretched summer, only 114 against the West Indians redeeming his indifferent figures. Clift topped the bowling with 74 wickets, average 20.17, and deservedly was awarded his cap. Higgs took 55 wickets. McVicker had another cheerful season, then announced his retirement. Illingworth was not bowling so much, but his wickets were still cheap and he scored some valuable runs; his captaincy was as alert as ever.

The excellent weather and the positive, successful cricket brought in the crowds and as a result the profit on the season of £12,556 was the largest yet made by Leicestershire.

The County's only representative on the winter Test tour was Roger Tolchard, who went as reserve wicketkeeper, but played in four Tests as a batsman. His first Test innings, at Calcutta, was a dogged 67. He did not play in the Centenary Test in Melbourne and in fact never appeared for England in England.

With McVicker gone, Leicestershire were looking for a replacement and found two – Alan Ward the Derbyshire and England fast bowler had been released by his county at the end of 1976 and he and Ken Shuttleworth, another England fast bowler, but from Lancashire, were both engaged.

Alan Ward was 29. He had been hailed as England's white hope in 1969, but his career had been dogged by injury, though in 1976 he had been reinstated in the England side for the Headingley Test after a break of five years.

Shuttleworth was three years older than Ward. His debut for

Lancashire had been in 1964 and to date he had taken 524 first-class wickets at 24 runs each. Ward had taken 423 at 22 runs each.

In addition to McVicker, Schepens and the reserve wicketkeeper, Humphries, left Grace Road at the close of 1976; Humphries moved to Worcestershire where he became the regular first team 'keeper.

Season 1977 was the first in which the County Championship was sponsored, Schweppes being the company involved. The number of Championship matches was increased to 22 and the points for a win increased to 12. The headlines almost throughout the season were swallowed up by the Packer Circus, but no Leicestershire player was immediately involved in this revolution.

The Championship season began with rain. All three days of Leicestershire's match against Yorkshire at Headingley were affected, and what play there was, was all in Yorkshire's favour. In the second match the County seemed to be doing better, having made 137 for five in reply to Worcestershire's 182, but rain washed out both the second and third days. Shuttleworth made his Leicestershire Championship debut in the third match and marked the occasion, not only with a hat-trick, but also the County's first victory. Shuttleworth took five for 38 in Surrey's second innings, their score tumbling from 60 for one to 71 for nine. Leicester won by eight wickets.

Leicestershire had even at this early stage suffered their first injury, in what was to be an injury-prone summer. Tolchard broke a finger. He recovered but later sprained an ankle and in all missed six Championship games. Dudleston replaced Tolchard behind the wicket and performed very effectively, but three weeks later, in another washed-out game, this time at Old Trafford, a nasty delivery from Croft broke Dudleston's arm, putting him out for several weeks.

After ten Championship matches Leicestershire still had just the Surrey victory to balance against two losses and seven draws. They were languishing in 13th place in the table.

The John Player League at the same date showed a complete contrast, with the County in first place, with seven wins out of eight games. One of the successes of the Sunday game was David Gower, who whilst batting in the middle order in first-class cricket opened the innings on Sundays. The Benson & Hedges record was three losses and one win, which put Leicestershire bottom of their group and out of the competition. The single win was at Taunton where Illingworth returned figures of 10-4-13-4 and Davison hit a sparkling 88 out of 127.

Gower had one day of glory in the Championship and that occurred in the eleventh game, which provided the County with a second win. Gower made an unbeaten 144 of which 96 came in boundaries. The opponents were Hampshire and victory was by six wickets. It seemed to mark a change in Leicestershire's fortunes in the three-day matches, and further wins against Glamorgan, Middlesex, Derbyshire and in the final match, Notts, pushed the County into fifth place, a fall of only one position compared with 1976 and in the circumstances quite creditable.

In the Sunday League two losses were suffered in the second half of the summer and this allowed Essex to catch up. In fact prior to the matches played on 28 August, Essex were four points in the lead. Leicestershire met, and crushed, Warwickshire on this day, Gower making a splendid 135 not out in a total of 226 for one; Warwickshire were dismissed for 119. On the same day Essex fell to Yorkshire and this placed Essex and Leicestershire level on points with one game to play. Glamorgan came to Grace Road for this vital match; Essex were at home to Worcestershire. Glamorgan batted first and were unable to score runs – they made a paltry 117 all out; Leicestershire strolled to victory. Essex had a sterner fight but still won by 34 runs. The title therefore had to be decided on most wins, since each team had 52 points, and Leicestershire won the trophy with 13 wins, against Essex's 12.

For once Leicestershire made some appreciable headway in the Gillette Cup. Hertfordshire were beaten in the first round, Gower making a century, and Essex were beaten at Southend in the second round, Davison scoring 99 and Steele taking five for 19. In the third round Northants were beaten, Davison scoring 80. Leicestershire met Glamorgan in the semi-finals, but this time the batting failed and the Welsh county had few problems scoring the 173 needed to win.

Apart from the injuries to Dudleston and Tolchard, the County also lacked Clift for several matches and their new acquisitions, Ward and Shuttleworth, had strains which kept them off the field at times. McVicker was persuaded to return and played a valuable part in several Sunday games. Jeff Tolchard also played in six Championship games, having not played a single one in 1976.

Balderstone topped the batting table and was the only player to top 1,000 Championship runs, though in all matches Davison also reached the target. In comparison with 1976 Davison had a modest return. Steele, after his poor batting in 1976 returned to his best, though his bowling was not so effective.

The bowling was a story of collective efficiency. Eight players took more than 20 Championship wickets, but the most was exactly 50 by Birkenshaw, who took 59, average 25.69, in all first-class games. Higgs performed the hat-trick against Hampshire at Grace Road and in all had 38 victims at 26 runs each.

Aside from Shuttleworth and Ward, a third fast bowler made his County debut during the summer, Les Taylor from Earl Shilton. His only first-class games in 1977 were against Oxford University and the Australians, but he also appeared in four Sunday League matches. It was not long, however, before he was regarded as one of the most promising fast bowlers in England and in 1981 he took 75 first-class wickets. The winter of 1981–82 saw him decide to tour South Africa with the English 'rebel' side and it was not therefore until 1985 that he finally gained an England cap.

In December 1977 came the announcement that Yorkshire had signed Illingworth as team manager starting in April 1979, Illingworth having a three-year contract. His contract with Leicestershire was due to finish at the close of the 1978 season, but there had been some idea that he might stay on at Grace Road. The announcement of the signing of the contract with Yorkshire made the break definite, and thus 1978 was to be Illingworth's last summer with Leicestershire.

During Illingworth's captaincy, Leicestershire had won the County Championship once, the John Player League twice and the Benson & Hedges Cup twice. No other major honours had been secured in the entire history of the Club. It was therefore disappointing that the County were unable to capture any trophy in Illingworth's final summer. The captain himself, now 46, was not the formidable all-rounder he had been and his achievements in terms of runs and wickets in 1978 were modest. The most exciting player in the side was David Gower, but, unfortunately for the County, the England selectors thought highly of him and he played in all six 1978 Tests and all four limited-over internationals. He won abundant praise for his batting in both categories and scored maiden hundreds in both. It meant that he turned out in only nine Championship games and also missed many Sunday League fixtures. On the positive side, Davison was back at his best and was clearly the County's most reliable batsman. He hit four of the County's eleven first-class hundreds and was seventh in the overall first-class averages with 1,644 runs, average 51.37. The wicketkeeper, Tolchard, came second in the Leicestershire batting table, though he had 16 not outs to boost his average. Steele began the season well, hitting three hundreds by mid-June and was averaging well over fifty on 1 July, but his final record

JACK BIRKENSHAW

Starting his career in first-class cricket as a 17-year-old with Yorkshire in 1958, Jack Birkenshaw moved to Leicestershire for the 1961 season and remained with the County for 20 years. A stubborn left-hand batsman, he never gave up and his was a very difficult wicket to obtain. As an off-break bowler he turned the ball quite considerably, but also made the best use of a deceptive flight. He was capped by Leicestershire in 1965 and was one of the best all-rounders in the country. All five of his England caps were gained overseas – on the 1972–73 tour to India and Pakistan and the following winter in West Indies. The arrival of Illingworth at Grace Road in 1969 rather pushed him into the background, since clearly the captain was the principal off-spinner, and his best season as a bowler remained 1967 when he took 111 wickets at 21.41 runs each.

After leaving Grace Road in 1980, he spent one season with Worcestershire then in 1982 joined the first-class umpires list.

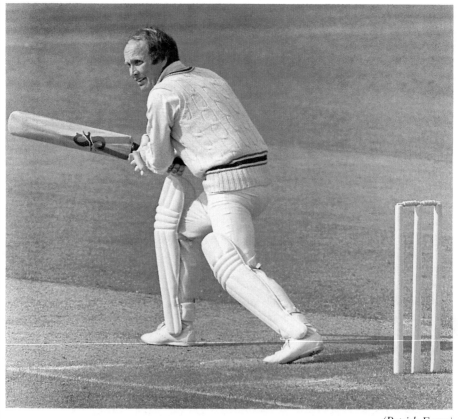

(Patrick Eagar)

was 1,182 runs, average 38.12. The rest of the batting was distinctly patchy, Dudleston in particular having a poor summer. Higgs returned the best bowling figures and his colleagues all performed adequately.

Up to 11 July, Leicestershire were in the race for the Championship, having won three matches, against Gloucestershire at home, and Hampshire and Derbyshire away, but then came three successive defeats at the hands of Middlesex, Somerset and Kent. A draw followed against Sussex, but immediately afterwards Kent again won. By now Leicestershire were over 100 points behind the leaders and in fact won only one more game, so had no interest in the destination of the title.

In the Sunday League, Leicestershire stayed with the leaders, spending much of the summer in fifth or sixth place. The County then won their last five matches and this great burst pushed them level on points with both Hampshire and Somerset at the top of the table. All three sides had won a total of eleven matches each and all three had an identical 'away win' record, so the title depended on run rate and went to Hampshire, whose rate had been the best throughout the year.

In the Benson & Hedges Cup, the County did not get into the knock-out section and though they beat Hampshire in their first Gillette Cup game, they were beaten by Essex in the following round, when rain reduced the 'game' to a 10-over slog. Essex hit 73 and Leicestershire 70.

Taylor, the powerfully built ex-miner, made a definite impact in both three-day and one-day matches during the season, and three new bowlers also appeared. Jon Agnew, an 18-year-old right-arm fast bowler from Uppingham School played in four matches. Very tall and slim he started as a tearaway fast bowler, but achieved greater success when later reducing pace to concentrate on accuracy and movement. Perhaps he would have achieved greater success at Test level had selection come later – in 1987 or 1988, rather than in 1984 and 1985. Being strangely ignored by the England selectors in those years when he was enjoying most success – 101 wickets in 1987 and 93 in 1988 – caused disillusionment, and he retired after the 1990 season to write for a national newspaper.

Gordon Parsons, another right-arm pace bowler and a useful left-hand batsman, took a while to achieve any marked success, but in 1984 when he scored 853 runs and took 67 wickets, he looked as though he had blossomed into a genuine all-rounder. Following a poor season in 1985, he was not retained and moved to Warwickshire. He returned to Leicestershire in 1989. From

1983 to 1989, he spent his winters playing in the Currie Cup Competition.

The third young bowler was the slow left-arm spinner, Nicholas Cook. Born in Leicester, Cook gained a regular first-team place in 1980 and in 1983 was capped by England, taking five for 35 and three for 90 on his debut (*v* New Zealand at Lord's). He left the Grace Road Staff at the end of the 1985 season and joined Northants.

The departure of Illingworth left the County therefore with four of the most promising young players in England: Gower, aged 21; Taylor, aged 24; Agnew, aged 18; and Cook, aged 22. The immediate future had a distinctly rosy glow.

A NEW ERA

THE COUNTY CLUB CELEBRATED ITS centenary year in 1978 and the Appeal Fund which had been launched to coincide with the anniversary had been exceedingly successful, raising £200,000. In addition the Club had had a surplus on its annual accounts for the tenth successive year and the winter of 1978–79 was spent in a large renovation and rebuilding programme for the Grace Road ground. Two-thirds of the pavilion was demolished and a new pavilion suite created which contained dining room, members' room, indoor cricket school and sponsors' boxes. More permanent seating was planned and the total cost of the work was in the region of £250,000.

The captain of the 1979 side was Ken Higgs and the playing staff under him lacked only Illingworth of the regular 1978 first team players – Ward had also gone, but he had played in just one Championship game in 1978. Gower had spent the winter with the England team in Australia and topped the Test tour batting, though it should be noted that Australia lacked their Packer players. Tolchard had also gone out on tour, but injured a cheekbone when batting at Newcastle and flew home early. He recovered in time for the start of the English season, but far more serious was the injury which Agnew suffered. He went to Australia under the Whitbread sponsorship scheme, then played for the England Under-19 side which toured Australia. During the tour Agnew developed back trouble and came home early in order to consult specialists. As it turned out his back problem prevented him playing nearly all summer.

Rain was the dominant factor of the first month of the summer. All six of Leicestershire's opening first-class matches were drawn. The first two at Grace Road, against New Zealand and Hampshire, were abandoned without a ball being bowled. There followed two successive defeats at the hands of Kent, by eight wickets, and Essex by 99 runs. Not until 26 June did Leicestershire win a Championship game and that was largely due to an innings of 85 by Tolchard, for which he batted four and a half hours. The victory, over Notts, was by three wickets. Excellent bowling by Taylor provided a much more convincing win at Maidstone in July, when the margin was an innings and the game was over in two days. The two other Championship wins were against Glamorgan, also by an innings, and Essex, when Cook took six for 57 and Steele hit an unbeaten hundred. The competition that year was a one-horse affair, Essex being proclaimed Champions with several matches still to play, so that Leicestershire's win over Essex right at the end of the summer had no bearing on the destination of the title.

The County fared poorly in the limited-overs competitions. In the Gillette Cup, the opening match against Devon at Grace Road was marked up as one of cricket's curiosities. Roger Tolchard was Leicestershire's wicketkeeper and his brother Jeff kept wicket for Devon, whilst Ray, another brother, also played for Devon. Leicestershire won the game by nine wickets. In the second round, Dudleston hit a century before lunch off the Worcestershire attack and the Leicestershire total reached 326 for six. Worcestershire never appeared to challenge the target and the margin of victory was 143 runs. In the quarter-finals, Leicestershire went to Northampton and though Dudleston made a fine 59, he received very little support. Northants went on to win by eight wickets.

A single win in the group matches of the Benson & Hedges Cup meant that Leicestershire progressed no further. The Sunday League was marred in its early stages by rain, no play taking place in three out of the first five Leicestershire games. The County's results in the other matches were variable and at no time did they challenge for the title.

Briers was promoted to open the batting with Steele and scored two centuries, but his batting was inconsistent and he was dropped down the order, then left out of the team altogether for several games. Balderstone, Steele, Dudleston and Davison all reached 1,000 runs; the first two had the best averages, but the Rhodesian had a moderate summer and failed to hit a single hundred. Clift hit 741 runs at an average of 30 as well as taking 50 wickets and was the side's principal all-rounder. Birkenshaw missed half the season due to injury and Gower was also often absent due to England selection.

Higgs and Taylor usually opened the bowling and both had good years. Cook, the left-arm spinner, was given plenty of opportunity and took six wickets in an innings in each of the final two home games and ended with 32 championship wickets at 25 runs each.

There was a perplexing headline in December for Leicestershire supporters when it was announced that the County had signed Mike Garnham, the Gloucestershire wicketkeeper, whose reason for moving was that he was unable to command a regular first team place in the Gloucestershire side. What therefore was the position of Roger Tolchard? In the event, Tolchard

Barry Dudleston was a valuable opening or middle-order batsman for the County throughout their successful run in the 1970s. (Patrick Eagar)

retained his position and Garnham languished in the Second Eleven.

Garnham, though only 19, was much travelled, having been born in Johannesburg and educated at Melbourne and Perth in Australia. He had then moved to Barnstaple in Devon and whilst there had toured India with ESCA. He had made his Gloucestershire debut in 1978 and was now studying at East Anglia University. He continued his wanderings; remaining with Leicestershire to 1985, he played for Cambridgeshire in the following three years and then in 1989 became the regular 'keeper for Essex.

The major change for 1980 was the appointment of Brian Davison to succeed Higgs as captain – Higgs played three matches early in the season and then officially retired from first-class cricket to become coach and Second Eleven captain. He did, in fact, play one match in 1982 and two more in 1986, but a long, distinguished career, which began as far back as 1958, was

Brian Davison, the aggressive Rhodesian batsman, played for Leicestershire throughout the 1970s and captained the side in 1980. (Patrick Eagar)

ostensibly finished. His career record contained 1,536 wickets, he scored 3,648 runs and his safe hands secured 311 catches.

The rain that had fallen so abundantly in May 1979 continued in 1980 and only one Saturday at Grace Road during the whole season was not affected by rain. In these circumstances it was surprising and creditable that there was a financial surplus at the end – albeit only £806.

Including three outside the Championship, of the first 19 first-class Leicestershire games, three were lost and the rest drawn. Leicestershire finally won a match on 8 August and moved to 15th place in the table. The win, over Middlesex, was so convincing that it is even more surprising that it was the first one, especially as it was also Middlesex's first defeat. Cook took five for 17 to bowl Middlesex out in their second innings for 164 and Tolchard hit a century in Leicestershire's 351 – the margin was an innings and 100 runs. The match was over in two days.

The next game, against Kent at Grace Road, was drawn, the rain washing out the first two days. Somerset were then beaten at Taunton by 157 runs; Clift and Cook being the successful bowlers. Cook also excelled with the bat, being sent in at number three as nightwatchman and reaching his highest score of 75, with a six and ten fours.

Northants came to Grace Road to be defeated by three wickets in a high-scoring match of three declarations. Larkins and Williams shared a second-wicket stand of 322 for the opposition. Leicestershire in the fourth innings were set 382 in 330 minutes and won with nine balls to spare. In the final match of the season, Leicestershire managed another win, beating Hampshire, the wooden-spoonists, by an innings and 34 runs in two days. So 81 of Leicestershire's 157 Championship points came in the final six matches and they moved from the basement to a respectable ninth place.

Three wins in the first four matches gave Leicestershire a good start in the Sunday League, but they then faltered and were only in mid-table at the half-way stage. The second part of the summer provided five more wins and on 10 August it appeared as if Leicestershire might take the title, being then four points behind the leaders with a game in hand. Warwickshire at this time were in front and the crucial game was the meeting of the two counties at Grace Road on 31 August. Warwickshire won by six wickets with two overs to spare and as Leicestershire also lost their final match, they had to settle for fourth place. Leicestershire's season in the Gillette Cup was brief, as they lost their only match to Essex. They also failed to qualify for the Benson & Hedges knock-out section,

ROGER WILLIAM TOLCHARD

One of the select band of wicketkeepers to obtain more than 1,000 dismissals and score over 10,000 first-class runs, Roger Tolchard gained his Leicestershire County cap at the age of 20, having previously played for his native Devon whilst still a schoolboy. His opportunities to represent England were very limited owing to the presence of Alan Knott and Bob Taylor. He went to India with the 1976–77 England touring side and won a place in the Test team as a batsman, demonstrating what grit and determination can do. Knott was the wicketkeeper on this tour. In 1978–79 Tolchard travelled as Bob Taylor's understudy on the visit to Australia. He batted brilliantly when everyone else failed in the match against Western Australia, which followed immediately after the first Test. Almost certainly Tolchard would have, as in India, secured a place in the Test team purely as a batsman for the last two Tests, but he was hit in the face by the ball and broke his cheek bone. This injury ended his tour and Bairstow was sent as a replacement. His Test career thus extended to only four matches on the 1976–77 tour. He captained Leicestershire for his last three years on the staff at Grace Road, leaving at the close of the 1983 season. Two of his brothers also played for Devon and brother Jeff appeared for Leicestershire between 1970 and 1977.

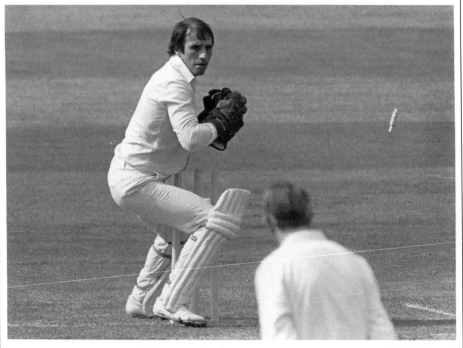

(Patrick Eagar)

although Gower did score an undefeated 114 against Derbyshire.

Gower at last played an almost full season for Leicestershire. West Indies were touring England, and Gower failed to make much impression in the two limited-overs internationals and then made only 20 and 1 in the first Test. The selectors dropped him. The press made a great mountain out of this, but it certainly assisted Leicestershire's cause. Gower reached 1,000 runs for the County for the first time, but he was inconsistent, a criticism that could be levelled at all the batsmen, save Balderstone and Davison.

Balderstone had his most prolific season to date, finishing with 1,472 runs at an average of 43. Davison recovered the form which had eluded him in 1979. Steele just missed 1,000 runs, but did good work with the ball, his 40 wickets costing a mere 17.60 runs each. Most progress was made by Nick Cook, his left-arm spin being responsible for 75 wickets, the most in a Leicestershire season for eight years. The three other young bowlers, Agnew, Parsons and Taylor, turned in some good performances, but remained in the 'promising' category. Clift was second to Steele in the bowling averages and was a very useful man to have batting at number seven.

Two of the senior members of the playing staff, Birkenshaw and Dudleston, were unable to retain a regular place in the first team and at the end of the summer both left Grace Road. Birkenshaw moved to Worcestershire for 1981. He later became a first-class umpire, then joined Somerset as cricket manager and in 1991 returned to Grace Road again as coach. Dudleston went to Gloucestershire, then, like Birkenshaw, joined the first-class umpires' list. Two others to move on were Shuttleworth and Schepens. Shuttleworth took part in three Leicestershire first-class games in 1980, Schepens in just one.

Four young hopefuls made their first-class debuts for the County during 1980. R. A. Cobb and D. A. Wenlock were home-grown products from Leicester itself. Cobb, a batsman from Trent College, had toured overseas with England Young Cricketers in 1979 and 1980. Wenlock was a medium-pace bowler from Lutterworth Grammar School. Ian Butcher, brother of the Surrey cricketer, had appeared in two Sunday League matches for Leicestershire the previous year. Boon, from Doncaster, had played for Yorkshire Second Eleven in 1978 and 1979 and had captained England Young Cricketers in West Indies in 1980. A right-hand batsman he appeared in eight first-class games in 1980 and made a maiden fifty against Northants at Grace Road.

In December the Cricket Society's award for the 'Young

John Steele, an opening right-hand batsman and left-arm slow bowler, was a regular during the good years of the 1970s, moving on to Glamorgan in 1983. (Patrick Eagar)

Cricketer of the Year' went to Boon. In the same month Leicestershire signed the 19-year-old all-rounder, Grant Forster, who had come from Durham, but had had extensive trials with Northants and played one first-class game for that county.

One major disappointment for the County Club was the change of heart at the TCCB. Grace Road had been allocated one of the 1981 limited-overs internationals with Australia, but opponents of the innovation prevailed on the TCCB to alter its mind and the match was moved to Edgbaston. Leicestershire sought compensation and received £6,000.

Another innovation, however, was not thwarted. The Club organised a tour of Zimbabwe in March 1981. Zimbabwe had broken away from the South African Cricket Union in May 1980 and had applied for Associate Membership of the ICC; they gained admission in July 1981.

Davison and Clift were not available for the tour and Gower was with England in the West Indies. Roger Tolchard captained the County and two 'guest' players were included, John

Hampshire of Yorkshire and David Steele, who had moved to Derbyshire in 1979. All three first-class matches against Zimbabwe were drawn, the last being particularly exciting. With the scores level Leicestershire had two wickets remaining prior to the final ball being bowled. Cook, attempting a single off this delivery, was run out. John Hampshire scored 112, the only century of the tour, in this innings.

The major change for 1981 in the Leicestershire side was that Davison stepped down as captain and was replaced by Roger Tolchard. Davison had now qualified as an 'England' player by residence and the County could therefore sign a new overseas cricketer. The man chosen was Andy Roberts. The 30-year-old West Indian fast bowler had found himself dropped from the Test side in the middle of the series against England, his place being taken by Malcolm Marshall. Roberts, who came from Antigua, played for the Leeward Islands and had been engaged with Hampshire from 1973 to 1978. In 1980 he had toured England with the West Indies side and in 1981 had signed for Haslingden in the Lancashire League. His appearances for Leicestershire were thus going to be limited. The press criticised Leicestershire for engaging Roberts, pointing out that the County had three promising fast bowlers in Agnew, Taylor and Parsons and one of them would have to step down to allow Roberts to play. In reply Mike Turner stated that the know-how and experience of Roberts would be a great assistance to Leicestershire's young bowlers.

The first weeks of the Championship season were very disappointing. On 3 July, with a third of the matches played, Leicestershire languished at the foot of the table and had yet to record a win. They were handicapped after a few matches when Clift was injured and on 13 June Tolchard broke a bone whilst batting against Glamorgan. Gower began in splendid form, hitting three centuries. He then disappeared into the England side, playing in three limited-overs internationals and five Tests.

In the Sunday League, Leicestershire fared almost as badly, having won only two games at the halfway stage and being in tenth position. The one bright spot was the Benson & Hedges Cup, where two wins secured the County a place in the knockout section. In the quarter-finals they met Sussex at Hove. Balderstone captained the side in the absence of the injured Tolchard and it was the deputy captain who won the match with an innings of 67. The semi-final was at The Oval. Surrey made 191 for nine off their 55 overs. Leicestershire with the last two batsmen at the wicket required four with two deliveries left. Higgs and Parsons had already added 23 for the last wicket, but on the penultimate delivery the former was run out and Surrey went through to the final. Both of Leicestershire's matches in the Gillette Cup were rain-affected. In the first they took revenge on Surrey in a game limited to ten overs; in the second Northants required 21 runs off nine remaining overs at the end of the first day, bad light ending play early. No play was possible on the two other days allocated to the match and Northants were awarded a place in the semi-finals on faster scoring rate.

Returning to the Championship, Leicestershire had a change of fortune in the later matches. The first Championship win came at Coventry on 17 July, when Boon hit 83 and John Steele 64 in the Leicestershire total of 357 for nine declared. Warwickshire were bowled out for 136 and 160, Parsons, Taylor and Steele all having good returns. The first home win coincided with the first match away from Grace Road since 1966. Leicestershire played Notts on Hinckley Town's new ground some two miles from the town centre on the Leicester Road. Balderstone, Steele and Davison hit hundreds, the first two adding 206 in their opening stand. Notts were 231 behind on first innings, but fought back and Leicestershire's victory was by four wickets. Randall was involved in a controversial decision. He was adjudged run out when backing up, the bowler removing the bails, but Tolchard asked him to continue his innings.

The following match, at Grace Road against Sussex, provided much excitement. Leicestershire set Sussex 264 at five an over and the visitors were dismissed four runs short, when Cook bowled Arnold with the last possible ball.

Derbyshire, Lancashire and Northants were Leicestershire's other wins late in the season and this revival pushed the County to eighth place – one better than in 1980.

Gower, though playing in only 13 Championship games, hit 1,000 runs for the County and easily topped the table. Briers came second and his elegant batting brought favourable comments. Davison and Balderstone also topped 1,000. Cobb was promoted to open the batting with Balderstone in August and was very promising. Garnham stood in for Tolchard behind the stumps and continued to occupy that post even after Tolchard returned. Garnham was also very useful with the bat.

Taylor was easily the most impressive of the bowlers. He took 75 wickets at 21 runs each, which placed him tenth among those bowlers who captured 50 or more wickets during the season. Roberts played in 11 matches and took 37 wickets. Both Agnew and Parsons took wickets at 32 runs each and Cook was much more expensive than in the previous summer.

For the 13th consecutive year the Club made a profit – £15,200 – and further extensions were built at Grace Road during the winter months. The pavilion was added to, with offices on the ground floor and a balconied executive suite for the use of sponsors on the first.

Gower went with England to India in the winter of 1981–82 and, for once, batted consistently, averaging 46 in the six Tests, even though his highest score was 85. As soon as the tour ended, several England players re-formed to tour South Africa. Gower was not among them, but Les Taylor, who was already in the republic, was chosen as one of the squad and topped the bowling averages. The TCCB response to the tour was to ban all the players from selection for England for three years.

The only major player not to arrive for the 1982 season was Peter Booth. He was now in the shadow of the younger fast bowlers and had played in only five first-class games in 1981.

The press hailed the appointment of David Gower as the County's vice-captain as the 'most significant development' in the early season team reports; the thought of him leading England was no doubt uppermost in the journalists' minds.

The early season Championship results were favourable for Leicestershire. A victory in the first home match, when Surrey set Leicestershire 288 in 175 minutes and Davison responded with 111 in 120 minutes, was immediately followed by an innings win over Glamorgan at Sophia Gardens. Leicestershire made 327, then Roberts took five for 27 in dismissing the Welsh county for 134. Tolchard enforced the follow-on, Taylor took four for 31 and the game was all over by lunch on the third day. On 4 June therefore, the County was second in the table two points behind leaders Middlesex. There followed four drawn matches, plus another two against Cambridge University and Zimbabwe, then the first defeat at the hands of Derbyshire – the match was badly affected by rain and the result came after another run chase on the last afternoon. Leicestershire were slipping down the table, and the match on 7 July against Middlesex, still in the lead, was vital to any hopes the County had. Put in to bat, Leicestershire lost two wickets for nine runs. Davison then joined Balderstone. In 40 minutes the Rhodesian reached 50 and when he was out in the over before lunch he had reached exactly 100. Balderstone went on to 148 and the total was 399. Cook found that the wicket encouraged spin on the second day and he dismissed Middlesex for 160, taking six for 32. Tolchard enforced the follow-on; Middlesex put up a more determined front, but Leicestershire won by six wickets. It was the metropolitan county's first defeat.

Les Taylor's fast bowling won him a Test place after he had ruled himself out for a while through touring South Africa in 1981–2. He was a fine opening bowler for the County. (Patrick Eagar)

However, they still led the table while Leicestershire were in seventh place, 42 points behind.

After the success over Middlesex, which took place at Uxbridge, Leicestershire's next game was at another occasional county ground – Snibston Colliery. In fact it was the first time since 1966 that the County had played a home Championship game at that venue and it was not been used since. The reason for the unusual surroundings was that Grace Road staged the final of

Chris Balderstone was an all-rounder who left Yorkshire for Leicestershire and gave the County great service in the 1970s and 1980s, once playing cricket and then soccer for Doncaster Rovers on the same day. (Patrick Eagar)

the ICC Trophy on the same date. The visitors were Derbyshire and they repeated the defeat inflicted only a fortnight previously. Geoff Miller proved the decisive figure in the game, his spin bowling taking twelve for 138, while in contrast the spin of Cook seemed innocuous – his figures were one for 115.

The fortunes of Leicestershire then took a dramatic upturn. In brief the results from mid-July were:

July 17, 19, 20: beat Sussex at Hove by 13 runs

July 24, 26, 27: beat Essex at Grace Road by 25 runs

July 31, Aug 2: beat Gloucestershire at Grace Road by an innings and 45 runs

August 7, 9, 10: drew with Worcestershire at Worcester

August 11, 12: beat Nottinghamshire at Grace Road by ten wickets

August 14, 16, 17: drew with Lancashire at Grace Road

August 21, 23, 24: beat Somerset at Taunton by 160 runs

August 25, 26, 27: beat Essex at Colchester by six wickets

August 28, 30, 31: drew with Northants at Northampton

September 1, 2, 3: beat Glamorgan at Grace Road by an innings and 58 runs

These seven wickets pushed Leicestershire past all their rivals save Middlesex, and they were only two points behind when both counties had two matches to play. The first four of the above wins were all due to the bowlers in relatively low-scoring matches. Cook was particularly effective against Sussex with seven for 81 and against Essex with six for 51. The Gloucestershire game was a triumph for Taylor with five for 24 and three for 9, whilst Roberts took nine wickets in the Notts game at Grace Road. Cook dismissed Somerset cheaply at Taunton and Gower hit 111. In the Colchester game Balderstone played a lone, splendid innings of 114, carrying out his bat in a stay of six and a half hours. Cook picked up 12 wickets and then Davison reached three figures in the fourth innings. Davison hit another hundred against Glamorgan, as did Balderstone, but the man of the match was Roberts, whose figures were 14 for 94.

The stage was now set for an exciting last week of county cricket. Leicestershire's matches were both away from home – at Trent Bridge and Canterbury. Middlesex played Hampshire at Lord's and Worcestershire away.

On the first day at Trent Bridge, Leicestershire struggled. Notts reached 355 for seven off 100 overs and went on to 400 all out. Things went from bad to worse on the second day when Kevin Cooper made the ball swing and none of the Leicestershire batsmen, apart from Balderstone, who made 42, survived for long. The follow-on was enforced and the second innings was a repeat of the first, save that the spin of Hemmings and Bore did the damage. The match was over before tea on the third day, a defeat by an innings and 105 runs. Down at Lord's the spin of Edmonds dealt with Hampshire. Middlesex picked up 22 points against Leicestershire's three. The gap had widened to 21 points.

The only hope for Leicestershire now was heavy rain at Worcester (the venue of the final Middlesex game) and full points for Leicester at Canterbury. Unfortunately on the first day Middlesex bowled out Worcestershire for 168, picked up four bowling bonus points and clinched the title. As it happened whatever Middlesex did was of no consequence because Leicestershire were beaten by Kent. The one redeeming feature of the game was another century by Davison, his seventh of the summer which equalled the Leicestershire record.

Davison was the outstanding batsman of the year with 1,800 runs, average 54.55 and stood ninth in the first-class averages with only three England-qualified batsmen above him. He must have been close to selection for the 1982 Tests against the Indians and Pakistanis. As it was Gower was the County's sole representative at Test level, playing in all six Tests and four limited-overs internationals. Nick Cook was chosen for the England B side which opposed Pakistan at Grace Road in August, but the weather was dreadful and no one turned up to watch; Cook took three for 66.

Gower came second to Davison in the Leicestershire batting list, but played in only nine Championship games. Balderstone and Briers had very good summers and both topped 1,000 runs. Steele failed quite dramatically and his opening spot with Balderstone was taken over by Cobb, who batted soundly without making any big scores. The four main bowlers, Roberts, Steele, Taylor and Cook all had good returns, with Cook capturing most victims – 87 at 23.30. Roberts was still involved in League cricket and not available for all matches. Clift was very unfortunate. He damaged his Achilles' tendon and could play in only five matches.

Turning to the limited-overs competitions, Leicestershire won eight Sunday League matches, finishing fifth in the table. The relative success was due to the batting of Gower who scored 669 runs in nine innings and had he been available for all matches he would probably have beaten Clive Rice's 814 aggregate record for a Sunday League season.

In the Benson & Hedges Cup, there were red faces when Leicestershire were dismissed for 56 by the Minor Counties team and lost the match by 131 runs. This was, and still remains, the

Paddy Clift was a Rhodesian all-rounder who joined Leicestershire in 1975 and played his part in the successes for over a decade, including the 1985 Benson & Hedges Cup win. (Patrick Eagar)

lowest all-out score in the history of the competition. It must be said however that the pitch at Wellington had deteriorated badly following rain and had already been reported to the TCCB by the umpires before Leicestershire ventured on to it.

Leicestershire did win the other three matches in their group to gain a place in the knock-out section. They met Nottinghamshire at Trent Bridge in the quarter-finals and needed four off the last ball to win – only two runs came.

The NatWest Trophy first round saw Norfolk play at Grace Road and an easy win for the home side, but the second round brought defeat at Taunton, Garner having bowling figures of 12-7-23-4, though Gower batted at his best for 60.

Leicestershire had one representative on the England tour of Australia and New Zealand during the 1982–83 winter. A single line in the report of the tour says it all: 'In Gower England had the outstanding batsman of the Australian season. His elegant style, powered by fine timing, was much admired.'

The main addition to the playing staff for 1983 was George Ferris, an 18-year-old fast bowler from Antigua. His experience of first-class cricket was limited to two games for Leeward Islands in 1982–83, though he had bowled with great success for his native island in the Leeward Islands Tournament of June 1982, taking 20 wickets at 10 runs each. The following month he had come to England with the West Indies Young Cricketers and it was his bowling on this tour that brought him to the attention of the County. It was anticipated that he would replace Roberts, who would be absent for some matches due to the World Cup.

Leicestershire's summer got off to a bad start, even before it had begun! Les Taylor collided with Parsons whilst exercising in the gym and broke his right elbow – Taylor missed several early matches as a result. At the halfway stage in the Championship, Middlesex and Essex were well ahead of the field, but Leicestershire with three wins were still in contention in fifth place. The fact that the County's first win was a convincing victory over Essex demonstrated that Leicestershire had the ability to beat the best sides. The success was very much a team effort both in terms of batting and bowling. The second win coincided with Ferris's Championship debut. His figures in the first innings were 17.5-8-29-5 and Derbyshire, at Derby, were all out for 79 in reply to Leicestershire's 251 for nine declared. Ferris took three more wickets in the second innings and Derbyshire lost by an innings. In the following match another 18-year-old made his mark. Ian Butcher in his first Championship game at Grace Road opened the Leicestershire batting and hit 103 out of a total of 246 for nine declared. In the second innings he saved the County from defeat, being 76 not out when the match ended with Leicestershire on 161 for nine, still requiring 138 to win.

The third victory, over Glamorgan at Hinckley, was a second triumph for Ferris, his first innings analysis being 21-5-42-7 as Glamorgan were dismissed for 109, just avoiding the follow-on.

July provided the County with three more Championship wins – at Harrogate against Yorkshire, due to the bowling of Clift and

Ferris; at Hereford against Worcestershire, when Balderstone carried his bat through the first innings and made 63 in the second; and at Grace Road, with Roberts destroying Sussex.

The beginning of August provided Taylor with splendid figures, 11 for 102, against Notts, which brought victory by 50 runs. Leicestershire were now third and pressing Middlesex and Essex closely. The County went to Chelmsford for a crucial match. Batting first, Leicestershire made 301, of which Davison contributed 106. Ferris completely overwhelmed Essex, who were dismissed for 129, the Antiguan taking six for 43. Tolchard enforced the follow-on, but could not shift Gooch, who remained five hours for 110 and the game was drawn. Victory would have meant second place for Leicestershire. A draw against Warwickshire was followed by defeat at the hands of Kent and the Championship, with four matches to go was slipping away. Northants came to Grace Road and Leicestershire required 100 off 13 overs in the final innings – they achieved the target with 10 deliveries unused. Kent were beaten in the next game, Balderstone making 112. The final two games were drawn and Leicestershire finished in fourth place, behind Essex, Middlesex and Hampshire.

In the Sunday League the County were among the also-rans, due in part to no fewer than five 'no result' games, but they claimed only four wins against seven losses. The Benson & Hedges competition was rain-ruined, two of the County's four group matches being washed out. The NatWest Trophy saw the Tolchard family in action again when Leicestershire met Devon in the first round, but the second round saw defeat at the hands of Gloucestershire, when Zaheer hit 158, after Gower had made 138. So all in all Leicestershire did not enjoy their limited-overs cricket in 1983.

The feature of the season was the bowling of Ferris, who captured 53 first-class wickets in 13 matches. Clift, at last free from injury, had a very good summer with both bat and ball. He topped the bowling table with 83 wickets at 19.18 each, as well as scoring 843 runs. His maiden century, 100 not out in the penultimate game at Hove, came in only 50 minutes off 58 balls and is the fastest hundred ever scored for the County. Taylor shook off the effects of his broken elbow and captured 69 wickets for just 20 runs each. Nick Cook, although not enjoying as much success for the County as in the previous three seasons, was called at the last minute into the England team for the third Test at Lord's, replacing the injured Edmonds. His success was instant – five for 35 in the first innings and eight wickets in the match. Retained for

Slow left-arm bowler Nick Cook plugged away for the County from 1978, and made his Test debut in 1983, but soon afterwards he decided to throw in his lot with Northamptonshire. (Patrick Eagar)

the final Test at Trent Bridge, he responded with another five-wicket haul, five for 63, in the first innings and nine wickets in the match.

Gower was selected for all four Tests and scored two hundreds for England. He played in 15 Leicestershire first-class matches and hit 849 runs, with three more hundreds.

The mainstays of the County batting were therefore Davison (1,417 runs) and Balderstone (1,478 runs). Butcher finished 27 runs short of a thousand and made three centuries. Briers hit 201 not out at Edgbaston and 1,289 runs altogether at an average of 40.

James Whitaker made his debut in 1983. A product of Uppingham School, he had captained the Eleven in 1981 and topped the school batting averages that season, when he also turned out for Leicestershire Second Eleven. Born in Skipton, Yorkshire, he is a fine right-hand batsman and probably one of the hardest hitters of the ball in county cricket. His eagerness to attack the bowling right from the start of each innings has caused some early dismissals and is the main reason why he has, to 1992, only played once for England.

Another 1983 debutant was J. P. Addison, a 17-year-old batsman from Staffordshire, who hit 51 when opening the batting against the New Zealanders. He had made his debut for Leicestershire Second Eleven at the age of 15. His first-class career, however, was destined to be very limited and he returned to being a leading batsman for his native county.

The final first-class match of the season – the drawn game with Lancashire – turned out to be not only Tolchard's last match for the County, but also a headline hitter. The first day and a half was lost through rain. Lancashire made 236, and when Leicestershire reached 150 for four at 3 o'clock on the final afternoon Tolchard declared in the hope that Lancashire might be generous, score a few quick runs and then set Leicestershire a target. What happened in reality was that Fowler and O'Shaughnessy opened the batting against Gower and Whitaker, who purposely bowled long hops and full tosses. O'Shaughnessy reached 100 in 35 minutes; the pair added 200 in 43 minutes and Fowler took 46 minutes to score his hundred. Clive Lloyd, the Lancashire captain, did not declare and the match ended in farce. The press had a field day. O'Shaughnessy was taken to meet P. G. H. Fender, who long ago had also scored a century in 35 minutes and the statisticians debated whether the new 'record' should count.

In the midst of all this hilarity, Mike Turner, the Leicestershire Secretary was more concerned with real life. The financial position of the County, which had been sound for more than a decade, was now giving some cause for concern. Savings had to be made and one area which was looked at was the salaries of the playing staff. Two players, Roberts and Davison, had announced their departure, and two more, Tolchard and Steele, were not re-engaged for 1984. The retirement of these four major figures from Grace Road meant the end of an era. Davison had already been in dispute with the Club over the financial terms of his contract and had agreed to play in 1983 only when a local

Peter Willey, the Northants and England all-rounder, was signed by Leicestershire in 1984 as vice-captain to Gower, and his competitive nature immediately enlivened the side. (Patrick Eagar)

businessman made up the difference between what Davison asked for and what the Club were prepared to pay. Midway through 1983 the Tasmanian Cricket Council offered Davison full-time employment and he asked to be released from his Leicestershire contract, which still had a year to run. The Club agreed provided he did not sign for another county.

273

John Steele had scored 12,814 runs and taken 448 wickets since joining Leicestershire in 1970. He moved on to Glamorgan and spent the next three seasons playing for the Welsh county, before becoming their Second Eleven captain and coach.

DISAPPOINTMENT AND DEPARTURES

'THE DECISION BY LEICESTERSHIRE to make David Gower captain will give him valuable and necessary experience if one day he is to captain England,' commented *The Cricketer* magazine at the end of November 1983. On 12 March 1984 Gower walked out on to the field at Faisalabad as England's captain, replacing Willis who was indisposed. Gower hit 152 and completed 4,000 Test match runs. In the next Test he hit 173 not out, again as captain. Both matches were drawn.

Back in England a few weeks later, he surveyed the resources of the County he was to lead for the first time as 'official' captain. Peter Willey, the Northants all-rounder, had been signed up and appointed as vice-captain. Willey had made his debut for Northants at the age of 16 in 1966 and played 20 Tests for England between 1976 and 1981. After this he had gone with the rebel team to South Africa and been banned from Test cricket for three years.

There was a pre-season query over the availability of Ferris, as it was expected that he might tour England with the West Indies; the County therefore held on to the registration of Roberts, just in case. Ferris was not chosen for West Indies, but after playing in a single Sunday League match, he suffered a stress fracture of the knee and this kept him out of cricket for the rest of the summer except for a single match when he again broke down.

In the Championship Leicestershire were unbeaten until the end of the June and led the field, but this pace was not maintained and in the second half of the summer only two further Championship wins were recorded, making eight in all. Leicestershire therefore finished in fourth place for the second successive year. Gower was appointed as captain of England and thus played in only nine Championship games, the side being led in the rest of the matches by Peter Willey. The latter's personal form was a revelation and he certainly set a splendid example to his new colleagues. Six centuries flowed from his bat in a total of 1,472 runs at an average of almost 36. Added to this were 43 wickets and 17 catches. He also became the first Leicestershire batsman to hit a century on his first-class debut for the County, scoring 141 not out against Cambridge at Fenner's. In the second innings of the same match the young South Australian, Michael Haysman, repeated the feat, making 102 not out. This talented 23-year-old had come to the County as part of an exchange agreement between Leicestershire and Glenelg CC, near Adelaide. Because of the restrictions on overseas players in county cricket his opportunities were very limited and at the close of the summer he decided to return to Australia. These two centuries set the tone for a high-scoring season in which the County amassed 23 centuries, equalling the record set in 1937. Willey, in fact, went on to hit a second hundred in his first Championship game for the County, at Chesterfield, where Leicestershire beat Derbyshire by eleven runs. Another record early in the season also involved Willey, when he and Boon hit 290 for the first wicket against Warwickshire at Grace Road.

The main support for Willey came from the experienced Balderstone, who was as dependable as ever and hit 1,260 runs, and three of the younger generation, Boon, Butcher and Whitaker, all of whom reached 1,000 runs for the first time. Butcher hit five centuries and generally opened the batting with Balderstone.

In contrast Nigel Briers had a poor summer, averaging only 18 with a total of 616 runs. Garnham began the season as first-choice wicketkeeper, but his volatile personality tended to upset the tranquillity of the dressing room and he was eventually suspended for 'breaches of club discipline'. This gave a chance to the 19-year-old Philip Whitticase, who kept wicket in eight matches and gained many admirers for his neat and unobtrusive style behind the stumps.

On paper Leicestershire had the strongest pair of opening bowlers in the country, George Ferris and Les Taylor. As has been noted Ferris suffered an injury which kept him out of Championship cricket; Taylor injured his elbow again and bowled only 142 overs through the season. Fortunately Jonathan Agnew at last fulfilled his potential and so well did he perform that he gained a place in two Tests – the final match against West Indies and the match against Sri Lanka. His best Championship performance was five wickets in each innings against Surrey; he also took eight for 47 against Cambridge. In all he took 80 wickets for the County during the year. Andy Roberts was persuaded to come out of retirement to fill the gap left by Taylor and Ferris and took 33 wickets in eight matches.

Clift missed some early matches due to injury, but then bowled well and captured 63 wickets. Parsons had a good summer with both bat and ball, hitting 853 runs and taking 67 wickets, but Nick Cook found the pitches not at all to his liking, his wickets costing over 40 runs each. Despite this the Test selectors still had faith in him and he appeared in three Tests.

The Club caused some newspaper comment over the inclusion of Ian Carmichael in the side. A fast bowler, he had been playing for South Australia, and it appeared should be registered as an overseas player, but as he was born in Yorkshire he rightly claimed to be qualified as an English cricketer. In the event his bowling proved somewhat expensive and he left the County at the end of the summer.

Although Leicestershire hit the highest Sunday League total of 1984 – 291 for five against Glamorgan at Swansea – the County made little impact on the John Player League and finished 13th equal (or second from bottom).

There was little success either in the Benson & Hedges competition, where with two wins Leicestershire did not qualify for the knock-out section. The County were unfortunate in that Gower was unable to play due to blood poisoning, which confined him to hospital for a spell.

Wiltshire were crushed in the NatWest Trophy, when Leicestershire reached their highest total ever in the competition, 354 for seven, Whitaker making 155, another record. The latter lasted only a few weeks since Gower hit 156 off the Derbyshire attack in the next round – victory was by 120 runs. In the quarter-finals Leicestershire were beaten by Northants, the margin being three wickets. No less than four players received their caps during the year, Willey, Agnew, Butcher and Parsons.

Season 1985 proved a complete change from its predecessor. At no time did Leicestershire appear in the County Championship race and so poorly did they perform that they finished 16th; in the Benson & Hedges competition however they took the title and thus obtained their first major trophy since 1977.

The weather had much to do with the Championship results. According to the Annual Report a total of 6,969 minutes playing time were lost through bad weather in the Britannic competition, a quarter of the possible total.

The first match – against Yorkshire at Grace Road – was unfinished due to a snowstorm allied to rain and bad light. The County travelled to Oxford and found the undergraduates easy meat. Garnham hit a maiden first-class hundred whilst Oxford were all out for 24, equalling the lowest total ever against the County. Parsons enjoyed himself with figures of 11-5-11-6. Back to the more serious stuff, a sequence of 13 matches amounted to twelve draws and a solitary victory. This was at Hinckley where Warwickshire succumbed by four wickets. Two early declarations following a first day lost through rain were necessary to provide this definite result.

The match against the Australians was arranged for four days. It came immediately prior to the first Test and the tourists were anxious to give their bowlers a hard workout. The Leicestershire batsmen obliged. Balderstone made 134 and Gower 135. The pair added 253 for the second wicket and the Leicestershire total amounted to 454. The Australians replied with 466, of which W. B. Phillips made 128 and Ritchie 115. Rain meant that the match was more or less confined to the two first innings.

A century by Willey and some good bowling from Clift, which included a hat-trick, enabled Leicestershire to beat Derbyshire at Chesterfield on 15 July. Whitticase held seven catches in this game. Championship cricket then came to a halt for nearly two weeks, whilst Benson & Hedges matches were in progress. Kent came to Grace Road for the next three-day game and Agnew distinguished himself by capturing nine for 70 in the first innings. Agnew in fact had a splendid opportunity to take all ten wickets in the innings, since he obtained the first nine and then needed to dismiss only Kevin Jarvis, the Kent number eleven, whose career batting average was 3. However Jarvis survived briefly and was dismissed off the bowling of Clift. This match, despite the efforts of Agnew, was drawn, as were the next four. Despondency set in and three of the final five matches ended in defeat, though Gower managed a century off the Sussex attack.

All this contrasted sharply with the performances in the Benson & Hedges Cup. Leicestershire qualified for the knock-out section by winning three out of four of their group matches – the single loss was by a solitary run against Yorkshire. Balderstone gained two Gold Awards and Whitaker one in these group matches.

The quarter-final was staged at Southampton. In an exciting finish Leicestershire took the final Hampshire wicket with the penultimate ball and claimed victory by four runs. The semi-final proved much easier. Kent came to Grace Road and were dismissed for 101. The home batsmen took just 22 overs to win the game which finished at 4.20 – it was the first day of first eleven cricket at Leicester in which there was uninterrupted sunshine.

The final at Lord's began on a damp wicket with overcast conditions. Gower put Essex in. Accurate bowling, especially by Taylor, restricted the run flow and Essex could reach only 213 for eight off 55 overs. Leicestershire lost both openers with 33 runs on the board. Gower was joined by Willey and the pair added 83 in 17 overs, before the captain was brilliantly caught in the covers by Lilley. Whitaker and Briers came and went and 79 runs were still required with 15 overs left. Garnham, however, was equal to the task and with Willey firmly in place, the target was reached

Another Benson & Hedges Cup success in 1985. Skipper David Gower, holding up the trophy, shares the limelight with vice-captain Peter Willey, who was Man of the Match in the final. (Patrick Eagar)

with three overs to spare. Willey's 86 not out gained him the Gold Award – an easy choice for the adjudicator, Denis Compton. The jubilant spectators cheered the victorious side who stood on the dressing room balcony, Gower holding the trophy aloft.

In the two other limited-overs competitions Leicestershire did not fare so well. Following an easy first round against Minor County opposition in the NatWest Trophy, they went out to Hampshire in the second round, the margin being four wickets. Five matches in the Sunday League were washed out, but the County still seemed set for a good overall result until it came to the final three matches, all of which were lost. They finished 6th equal.

Gower captained England in all six Tests and his batting record against Australia was quite exceptional – 732 runs in nine innings with three centuries. With Taylor, Agnew and Willey also chosen for England, the County had four representatives in a series for the first time.

Four batsmen reached 1,000 runs for the County in 1985. Willey came out at the head of the table with 1,253 runs and an average of 46.61. Russell Cobb had more opportunities, taking

BENSON AND HEDGES CUP FINAL LEICESTERSHIRE *v* ESSEX

Played at Lord's, 20 July 1985

LEICESTERSHIRE WON BY FIVE WICKETS

ESSEX

*G. A. Gooch	b Willey	57
B. R. Hardie	c and b Clift	25
P. J. Prichard	b Taylor	32
K. S. McEwan	c Garnham b Taylor	29
D. R. Pringle	c Agnew b Taylor	10
C. Gladwin	b Clift	14
A. W. Lilley	b Agnew	12
†D. E. East	not out	7
S. Turner	run out	3
N. A. Foster	not out	6
J. K. Lever		
Extras	b 1, lb 15, w 1, nb 1	18
Total	(8 wkts, 55 overs)	213

Fall: 1-71, 2-101, 3-147, 4-163, 5-164, 6-191, 7-195, 8-198

BOWLING	O	M	R	W
Willey	11	0	41	1
Clift	11	1	40	2
Agnew	11	1	51	1
Taylor	11	3	26	3
Parsons	11	0	39	0

LEICESTERSHIRE

J. C. Balderstone	c Prichard b Pringle	12
I. P. Butcher	c Prichard b Turner	19
*D. I. Gower	c Lilley b Foster	43
P. Willey	not out	86
J. J. Whitaker	b Gooch	1
N. E. Briers	lbw b Gooch	6
†M. A. Garnham	not out	34
P. B. Clift		
G. J. Parsons		
J. P. Agnew		
L. B. Taylor		
Extras	b 2, lb 9, w 2, nb 1	14
Total	(5 wkts, 52 overs)	215

Fall: 1-33, 2-37, 3-120, 4-123, 5-135

BOWLING	O	M	R	W
Lever	11	0	50	0
Foster	11	2	32	1
Pringle	10	0	42	1
Turner	10	1	40	1
Gooch	10	1	40	2

Umpires: H. D. Bird and K. E. Palmer
*Captain; †Wicketkeeper

Gower's place when he was away with England. Cobb made 601 runs and impressed with his solid technique. The disappointment among the regular batsmen was Briers, whose form remained moderate for the second successive year.

The bowling averages help to explain the lack of success in first-class matches. Taylor was the leading figure but he could claim only 56 wickets at 21 runs each; Agnew took 55, Clift 47 and Willey 35. Ferris had recovered from his 1984 injury, but his form was very variable. Parsons was expected to continue where he left off in 1984, but failed so badly that he was dropped from the side and released at the close of the year. He joined War-wickshire in 1986. Even more disappointing was the form of Cook. His 29 Championship wickets cost 42 runs each. He claimed that the home wickets were designed purely for the seam attack and at the end of the summer he was reluctantly released by the County. He joined Northants in 1986. A bright spot amidst the gloom was the debut of Phillip DeFreitas. Though born in Dominica, he had been living in England since 1976 and been educated in Willesden. In 1984 he had been on the ground staff at Lord's and had joined Leicestershire at the start of the year. In nine first-class matches he took 27 wickets at a reasonable cost. Extremely raw and volatile in temperament he was regarded by critics as an England bowler in the making.

Garnham, the regular first eleven wicketkeeper, though only

The Leicestershire team in 1985. Left to right, back: G. Blackburn (Scorer), M. Garnham, I. Butcher, J. Agnew, L. Taylor, N. Cook, G. Parsons, J. Whitaker. Front: P. Clift, C. Balderstone, D. Gower (Captain), P. Willey, N. Briers. (Patrick Eagar)

25, announced his retirement at the end of the season, in order to take up a business career, but he later had second thoughts and returned to county cricket, playing with success for Essex. Tim Boon was not seen in the Leicestershire side during the summer due to a serious road accident – he resumed his career in 1986.

Despite a dreadful spate of injuries, Leicestershire's County Championship record improved in 1986 with wins increasing from two to five and seventh place in the table being secured. As usual Gower was absent playing for England, though he lost the captaincy to Gatting. Willey, the official County vice-captain, was unable to play until June due to a knee operation. Briers was made captain in the absence of both Gower and Willey, but sustained a broken arm in the Sussex match at Hove. Clift was given the post, but missed the last eight weeks of the season due to a knee injury and Balderstone was the fifth player called upon to lead the side during the summer.

The successive captains were not the only players to suffer injury. Whitaker fractured bones in both hands after being hit by a delivery from Marshall; Whitticase, the wicketkeeper, and Paul Gill his young deputy, both had hand injuries. Nearly all the bowlers were away with injuries at one time or another.

In these circumstances it was pleasing to note how well the younger players responded to unexpected demands. The outstanding figure was DeFreitas. He not only took 91 wickets at 22.78 runs each, but also hit 645 aggressive runs, including a maiden century against Kent at Canterbury. He was chosen to play for the TCCB XI against the New Zealanders in August and then gained a place on the England tour to Australia during the winter. If DeFreitas was the outstanding bowler, then Whitaker was the outstanding batsman. He finished second to Greenidge in the national averages with 1,526 runs, average 66.34, was named as one of *Wisden*'s Five Cricketers of the Year, and like DeFreitas found himself going to Australia with the England side. Aged 24, Whitaker had assumed the role vacant since Davison left the County. His sharp eyesight allowed him to get away with shots which would cause the downfall of a less talented player and he had the ability to make aggressive strokes off both the front and the back foot. Runs generally came off his bat at a fast rate and he quite deliberately attacked the bowling in the same manner whether the match was first-class or limited-overs.

These two young England cricketers – both were to gain Test caps in Australia – made Leicestershire into an exciting side once more. The County brought in two newcomers to try to strengthen the attack. The first was Laurie Potter, the Kent all-rounder, who, it was hoped, would fill the gap left by Cook, as Potter's main asset was his slow left-arm bowling. He was 24 and had played for Kent since 1981. The Antiguan, Winston Benjamin, was brought in as a back-up seam bowler for Ferris. Benjamin had played for Cheshire in 1985 and for the Leeward Islands in the winter of 1985–86. He had plenty of fire and pace, but tended at this stage of his career to be erratic. Potter played in virtually every match, but made little impression; Benjamin took 46 rather expensive wickets, though he had days of success.

In the County Championship the only definite result in the first five matches was a defeat at the hands of Notts, when both sides forefeited an innings. There was another defeat, inflicted by Gloucestershire, before two wins, against Surrey and Sussex. The outstanding match of the summer was the return with Notts at Grace Road. Whitaker hit 200 not out, with 30 fours and three sixes and Benjamin took six for 33, dismissing Notts or 58. Victory was by 275 runs.

Hampshire were the next visitors to Grace Road and with a rising injury list, Leicestershire included Peter Bowler. The young Devon-born batsman proceeded to hit a century on his first-class debut, the first Leicestershire player to do so (Willey and Haysman had made 100s on their Leicestershire debuts but had previously played in first-class cricket). Bowler went on to score 62 in the second innings of this drawn match.

DeFreitas produced the best bowling figures of his short career at Chalkwell Park, Southend. Having taken six for 42 in the first innings, he followed up with seven for 44 in the second. Leicestershire beat Essex inside two days by ten wickets.

These victories pushed the County well up the Championship table, but unfortunately only one more game was won all summer, this being against Yorkshire at Grace Road in the first week of August. Whitaker, who had just recovered from his broken fingers, hit 100 and 82, both not out, and Ken Higgs, drafted in due to the absence of the regular attack, took five for 22.

Results in the limited-overs competitions were unimpressive. Only one match was won in the Benson & Hedges preliminary group competition and that was against Minor Counties. In the NatWest Trophy, the first opponents were Ireland who were outclassed. Willey and Gower put on a record 209 for the third wicket, both batsmen hitting hundreds. In the second round Gloucestershire were beaten at Bristol, but in the quarter-finals Leicestershire were easily defeated by Lancashire in a match interrupted by rain.

Philip DeFreitas made an impact as an exciting all-rounder right from his debut for the County in 1985 and was capped within two years; but after a hiatus in his Test career he went to Lancashire in 1989 to revive his fortunes. (Patrick Eagar)

Disappointing form was displayed in the Sunday League, only five matches were won, against ten losses.

It was thought that Gower and the side would benefit if the cares of captaincy were removed from his shoulders. He had asked to be rested from the three final matches of the season because of 'mental and physical exhaustion' and Mike Turner recommended to the County Committee that he be 'rested' from the captaincy for 1987, especially as he had the extra tasks involved in organising his benefit during that coming summer.

The three Leicestershire players touring with England during the winter achieved mixed results. Gower began poorly, because, it is said, he was not appointed vice-captain, but he proved as good as ever in the later matches and came second in the Test batting table. DeFreitas was the youngest tourist. His final figures do not appear impressive, but he bowled aggressively, worried most of the batsmen and fielded brilliantly in the deep. Whitaker had few opportunities, but played in the Adelaide Test when Botham withdrew through injury. This Test created a County record since it was the first time three Leicestershire men had been in the same England side.

On paper Leicestershire had a match-winning side for the 1987 season, but the dressing room seemed filled with problems. Willey was appointed captain in succession to Gower and this created an immediate change of gear, the sergeant-major style of Willey contrasting sharply with the laid-back approach of Gower. This change of emphasis seemed to affect DeFreitas and some horseplay in the dressing room between DeFreitas and Agnew was built up out of proportion and then came under the magnifying glass of the press. DeFreitas lost his place in the England side and was suspended from the County eleven for disciplinary reasons. The number of runs and wickets he took for the County was therefore more or less half that of twelve months before.

Clift intimated before the season began that 1987 would be his last summer and that he would prefer to operate as a spin bowler due to his 1986 knee injury. When he found himself omitted from the County side for the first Sunday League match, his reaction was to apply to be released from his contract. This problem was smoothed over. Ian Butcher was also unhappy at not retaining a regular first team place and requested that his contract should not be renewed.

All in all Willey had a great deal to contend with. He led by example and did not suffer fools gladly, but by the season's end he had had enough and resigned as captain.

Surprisingly in view of the apparent rancour, the overall playing performance of the County was good. Leicestershire finished third in the Championship – only the fifth time in their history that they had ended in the top three. Eight matches were won, three lost and 13 drawn. The pattern at the start mirrored 1986 with a single defeat and no wins from the first seven matches. At this stage they were languishing at the foot of the table. Then came a sudden reversal of fortunes. Commencing with the Sussex match came three victories in a row. Sussex lost by four wickets; Derbyshire were vanquished by 47 runs; Surrey were hammered to the tune of an innings and 24 runs. The first two of these games were at Grace Road, the last at The Oval.

DAVID IVON GOWER

Although David Gower now plays for Hampshire, he will always be regarded as a Leicestershire cricketer and by many as the best batsman the County ever had. A batsman who can time his shots to perfection, Gower accumulates runs without apparent energy or show of force. From his first days in county cricket he was hailed as a potential England cricketer and has now played in over 100 Tests. His cool, subtle approach to both batting and captaincy has led some sections of the press to accuse him of being casual and lazy, and on some occasions it can be said

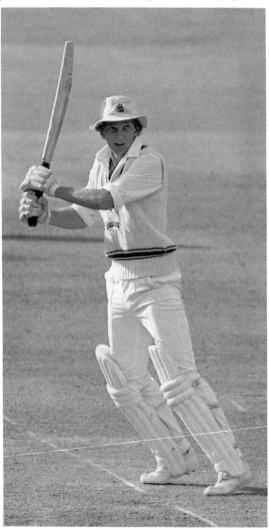

that he lacked the killer instinct which was part of the make-up of such players as Bradman.

His career in county cricket has perhaps been ruined by the continual demands on his time by England; any player appearing in all the Tests and limited-overs internationals in a season misses half the county matches, and when that player is also the captain of his County, as Gower was, the almost weekly switch from Test to county can be disturbing.

By the age of 21, Gower had received the accolade as '*Wisden* Cricketer of the Year' and virtually every winter between the mid-1970s and the mid-1980s toured overseas. He captained both England and Leicestershire from 1984 to 1986 and after being relieved of both posts, was reappointed County captain in 1988 and England captain in 1989, but lost his place in the England side after England lost the Ashes.

(Patrick Eagar)

Jonathan Agnew, a fast bowler who became the first Leicestershire bowler to claim 100 wickets for 11 years in 1987, when the County finished third in the Championship. Agnew, somewhat disappointed by non-recognition by the national selectors, retired to become, in 1990, the BBC cricket correspondent. (Patrick Eagar)

Then came a tense draw at Taunton with Leicestershire at the end needing 27 with two wickets in hand. Middlesex were beaten by an innings at Grace Road. The wins were mainly the work of the bowlers, Agnew, Clift and Ferris. The second half of the summer produced four more wins, in two of which Agnew played a leading part, taking eleven wickets against Derbyshire and ten against Northants.

Gower topped the batting table, but played in only 14 matches, scoring 913 runs at an average of 53.70. Briers at last found his form and hit 1,257 runs at 44.89. Willey, Whitaker and Boon also exceeded 1,000. Agnew captured 101 wickets, the first Leicestershire bowler to claim over 100 since Birkenshaw in 1968. Ferris showed improved form with 52 wickets at 22 runs each, but DeFreitas, beset by problems, fell right away both as batsman and bowler. Potter having failed to provide any bite to the spin department the County signed Peter Such, the 22-year-old off-spinner from Nottinghamshire. He performed creditably with 41 wickets at 30 runs each. A younger debutant was the 18-year-old Chris Lewis, who had an outstanding record in the Second Eleven and was therefore given four first-class matches – his talent was patently obvious.

Behind the stumps Whitticase continued to progress, being responsible for 69 dismissals, and he was awarded his County Cap.

In the three limited-overs competitions the best results were obtained in the NatWest Trophy. Oxfordshire were easily beaten in the first round – Cobb gaining the Man of the Match Award with 66 not out. Willey hit 154 in the second round match at home against Hampshire – Hampshire made a record 326 for nine for a team batting second, but still lost by 15 runs. DeFreitas bowled out Yorkshire in the quarter-finals for 200, taking five for 34 and bringing victory by 36 runs. The semi-final was staged at Grace Road against Northamptonshire, who made 249 for six. Stoppages for bad light meant that Leicestershire's reply on the first day was restricted to 37 for two. On the second day they collapsed to 164 all out.

The weather ruined Leicestershire's Sunday League programme, seven matches ending with no result. The County finished 12th. As in 1986 only one Benson & Hedges match was won; this was against Notts when Benjamin performed the hat-trick and took five for 26.

Grace Road was enhanced by the addition of a clock-tower, the cost of which came from a bequest and generous donations in money and kind. In a further effort to improve the appearance of the ground one hundred rhododendron bushes were planted along the side of the Hawkesbury Road car park. It is a sad reflection on the times in which we live that 25 were stolen during the season.

No fewer than six of the playing staff had departed before the 1988 season began. Clift and Butcher had made it clear in 1987

The County Ground, Grace Road, in 1987, with Leicestershire playing Nottinghamshire.
(Patrick Eagar)

that they wished to leave; Bowler went to Derbyshire and had a brilliant summer; Billington, Blackett and Gill had made little impression in first-class cricket. David Billington was a Lancashire-born right-hand batsman who had been at Loughborough University; Mark Blackett, another right-hander, came from Edmonton, North London; and Paul Gill was the deputy wicketkeeper.

In an attempt to remove the dressing-room squabbles, the playing staff went to the Isle of Wight for a week before the 1988 season and received lectures from Dr Martin Landau-North in 'relaxation techniques and positive thinking'. Mike Turner also worked hard during the winter to eliminate possible areas of conflict. The club re-appointed Gower as captain with Briers as vice-captain.

The major change to the County Championship in 1988 was the introduction of some four-day matches. There were to be 16 three-day games, one against each of the other counties and six four-day games, three at the start of the season and three at the end.

Leicestershire began their season with a warm-up at Oxford and the potential of Lewis was immediately apparent for he took ten for 70. The County won by an innings. Lewis followed this up with five for 73 in the first Championship match – a drawn game with Derbyshire. Then Agnew took eleven for 122 as Leicestershire beat Northants by an innings. With Ferris and Taylor still on ice, as it seemed, everything looked most promising for 1988. The third Championship match brought another innings win, Agnew picking up another nine wickets and De-Freitas also bowling well – the defeated opposition was Kent. Two wins in June, against Sussex at Grace Road with Agnew again being the destroyer, and against Gloucestershire at Gloucester, with Agnew once more in control, kept Leicestershire in fourth place in the table. The second half of the summer, however, produced only two more victories and Leicestershire had to be content with seventh place.

The batting was a great disappointment – not a single Leicestershire player in the top 30 places in *Wisden*'s batting list. Willey failed to reach 1,000 runs and his average fell to 25; only Gower's average exceeded 40. DeFreitas had one great innings when he hit a century in 95 minutes off the Notts attack at Worksop. Another bowler, Taylor, surprised himself by hitting 60 in under half an hour, batting at number eleven – there were six sixes and five fours in his innings, but it did not prevent Essex winning by an innings.

Winston Benjamin, the Antiguan-born fast bowler, made his debut for Leicestershire in 1986 and his debut for the West Indies less than two years later. (Patrick Eagar)

The Test series against West Indies proved a disaster for England; Gower was dropped in an attempt to solve some problems, but what caused more surprise was the way the selectors managed to ignore Agnew. He took 93 wickets, with only Stephenson and Cooper, both Notts, having a larger aggregate. DeFreitas with 61, Ferris 62 and Lewis 42 all gave excellent support, but the two spinners, Potter and Such, were not over-used. Potter's batting improved and he scored his maiden Leicestershire hundred.

The results in the limited-overs matches were quite terrible. Only four wins came on Sunday and there were no notable individual performances. The County failed to qualify for the knock-out section of the Benson & Hedges Cup and in the NatWest Trophy they were removed by Gloucestershire in the second round.

DeFreitas remained unhappy at Grace Road and, as in 1987, was dropped for some matches, officially due to 'lack of effort'. The Committee agreed that it was in the best interests of both Club and player if he was released, despite having a year of his contract to run. He joined Lancashire in 1989 and greatly to his credit matured to become a successful and important member of the England team.

DeFreitas was the only player of any consequence to leave Grace Road in the winter of 1988–89, so, on paper, the County remained capable of challenging for all the trophies in 1989. One pre-season blow for the County, though not the player, was the announcement on 5 April that Gower was reappointed as captain of England for the home series against Australia.

Gower celebrated with a career-best 228 in the first Championship match of the summer, Glamorgan being the opposition. Rain on the final day caused the match to be drawn. Unfortunately Gower did not repeat this performance and his total number of runs for the County in first-class matches amounted to 719. He played in only 11 matches and spent much of his time with the England team. His batting in the Tests brought 383 runs and another Test hundred, but his captaincy came in for increasing criticism as England failed in one Test after another. It came as no surprise when the selectors announced that he would be relieved of the captaincy, but the press were amazed when Gower was omitted from the England side to tour West Indies in the winter. He was also left out of the 'A' team to visit Zimbabwe. In November Gower tendered his resignation as County captain and then came the announcement that he would leave Leicestershire and play for Hampshire in 1990. He had scored 10,685 runs for the County and hit 24 hundreds, but right from the very start of his first-class career his selection for international matches had meant that he played a restricted role in county cricket.

So the pattern of Leicestershire cricket in the 1980s continued until the end of the decade – a collection of very talented players who for a variety of reasons rarely formed a coherent combination.

The results in 1989 were not outstanding. Four Championship wins placed the county 13th in the table. Derbyshire were beaten at Chesterfield in mid-May when Benjamin took six for 26 and Lewis five for 69. At the end of June came the second success,

James Whitaker, an exciting batsman whose form in the mid-1980s won him a lone Test cap in 1986–7, and who is now trying to recapture the edge that will lead to more. (Patrick Eagar)

Agnew, 11 for 93, and Lewis 8 for 80, dismissing Notts for 116 and 135. Potter made 121 not out in the Leicestershire total of 352 for six. On a crumbling wicket, which was reported to Lord's, Leicestershire beat Glamorgan at Sophia Gardens on 28 July and the fourth win was against Derbyshire when, after the match was very even for the first half, Derbyshire collapsed in their second innings, all out 78. Benjamin took five for 25, Lewis five for 40. Briers and Boon knocked off the runs without a wicket being lost.

All the other matches were lost or drawn, but there were some good individual performances. Benjamin achieved a hat-trick and figures of seven for 54 against the Australians. Paul Nixon, the understudy for Whitticase held eight catches on his first-class debut against Warwickshire at Hinckley. Not yet 19 years of age he had been signed on during the winter from the Lord's groundstaff.

There was no joy in the limited-overs competitions. Only five wins were achieved in the Sunday League and the club finished 14th equal. The basic defect was the unreliable batting; just four individual fifties were hit on Sunday, three by Whitaker and one by Gower.

Two wins out of the four Benson & Hedges group matches were insufficient to qualify Leicestershire for the knock-out section and in the NatWest competition, as so often, Leicestershire had an easy win against a Minor County – this time Shropshire – and were then removed from the trophy in the second round.

Five of the batsmen reached 1,000 first-class runs: Whitaker, Willey, Potter (for the first time), Briers and Boon, but the two highest Leicestershire batsmen in the overall averages were Gower in 40th place and Whitaker one place below. However Benjamin and Lewis were both well to the fore in the bowling table and it was unfortunate that the latter missed half the season through injury. Ferris was only seen in five matches. Parsons re-appeared in the County's ranks having come back after his three seasons with Warwickshire. He had no outstanding analyses, but performed with his usual whole-hearted endeavour. Peter Such became disillusioned with his lack of success and opportunity and declined re-engagement for 1990, preferring to move to Essex.

Whitaker and Lewis were selected for the England 'A' squad going to Zimbabwe, but no sooner had the team arrived in Africa than Lewis was summoned to the West Indies to reinforce the main England team. He played in two first-class matches and the final limited-overs international.

After showing a surplus in each of the preceding 20 years, the County made a loss of £3,186 in 1989.

The County were concerned at the lack of success in spite of the apparent talent on the groundstaff and soon after the end of the 1989 season, Mike Turner took the bold step of signing up Bobby Simpson, the Australian team manager, as County Cricket Manager on a two-year contract. Simpson had completely revived the sagging confidence of the Australian team and was regarded as

After Bobby Simpson had led the Australian tourists to an overwhelming win in England in 1989, Mike Turner signed him as County Cricket Manager for two years. (Patrick Eagar)

primarily responsible for the great success the side had had in England in 1989.

Gower having left, a new captain was required and Briers, the vice-captain, was appointed, with Whitaker as his stand-in. There was some adverse comment on Briers' appointment since 1990 was also his benefit season. In fact he thrived on the added responsibility and work load. As a batsman he scored more runs than in any previous summer, failing by just four to complete 2,000. He hit five centuries and averaged fractionally under 50, topping the County averages by a fair margin. A more positive approach to the captaincy might have earned him more laurels, but the fact that the County rose to seventh place in the Championship was pleasing enough, though the limited-overs results remained pretty dismal.

The 1990 season in general saw the introduction of bland pitches which made the bowlers work harder. The threat of a 25-point penalty for an unsatisfactory pitch made the groundsmen cautious and the reduction of the size of the seam on the ball did nothing to assist the bowlers. In addition the hot, dry summer made runs come more quickly.

The campaign began with a nine-wicket victory at Sophia Gardens. Lewis, in a very hostile performance, took ten for 119. He was by now a marked man, and was selected for all four Texaco Trophy matches as well as three Tests, one against New Zealand and two against India. This of course meant that he missed nine County Championship games.

Evidence of the way the wickets were destined to play through 1990 came in the second match at Chelmsford. Briers won the toss and took the total to 145 before the first wicket fell. Lewis scored 189 not out in six hours and the total reached 520. Essex were undaunted. They replied with the highest score the county had ever made, 761 for six, with two double centuries, Gooch, 215, and Prichard 245. This pair added 403 for the second wicket, another Essex record. In the closing stages of the innings Neil Foster hit his maiden hundred off 79 balls. Leicestershire in their second innings were 249 for three when the players went home.

With David Gower leaving the County, the new captain for 1990 was Nigel Briers, who had made his debut in 1971 aged 16 years 104 days. Briers led by example, just missing 2,000 runs and easily topping the averages. (Patrick Eagar)

The third match did produce a result. Briers carried his bat through the innings for 157 out of 359, but Notts won by five wickets. Whitticase suffered a badly broken finger during the game and missed all but the last two matches of the summer. The County were fortunate that Nixon proved a very competent reserve keeper. He disposed of 50 victims behind the stumps and steadily improved as a batsman.

Five drawn matches followed, but the New Zealand tourists were beaten by four wickets in a one-day game, then immediately afterwards Middlesex won a match of declarations. A similar game followed, except this time Leicestershire won, when in the final innings Derbyshire disintegrated, being all out for 130. The pattern was repeated for a third time at Gloucester, Agnew taking five for 70 as the home side lost by 111 runs.

The most exciting game of the summer was against Worcestershire at Grace Road. Leicestershire were set 265 to win from 56 overs. The target was well in sight with 23 runs required off 27 balls and five wickets in hand. The batsmen then lost their nerve and poor Nixon was left needing to make two to win off the last ball with one wicket to fall. He was run out trying to scramble a single to tie the match. The summary at the season's end was six wins, seven losses and nine draws.

Leicestershire did not move as far as the second round of the NatWest Trophy, being beaten in the initial match by Hampshire; again Nixon was asked to make three off the last ball and was run out. Only one match was won in the Benson & Hedges Cup, and poor batting meant that the County were always near the foot of the Sunday League table – they finished 16th.

Whitaker and Boon, as well as Briers, made the most of the generally favourable batting wickets and both returned good figures. Willey and Potter also completed 1,000 runs. Justin Benson, a 23-year-old batsman born in Dublin, was given a long run and hit 725 runs, including a maiden hundred against the Indian tourists. Lewis and Benjamin both had batting averages in the 30s, but owed this to a single hundred each.

The most successful bowler was Agnew with 59 wickets, but they cost 37 runs apiece and top of the bowling table was David Millns, who had joined the side at the start of the summer after two years in and out of his native Notts side. He played in eight Championship matches and took 25 wickets. Another newcomer was the left-arm seamer Alan Mullally, who had been born in England, but learnt his cricket in Perth, Western Australia. He certainly bowled better than his figures of 38 wickets at 38 runs each suggest. The two West Indian fast bowlers, Ferris and

ESSEX *v* LEICESTERSHIRE

Played at Chelmsford, 3, 4, 5, and 7 May 1990

DRAWN

LEICESTERSHIRE	FIRST INNINGS		SECOND INNINGS	
T. J. Boon	lbw b Such	90	c Waugh b Childs	89
*N. E. Briers	c Garnham b Such	65	c Garnham b Such	104
J. J. Whitaker	c and b Such	31	b Stephenson	15
L. Potter	c Prichard b Waugh	62	not out	16
J. D. R. Benson	c Shahid b Foster	8	not out	10
C. C. Lewis	not out	189		
†P. Whitticase	lbw b Waugh	0		
M. I. Gidley	c and b Shahid	9		
J. P. Agnew	lbw b Shahid	37		
G. J. F. Ferris	c Waugh b Foster	11		
A. D. Mullally	b Foster	3		
Extras	b 1, lb 9, w 4, nb 1	15	b 5, lb 3, w 1, nb 6	15
Total		520	(3 wkts)	249

1st inns: 1-145, 2-178, 3-197, 4-214, 5-303, 6-309, 7-458, 8-460, 9-498
2nd inns: 1-170, 2-205, 3-236

BOWLING	O	M	R	W	O	M	R	W
Foster	41	8	102	3	8	2	30	0
Andrew	20	3	72	0	9	1	31	0
Waugh	23	5	76	2				
Childs	41	14	88	0	33	10	93	1
Such	43	7	118	3	19	9	29	1
Shahid	13	1	54	2	11	3	42	0
Stephenson					9	5	16	1

ESSEX	FIRST INNINGS	
*G. A. Gooch	c Whitticase b Lewis	215
J. P. Stephenson	c Lewis b Mullally	35
P. J. Prichard	c Briers b Mullally	245
M. E. Waugh	b Lewis	43
B. R. Hardie	not out	74
†M. A. Garnham	b Lewis	0
N. A. Foster	run out	101
N. Shahid		
J. H. Childs		
S. J. W. Andrew		
P. M. Such		
Extras	b 9, lb 20, w 3, nb 16	48
Total	(6 wkts dec)	761

1st inns: 1-82, 2-485, 3-551, 4-587, 5-589, 6-761

BOWLING	O	M	R	W
Mullally	31	3	124	2
Agnew	35.5	4	170	0
Ferris	23	2	100	0
Lewis	28	3	115	3
Potter	14	0	91	0
Gidley	25	3	121	0
Benson	2	0	11	0

Umpires: K. E. Palmer and D. R. Shepherd
*Captain; †Wicketkeeper

Benjamin, played in five and 11 Championship games respectively. Both decided to leave county cricket at the end of the season, the former to go into League cricket and the latter retiring due to continued knee injury problems. Les Taylor finally retired at the end of the summer; he had played in only one Championship match, but had been used for many of the one-day games. Taylor was now aged 37. Though seven years his junior, Agnew also announced his retirement in order to pursue a full-time career in journalism. Another figure who would be absent in 1991 was Ken Higgs, whose playing career with Leicestershire had begun in 1972. Since 1980 he had been the County's coach.

The season was disappointing financially with a deficit of £18,230.

Chris Lewis was the only Leicestershire representative in the senior English party touring Australia and New Zealand during the winter of 1990–91; no one from the County was selected for the England 'A' team to Pakistan and Sri Lanka. Lewis played in the first Test match and two other first-class matches, and then incurred an injury to his back, which eventually necessitated a return to England. For some time this was thought to be serious, but following a course of treatment, including some time spent at Lilleshall, he was fit again for the beginning of the 1991 season.

After the improvement shown in the previous season, 1991 was to prove a crashing disappointment. Languishing at the foot of the table for much of the summer, Leicestershire did not record their first Championship victory until 12 August, when Kent were beaten by five wickets at Grace Road. Of the 16 Championship games prior to this, five had been lost and the remainder drawn. Nigel Briers, again appointed captain, was the only consistent batsman during this unfortunate sequence of matches. Of the five individual hundreds, he had made four, the other coming from Tim Boon. The bowling had lacked penetration and was expensive.

The victory over Kent came 50 weeks after the previous Championship win, that being in the identical fixture of 1990. In the 1991 engagement the home side were all out of 282; John Maguire then bowled an inspired spell taking seven for 57 and Kent were dismissed for 130: at one stage they were 57 for eight. The follow-on was enforced with quite different results. Kent hit 403 for four, then declared setting a target of 252 off 62 overs. Briers and Boon opened with a stand of 111, Whitaker smashed 70 off 74 balls before falling to a blinding catch at long-on by Graham Cowdrey, and Leicestershire won with nine balls to spare.

Chris Lewis, Leicestershire's newest Test player, established himself in the England side in 1991, having seemingly overcome problems of temperament. (Patrick Eagar)

John Maguire, born in Australia in 1956, had made his Sheffield Shield debut for Queensland in 1977. After three Tests and 23 limited-overs internationals for Australia, he went on two unofficial tours to South Africa and was banned from Test cricket. Most of his recent first-class cricket has been played, with some success, in South Africa. He is a right-arm fast-medium bowler, strong and exceptionally fit and a glutton for hard work.

Following the Kent match, Leicestershire travelled to Bournemouth and were involved in a second thrilling finish, but this time ended on the losing side. In Leicestershire's first innings of 394 for six declared, Benson and Whitticase broke the County record by putting on an unbeaten 219 for the seventh wicket. Benson's 133 was his first Championship hundred and Whitticase made his maiden first-class hundred. Hampshire declared their innings 132 runs in arrears; Briers made the third declaration of the match, which set Hampshire 283 from 66 overs. The southern county won off the penultimate delivery with two wickets in hand, despite two run-outs in the final over.

Going from Bournemouth to Derby, Leicestershire produced one of the surprises of the summer by beating Derbyshire by an innings and 131 runs inside two days. The architect behind this change of fortune was David Millns, who recorded not only the best figures of his career, but also the best in English first-class cricket in 1991. Millns' analysis was nine for 37; Derbyshire were dismissed for 117. His figures were the best in English first-class cricket since 1975 and a new record for Leicestershire v Derbyshire. In reply Leicestershire made 392, only the captain failing to reach double figures – he was out for a duck – and the highest scorer was Whitticase with 93. Derbyshire followed on and struggled to 144. This time however the wickets were shared around, though Millns took three more to register twelve in the match.

A week later Derbyshire came to Grace Road and had their revenge, winning by 195 runs in a four-day game. Bowler had the pleasure of scoring a century against his old county and Azharuddin reached 212. High scoring by the opposition continued in the next match when Essex reached 621 to win by nine wickets, also at Grace Road. Peter Hepworth scored his maiden Championship hundred in this match, having made an identical score, 115, earlier in the season at Cambridge.

The final match of the season arrived with Leicestershire needing to win their game, and Somerset to lose, for Leicestershire to avoid the wooden spoon. Somerset duly obliged by losing a close and exciting match with Warwickshire by the narrow margin of five runs. Leicestershire's younger brigade played a vital role in beating Kent by the emphatic margin of 90 runs. Hepworth made 97 in the first innings and his occasional spinners picked up three valuable wickets. Millns took five for 65 in the first innings and gained his County cap.

A disappointing season ended with Leicestershire therefore in 16th position, only four points above Somerset. There was little consolation in the limited-overs competitions. In the Refuge League, five wins and ten losses left the County in 14th place and there were no individual performances worthy of recall. Only one match was won in the Benson & Hedges group competition and that was against Scotland. Tim Boon hit 103 in this match; against Kent Whitaker made exactly 100.

Shropshire were defeated in the first round of the NatWest Trophy, but Leicestershire were removed in the second round, when Northants thundered to victory by nine wickets.

The first-class averages were headed by Briers with 1,485 runs, average 39.07. Though not as prolific as in 1990, he reinforced the general view that he thrives on hard work and responsibility. Whitaker totalled 1,289 runs at an average of 38. The other three batsmen to reach 1,000, Boon, Potter and Hepworth, all improved as the season wore on. Hepworth generally batted at number three, missed only one game, and at last his promise blossomed into something more.

The find of the season was 19-year-old Benjamin Smith, a stylish right-hand batsman. He graduated through the Leicestershire Young Cricketers sides and in 1991 represented England at Under-19 level against Australia. Playing 15 first-class matches for the County he made 674 runs at an average of 37.44, although his top score was only 71; just once in 23 innings did he fail to reach double figures.

Peter Willey, in his 26th season of first-class cricket, struggled with both bat and ball, and after 12 matches was omitted from the side. He was offered a release from his contract which still had a year to run and considered joining the new first-class county, Durham, for 1992. No one can criticise the spirit and determination with which he had pursued his county career over a quarter of a century.

Chris Lewis was selected for the fourth and fifth Tests against the West Indies and now made his mark at international level. In the Edgbaston Test he took six for 111 off 35 overs, as well as leading England's fight-back in the second innings. Going for his strokes at every opportunity, Lewis made 65 off 94 balls with ten boundaries; he was eventually caught in the covers and departed, cursing himself all the way back to the pavilion. At The Oval, he remained undefeated for a slightly more restrained 47, but did not take a wicket. He was also chosen for two out of the three limited-overs internationals. To Leicestershire he remained something of an enigma. Late in the season came the announcement from Lewis that he wished to leave the County, because he felt Leicestershire would not be in contention for honours in the near future and this would not help his international career. This view was not accepted and Mike Turner spent some time trying to dissuade him, but apparently to no avail. The situation naturally caused some upset in the dressing room and Lewis was omitted from the team in some of the closing matches.

Because of his absence from the side, Lewis took only 40 wickets for Leicestershire, but he headed the bowling table with an average of 23.80. John Maguire finished with 77 wickets at 31.64 and played in every match. David Millns took 63 wickets, improving out of all recognition. In the absence of Peter Willey, Potter had a lot of bowling to do; he proved very expensive. Another newcomer to the side in 1991 was Craig Wilkinson, a Lancashire-born seam bowler, who had emigrated early in life to Australia and learnt his craft in grade cricket in Western Australia. Playing in 14 matches, his 23 wickets cost 43.85 runs each and he obviously needed a little time to acclimatise to first-class cricket.

Leicestershire are now close to completing their first hundred years as a first-class county. For most of that time, indeed right up to the end of the 1960s, they were among the 'also rans', though sometimes showing tantalisingly brief glimpses of talent, which was always there in the form of individuals, even if those individuals failed to gel as a unit.

In 1953 and 1967 the County were placed third in the Championship, but each of these seasons was followed, not as expected by a determined final push to take the title, but by an abrupt descent to the lower depths once again. The arrival of Raymond Illingworth and the application of his leadership forced latent talent to blossom simultaneously amongst the eleven. The Championship was won in 1975 and between 1970 and 1984 the County remained in the top half of the table and generally in contention for first place. And, during the same period, through shrewd and careful management, the Club enjoyed 19 years of profits enabling significant re-development of the Grace Road ground. Since 1985 however the term 'under-achievers' has been increasingly used to describe the County side. Perhaps 1992 will bring success and be the season of the running fox?

STATISTICAL SECTION

BIOGRAPHICAL DETAILS
OF LEICESTERSHIRE PLAYERS

NAME AND EXTENT OF CAREER	BIRTHPLACE	DATE OF BIRTH	DATE OF DEATH
Alan Wesley Abbott *1946*	Sutton-in-the-Elms	15.11.1926	
Robert Alfred Adcock *1938*	Ibstock	3.11.1916	
Jonathan Paul Addison *1983*	Leek, Staffordshire	14.11.1965	
Charles Agar *1898–1900*	Birstall	1877	10.11.1921
Jonathan Philip Agnew *1978–1990*	Macclesfield, Cheshire	4. 4.1960	
Thomas Charlesworth Allsopp *1903–1905*	Leicester	18.12.1880	7. 3.1919
Norman Foster Armstrong *1919–1939*	Loughborough	22.12.1892	19. 1.1990
William Ewart Astill *1906–1939*	Ratby	1. 3.1888	10. 2.1948
John Bacon *1895*	Cosby	1872	16.10.1942
Peter Henry Christopher Badham *1933*	Bagworth	11. 2.1911	10. 4.1983
William Henry Bailey *1896*	Melton Mowbray	2.10.1870	19.10.1930
John Christopher Balderstone *1971–1986*	Longwood, Huddersfield, Yorks	16.11.1940	
Frank Bale *1920–1928*	Leicester	7. 1.1891	16. 1.1969
George Armstrong Ball *1933–1936*	Barwell	27. 2.1914	
Herbert Milburn Bannister *1912–1921*	Lutterworth	3. 6.1889	18. 6.1959
Roy James Barratt *1961–1970*	Aylestone, Leicester	3. 5.1942	
Walter Karl Beisiegel *1934*	Uppingham, Rutland	13. 7.1907	8. 1.1973
Winston Keithroy Matthew Benjamin *1986–1990*	All Saints, Antigua	31.12.1964	
William Ewart Benskin *1906–1924*	Leicester	8. 4.1880	1. 6.1956
Justin David Ramsay Benson *1988–1991*	Dublin, Ireland	1. 3.1967	
William Berridge *1923–1924*	Leicester	7. 9.1892	1. 4.1968
William Claude Morpott Berridge *1914–1922*	Enderby	2.12.1894	25. 2.1973
George Leslie Berry *1924–1951*	Dorking, Surrey	28. 4.1906	5. 2.1985
David James Billington *1985*	Leyland, Lancashire	6.12.1965	
Harold Dennis Bird *1960–1964*	Barnsley, Yorkshire	19. 4.1933	
Jack Birkenshaw *1961–1980*	Rothwell, Yorkshire	13.11.1940	
Mark Blackett *1985*	Edmonton, London	3. 2.1964	
Cecil Arthur Boden *1911–1913*	Countesthorpe	18.12.1890	31. 5.1981

Timothy James Boon *1980–1991*	Balby, Doncaster, Yorks	1.11.1961	
Brian Joseph Booth *1964–1973*	Billinge, Lancashire	3.10.1935	
Peter Booth *1972–1981*	Shipley, Yorkshire	2.11.1952	
Brian Stanley Boshier *1953–1964*	Leicester	6. 3.1932	
Peter Duncan Bowler *1986*	Plymouth, Devon	30. 7.1963	
Frederick James Bowley *1930–1931*	Ratby	20. 2.1909	
Herrick Browett Bowley *1933–1937*	Kirby Muxloe	10. 1.1911	12.1991
James Cecil Bradshaw *1923–1933*	Romford, Essex	25. 1.1902	8.11.1984
James William Montgomery Bradshaw *1935–1938*	Oakham, Rutland	23.11.1906	5.12.1938
Stanley William Bradshaw *1923*	Leicester	16. 1.1898	9. 1.1980
Walter Harry Bradshaw *1929*	Teddington, Middlesex	2. 8.1906	
Nigel Edwin Briers *1971–1991*	Southfields, Leicester	15. 1.1955	
Norman Briers *1967*	Highfields, Leicester	10. 2.1947	
Ernest Alfred Broughton *1928–1933*	Wigston	22. 4.1905	19. 2.1982
Peter Norman Broughton *1960–1962*	Castleford, Yorkshire	22.10.1935	
Cecil Leonard Morley Brown *1920–1921*	Melton Mowbray	16. 7.1895	6.12.1955
Joseph Henry Brown *1898–1905*	Earl Shilton	26. 1.1872	5.1915
Lewis Brown *1896–1903*	Earl Shilton	12. 3.1874	14.10.1951
William Brown *1910–1919*	Old Woodhouse	11. 4.1888	3. 9.1964
Geoffrey Worth Burch *1958–1964*	Braunstone, Leicester	12. 4.1937	
John Willder Burdett *1919*	Blaby, Leicester	16. 8.1888	16. 4.1974
Henry Burgess *1900–1902*	Carlton-Curlieu	1879	16. 4.1964
John Burgess *1902–1913*	Carlton-Curlieu	22.11.1880	2.11.1953
Ian Paul Butcher *1980–1987*	Farnborough, Kent	1. 7.1962	
Albert Callington (known as Albert Lord) *1920–1926*	Barwell	28. 8.1888	29. 3.1969
Ian Robert Carmichael *1984*	Hull, Yorkshire	17.12.1960	
John William Carter *1959*	Oxford	23. 6.1935	
Edward Lacy Challenor *1906–1913*	Speightstown, Barbados	10. 3.1873	15. 9.1935
Matt Chapman *1894–1895*	Arnesby	13. 4.1865	1909
Thomas Alan Chapman *1946–1950*	Barwell	14. 5.1918	19. 2.1979
Peter Ralph Cherrington *1938*	Newark, Notts	24.11.1917	20. 1.1945
A. Clarke *1902*			

Basil Frederick Clarke *1922*	Madras, India	26. 9.1885	4. 5.1940
Patrick Bernard Clift *1975–1987*	Salisbury, Rhodesia	14. 7.1953	
Russell Alan Cobb *1980–1989*	Leicester	18. 5.1961	
Arthur Cobley *1897–1904*	Barwell	5.10.1874	21. 4.1960
Geoffrey Coe *1963*	Earl Shilton	29. 3.1943	
Samuel Coe *1896–1923*	Earl Shilton	3. 6.1873	4.11.1955
Charles Alfred Richard Coleman *1926–1935*	Gumley	7. 7.1906	14. 6.1978
David John Constant *1965–1968*	Bradford-on-Avon, Wilts	9.11.1941	
Nicholas Grant Billson Cook *1978–1985*	Broughton-Astley	17. 6.1956	
Walter Berkeley Cornock *1948*	Waverley, New South Wales	1. 1.1921	
Percy Corrall *1930–1951*	Aylestone Park, Leicester	16. 7.1906	
John Cotton *1965–1969*	Newstead, Notts	7.11.1940	
Sydney Samuel Coulson *1923–1927*	South Wigston	17.10.1898	3.10.1981
Reginald Trevor Crawford *1901–1911*	Leicester	11. 6.1882	15.11.1945
Vivian Frank Shergold Crawford *1903–1910*	Leicester	11. 4.1879	21. 8.1922
Bernard Cromack *1959–1968*	Rothwell, Yorkshire	5. 6.1937	
Graham Frederick Cross *1961–1976*	Leicester	15.11.1943	
John Stafford Curtis *1906–1921*	Barrow-upon-Soar	21.12.1887	8. 3.1972
William Frederick Curtis *1911–1920*	Leicester	29. 5.1881	23.12.1962
Arthur Edward Davis *1901–1908*	Leicester	4. 8.1882	4.11.1916
Brian Fettes Davison *1970–1983*	Bulawayo, Rhodesia	21.12.1946	
George Owen Dawkes *1937–1939*	Aylestone Park, Leicester	19. 7.1920	
Edward William Dawson *1922–1934*	Paddington, London	13. 2.1904	4. 6.1979
Phillip Anthony Jason DeFreitas *1985–1988*	Scotts Head, Dominica	18. 2.1966	
John Adrian Frederick March Phillips De Lisle *1921–1930*	Kensington, London	27. 9.1891	4.11.1961
Charles Stewart Dempster *1935–1939*	Wellington, New Zealand	15.11.1903	14. 2.1974
Charles Edmund de Trafford *1894–1920*	Trafford Park, Manchester	21. 5.1864	11.11.1951
John Edward Dickinson *1933–1935*	Ashby-de-la-Zouch	20. 5.1914	
Alexander Willoughby Dickson (also known as Dixon) *1900*	West Derby, Liverpool	1876	1. 3.1953
Robert Anthony Diment *1955–1958*	Tortworth, Glos	9. 2.1927	
Ivan D'Oliveira *1967*	Cape Town, South Africa	19. 3.1941	

Name	Years	Place	Born	Died
Neville Thomas Dowen	1925–1938	Bulwell, Notts	18. 8.1901	25.10.1964
Cyril Henry Drake	1939	Highfields, Leicester	9. 1.1922	
Barry Dudleston	1966–1980	Bebington, Cheshire	16. 7.1945	
Norman Leonard Dunham	1949	Quorn	9.12.1925	
Charles Leslie Edgson	1933–1939	Morcott, Rutland	22. 8.1915	28. 6.1983
Richard Harold Edmunds	1989	Oakham, Rutland	27. 5.1970	9.12.1989
Arthur Emmett	1902	Halifax, Yorkshire	1873	1935
Maurice William Etherington	1948	North Hammersmith, London	24. 8.1916	
Gwynn Evans	1949	Bala, Merioneth	13. 8.1915	
Michael Evans	1946	Leicester	3. 5.1908	14.11.1974
Sir William Lindsay Everard	1924	Knighton, Leicester	13. 3.1891	11. 3.1949
George John Fitzgerald Ferris	1983–1990	Urlings Village, Antigua	18.10.1964	
William Finney	1894	Newtown, Montgomery	13. 8.1866	8. 5.1927
Jack Firth	1951–1958	Cottingley, Yorkshire	27. 6.1917	7. 9.1981
William Henry Flamson	1934–1939	Heather, Leicester	12. 8.1904	9. 1.1945
Grant Forster	1980–1982	Seaham, Co. Durham	27. 5.1961	
Frederick George Foulds	1952–1956	West End, Leicester	23. 4.1935	
Gustavus Henry Spencer Fowke	1899–1927	Brighton, Sussex	14.10.1880	24. 6.1946
Joseph Brankin Frisby	1938	Carlton-Curlieu	26. 2.1908	2.11.1977
Leslie Robin Gardner	1954–1962	Ledbury, Herefordshire	23. 2.1934	
Michael Anthony Garnham	1980–1988	Johannesburg, S. Africa	20. 8.1960	
George Geary	1912–1938	Barwell	9. 7.1893	6. 3.1981
Frederick Geeson	1895–1902	Redmile	23. 8.1862	2. 5.1920
Arthur Clive Johnson German	1923–1924	Ashby-de-la-Zouch	28. 6.1905	2. 2.1968
Harry German	1896–1898	Measham	1865	14. 6.1945
Alfred Leonard Gibson	1946	Devon, Jamaica	13. 2.1912	
Martyn Ian Gidley	1989–1991	Leicester	30. 9.1968	
Ernest Harry Gill	1901	Mountsorrel	1877	1950
George Cooper Gill	1903–1906	Mountsorrel	18. 4.1876	21. 8.1937

Paul Gill *1986* Greenfield, 31. 5.1963
Manchester

Christopher Gimson *1921* Leicester 24.12.1886 8.11.1975
Joseph Edward Glennon *1921* Whitwick 1889 26. 6.1926
Donald Goodson *1950–1953* Eastwell 15.10.1932
Thomas Jeffrey Goodwin *1950–1959* Bignall End, 22. 1.1929
Staffs

David Ivon Gower *1975–1989* Tunbridge 1. 4.1957
Wells, Kent

Henry Canning Graham *1936–1937* Belfast, N. 31. 5.1914 3.1982
Ireland

Frank Davis Gray *1895* Leicester 2. 7.1873 23. 2.1947
Stephen Greensword *1963–1966* Gateshead, Co. 6. 9.1943
Durham

George Grewcock *1899* Barwell 1862 8.1922
Lloyd Archibald Hales *1947* Leicester 27. 6.1921 12. 9.1984
Maurice Raymond Hallam *1950–1970* Leicester 10. 9.1931
Arthur Harry Hampson *1905–1906* Earl Shilton 1878 24.11.1952
Gordon Andrew Robert Harris *1986* Edmonton, 11. 1.1964
London

Dawson Gascoigne Harron *1951* Langley Park, 12. 9.1921 21. 7.1988
Co. Durham

Douglas John Harrop *1972* Cosby 16. 4.1947
Frederick Hassall *1894* Nantwich, 1868 1945
Cheshire

Christopher James Hawkes *1990* Loughborough 14. 7.1972
Ernest George Hayes *1926* Peckham, 6.11.1876 2.12.1953
London

Michael Donald Haysman *1984* North Adelaide, 22. 4.1961
South
Australia

John William Haywood *1901–1903* Harby 17. 4.1878 2. 2.1963
Paul Raymond Haywood *1969–1973* Leicester 30. 3.1947
Sir Arthur Grey Hazlerigg (created 1st Baron Ayr, Scotland 17.11.1878 25. 5.1949
Hazlerigg in 1945) *1907–1910*
Sir Arthur Grey Hazlerigg (succeeded as 2nd South 24. 2.1910
Baron Hazlerigg in 1949) *1930–1934* Kensington,
London

Peter Nash Hepworth *1988–1991* Ackworth, 4. 5.1967
Yorkshire

Geoffrey Alfred Hickinbottom *1959* West End, 15.11.1932
Leicester

Frank Hickley *1921* Leicester 14.12.1895 28.10.1972
Malcolm Francis Hickman *1954–1957* Market 30. 6.1936
Harborough

Kenneth Higgs *1972–1986* Kidsgrove, 14. 1.1937
Staffs

George Whiteside Hillyard *1894–1896* Hanwell, 6. 2.1864 24. 3.1943
Middlesex

R. H. Hincks *1895*
John Preston Hings *1934* Leicester 22.12.1910
John Holland *1894–1896* Nantwich, 7. 4.1869 22. 8.1914
Cheshire

Name	Years	Place	Born	Died
Kenneth Holland	*1935*	Rowley Fields, Leicester	29.3.1911	21. 7.1986
Arthur Howard	*1921*	Ashby-de-la-Zouch	1882	5. 8.1946
Jack Howard	*1946–1948*	Belgrave, Leicester	24.11.1917	
Frederick John Hudson	*1901*	Bottesford	22.11.1878	7.10.1966
David John Humphries	*1974–1976*	Alveley, Shropshire	6. 8.1953	
William Sydney Hurd	*1932–1934*	Ashby-de-la-Zouch	9.1908	
Leonard Staughton Hutchinson	*1923–1925*	Anstey	16. 4.1901	2.10.1976
Raymond Illingworth	*1969–1978*	Pudsey, Yorkshire	8. 6.1932	
Clive Clay Inman	*1961–1971*	Colombo, Ceylon	29. 1.1936	
Victor Edward Jackson	*1938–1956*	Sydney, New South Wales	25.10.1916	30. 1.1965
Peter Heath Jaques	*1949*	Aylestone, Leicester	20.11.1919	
James Edward Frisby Jarvis	*1900*	Leicester	1875	24. 1.1962
Stanley Jayasinghe	*1961–1965*	Badulla, Ceylon	19. 1.1931	
Thomas Jayes	*1903–1911*	Ratby	17. 4.1877	16. 4.1913
Howard William James Jeffery	*1964*	Workington, Cumberland	5. 5.1944	
Wilfrid Wykeham Jelf	*1911*	Halifax, Nova Scotia	22. 7.1880	17.10.1933
John Michael Josephs	*1946–1953*	Hendon, Middlesex	16. 1.1924	
Francis Matthew Joyce	*1911–1920*	Blackfordby	16.12.1886	23. 9.1958
John Hall Joyce	*1894*	Blackfordby	5.12.1868	17. 4.1938
Ralph Joyce	*1896–1907*	Ashby-de-la-Zouch	28. 8.1878	12. 3.1908
Raymond Julian	*1953–1971*	Cosby	23. 8.1936	
Edwin King	*1925*	Braunstone	1884	7. 7.1952
Harry King	*1912–1920*	Leicester	6.11.1881	30. 6.1947
James King	*1899–1905*	Lutterworth	3. 5.1869	8. 3.1948
John Herbert King	*1895–1925*	Lutterworth	16. 4.1871	18.11.1946
John William King	*1929*	Leicester	21. 1.1908	25. 3.1953
David Kirby	*1959–1964*	Darlington, Co. Durham	18. 1.1939	
George Alan Knew	*1972–1973*	Leicester	5. 3.1954	
George Frank Knew	*1939*	Wigston, Leicester	13.10.1920	
Albert Ernest Knight	*1895–1912*	Leicester	8.10.1872	25. 4.1946
Barry Rolfe Knight	*1967–1969*	Chesterfield, Derbyshire	18. 2.1938	
Peter Hans Konig	*1949*	Vienna, Austria	16.10.1931	
Jack Lee	*1947*	Sileby	4.11.1920	
Nevill Bernard Lee	*1922–1924*	Barlestone	13. 8.1898	21. 7.1978
Gerald Lester	*1937–1958*	Long Whatton	27.12.1915	

Clairmonte Christopher Lewis 1987–1991	Georgetown, Guyana	14. 2.1968	
Graham Anthony Richard Lock 1965–1967	Limpsfield, Surrey	5. 7.1929	
Hugh Logan 1903	East Langton, Market Harborough	10. 5.1885	24. 2.1919
Alexander Lorrimer 1894–1896	Aylestone, Leicester	9. 1.1859	2. 2.1947
David Lorrimer 1894–1895	Aylestone, Leicester	16. 1.1865	12.11.1925
Robert MacDonald 1899–1902	Melbourne, Australia	14. 2.1870	5.1945
Graham Douglas McKenzie 1969–1975	Cottesloe, W. Australia	24. 6.1941	
Norman Michael McVicker 1974–1976	Whitefield, Radcliffe, Lancs	4.11.1940	
John Norman Maguire 1991	Murwillumbah, New South Wales	15. 9.1956	
Thomas Marlow 1900–1903	Anstey	1879	13. 8.1954
William Henry Marlow 1931–1936	Wigston	13. 2.1900	16.12.1975
Peter Thomas Marner 1965–1970	Greenacres, Oldham, Lancs	31. 3.1936	
Harold Henry Marriott 1894–1902	Oadby, Leicester	20. 1.1875	15.11.1949
Damien Richard Martyn 1991	Australia	21.10.1971	
Albert John Matthews 1965–1968	Fearn, Inverness	29. 4.1944	
Robin Birkby Matthews 1971–1973	Stockton-on-Tees, Co. Durham	30. 1.1944	
Alfred Shipley Matts 1921	Barrow-on-Soar	2. 4.1893	20. 6.1970
John William Middleton 1914–1921	Stoney Stanton	26.10.1890	16. 9.1966
David James Millns 1990–1991	Clipstone, Notts	27. 2.1965	
Frederick Mills 1921–1923	Leicester	1898	4.11.1929
John Mitten 1961–1963	Davyhulme, Manchester	30. 3.1941	
Arthur Mounteney, jnr. 1911–1924	Loughborough	11. 2.1883	1. 6.1933
Harold Mudge 1937	Stanmore, New South Wales	14. 2.1914	
Alan David Mullally 1990–1991	Southend, Essex	12. 7.1969	
Donald Francis Xavier Munden 1960–1961	Leicester	17.10.1934	
Paul Anthony Munden 1957–1964	Barrow-on-Soar	5.11.1938	
Victor Stanislaus Munden 1946–1957	Leicester	2. 1.1928	
Rowland Needham 1911	Huncote	1878	28. 4.1963

Alfred Edwin Newcomb *1911*	Market Harborough	1873	4. 2.1932
Paul Andrew Nixon *1989–1991*	Carlisle, Cumberland	31.10.1970	
Michael Eric John Charles Norman *1966–1975*	Northampton	19. 1.1933	
Edwin Freame Odell *1912*	Leicester	2.12.1883	11. 3.1960
William Ward Odell *1901–1914*	Leicester	5.11.1881	4.10.1917
Frederick Osborn *1911–1913*	Leicester	10.11.1889	11.10.1954
Donald Straker Oscroft *1928*	St Pancras, London	12. 4.1908	19. 2.1944
Charles William Christopher Packe *1929–1934*	Pietermaritz-burg, South Africa	2. 5.1909	1. 7.1944
Michael St John Packe *1936–1939*	Eastbourne, Sussex	21. 8.1916	20.12.1978
Robert Julian Packe *1933*	Hounslow, Middlesex	8. 7.1913	24.10.1935
Charles Henry Palmer *1950–1959*	Old Hill, Staffordshire	15. 5.1919	
George Harry Palmer *1938–1939*	Ibstock	24.10.1917	
John Palmer *1906*	Ibstock	1881	14. 6.1928
William Richard Parkins *1950*	Glenfield	20. 8.1925	1.11.1969
Ernest William Parkinson *1920*	Sileby	28. 4.1894	14. 4.1978
Gordon James Parsons *1978–1991*	Slough, Bucks	17.10.1959	
Albert Payne *1906–1907*	Leicester	1885	7. 5.1908
Kenneth George Peake *1946*	New Found Pool, Leicester	24. 7.1920	
John Devereaux Dubricious Pember *1968–1971*	Creaton, Northants	8. 6.1940	
Edmund Frederick Phillips *1957–1959*	Bridgnorth, Shropshire	12. 1.1932	
Harry Gordon Pickering *1947*	Hackney, London	18. 1.1917	4. 3.1984
Laurie Potter *1986–1991*	Bexleyheath, Kent	7.11.1962	
Arthur Dick Pougher *1894–1901*	Leicester	19. 4.1865	20. 5.1926
John Powers *1895–1906*	Barwell	1868	9.11.1939
Rodney Lynes Pratt *1955–1964*	Stoney Stanton	15.11.1938	
William Ewart Pratt *1920–1930*	Hinckley	2. 7.1895	27. 5.1974
Francis Thomas Prentice *1934–1951*	Knares-borough, Yorkshire	22. 4.1912	10. 7.1978
Frederick John Randon *1894*	Hathern	18.11.1873	15. 1.1949
Kenneth Raynor *1923*	Wellington, Berkshire	23. 5.1886	15. 4.1973
Alan Chambers Revill *1958–1960*	Sheffield, Yorkshire	27. 3.1923	
Riaz-ur-Rehman *1966*	India	1940	10. 7.1966
Alan Sedgwick Rice *1954*	West End, Leicester	29.8.1929	

Anthony Riddington *1931–1950*	Countesthorpe	22.12.1911	
Edwin Riley *1895*	Stoney Stanton	1867	4. 5.1936
Harold Riley *1928–1937*	Stoney Stanton	3.10.1902	24. 1.1989
William Nairn Riley *1911–1914*	Appleby Magna	24.11.1892	20.11.1955
Anderson Montgomery Everton Roberts *1981–1984*	Urlings Village, Antigua	29. 1.1951	
Michael Harrison Rose *1963–1964*	Hereford	8. 4.1942	
George Boyd Franklin Rudd *1913–1932*	Clarendon Park, Leicester	3. 7.1894	4. 2.1957
George Edward Rudd *1894–1901*	York	14. 1.1866	16. 9.1921
Gordon Hedley Salmon *1913–1924*	Leicester	1. 8.1894	13. 6.1978
Murray Alfred James Sargent *1951–1952*	North Adelaide, South Australia	23. 8.1928	
Philip Frederick Saunders *1951–1952*	Adelaide, South Australia	28. 4.1929	
John Scholes Savage *1953–1966*	Ramsbottom, Lancashire	3. 3.1929	
Martin Schepens *1973–1980*	Barrow-upon-Soar	12. 8.1955	
Aubrey Temple Sharp *1908–1935*	Whitwick	23. 3.1889	15. 2.1973
Sir John Aubrey Taylor Sharp *1937–1946*	Blaby	6. 8.1917	15. 1.1977
Patrick Sherrard *1938*	Mickleover, Burton-on-Trent, Staffs	7. 1.1919	
John Shields *1906–1923*	Loudoun, Ayrshire	1. 2.1882	11. 5.1960
George Shingler *1920–1921*	Leicester	1882	5.1946
Alan Wilfred Shipman *1920–1936*	Ratby	7. 3.1901	12.12.1979
William Shipman *1908–1921*	Ratby	1. 3.1886	26. 8.1943
Kenneth Shuttleworth *1977–1980*	St Helens, Lancashire	13.11.1944	
Thomas Edgar Sidwell *1913–1933*	Belgrave	30. 1.1888	8.12.1958
Alexander Skelding *1912–1929*	Leicester	5. 9.1886	18. 4.1960
Arthur Smith *1897–1901*	Barlestone	1872	3.10.1952
Benjamin Francis Smith *1990–1991*	Corby, Northants	3. 4.1972	
Graham Stuart Smith *1949*	Leicester	4. 7.1923	
Haydon Arthur Smith *1925–1939*	Groby	29. 3.1901	7. 8.1948
John Willoughby Dixie Smith *1921*	Blaby	11. 3.1882	2.10.1959
John Westwood Rowley Smith *1950–1955*	Clarendon Park, Leicester	28. 7.1924	12.12.1991
Kenneth Desmond Smith *1950–1951*	Bishop Auckland, Co. Durham	29. 4.1922	
Michael John Knight Smith *1951–1955*	Westcotes, Leicester	30. 6.1933	

Peter Thomas Smith *1956–1957*	Leicester	5.10.1934	
Raymond Charles Smith *1956–1964*	Duddington, Northants	3. 8.1935	
Walter Alfred Smith *1930–1946*	Evington, Leicester	23. 2.1913	
Gerald Arthur Smithson *1951–1956*	Spofforth, Yorkshire	1.11.1926	6. 9.1970
Horace Charles Snary *1921–1933*	Whissendine, Rutland	22. 9.1897	26.12.1966
Lawrence Arthur Spence *1952–1954*	Blaby	14. 1.1932	
Charles Terrance Spencer *1952–1974*	Braunstone, Leicester	18. 8.1931	
James Sperry *1937–1952*	Thornton	19. 3.1910	
Clement Edwin Starmer *1925*	Cosby	2.12.1895	25. 7.1978
John Frederick Steele *1970–1983*	Brown Edge, Staffordshire	23. 7.1946	
Francis Wilfrid Stocks *1894–1903*	Market Harborough	10.12.1873	21. 5.1929
Charles Cecil Stone *1895–1896*	Knighton, Leicester	13. 6.1865	11.11.1951
Terry Kevin Stretton *1972–1975*	Cosby	23. 5.1953	
Peter Michael Stringer *1970–1972*	Gipton, Leeds, Yorks	23. 2.1943	
Walter Sturman *1909–1912*	Leicester	29. 8.1882	7.1958
Peter Mark Such *1987–1989*	Helensburgh, Scotland	12. 6.1964	
Stuart Johnston Symington *1948–1949*	Bexhill, Sussex	16. 9.1926	
Claude Hilary Taylor *1922–1927*	Leicester	6. 2.1904	28. 1.1966
James Alexander Simson Taylor *1937*	Weston-super-Mare, Somerset	19. 6.1917	
Leslie Brian Taylor *1977–1990*	Earl Shilton	25.10.1953	
Lloyd Tennant *1986–1991*	Walsall, Staffordshire	9. 4.1968	
Arthur Paul Thompson *1937*	Leicester	1. 3.1914	
Herbert Thompson *1908–1910*	Leicester	14. 5.1886	8. 8.1941
Thomas Thompson *1963–1964*	Workington, Cumberland	24. 2.1934	
John Arthur Curzon Thornton *1921*	Stoneygate, Leicester	24. 2.1902	
Laurence Denis Thursting *1938–1947*	Lambeth, London	9. 9.1915	
Eric Warrington Tilley *1946*	Whatstandwell, Derbyshire	22. 9.1913	1.12.1977
Jeffrey Graham Tolchard *1970–1977*	Torquay, Devon	17. 3.1944	
Roger William Tolchard *1965–1983*	Torquay, Devon	15. 6.1946	
William Tomlin *1894–1899*	Broughton-Astley	15. 9.1866	11. 5.1910
Maurice Tompkin *1938–1956*	Countesthorpe	17. 2.1919	27. 9.1956
Joseph Toon *1902–1909*	Ratby	5. 6.1879	7. 3.1950
Francis Michael Turner *1954–1959*	Leicester	8. 8.1934	

Robert Frewin Turner *1909–1911*	Leicester	15. 7.1885	15. 2.1959
Bernard Tyler *1926–1928*	Ridlington, Rutland	29. 4.1902	10.11.1987
Geoffrey Francis Uvedale Udal *1946*	Holborn, London	23. 2.1908	5.12.1980
John van Geloven *1956–1965*	Guiseley, Yorkshire	4. 1.1934	
Edwin William Walker *1930*	Coalville	27.12.1909	
John Edward Walsh *1937–1956*	Sydney, New South Wales	4.12.1912	20. 5.1980
George Walton *1894–1895*	Belgrave	3.12.1863	30. 6.1921
Alan Ward *1977–1978*	Dronfield, Derbyshire	10. 8.1947	
Thomas Warren *1894–1895*	Hathern	8.10.1959	1936
George Sutton Watson *1934–1950*	Milton Regis, Kent	10. 4.1907	1. 4.1974
Willie Watson *1958–1964*	Bolton-on-Dearne, Yorkshire	7. 3.1920	
Charles George Watts *1924*	Hinckley	4. 9.1894	30. 1.1979
Arthur Geoffrey Gascoigne Webb *1933–1938*	Newington, Kent	17. 8.1896	6. 4.1981
David Alan Wenlock *1980–1982*	Leicester	16. 4.1959	
Albert Richard West *1939*	Earl Shilton	7.11.1920	8. 6.1985
Alan Gibbons Weston *1933–1934*	Leicester	30. 9.1907	
Alan Wharton *1961–1963*	Heywood, Lancashire	30. 4.1923	
John James Whitaker *1983–1991*	Skipton, Yorkshire	5. 5.1962	
Harry Whitehead *1898–1922*	Barlestone	19. 9.1874	14. 9.1944
John Parkinson Whiteside *1894–1906*	Fleetwood, Lancashire	11. 6.1861	8. 3.1946
Philip Whitticase *1984–1991*	Marston Green, Solihull	15. 3.1965	
Searson Harry Wigginton *1930–1934*	Leicester	26. 3.1909	15. 9.1977
Craig William Wilkinson *1991*	Wardle, Lancashire	19. 3.1963	
Peter Willey *1984–1991*	Sedgefield, Co. Durham	6.12.1949	
Edward Lovell Williams, *1949*	Shaftesbury, Dorset	15. 9.1925	
Cecil John Burditt Wood *1896–1923*	Northampton	21.11.1875	5. 6.1960
Edwin James Wood *1907*	Loughborough	1868	
Arthur Woodcock *1894–1908*	Northampton	23. 9.1865	14. 5.1910
Charles Robert Dudley Wooler *1949–1951*	Bulawayo, Rhodesia	30. 6.1930	
Frederick Wright *1895–1897*	Sysonby	20. 6.1855	20.11.1929
Harold Wright *1912–1914*	Barrow-upon-Soar	19. 2.1884	14. 9.1915
Samuel Reginald Wright *1896–1897*	Markfield	4. 1.1869	25. 1.1947
Geoffrey Noel Wykes *1923*	Clarendon Park, Leicester	22.11.1890	1. 5.1926

CAREER RECORDS OF LEICESTERSHIRE PLAYERS, 1894–1991

The following career records cover all first-class matches played by Leicestershire since their elevation to first-class status in 1894, a total of 2,270 matches.

Name	Inns	NO	Runs	HS	Avge	100s	Runs	Wkts	Avge	BB	5wI
Abbott A. W.	2	–	5	5	2.50	–	8	–	–	–	–
Adcock R. A.	9	–	89	27	9.89	–	29	1	29.00	1/29	–
Addison J. P.	2	–	67	51	33.50	–	–	–	–	–	–
Agar C.	40	6	381	48	11.21	–	1711	38	45.03	4/80	–
Agnew J. P.	221	45	2081	90	11.82	–	18144	632	28.70	9/70	36
Allsopp T. C.	53	17	337	32	9.36	–	2417	83	29.12	6/85	4
Armstrong N. F.	637	61	19002	186	32.99	36	4459	110	40.54	4/21	–
Astill W. E.	1017	131	19875	164*	22.43	13	49396	2130	23.19	9/41	127
Bacon J.	8	1	42	14	6.00	–	21	1	21.00	1/18	–
Badham P. H. C.	2	–	18	15	9.00	–	29	–	–	–	–
Bailey W. H.	4	–	49	15	12.25	–	–	–	–	–	–
Balderstone J. C.	532	55	17627	181*	36.95	32	7241	271	26.71	6/25	5
Bale F.	202	53	1426	52	9.57	–	6431	231	27.84	5/62	3
Ball G. A.	17	2	206	44*	13.73	–	–	–	–	–	–
Bannister H. M.	20	3	227	64	13.35	–	793	26	30.50	5/90	1
Barratt R. J.	88	16	604	39	8.39	–	4007	141	28.42	7/35	7
Beisiegel W. K.	17	2	185	33	12.33	–	–	–	–	–	–
Benjamin W. K. M.	63	15	1183	101*	24.64	1	4162	158	26.34	7/54	13
Benskin W. E.	152	47	797	26	7.59	–	7813	302	25.87	8/86	15
Benson J. D. R.	48	7	1231	133*	30.02	2	346	3	115.33	1/18	–
Berridge W.	21	–	146	33	6.95	–	27	–	–	–	–
Berridge W. C. M.	38	5	406	61	12.30	–	804	29	27.72	5/58	1
Berry G. L.	1050	56	30143	232	30.32	45	606	10	60.60	1/1	–
Billington D.	1	–	19	19	19.00	–	–	–	–	–	–
Bird H. D.	145	8	2701	104	19.72	1	22	–	–	–	–
Birkenshaw J.	573	109	11040	131	23.79	4	24058	908	26.50	8/94	37
Blackett M.	4	2	41	28*	20.50	–	–	–	–	–	–
Boden C. A.	19	–	196	40	10.32	–	–	–	–	–	–
Boon T. J.	309	36	8669	144	31.75	10	350	7	50.00	3/40	–
Booth B. J.	388	35	10113	171*	28.65	13	1410	35	40.29	4/56	–
Booth P.	80	21	767	58*	13.00	–	4549	162	28.08	6/93	1
Boshier B. S.	225	92	565	30	4.25	–	11608	505	22.99	8/45	23
Bowler P. D.	11	1	249	100*	24.90	1	57	–	–	–	–
Bowley F. J.	17	7	33	6	3.30	–	770	23	33.48	4/46	–
Bowley H. B.	18	1	113	25	6.65	–	919	17	54.06	4/17	–
Bradshaw J. C.	286	20	5051	140	18.99	3	80	–	–	–	–
Bradshaw J. W. M.	3	–	95	82	31.67	–	103	1	103.00	1/25	–
Bradshaw S. W.	6	–	9	5	1.50	–	–	–	–	–	–
Bradshaw W. H.	5	–	38	20	7.60	–	–	–	–	–	–
Briers N. E.	505	49	14605	201*	32.22	23	988	32	30.87	4/29	–
Briers N.	1	–	1	1	1.00	–	31	–	–	–	–
Broughton E. A.	38	1	482	61	13.03	–	18	–	–	–	–
Broughton P. N.	28	15	143	17*	11.00	–	2065	69	29.93	6/111	4

Name	Inns	NO	Runs	HS	Avge	100s	Runs	Wkts	Avge	BB	5wI
Brown C. L. M.	11	–	74	33	6.73	–	–	–	– –	–
Brown J. H.	28	3	305	53★	12.20	–	325	7	46.43	2/6	–
Brown L.	110	7	1660	110	16.12	1	385	7	55.00	3/39	–
Brown W.	72	23	347	35	7.08	–	3161	114	27.73	7/51	4
Burch G. W.	79	10	1067	64★	15.46	–	3	–	– –	–
Burdett J. W.	2	–	1	1	0.50	–	–	–	– –	–
Burgess H.	11	1	53	20	5.30	–	524	11	47.64	3/106	–
Burgess J.	18	–	230	39	12.78	–	–	–	– –	–
Butcher I. P.	153	9	4432	139	30.77	9	28	1	28.00	1/2	–
Callington A. ★	235	12	3864	102	17.33	1	1060	39	27.18	5/40	2
Carmichael I. R.	6	3	6	4★	2.00	–	661	17	38.88	5/84	1
Carter J. W.	14	–	209	41	14.93	–	–	–	– –	–
Challenor E. L.	19	–	256	28	13.47	–	15	–	– –	–
Chapman M.	52	6	595	56	12.93	–	30	–	– –	–
Chapman T. A.	85	3	1137	74	13.87	–	6	–	– –	–
Cherrington P. R.	14	–	85	33	6.07	–	127	–	– –	–
Clarke A.	–	–	–	–	–	–	70	2	35.00	2/70	–
Clarke B. F.	9	1	51	20	6.38	–	–	–	– –	–
Clift P. B.	284	58	5825	106	25.77	2	14010	586	23.90	8/17	19
Cobb R. A.	187	15	4229	91	24.58	–	46	–	– –	–
Cobley A.	18	–	139	22	7.72	–	142	1	142.00	1/9	–
Coe G.	–	–	–	–	–	–	77	2	38.50	1/26	–
Coe S.	768	69	17367	252★	24.85	19	10685	326	32.78	6/38	2
Coleman C. A. R.	170	10	2403	114	15.02	1	3576	100	35.76	5/30	1
Constant D. J.	79	12	1385	80	20.67	–	36	1	36.00	1/28	–
Cook N. G. B.	151	47	1316	75	12.65	–	11660	395	29.52	7/63	14
Cornock W. B.	43	2	801	60	19.54	–	1007	15	67.13	3/46	–
Corrall P.	418	125	2831	64	9.66	–	–	–	– –	–
Cotton J.	99	39	568	30★	9.47	–	6029	242	24.91	9/29	6
Coulson S. S.	94	6	1094	80	12.43	–	–	–	– –	–
Crawford R. T.	160	10	2502	99★	16.68	–	4228	147	28.76	5/29	6
Crawford V. F. S.	281	16	6918	172★	26.11	8	592	14	42.29	3/14	–
Cromack B.	55	2	626	55	11.81	–	1006	38	26.47	6/48	1
Cross G. F.	128	15	2079	78	18.40	–	2756	92	29.96	4/28	–
Curtis J. S.	57	4	868	66	16.38	–	2334	71	32.87	7/75	4
Curtis W. F.	8	–	69	38	8.63	–	–	–	– –	–
Davis A. E.	31	4	334	55	12.37	–	–	–	– –	–
Davison B. F.	483	53	18537	189	43.11	37	1594	44	36.23	4/99	–
Dawkes G. O.	92	12	1147	81	14.34	–	–	–	– –	–
Dawson E. W.	297	10	7705	146	26.85	10	12	–	– –	–
DeFreitas P. A. J.	83	8	1641	113	21.88	2	5362	225	23.83	7/44	15
De Lisle J. A. F. M. P.	50	4	530	88	11.52	–	–	–	– –	–
Dempster C. S.	108	13	4659	207★	49.04	18	52	2	26.00	1/14	–
De Trafford C. E.	413	9	8080	137	20.00	5	95	2	47.50	2/47	–
Dickinson J. E.	4	–	27	16	6.75	–	63	–	– –	–
Dickson A. W.	9	1	36	18	4.50	–	266	5	53.20	2/79	–
Diment R. A.	100	5	1592	71	16.76	–	4	–	– –	–
D'Oliveira I.	1	–	–	–	–	–	–	–	– –	–
Dowen N. T.	12	–	187	44	15.58	–	25	–	– –	–
Drake C. H.	11	3	43	13	5.38	–	605	19	31.84	5/21	1
Dudleston B.	438	44	12483	202	31.68	27	811	30	27.03	4/6	–
Dunham N. L.	2	1	15	12★	15.00	–	60	–	– –	–

Name	Inns	NO	Runs	HS	Avge	100s	Runs	Wkts	Avge	BB	5wI
Edgson C. L.	24	–	321	49	13.38	–	–	–	–	–	–
Edmunds R. H.	3	–	17	17	5.66	–	113	3	37.66	2/38	–
Emmett, A.	4	–	12	10	3.00	–	240	5	48.00	3/48	–
Etherington M. W.	5	1	41	27	10.25	–	178	3	59.33	2/60	–
Evans G.	15	2	192	65★	14.77	–	664	16	41.50	4/49	–
Evans M.	4	1	26	14★	8.67	–	130	6	21.67	3/30	–
Everard W. L.	2	–	3	3	1.50	–	–	–	–	–	–
Ferris G. J. F.	76	26	550	36★	11.00	–	5802	224	25.90	7/42	9
Finney W.	5	1	29	14★	7.25	–	123	3	41.00	1/7	–
Firth J.	325	88	3362	90★	14.19	–	–	–	–	–	–
Flamson W. H.	67	20	351	50★	7.47	–	4971	151	32.92	7/46	7
Forster G.	4	2	45	22★	22.50	–	175	1	175.00	1/29	–
Foulds F. G.	4	–	1	1	0.25	–	–	–	–	–	–
Fowke G. H. S.	260	27	4325	104	18.56	1	738	13	56.77	2/13	–
Frisby J. B.	1	–	4	4	4.00	–	–	–	–	–	–
Gardner L. R.	227	19	4119	102★	19.80	2	199	5	39.80	3/54	–
Garnham M. A.	100	16	2033	100	24.20	1	–	–	–	–	–
Geary, G.	704	112	11688	122	19.74	7	34708	1759	19.73	10/18	110
Geeson F.	228	46	3378	104★	18.56	1	11111	411	27.03	7/33	21
German A. C. J.	6	–	73	36	12.17	–	–	–	–	–	–
German H.	9	–	69	13	7.67	–	–	–	–	–	–
Gibson A. L.	3	–	17	11	5.67	–	–	–	–	–	–
Gidley M. I.	15	3	235	80	19.58	–	655	6	109.16	2/58	–
Gill E. H.	5	3	23	11★	11.50	–	413	12	34.42	3/61	–
Gill G. C.	112	8	1553	100	14.93	1	4535	179	25.34	9/89	11
Gill P.	11	4	68	17	9.71	–	–	–	–	–	–
Gimson C.	15	1	166	40	11.86	–	32	–	–	–	–
Glennon J. E.	4	–	12	7	3.00	–	–	–	–	–	–
Goodson D.	13	4	36	22★	4.00	–	394	7	56.29	3/43	–
Goodwin T. J.	167	80	474	23★	5.45	–	10108	335	30.17	8/81	15
Gower D. I.	307	33	10685	228	38.99	24	197	3	65.66	3/47	–
Graham H. C.	38	4	589	75	17.32	–	37	1	37.00	1/9	–
Gray F. D.	2	–	17	9	8.50	–	–	–	–	–	–
Greensword S.	68	7	888	57	14.56	–	808	24	33.67	3/22	–
Grewcock G.	6	–	4	1	0.67	–	308	8	38.50	4/93	–
Hales L. A.	4	–	76	62	19.00	–	38	–	–	–	–
Hallam M. R.	883	56	23662	210★	28.61	31	141	4	35.25	1/12	–
Hampshire J. H.	6	1	254	112	50.80	1	–	–	–	–	–
Hampson A. H.	18	4	100	23	7.14	–	–	–	–	–	–
Harris G. A. R.	2	1	6	6	6.00	–	34	–	–	–	–
Harron D. G.	14	2	186	53	15.50	–	–	–	–	–	–
Harrop D. J.	2	1	11	11★	11.00	–	–	–	–	–	–
Hassall F.	7	–	57	20	8.14	–	25	–	–	–	–
Hawkes C. J.	2	1	5	3	5.00	–	40	–	–	–	–
Hayes E. G.	7	–	254	99	36.29	–	91	3	30.33	2/28	–
Haysman M. D.	10	4	230	102★	38.33	1	–	–	–	–	–
Haywood J. W.	5	–	37	16	7.40	–	240	4	60.00	2/81	–
Haywood P. R.	82	8	1570	100★	21.22	1	324	9	36.00	4/60	–
Hazlerigg Sir A. G.	108	28	866	55★	10.83	–	44	–	–	–	–
Hazlerigg A. G.	53	4	1151	97	23.49	–	1120	29	38.62	4/64	–
Hepworth P. N.	60	6	1499	115	27.75	2	463	14	33.07	3/51	–
Hickinbottom G. A.	7	5	6	4★	3.00	–	–	–	–	–	–

317

Name	Inns	NO	Runs	HS	Avge	100s	Runs	Wkts	Avge	BB	5wI
Hickley F.	3	–	34	27	11.33	–	18	1	18.00	1/8	–
Hickman M. F.	22	2	232	40	11.60	–	–	–	– –		–
Higgs K.	120	66	677	98	12.53	–	9324	371	25.13	7/44	11
Hillyard G. W.	59	3	531	36	9.48	–	2240	101	22.18	6/74	7
Hincks R. H.	4	–	15	14	3.75	–	29	2	14.50	1/3	–
Hings J. P.	4	–	18	10	4.50	–	4	–	– –		–
Holland J.	80	3	1326	65	17.22	–	54	–	– –		–
Holland K.	2	–	2	2	1.00	–	146	3	48.67	1/9	–
Howard A.	6	–	60	27	10.00	–	–	–	– –		–
Howard J.	66	14	589	38*	11.33	–	5	–	– –		–
Hudson F. J.	2	–	1	1	0.50	–	38	–	– –		–
Humphries D. J.	9	3	147	62*	24.50	–	–	–	– –		–
Hurd W. S.	4	–	7	5	1.75	–	28	–	– –		–
Hutchinson L. S.	15	1	65	14	4.64	–	64	1	64.00	1/9	–
Illingworth R.	237	56	5341	153*	29.51	4	7547	372	20.29	8/38	14
Inman C. C.	398	40	12364	178	34.54	19	55	–	– –		–
Jackson V. E.	550	46	14379	170	28.53	21	22461	930	24.15	8/43	43
Jaques P. H.	2	–	69	55	34.50	–	–	–	– –		–
Jarvis J. E. F.	2	1	–	–	–	–	–	–	– –		–
Jayasinghe S.	198	10	5223	110*	27.78	3	371	8	46.38	2/43	–
Jayes T.	203	20	2696	100	14.73	1	12537	528	23.74	9/78	41
Jeffery H. W. J.	3	1	6	6	3.00	–	103	2	51.50	2/77	–
Jelf W. W.	6	–	6	6	1.00	–	–	–	– –		–
Josephs J. M.	14	2	116	25*	9.67	–	86	1	86.00	1/21	–
Joyce F. M.	27	1	431	73	16.58	–	684	17	40.24	5/117	1
Joyce J. H.	1	–	18	18	18.00	–	47	2	23.50	2/33	–
Joyce R.	88	4	1586	102	18.88	1	590	11	53.64	2/36	–
Julian R.	288	23	2581	51	9.74	–	–	–	– –		–
King E.	4	1	33	31*	11.00	–	–	–	– –		–
King H.	6	1	29	11	5.80	–	64	–	– –		–
King Jas.	10	2	83	24*	10.38	–	146	2	73.00	2/71	–
King J. H.	896	64	22618	227*	27.19	32	27780	1100	25.25	8/17	64
King J. W.	15	2	154	56	11.85	–	–	–	– –		–
Kirby D.	116	2	2234	118	19.60	2	1104	29	38.07	4/23	–
Knew G. A.	6	1	59	25	11.80	–	–	–	– –		–
Knew G. F.	8	–	78	42	9.75	–	100	1	100.00	1/58	–
Knight A. E.	663	36	18142	229*	28.93	31	71	1	71.00	1/28	–
Knight B. R.	67	20	1245	93*	26.49	–	2898	112	25.88	8/82	4
Konig P. H.	1	–	3	3	3.00	–	–	–	– –		–
Lee J.	2	–	3	3	1.50	–	13	1	13.00	1/13	–
Lee N. B.	12	1	117	62	10.64	–	6	–	– –		–
Lester G.	649	54	12857	143	21.61	9	10882	307	35.45	6/42	7
Lewis C. C.	85	11	1876	189*	25.35	1	4604	179	25.72	6/22	9
Lock G. A. R.	84	11	1325	81*	18.15	–	5116	272	18.81	8/85	22
Logan H.	2	–	13	12	6.50	–	–	–	– –		–
Lorrimer A.	12	–	174	46	14.50	–	–	–	– –		–
Lorrimer D.	16	–	194	46	12.13	–	–	–	– –		–
MacDonald R.	52	10	1300	147*	30.95	3	72	–	– –		–
McKenzie G. D.	161	40	1830	55	15.12	–	10337	465	22.23	7/8	21
McVicker N. M.	77	20	1364	83*	23.93	–	3592	148	24.27	6/19	5
Maguire J. N.	24	7	237	44*	13.94	–	2437	77	31.64	7/57	4
Marlow T.	22	8	46	10*	3.29	–	846	31	27.29	6/50	2

Name	Inns	NO	Runs	HS	Avge	100s	Runs	Wkts	Avge	BB	5wI
Marlow W. H.	158	33	1117	64	8.94	–	7615	261	29.18	7/90	12
Marner P. T.	226	21	6910	137	28.20	8	6989	245	28.53	7/29	12
Marriott H. H.	71	1	1162	103	16.60	2	236	4	59.00	2/53	–
Martyn D. R.	2	1	95	60★	95.00	–	–	–	–	–	–
Matthews A. J.	20	3	167	32	9.82	–	786	24	32.75	4.87	–
Matthews R. B.	18	8	89	16★	8.90	–	1338	48	27.88	7/51	1
Matts A. S.	2	–	3	3	1.50	–	54	1	54.00	1/54	–
Middleton J. W.	45	–	478	37	10.62	–	60	–	–	–	–
Millns D. J.	34	13	329	44	15.66	–	2619	94	27.86	9/37	5
Mills F.	7	2	69	30★	13.80	–	–	–	–	–	–
Mitten J.	23	2	259	50★	12.33	–	–	–	–	–	–
Mounteney A. Jnr.	267	12	5306	153	20.81	6	504	17	29.65	3/38	–
Mudge H.	2	–	25	19	12.50	–	80	–	–	–	–
Mullally A. D.	18	6	113	29	9.41	–	1545	39	39.61	4/59	–
Munden D. F. X.	13	–	98	34	7.54	–	13	–	–	–	–
Munden P. A.	85	6	1193	77	15.10	–	–	–	–	–	–
Munden V. S.	370	43	5681	102	17.37	2	10433	368	28.35	6/33	14
Needham R.	2	1	31	16	31.00	–	75	2	37.50	2/75	–
Newcomb A. E.	2	–	1	1	0.50	–	74	1	74.00	1/26	–
Nixon P. A.	34	12	552	46	25.09	–	–	–	–	–	–
Norman M. E. J. C.	258	26	6697	221★	28.87	9	80	–	–	–	–
Odell E. F.	1	–	–	–	–	–	42	2	21.00	2/42	–
Odell W. W.	266	44	3079	75	13.87	–	15219	649	23.45	8/20	39
Osborn F.	3	–	14	14	4.67	–	–	–	–	–	–
Oscroft D. S.	7	1	104	50	17.33	–	–	–	–	–	–
Packe C. W. C.	34	–	602	61	17.71	–	35	1	35.00	1/21	–
Packe M. St J.	54	3	909	118	17.82	1	14	1	14.00	1/0	–
Packe R. J.	5	2	25	12	8.33	–	68	1	68.00	1/31	–
Palmer C. H.	407	26	12587	201	33.04	24	6565	291	22.56	8/7	5
Palmer G. H.	6	1	31	14★	6.20	–	320	12	26.67	3/36	–
Palmer J.	6	1	27	13	5.40	–	209	8	26.13	3/14	–
Parkins W. R.	10	–	125	39	12.50	–	–	–	–	–	–
Parkinson E. W.	4	–	26	18	6.50	–	100	–	–	–	–
Parsons G. J.	191	48	2705	69	18.91	–	10693	323	33.10	6/11	8
Payne A.	9	3	15	7★	2.50	–	–	–	–	–	–
Peake K.	2	1	2	1★	2.00	–	52	–	–	–	–
Pember J. D. D.	25	10	271	53	18.07	–	1370	43	31.86	5/45	1
Phillips E. F.	54	7	629	55	13.38	–	–	–	–	–	–
Pickering H. G.	10	–	235	79	23.50	–	–	–	–	–	–
Potter L.	198	28	5031	121★	29.59	3	3215	73	44.04	4/116	–
Pougher A. D.	160	10	3197	114	21.31	5	5343	262	20.39	8/40	15
Powers J.	17	1	195	25	12.19	–	–	–	–	–	–
Pratt R. L.	153	20	1810	80	13.61	–	6418	253	25.37	7/47	11
Pratt W. E.	17	1	166	29★	10.38	–	52	–	–	–	–
Prentice F. T.	421	24	10997	191	27.70	17	5847	117	49.97	5/46	2
Randon F.	5	2	5	5	1.67	–	128	4	32.00	3/20	–
Raynor K.	2	–	–	–	–	–	12	1	12.00	1/12	–
Revill A. C.	116	11	2545	106★	24.24	1	71	3	23.67	2/29	–
Riaz-ur-Rehman	2	–	22	18	11.00	–	–	–	–	–	–
Rice A. S.	2	–	15	13	7.50	–	269	8	33.63	3/34	–
Riddington A.	214	17	3650	104★	18.53	1	3232	83	38.94	5/34	1
Riley E.	3	1	13	8★	6.50	–	7	–	–	–	–

Name	Inns	NO	Runs	HS	Avge	100s	Runs	Wkts	Avge	BB	5wI
Riley H.	147	11	2346	101	17.25	1	173	5	34.60	2/32	–
Riley W. N.	52	1	802	100	15.73	1	157	5	31.40	2/12	–
Roberts A. M. E.	52	9	895	89	20.81	–	3067	141	21.75	8/56	11
Rose M. H.	6	–	35	18	5.83	–	–	–	– –	–
Rudd G. B. F.	159	7	2916	114	19.18	1	713	18	39.61	3/38	–
Rudd G. E.	36	6	379	47	12.63	–	537	12	44.75	5/118	1
Salmon G. H.	86	5	1273	72	15.72	–	31	–	– –	–
Sargent M. A. J.	21	4	240	52	14.12	–	–	–	– –	–
Saunders P. F.	11	4	93	30	13.29	–	190	6	31.67	3/57	–
Savage J. S.	392	127	1945	33	7.34	–	19969	816	24.47	8/50	42
Schepens M.	28	5	407	57	17.70	–	13	–	– –	–
Sharp A. T.	228	25	5220	216	25.71	8	78	–	– –	–
Sharp J. A. T.	8	–	28	16	3.50	–	172	7	24.57	4/63	–
Sherrard P.	1	–	53	53	53.00	–	–	–	– –	–
Shields J.	209	41	1377	63	8.20	–	4	–	– –	–
Shingler G.	8	–	76	26	9.50	–	85	–	– –	–
Shipman A. W.	656	71	13605	226	23.26	15	15148	597	25.37	7/62	16
Shipman W.	187	14	2474	69	14.30	–	9962	366	27.22	9/83	16
Shuttleworth K.	42	15	509	44	18.85	–	2674	99	27.01	6/17	3
Sidwell T. E.	601	84	7904	105	15.29	3	–	–	– –	–
Skelding A.	257	92	1117	33	6.77	–	14630	593	24.67	8/44	35
Smith A.	7	1	16	9	2.67	–	135	5	27.00	3/40	–
Smith B. F.	25	6	693	71	36.47	–	91	1	91.00	1/5	–
Smith G. S.	2	–	29	22	14.50	–	–	–	– –	–
Smith H. A.	500	82	4603	100*	11.01	1	27968	1076	25.99	8/40	66
Smith J. W. D.	4	–	30	25	7.50	–	17	–	– –	–
Smith J. W. R.	3	–	5	4	1.67	–	–	–	– –	–
Smith K. D.	43	7	621	70*	17.25	–	103	3	34.33	2/37	–
Smith M. J. K.	50	1	1232	72	25.14	–	–	–	– –	–
Smith P. T.	24	2	152	40	6.91	–	–	–	– –	–
Smith R. C.	156	37	1115	36	9.37	–	5514	203	27.16	7/54	11
Smith W. A.	44	4	754	125*	18.85	1	122	3	40.67	1/4	–
Smithson G. A.	261	21	5305	111*	22.10	6	22	–	– –	–
Snary H. C.	249	114	2156	124*	15.97	1	10170	419	24.27	7/31	12
Spence L. A.	34	6	326	44	11.64	–	9	–	– –	–
Spencer C. T.	674	140	5796	90	10.85	–	35515	1320	26.91	9/63	45
Sperry J.	264	98	1184	35	7.13	–	13910	490	28.39	7/19	19
Starmer C. E.	4	–	19	8	4.75	–	–	–	– –	–
Steele D. S.	6	–	120	52	20.00	–	79	4	19.75	3.29	–
Steele J. F.	499	63	12814	195	29.39	20	11797	448	26.33	7/29	11
Stocks F. W.	74	11	620	58	9.84	–	3548	134	26.48	8/56	9
Stone C. C.	14	–	106	55	7.57	–	–	–	– –	–
Stretton T. K.	7	3	20	6*	5.00	–	338	4	84.50	2/71	–
Stringer P. M.	46	13	232	22	7.03	–	2076	56	37.07	5/43	1
Sturman W.	36	9	273	46	10.11	–	–	–	– –	–
Such P. M.	31	13	55	14	3.05	–	2212	66	33.51	4/14	–
Symington S. J.	40	6	744	65	21.88	–	1448	36	40.22	5/45	1
Taylor C. H.	68	5	1327	123	21.06	4	397	7	56.71	2/6	–
Taylor J. A. S.	4	–	49	22	12.25	–	52	1	52.00	1/11	–
Taylor L. B.	171	73	941	60	9.60	–	12613	502	25.12	7/28	16
Tennant L.	13	5	110	23*	13.75	–	503	15	33.53	4/54	–
Thompson A. P.	4	1	11	5	3.67	–	–	–	– –	–

Name	Inns	NO	Runs	HS	Avge	100s	Runs	Wkts	Avge	BB	5wI
Thompson H.	18	–	233	72	12.94	–	–	–	–	–	–
Thompson T.	14	5	43	12	4.78	–	497	17	29.24	3/53	–
Thornton J. A. C.	5	3	53	19*	26.50	–	72	1	72.00	1/21	–
Thursting L. D.	45	10	882	94	25.20	–	660	13	50.77	3/34	–
Tilley E. W.	3	–	3	2	1.00	–	256	10	25.60	3/33	–
Tolchard J. G.	108	16	1863	78	20.25	–	5	–	–	–	–
Tolchard R. W.	610	163	13895	126*	31.09	12	34	1	34.00	1/4	–
Tomlin W.	127	11	2353	140	20.28	4	346	8	43.25	3/49	–
Tompkin M.	608	26	18590	186	31.94	29	105	1	105.00	1/1	–
Toon J.	19	4	159	39	10.60	–	477	10	47.70	4/114	–
Turner F. M.	16	5	196	28*	17.82	–	223	3	74.33	3/56	–
Turner R. F.	34	1	525	41	15.91	–	367	9	40.78	2/2	–
Tyler B.	7	–	17	10	2.43	–	88	2	44.00	1/3	–
Udal G. F.	4	1	4	2*	1.33	–	53	–	–	–	–
Van Geloven J.	428	43	7505	157*	19.49	5	13688	480	28.52	7/56	14
Walker E. W.	2	1	2	1*	2.00	–	21	1	21.00	1/21	–
Walsh J. E.	437	46	6892	106	17.63	2	27335	1127	24.25	8/40	96
Walton G.	14	1	88	24	6.77	–	424	17	24.94	4/64	–
Ward A.	15	4	81	19	7.36	–	1026	37	27.73	4/37	–
Warren T.	24	2	302	33	13.73	–	–	–	–	–	–
Watson G. S.	374	18	8399	145	23.59	5	51	1	51.00	1/21	–
Watson W.	210	28	7728	217*	42.46	18	52	–	–	–	–
Watts C. G.	1	–	16	16	16.00	–	–	–	–	–	–
Webb A. G. G.	5	–	27	11	5.40	–	–	–	–	–	–
Wenlock D. A.	13	4	148	62	16.44	–	268	7	38.29	3/50	–
West A. R.	5	–	50	22	10.00	–	205	2	102.50	2/46	–
Weston A. G.	9	1	72	31*	9.00	–	–	–	–	–	–
Wharton A.	137	12	3523	135	28.18	6	212	7	30.29	2/55	–
Whitaker J. J.	310	40	10820	200*	40.07	23	182	1	182.00	1/41	–
Whitehead H.	676	25	15010	174	23.06	14	3351	106	31.61	5/80	1
Whiteside J. P.	337	139	1262	50	6.37	–	–	–	–	–	–
Whitticase P.	159	36	2901	114*	23.58	1	7	–	–	–	–
Wigginton S. H.	85	4	1426	120*	17.60	1	90	3	30.00	2/14	–
Wilkinson C. W.	13	2	138	41	12.54	–	1009	23	43.86	4/59	–
Willey P.	278	29	8370	177	33.61	19	6593	187	35.25	6/43	6
Williams E. L.	2	–	17	14	8.50	–	33	2	16.50	2/33	–
Wood C. J. B.	763	52	21872	225	30.76	34	6638	169	39.28	6/79	3
Wood E.	2	–	1	1	0.50	–	–	–	–	–	–
Woodcock A.	199	36	1358	62*	8.33	–	10814	486	22.25	9/28	32
Wooler C. R. D.	76	14	676	49*	10.90	–	3233	107	30.21	5/47	3
Wright F.	10	–	110	31	11.00	–	365	17	21.47	5/78	1
Wright H.	19	4	218	44	14.53	–	20	–	–	–	–
Wright S. R.	4	–	75	65	18.75	–	185	2	92.50	1/14	–
Wykes G. N.	4	–	2	2	0.50	–	–	–	–	–	–

Notes

1. Shields' total matches include *v* Indians in 1911, when he started playing, and was replaced.
2. Agnew's figures *v* Essex at Chelmsford in 1983, when he substituted for Cook, who was called away to the Third Test.

★A. Callington played as A. C. Lord.

RESULTS OF ALL INTER-COUNTY FIRST-CLASS MATCHES 1894–1991

Year	DY	EX	GM	GS	HA	KT	LA	MX	NR	NT	SM	SY	SX	WA	WO	YK	P	W	L	D	T	Pos.
1894	LL	WD			DL			W		DW		L				WL	12	4	5	3		–
1895	DL	WD	LL		LL					WL		WL	LD			LL	16	3	10	3		12TH
1896	LD	DL		WL	LD					LL		WD				LL	14	2	8	4		13TH
1897	WD	DL		LL	LL					LL		LL				LD	14	1	10	3		13TH
1898	LW	DL		LD	DL	LL				DL		DL				LL	16	1	10	5		13TH
1899	DD	DL		DD	WL	LD				LD		DL	WL			LL	18	2	8	8		13TH
1900	DW	LD		DW	DL	WL		LL				LD	DL	LD	DL	LL	22	3	11	8		14TH
1901	WD	L		DL	LD					LW		LD	LD	LW	WL	LL	19	4	10	5		12TH
1902	DL	DD		DW	DD					DL		DD	DD	DL	WL	D	19	2	4	13		11TH
1903	LW	DL		DD	LL					DD		LL	DD	LD	LD	LL	20	1	10	9		14TH
1904	WL	WL		WW	LD					DD		DL	DL	WL	WD	DD	30	6	6	8		7TH
1905	WW	WW		WW	LD			DW		DD		DD	LD	WD	LL	DL	22	8	5	9		5TH
1906	WL	LL		DL	LL	LL		WL	LL	LL			DD	DW	LD		22	3	14	5		15TH
1907	WW	DW		WD	LL	LL		WW	LL	LL			LD			DL	20	6	10	4		11TH
1908	WD	DD		LD	LL	LL		WD	LD		LD	DW	W			LD	21	4	8	9		13TH
1909	WL	D		LD	LL	LD		WL	LW		LD	DD	DD			LL	21	3	10	8		13TH
1910	LL				WL	WL		WL	LL		LW	LL	LW			DW	18	6	11	1		10TH
1911	DD			LD	LL	LD		LL	LL		LL	DL	LL	LL	LW		22	1	16	5		15TH
1912	LD			WL	LL	LL		LD	LL		DD	LW	WD	DL	LL		22	3	13	6		13TH
1913	WD			DD	LL	LL		LD	LL		LL	LD	LW	WW	LL		22	4	13	5		14TH
1914	DL	WL			LL	DL	WL	WL	DL			L	DL	LD	DW	DD	23	4	11	8		13TH
1919	LW		WL					DD			DD	DL			DW	DL	14	3	4	7		9TH
1920	WW		LL	WD	LL	LL		LW	LW	WW	LL	LL	DL			LD	24	7	14	3		13TH
1921	LW		WW	LL	LL	LL	LW	WW	LL	WD	LL	WL	WW			LD	26	10	14	2		11TH
1922	WD		WD	WW	DD	DL	LL	WD	LL	LD	LL	LW	DL			DL	26	6	11	9		14TH
1923	LD		DW	LL	WD	WL	LL	WW	LL			DL	LL	DD		LL	26	5	13	6		14TH
1924	DW	WW	LD	WL	WW	LL	LL	DD	DL			L	LL	WD		LL	25	7	12	6		11TH
1925	DW	LW	WW	WW	LL	LL	LL	WD	LL			LD	DL	LD		LD	26	7	13	6		12TH
1926	W	WL	DW	DL	LD	LL	LW	DD	LL			DL	LD	DD	WL	LD	27	5	12	10		13TH
1927	WD	DW	DW	WD	DD	DD	DD		DL	DL		LD	WW	DD	WD	DD	28	7	3	18		7TH
1928	DL	DD	DD	DW	WD	DD	DD		WD	DL		DD	LD	DW	WW	LD	28	6	4	18		9TH
1929	DW	DD	WW	WL	LL	LL	DD	LW	DD	DD	WW	WD			DW	DD	28	9	6	13		9TH
1930	DD		DD	DL	DW		LL	DW	WD	LL	LD	WL	DD	DD	LL	LD	28	4	10	14		12TH
1931	DD	DD	DD	DL	WL	LL			DD	DD	DD	DL	DL	DD	WD	DL	28	2	7	19		16TH
1932	DL	LD	LW		DD	LL	DL	WD	WW	LW	DD		LL	DD	WD	LL	28	6	11	11		12TH
1933	LL		DW	LL	DD	LL	LL		LW	LD		DL	WL	LD	DL	LL	26	3	15	8		17TH
1934	LL	LD	DW	WL	DD		DL		WW	LW		LD	LD	DD	LW		24	6	9	9		12TH
1935	LD		LL	DL	WW	LW	WL	WW	LL				WW	DW	WW	DL	24	11	9	4		6TH
1936	LL		LD	LD	DD			DL		DD	DD	DD	DD	WD	WD	DD	24	2	5	17		15TH
1937	LL		LL	DL	DW	LL	DD		DD	LD	DD		DD	LD	DL	DL	26	1	11	14		16TH
1938	DL		DD	WL	DD	WL	DL		WD	DD	DL		DL	WD	LD	LL	26	4	9	13		15TH
1939	LD		DD		WL	LL	D		LD	DD	LL		LL	LL	LD	LL	23	1	14	8		17TH
1946	WW	DD	L	LL	L	LW	LL	L	DW	W	LL	L	W	LL	WD	DD	26	7	13	6		11TH
1947	LW	DD	D	LL	W	LL	LL	L	WL	W	LL	L	D	DW	LW	DL	26	6	14	6		14TH
1948	LL	DD	WW	L	LD	L	L	DL	DW	DD	L	LD	WW	LL	D	W	26	6	11	9		11TH
1949	LD	LL	DW	L	LL	L	D	LL	DDD	WL	L	DW	DL	DL	D	L	27	3	14	10		17TH
1950	WD	DL	WL	D	LW	LL	DL	DL	LL	DD	L	DL	D	LD	DL	L	28	3	13	12		16TH
1951	DL	DD	LD	D	DD	LW	DD	DD	DD	DD	W	DW	L	DL	LW	L	28	4	7	17		15TH
1952	DL	LL	L	DL	WW	WW	W	W	DD	D	WW	DD	WD	LL	DD	LL	28	9	9	10		6TH
1953	WL	DW	D	LW	LD	DW	D	L	DW	L	WW	LD	LD	DD	WW	DW	28	10	7	11		3RD
1954	LD	WD	LD		LD	WW	D	LD	DL	DL	D	DL	D	LD	DL	T	26	3	9	13	1	16TH
1955	DD	WW	WW	W	WL	DW	LL	WL	DL	WL	D	LL	W	LD	DW	L	28	11	10	7		6TH
1956	LL	WD	L	LL	LD	DD	L	L	DD	L	DW	LL	WD	DD	LD	DD	28	3	12	13		17TH
1957	LL	LD	L	LD	LL	DD	W		LL	L	LD	LL	WD	LD	LD	DL	27	2	16	9		17TH
1958	WL	DW	WW	L	DL	LL	LL	LD	LW	WL	L	LD	D	DD	LW	D	28	7	13	8		12TH
1959	DD	WL	WL	L	WL	DD	WL	LW	LL	LD	L	DD	L	LL	LL	L	28	5	16	7		16TH
1960	DL	L	LL	DL	DD	W	LL	L	DD	DD	WD	L	LL	DD	DD	LL	28	2	13	13		17TH
1961	LL	L	WL	DL	LL	W	DD	L	WD	DW	DW	W	LW	LL	WL	LW	28	9	13	6		9TH

Year	DY	EX	GM	GS	HA	KT	LA	MX	NR	NT	SM	SY	SX	WA	WO	YK	P	W	L	D	T	Pos.
1962	LD	L	LD	DL	LD	L	DD	L	DW	DD	DL	L	WL	LD	DD	LD	28	2	12	14		17TH
1963	DD	DW	L	LL	LL	DL	D	D	LW	D	LL	DD	LL	DD	DW	LL	28	3	13	12		16TH
1964	DL	LL	W	WL	WL	DL	L	L	LL	L	DL	D	LL	LL	LL	DD	27	3	18	6		16TH
1965	DL	DD	LL	L	WL	DD	WD	WL	LD	WD	D	WL	D	DL	DL	L	28	5	11	12		14TH
1966	DW	DW	DW	D	DD	LW	WW	DD	DL	WD	L	DD	L	LD	LW	L	28	8	7	13		8TH
1967	LW	WD	W	WW	WD	WD	D	D	DW	D	WD	LD	DD	DD	DW	L	27	10	3	14		3RD
1968	DD	DL	D	WW	LD	LW	D	D	LL	D	LW	DD	LD	DW	WL	LL	28	6	10	12		9TH
1969	WD	DL	D	L	WL	DD	D	D	DW	DD	D	L	W	DL	L	DL	24	4	7	13		14TH
1970	WD	LD	W	D	DD	LL	L	W	DD	WD	D	D	D	LW	D	DL	24	5	6	13		15TH
1971	DD	DD	WW	D	D	D	W	L	WD	DL	D	DD	DW	D	DW	D	24	6	2	16		5TH
1972	DD	DW	D	W	W	D	D	D	DD	WD	W	W	L	D	L	D	20	6	2	12		6TH
1973	WW	WD	L	D	D	D	D	DD	DW	D	D	D	L	L	D		19	4	3	12		9TH
1974	DD	DL	L	W	L	D	W	DL	DW	L	L	W	W	W	W		20	7	7	6		4TH
1975	DW	DW	W	D	W	W	D	WW	WW	W	L	D	W	D	D		20	12	1	7		1ST
1976	DW	DL	D	W	W	W	D	W	LD	DW	L	D	W	W	D	W	20	9	3	8		4TH
1977	LW	DD	WD	L	W	LD	D	W	DD	DW	D	W	D	L	D	D	22	6	4	12		5TH
1978	WD	DD	DD	W	W	LL	W	L	DD	DD	L	D	D	D	L		22	4	5	13		6TH
1979	DD	LW	DW	L		LW	L	L	DD	DW	D	D	D	D	D	D	21	4	5	12		6TH
1980	DD	DL	DD	D	W	DD	D	W	DW	DL	W	D	D	D	D	D	22	4	2	16		9TH*
1981	DW	DL	DD	D	D	DL	W	L	W	LW	L	D	W	W	D	L	21	6	6	9		8TH
1982	LL	WW	WW	W	D	DL	W	D	DD	WL	W	W	W	D	D		22	10	4	8		2ND
1983	DW	WD	W	D	D	LW	D	L	DW	DW	L	DD	WD	D	W	DW	24	9	3	12		4TH
1984	WD	D	D	DW	W	D	L	D	WD	DD	DL	W	D	WW	DW	DD	24	8	2	14		4TH
1985	DW	D	DD	D	DL	D	DD	DL	DD	DD	D	D	L	W	D	DD	24	2	3	19		16TH
1986	DD	WL	L	L	D	DL	D	D	DD	LW	D	WL	WD	D	L	DW	24	5	7	12		7TH
1987	WW	D	D	WW	D	D	L	W	DW	LD	DD	W	DD	DD	LD		24	8	3	13		3RD
1988	DD	DL	DD	W	D	WD	D	L	WD	DD	W	D	W	W	D	L	22	6	3	13		7TH*
1989	WW	DL	DW	L	L	DD	D	D	LD	WD	L	L	D	D	L	L	22	4	8	10		13TH
1990	WD	DD	WD	W	D	LW	D	L	DL	LD	D	L	L	W	L	W	22	6	7	9		7TH
1991	WL	DL	DD	L	L	WW	L	D	DD	LD	D	D	L	L	D	D	22	3	8	11		16TH

Notes:

1. All matches are included in the County Championship, with the exception of:
   (i) all matches in 1894, when Leicestershire, together with the other newly promoted counties, did not compete
   (ii) a first-class friendly match was played against Northamptonshire at Northampton in 1949. This match was drawn.
2. Seventeen matches have been abandoned without a ball bowled, and are not included in the tables or the matches played totals above. These are:

1894 Warwickshire (Edgbaston)
1901 Essex (Leyton)
1902 Yorkshire (Aylestone Road, Leicester)
1908 Warwickshire (Bulls Head Ground, Coventry)
1909 Essex (Leyton)
1914 Surrey (The Oval)
1924 Surrey (Aylestone Road, Leicester)
1926 Derbyshire (Chesterfield)
1939 Lancashire (Aylestone Road, Leicester)
1954 Gloucestershire (Grace Road, Leicester)
       Lancashire (Grace Road, Leicester)
1957 Middlesex (Lord's)
1964 Surrey (Ashby-de-la-Zouch)
1967 Yorkshire (Headingley)
1973 Gloucestershire (Bristol)
1979 Hampshire (Grace Road, Leicester)
1981 Northamptonshire (Northampton)

RESULTS OF ALL SUNDAY LEAGUE MATCHES 1969–1991

Year	DY	EX	GM	GS	HA	KT	LA	MX	NR	NT	SM	SY	SX	WA	WO	YK	P	W	L	T	NR	AB	Pos.
1969	W	L	L	L	L	L	L			W	W	L	W		W	W	13	6	7			3	11TH
1970	W	L	W		L	W	L	W	L	L	W	W		W	L	L	14	7	7			2	7TH
1971	W	W	L	W	W	L	L	W	L	W	W	W	W	L	W	L	16	10	6				4TH
1972	L	W	W	W	L	L	L	W	W	W	W	W	W	W	W	L	16	11	5				2ND
1973	W	W	W	W	W	W	L	L	L		W		L	L	W	L	14	8	6			2	5TH
1974	W		W	W	W	L	W	W	W	W	NR	W	T	W	W	W	15	12	1	1	1	1	1ST
1975	W	W	L	W	L	L	L	L	W	L	W	L	L	W	L	L	16	6	10				12TH
1976	L	L	L	W	W	L	W	W	L	W	W	W	L	W	W	W	16	10	6				2ND*
1977	W	W	W	W	W	W	W	L	L	L	W	W	W	W	W	W	16	13	3				1ST
1978	W	W	W	W		W	W	W	W	W	L	W		W	L	L	14	11	3			2	3RD
1979	W	L	W		W	L	W		L	L	W	W	L	W	NR		13	7	5		1	3	6TH*
1980	W	W	W	W	L	W	L		W	W	L	L	W	L	L	W	15	9	6			1	4TH
1981	L	L	L		L	W	L	W	L	W	W	W	L		L	L	14	5	9			2	14TH
1982	W	L	NR	W	W	W	W	L	W	L	L	L	L	W	W	W	16	9	6		1		3RD
1983	W	L	W		L		L	L	W	W	L	NR	L		L		12	4	7		1	4	11TH*
1984	L	L	W	W	W	NR	L	L	L	L	NR	L		NR	W	L	15	4	8		3	1	13TH*
1985	L	T	W	W	NR		NR	L	NR	NR	W	W	L	W	L	L	15	5	5	1	4	1	6TH*
1986	W	L	L	W	L		W	W	L	W	L	L	L	L	L	L	15	5	10			1	15TH
1987	L	NR		W	L	L	W	L	W	L		NR			L	NR	12	3	6		3	4	12TH
1988	L	W	W	L	L		L	NR	W		W	L	L	L	L	L	14	4	9		1	2	14TH*
1989	L	L		L	L	L	W	L	W	L	W	L	W	L	W	L	15	5	10			1	15TH*
1990	L	W	L	W	L	W	L	L	L	L	L	W	NR	L	L	L	16	4	11		1		15TH*
1991	L		W	L	W	L	L	W	L	L	W	L	L	L	W	L	15	5	10			1	13TH

Notes:
1. Matches designated 'NR' are instances where some play took place, and are included in the matches played total.
2. No play took place in 'AB' (abandoned) matches. These are therefore not included in the matches played total.

RESULTS OF ALL NATWEST TROPHY AND GILLETTE MATCHES 1963–1991

1963   *Prelim Round:* lost to Lancashire
1964   *1st Round:* bye; *2nd Round:* lost to Northamptonshire
1965   *1st Round:* bye; *2nd Round:* lost to Yorkshire
1966   *1st Round:* bye; *2nd Round:* lost to Surrey
1967   *1st Round:* lost to Somerset
1968   *1st Round:* bye; *2nd Round:* beat Somerset; *Q/Final:* lost to Middlesex
1969   *1st Round:* bye; *2nd Round:* beat Kent; *Q/Final:* lost to Sussex
1970   *1st Round:* bye; *2nd Round:* lost to Nottinghamshire
1971   *1st Round:* bye; *2nd Round:* beat Derbyshire; *Q/Final:* lost to Kent
1972   *1st Round:* bye; *2nd Round:* lost to Warwickshire
1973   *1st Round:* bye; *2nd Round:* beat Somerset; *Q/Final:* lost to Worcestershire
1974   *1st Round:* bye; *2nd Round:* beat Northamptonshire; *Q/Final:* lost to Kent
1975   *1st Round:* beat Staffordshire; *2nd Round:* beat Yorkshire; *Q/Final:* lost to Gloucestershire
1976   *1st Round:* bye; *2nd Round:* lost to Hampshire
1977   *1st Round:* beat Hertfordshire; *2nd Round:* beat Essex; *Q/Final:* beat Northamptonshire; *S/Final:* lost to Glamorgan

1978   *1st Round:* bye; *2nd Round:* beat Hampshire; *Q/Final:* lost to Essex
1979   *1st Round:* beat Devonshire; *2nd Round:* beat Worcestershire; *Q/Final:* lost to Northamptonshire
1980   *1st Round:* bye; *2nd Round:* lost to Essex
1981   *1st Round:* bye; *2nd Round:* beat Surrey; *Q/Final:* lost to Northamptonshire
1982   *1st Round:* beat Norfolk; *2nd Round:* lost to Somerset
1983   *1st Round:* beat Devonshire; *2nd Round:* lost to Gloucestershire
1984   *1st Round:* beat Wiltshire; *2nd Round:* beat Derbyshire; *Q/Final:* lost to Northamptonshire
1985   *1st Round:* beat Norfolk; *2nd Round:* lost to Hampshire
1986   *1st Round:* beat Ireland; *2nd Round:* beat Gloucestershire; *Q/Final:* lost to Lancashire
1987   *1st Round:* beat Oxfordshire; *2nd Round:* beat Hampshire; *Q/Final:* beat Yorkshire; *S/Final:* lost to Northamptonshire
1988   *1st Round:* beat Suffolk; *2nd Round:* lost to Gloucestershire
1989   *1st Round:* beat Shropshire; *2nd Round:* lost to Sussex
1990   *1st Round:* lost to Hampshire
1991   *1st Round:* beat Shropshire; *2nd Round:* lost to Northamptonshire

RESULTS IN BENSON AND HEDGES CUP 1972–1991

1972   First in Midlands Section; *Q/Final:* beat Lancashire; *S/Final:* beat Warwickshire; *Final:* beat Yorkshire
1973   First in Midlands Section; *Q/Final:* lost to Essex
1974   Second in Midlands Section; *Q/Final:* beat Kent; *S/Final:* beat Somerset; *Final:* lost to Surrey
1975   Second in Midlands Section; *Q/Final:* beat Lancashire; *S/Final:* beat Hampshire; *Final:* beat Middlesex
1976   First in Group B; *Q/Final:* lost to Worcestershire
1977   Fifth in Group A
1978   Third in Group C
1979   Fourth in Group B
1980   Third in Group A
1981   Second in Group A; *Q/Final:* beat Sussex; *S/Final:* lost to Surrey
1982   Second in Group A; *Q/Final:* lost to Nottinghamshire
1983   Third in Group A
1984   Third in Group A
1985   Second in Group B; *Q/Final:* beat Hampshire; *S/Final:* beat Kent; *Final:* beat Essex
1986   Fourth in Group A
1987   Fifth in Group A
1988   Third in Group A
1989   Third in group D
1990   Third in Group D
1991   Fourth in Group C

GROUNDS USED BY LEICESTERSHIRE IN FIRST-CLASS MATCHES 1894–1991

Ground	First	Last	P	W	L	D	AB
Leicester (Grace Road)	1894	1991	593	140	177	276	4
Leicester (Aylestone Road)	1901	1962	399	94	143	162	3
Ashby-de-la-Zouch (Bath Grounds)	1912	1964	43	9	19	15	1
Barwell (Kirkby Road)	1946	1947	3	1	2	–	–
Coalville (Fox & Goose)	1913	1914	2	2	–	–	–
Coalville (Town Ground)	1950	1950	1	–	1	–	–
Coalville (Snibston Colliery)	1957	1982	8	3	2	3	–
Hinckley (Ashby Road)	1911	1937	19	6	5	8	–
Hinckley (Coventry Road)	1951	1964	17	1	11	5	–
Hinckley (Leicester Road)	1981	1991	11	5	1	5	–
Loughborough (Park Road)	1913	1952	15	3	10	2	–
Loughborough (College Ground)	1928	1929	2	1	–	1	–
Loughborough (Brush Sports)	1953	1965	16	6	6	4	–
Melton Mowbray (Egerton Park)	1946	1948	3	–	3	–	–
Oakham (School Ground)	1935	1938	4	1	2	1	–
			1136	272	382	482	8

TEAM RECORDS

(1) HIGHEST AND LOWEST SCORE FOR LEICESTERSHIRE AGAINST EACH COUNTY

Opponents	Highest	Year	Lowest	Year
Derbyshire	541-4 dec at Glossop	1901	36 at Loughborough (Brush Sports)	1965
Essex	521 at Leyton	1914	45 at Brentwood	1957
Glamorgan	456-4 at Leicester (GR)	1975	33 at Ebbw Vale	1965
Gloucestershire	456 at Leicester (GR)	1984	49 at Gloucester	1977
Hampshire	535-8 dec at Leicester (AR)	1938	52 at Bournemouth	1931
Kent	432 at Tonbridge	1928	25 at Leicester (AR)	1912
Lancashire	493 at Leicester (AR)	1910	33 at Leicester (AR)	1925
Middlesex	479-6 dec at Lord's	1932	65 at Lord's	1971
Northamptonshire	477 at Leicester (AR)	1908	43 at Peterborough	1968
Nottinghamshire	468-8 dec at Trent Bridge	1926	53 at Trent Bridge	1932
Somerset	490 at Frome	1937	41 at Leicester (GR)	1957
Surrey	516-8 dec at The Oval	1929	35 and 35 (same match) at Leicester (GR)	1897
Sussex	609-8 dec at Leicester (GR)	1900	40 at Hove	1960
Warwickshire	438-3 dec at Edgbaston	1983	47 at Edgbaston	1900
Worcestershire	701-4 dec at Worcester	1906	52 at Worcester	1965
Yorkshire	458 at Hull	1937	34 at Headingley	1906

(2) HIGHEST AND LOWEST SCORE AGAINST LEICESTERSHIRE BY EACH COUNTY

Opponents	Highest	Year	Lowest	Year
Derbyshire	509 at Glossop	1906	36 at Chesterfield	1905
Essex	761-6 dec at Leicester (GR)	1990	53 at Leicester (GR)	1977
Glamorgan	469-7 dec at Leicester (AR)	1937	24 at Leicester (GR)	1971
Gloucestershire	518-9 dec at Leicester (AR)	1933	57 at Gloucester	1925
Hampshire	548-6 dec at Southampton	1927	58 at Leicester (AR)	1907
Kent	551-9 at Maidstone	1962	56 at Oakham	1935
Lancashire	590 at Leicester (GR)	1899	73 at Leicester (AR)	1935
Middlesex	637-4 dec at Leicester (GR)	1947	41 at Lord's	1974
Northamptonshire	510-8 dec at Northampton	1939	35 at Northampton	1907
Nottinghamshire	739-7 dec at Trent Bridge	1903	58 at Leicester (GR)	1974 and 1986
Somerset	528 at Leicester (GR)	1983	61 at Leicester (AR)	1929
Surrey	576 at The Oval	1947	35 at Leicester (GR)	1894
Sussex	686-8 at Leicester (GR)	1900	66 at Leicester (AR)	1935
Warwickshire	605 at Leicester (GR)	1899	48 at Coventry (Bulls Head)	1919
Worcestershire	561 at Leicester (AR)	1901	40 at Worcester	1971
Yorkshire	660 at Leicester (GR)	1896	47 at Leicester (AR)	1911

(3) HIGHEST AND LOWEST SCORES FOR LEICESTERSHIRE IN LIMITED-OVERS MATCHES

Competition	Score	Opponents and Venue	Year
Highest			
JP/Refuge League	291-5 (40 overs)	Glamorgan at Swansea	1984
Benson & Hedges Cup	327-4 (55 overs)	Warwickshire at Coventry	1972
Gillette/NatWest Trophy	354-7 (60 overs)	Wiltshire at Swindon	1984
Lowest			
JP/Refuge League	36 (25.4 overs)	Sussex at Leicester (GR)	1973
Benson & Hedges Cup	56 (26.2 overs)	Minor Counties at Wellington	1982
Gillette/NatWest Trophy	56 (26.2 overs)	Northamptonshire at Leicester (GR)	1964

(4) HIGHEST AND LOWEST SCORES AGAINST LEICESTERSHIRE IN LIMITED-OVERS MATCHES

Competition	Score	Opponents and Venue	Year
Highest			
JP/Refuge League	278-7 (40 overs)	Surrey at The Oval	1990
Benson & Hedges Cup	297-5 (55 overs)	Kent at Canterbury	1991
Gillette/NatWest Trophy	326-9 (60 overs)	Hampshire at Leicester (GR)	1987
Lowest			
JP/Refuge League	78 (34.3 overs)	Derbyshire at Leicester (GR)	1978
Benson & Hedges Cup	74 (32.4 overs)	Nottinghamshire at Leicester (GR)	1987
Gillette/NatWest Trophy	62 (34 overs)	Northamptonshire at Leicester (GR)	1974

INDIVIDUAL BATTING RECORDS

(1) DOUBLE CENTURIES IN FIRST-CLASS MATCHES

Score	Batsman	Opponents	Venue	Year
252*	S. Coe	Northamptonshire	Leicester (AR)	1914
232	G. L. Berry	Sussex	Leicester (AR)	1930
229*	A. E. Knight	Worcestershire	Worcester	1903
228	D. I. Gower	Glamorgan	Leicester (GR)	1989
227*	J. H. King	Worcestershire	Coalville (Fox & Goose)	1914
226	A. W. Shipman	Kent	Tonbridge	1928
225	C. J. B. Wood	Worcestershire	Worcester	1906
221*	M. E. J. C. Norman	Cambridge University	Cambridge	1967
217*	W. Watson	Somerset	Taunton	1961
216	A. T. Sharp	Derbyshire	Chesterfield	1911
210*	M. R. Hallam	Glamorgan	Leicester (GR)	1959
207*	C. S. Dempster	Sir Julien Cahn's XI	West Bridgford (Loughboro' Rd)	1935
207	G. L. Berry	Worcestershire	Ashby-de-la-Zouch	1928
205	J. H. King	Hampshire	Leicester (AR)	1923
203*	M. R. Hallam	Sussex	Worthing	1961
203	A. E. Knight	MCC	Lord's	1904
202	B. Dudleston	Derbyshire	Leicester (GR)	1979
201*	N. E. Briers	Warwickshire	Edgbaston	1983
201	C. H. Palmer	Northamptonshire	Northampton	1953
200*	C. J. B. Wood	Hampshire	Leicester (AR)	1905
200*	M. R. Hallam	Nottinghamshire	Trent Bridge	1962
200	M. R. Hallam	Derbyshire	Leicester (GR)	1959
200*	J. J. Whitaker	Nottinghamshire	Leicester (GR)	1986

(2) CENTURIES IN LIMITED-OVERS MATCHES
(a) John Player/Refuge Assurance League

Score	Batsman	Opponents	Venue	Year
152	B. Dudleston	Lancashire	Old Trafford	1975
135*	D. I. Gower	Warwickshire	Leicester (GR)	1977
132	J. J. Whitaker	Glamorgan	Swansea	1984
119*	N. E. Briers	Hampshire	Bournemouth	1981
115	D. I. Gower	Surrey	The Oval	1982
114*	D. I. Gower	Warwickshire	Leicester (GR)	1985
109*	B. Dudleston	Gloucestershire	Gloucester	1974
108	N. E. Briers	Yorkshire	Bradford	1984
107*	J. J. Whitaker	Surrey	The Oval	1984
107	D. I. Gower	Warwickshire	Leicestershire (GR)	1982
106	P. Willey	Glamorgan	Swansea	1984
105	L. Potter	Derbyshire	Leicester (GR)	1986
103	R. W. Tolchard	Middlesex	Lord's	1972

101*	N. E. Briers	Nottinghamshire	Leicester (GR)	1983
100	R. W. Tolchard	Worcestershire	Worcester	1974
100	D. I. Gower	Derbyshire	Leicester (GR)	1982

(b) Benson & Hedges Cup

Score	Batsman	Opponents	Venue	Year
158*	B. F. Davison	Warwickshire	Coventry	1972
114*	D. I. Gower	Derbyshire	Derby	1980
113*	J. C. Balderstone	Gloucestershire	Leicester (GR)	1981
112	L. Potter	Minor Counties	Leicester (GR)	1986
103*	I. P. Butcher	Minor Counties	Leicester (GR)	1986
103	T. J. Boon	Scotland	Leicester (GR)	1991
101*	J. C. Balderstone	Hampshire	Leicester (GR)	1975
101	I. P. Butcher	Yorkshire	Leicester (GR)	1985
100*	J. C. Balderstone	Worecestershire	Leicester (GR)	1976
100	J. C. Balderstone	Worcestershire	Worcester	1982
100	J. J. Whitaker	Kent	Canterbury	1991

(c) NatWest/Gillette Cup

Score	Batsman	Opponents	Venue	Year
156	D. I. Gower	Derbyshire	Leicester (GR)	1984
155	J. J. Whitaker	Wiltshire	Swindon	1984
154	P. Willey	Hampshire	Leicester (GR)	1987
138*	D. I. Gower	Gloucestershire	Leicester (GR)	1983
125	B. Dudleston	Worcestershire	Leicester (GR)	1979
121*	D. I. Gower	Ireland	Leicester (GR)	1986
119*	J. C. Balderstone	Somerset	Taunton	1973
118	B. Dudleston	Staffordshire	Stoke-on-Trent	1975
117*	D. I. Gower	Hertfordshire	Leicester (GR)	1977
108*	J. F. Steele	Staffordshire	Stoke-on-Trent	1975
106	M. R. Hallam	Lancashire	Old Trafford	1963
101*	J. Birkenshaw	Hampshire	Leicester (GR)	1976
101*	D. I. Gower	Shropshire	Telford	1989
101	P. Willey	Ireland	Leicester (GR)	1986

(3) CARRYING BAT THROUGH A COMPLETED FIRST-CLASS INNINGS

Batsman	Score	Total	Opponents	Venue	Year
J. C. Balderstone (3)	114*	(246)	Essex	Colchester (Castle Park)	1982
	100*	(198)	Worcestershire	Hereford	1983
	181*	(456)	Gloucestershire	Leicester (GR)	1984
G. L. Berry (4)	75*	(177)	Nottinghamshire	Leicester (AR)	1932
	58*	(126)	Derbyshire	Chesterfield	1939
	45*	(121)	South Africa	Leicester (GR)	1947
	109*	(236)	Somerset	Leicester (GR)	1949

T. J. Boon	75★	(163)	Zimbabwe	Salisbury	1980/81
N. E. Briers	157★	(359)	Nottinghamshire	Leicester (GR)	1990
	60★	(108)	Northamptonshire	Leicester (GR)	1991
E. W. Dawson	126★	(256)	Essex	Leyton	1928
C. S. Dempster	28★	(62)	Yorkshire	Bradford (Park Avenue)	1938
B. Dudleston	101★	(178)	Essex	Leyton	1971
M. R. Hallam	152★	(231)	Gloucestershire	Leicester (GR)	1961
J. Holland	46★	(95)	Surrey	Leicester (GR)	1894
A. E. Knight (5)	91★	(155)★	Surrey	The Oval	1903
	61★	(131)	Nottinghamshire	Trent Bridge	1908
	137★	(345)	Warwickshire	Edgbaston	1909
	74★	(182)	Surrey	Leicester (AR)	1911
	66★	(182)	Hampshire	Portsmouth	1911
F. T. Prentice	36★	(89)	Worcestershire	Hinckley (Ashby Rd)	1937
A. W. Shipman	100★	(212)	Lancashire	Old Trafford	1935
H. C. Snary	124★	(291)	India	Leicester (AR)	1932
W. Watson	79★	(132)	Yorkshire	Leicester (GR)	1959
H. Whitehead	130★	(271)	Lancashire	Leicester (AR)	1907
C. J. B. Wood (17)	21★	(98)	Yorkshire	Dewsbury	1898
	46★	(262)	Sussex	Leicester (AR)	1903
	118★	(322)	Yorkshire	Leicester (AR)	1903
	160★	(419)	Yorkshire	Leicester (AR)	1905
	200★	(507)	Hampshire	Leicester (AR)	1905
	56★	(112)	Lancashire	Leicester (AR)	1906
	105★	(393)	Essex	Southend (Southchurch Park)	1906
	110★	(220)	Northamptonshire	Northampton	1906
	84★	(159)	Lancashire	Leicester (AR)	1908
	38★	(116)	Derbyshire	Derby	1910
	78★	(270)	Kent	Leicester (AR)	1911
	54★	(151)	Northamptonshire	Leicester (AR)	1911
	54★	(164)	Warwickshire	Hinckley (Ashby Rd)	1911
	107★	(309)	Yorkshire	Bradford (Park Avenue)	1911 (1st innings)
	117★	(296)	Yorkshire	Bradford (Park Avenue)	1911 (2nd innings)
	38★	(179)	Lancashire	Leicester (AR)	1913
	164★	(392)	Warwickshire	Hinckley (Ashby Rd)	1913
H. Wright	26★	(63)	Hampshire	Southampton	1914

★9 wickets fell 1 player absent hurt.

(4) CENTURY IN EACH INNINGS OF A FIRST-CLASS MATCH

Scores	Batsman	Opponents	Venue	Year
165 and 111*	G. L. Berry	Essex	Clacton	1947
109 and 104	B. J. Booth	Middlesex	Lord's	1965
133 and 154*	C. S. Dempster	Gloucestershire	Gloucester	1937
210* and 157	M. R. Hallam	Glamorgan	Leicester (GR)	1959
203* and 154*	M. R. Hallam	Sussex	Worthing	1961
107* and 149*	M. R. Hallam	Worcestershire	Leicester (GR)	1965
111 and 100*	J. H. King	Northamptonshire	Leicester (AR)	1913
156 and 107*	M. Tompkin	Middlesex	Leicester (GR)	1952
129 and 108	A. Wharton	Middlesex	Leicester (GR)	1961
107* and 117*	C. J. B. Wood	Yorkshire	Bradford (Park Avenue)	1911

(5) CENTURY ON FIRST-CLASS DEBUT FOR LEICESTERSHIRE

Score	Batsman	Opponents	Venue	Year
100*	P. D. Bowler*	Hampshire	Leicester (GR)	1986
102*	M. D. Haysman	Cambridge Univ.	Cambridge	1984
141*	P. Willey	Cambridge Univ.	Cambridge	1984

He also scored 155 on debut for Derbyshire in 1988 – the only player to score a century on debut for two counties.

(6) 2,000 FIRST-CLASS RUNS IN A SEASON FOR LEICESTERSHIRE

Batsman	Total	Year
N. F. Armstrong	2,113	1933
G. L. Berry	2,446	1937
M. R. Hallam	2,096	1961
W. Watson	2,212	1959

(7) OPENING STANDS OF 100 IN BOTH INNINGS OF THE SAME MATCH

Scores	Batsman	Opponents	Venue	Year
124 and 139	G. L. Berry and G. Lester	Middlesex	Lord's	1948
143 and 204	M. R. Hallam and B. J. Booth	Worcestershire	Leicester (GR)	1965
136	D. J. Constant and B. J. Booth	Oxford Univ.	Oxford	1965
101	D. J. Constant and S. Greensword			
145 and 170	N. E. Briers and T. J. Boon	Essex	Chelmsford	1990

(8) HIGHEST INDIVIDUAL SCORES FOR LEICESTERSHIRE AGAINST EACH COUNTY

Opponents	Batsman	Score	Venue	Year
Derbyshire	A. T. Sharp	216	Chesterfield	1911
Essex	C. C. Lewis	189★	Chelmsford	1990
Glamorgan	D. I. Gower	228	Leicester (GR)	1989
Gloucestershire	J. C. Balderstone	181★	Leicester (GR)	1984
Hampshire	J. H. King	205	Leicester (AR)	1923
Kent	A. W. Shipman	226	Tonbridge	1928
Lancashire	W. Watson	158	Leicester (GR)	1961
Middlesex	N. F. Armstrong	183★	Lord's	1932
Northampton	S. Coe	252★	Leicester (AR)	1914
Nottingham	M. R. Hallam	200★	Trent Bridge	1962
Somerset	W. Watson	217★	Taunton	1961
Surrey	M. Tompkin	175★	The Oval	1951
Sussex	G. L. Berry	232	Leicester (AR)	1930
Warwickshire	N. E. Briers	201★	Edgbaston	1983
Worcestershire	A. E. Knight	229★	Worcester	1903
Yorkshire	N. F. Armstrong	186	Leicester (AR)	1928

INDIVIDUAL BOWLING RECORDS

(1) HAT-TRICKS IN FIRST-CLASS MATCHES

Player	Opponents	Venue	Year
J. H. King	Sussex	Hove	1903
T. Jayes	Northamptonshire	Leicester (AR)	1906
W. E. Benskin	Essex	Southend (Southchurch Park)	1906
T. Jayes	Kent	Maidstone	1907
W. W. Odell	Northamptonshire	Leicester (AR)	1908
W. Shipman	Derbyshire	Leicester (AR)	1909
J. H. King	Somerset	Weston-Super-Mare	1920
G. Geary	Gloucestershire	Bristol (Greenbank)	1922
V. E. Jackson	Derbyshire	Derby	1946
J. E. Walsh	Nottinghamshire	Loughborough (Park Road)	1949
V. E. Jackson	Surrey	Leicester (GR)	1950
V. S. Munden	Derbyshire	Ashby-de-la-Zouch	1953
J. S. Savage	Somerset	Loughborough (Brush Sports)	1961
J. Cotton	Surrey	The Oval	1965
G. A. R. Lock	Hampshire	Portsmouth	1967
J. Birkenshaw	Worcestershire	Worcester	1967
J. Birkenshaw	Cambridge University	Cambridge	1968
R. Illingworth	Surrey	The Oval	1975
J. C. Balderstone	Sussex	Eastbourne	1976
P. B. Clift	Yorkshire	Leicester (GR)	1976
K. Shuttleworth	Surrey	The Oval	1977

K. Higgs	Hampshire	Leicester (GR)	1977
L. B. Taylor	Middlesex	Leicester (GR)	1979
G. J. F. Ferris	Northamptonshire	Leicester (GR)	1983
P. B. Clift	Derbyshire	Chesterfield	1985
W. K. M. Benjamin	Australia	Leicester (GR)	1989

(2) HAT-TRICKS IN LIMITED OVERS MATCHES

(a) John Players/Refuge Assurance League

Player	Opponents	Venue	Year
G. D. McKenzie	Essex	Leicester (GR)	1972

(b) Benson & Hedges Cup

Player	Opponents	Venue	Year
G. D. McKenzie	Worcestershire	Worcester	1972
K. Higgs	Surrey	Lord's (Final)	1974
W. K. M. Benjamin	Nottinghamshire	Leicester (GR)	1987

(c) NatWest Trophy/Gillette Cup

None

(3) NINE/TEN WICKETS IN AN INNINGS

Bowler	Analysis	Opponents	Venue	Year
G. Geary	10-18	Glamorgan	Pontypridd	1929
A. Woodcock	9-28	MCC	Lord's	1899
J. Cotton	9-29	India	Leicester (GR)	1967
G. Geary	9-33	Lancashire	Ashby-de-la-Zouch	1926
D. J. Millns	9-37	Derbyshire	Derby	1991
W. E. Astill	9-41	Warwickshire	Edgbaston	1923
C. T. Spencer	9-63	Yorkshire	Huddersfield	1954
J. P. Agnew	9-70	Kent	Leicester (GR)	1985
T. Jayes	9-78	Derbyshire	Leicester (AR)	1905
W. Shipman	9-83	Surrey	The Oval	1910
G. C. Gill	9-89	Warwickshire	Edgbaston	1905

(4) FOURTEEN OR MORE WICKETS IN A MATCH

Bowler	Analysis	Opponents	Venue	Year
G. Geary	16-96	Glamorgan	Pontypridd	1929
J. E. Walsh	16-225	Oxford University	Oxford	1953
J. E. Walsh	15-100	Sussex	Hove	1948
A. Woodcock	15-136	Nottinghamshire	Leicester (GR)	1894

333

J. E. Walsh	15-164	Nottinghamshire	Loughborough (Park Road)	1949
A. Woodcock	14-72	MCC	Lord's	1899
G. Geary	14-86	Hampshire	Southampton	1926
J. E. Walsh	14-86	Glamorgan	Leicester (GR)	1948
A. D. Pougher	14-89	Essex	Leyton	1894
C. T. Spencer	14-94	Essex	Chelmsford	1959
A. M. E. Roberts	14-94	Glamorgan	Leicester (GR)	1982
G. Geary	14-98	Lancashire	Ashby-de-la-Zouch	1926
J. S. Savage	14-99	Northamptonshire	Northampton	1958
J. E. Walsh	14-107	Kent	Leicester (GR)	1946
A. Skelding	14-125	Northamptonshire	Northampton	1925
J. E. Walsh	14-181	Sussex	Leicester (GR)	1946

(5) SIX WICKETS IN A LIMITED-OVERS MATCH
(a) John Player/Refuge Assurance League

Bowler	Analysis	Opponents	Venue	Year
K. Higgs	6-17	Glamorgan	Leicester (GR)	1973

(b) Benson & Hedges Cup

Bowler	Analysis	Opponents	Venue	Year
L. B. Taylor	6-35	Worcestershire	Worcester	1982

(c) NatWest Trophy/Gillette Cup

Bowler	Analysis	Opponents	Venue	Year
K. Higgs	6-20	Staffordshire	Longton	1975

(6) 125 WICKETS IN A SEASON

Bowler	Runs	Wkts	Average	Year
J. E. Walsh	3224	170	18.96	1948
W. E. Astill	3212	153	20.99	1921
H. A. Smith	2950	150	19.67	1935
J. E. Walsh	3012	148	20.35	1946
J. E. Walsh	3328	147	22.63	1947
G. Geary	2392	140	17.08	1929
W. E. Astill	2617	138	18.96	1922
J. E. Walsh	3800	132	28.78	1949
G. Geary	2287	130	17.59	1931
G. Geary	1977	129	15.32	1935
G. A. R. Lock	2319	128	18.11	1967
W. E. Astill	2724	126	21.61	1928

The only bowler to take 100 wickets in a season since 1969 is J. P. Agnew (101 in 1987).

RECORD WICKET PARTNERSHIPS

(1) FIRST-CLASS MATCHES

Score		Batsmen	Opponents	Venue	Year
FIRST WICKET					
1	390	B. Dudleston *and* J. F. Steele	Derbyshire	Leicester (GR)	1979
2	380	C. J. B. Wood *and* H. Whitehead	Worcestershire	Worcester	1906
3	335	B. Dudleston *and* J. F. Steele	Glamorgan	Leicester (GR)	1975
SECOND WICKET					
1	289★	J. C. Balderstone *and* D. I. Gower	Essex	Leicester (GR)	1981
2	287	W. Watson *and* A. Wharton	Lancashire	Leicester (GR)	1961
3	254★	G. L. Berry *and* N. F. Armstrong	Sir L. Parkinson's XI	Blackpool	1935
THIRD WICKET					
1	316★	W. Watson *and* A. Wharton	Somerset	Taunton	1961
2	305	J. C. Balderstone *and* B. F. Davison	Nottinghamshire	Leicester (GR)	1975
3	291	A. E. Knight *and* J. H. King	MCC	Lord's	1904
FOURTH WICKET					
1	290★	P. Willey *and* T. J. Boon	Warwickshire	Leicester (GR)	1984
2	273★	P. Willey *and* P. D. Bowler	Hampshire	Leicester (GR)	1986
3	270	C. S. Dempster *and* G. S. Watson	Yorkshire	Hull	1937
FIFTH WICKET					
1	233	N. E. Briers *and* R. W. Tolchard	Somerset	Leicester (GR)	1979
2	226★	R. Macdonald *and* F. Geeson	Derbyshire	Glossop	1901
3	209★	B. F. Davison *and* R. W. Tolchard	Northamptonshire	Northampton	1978
SIXTH WICKET					
1	262	A. T. Sharp *and* G. H. S. Fowke	Derbyshire	Chesterfield	1911
2	237★	B. J. Booth *and* R. W. Tolchard	Surrey	Leicester (GR)	1971
3	231	V. F. S. Crawford *and* T. Jayes	Hampshire	Leicester (AR)	1908
SEVENTH WICKET					
1	219★	J. D. R. Benson *and* P. Whitticase	Hampshire	Bournemouth	1991
2	206	B. Dudleston *and* Birkenshaw	Kent	Canterbury	1969
3	194	W. W. Odell *and* H. Whitehead	Essex	Leicester (AR)	1905
EIGHTH WICKET					
1	164	M. R. Hallam *and* C. T. Spencer	Essex	Leicester (GR)	1964
2	150	G. Geary *and* T. E. Sidwell	Surrey	The Oval	1926
3	149	P. Whitticase *and* P. A. J. DeFreitas	Kent	Canterbury	1986

NINTH WICKET

1	160	W. W. Odell *and* R. T. Crawford	Worcestershire	Leicester (AR)	1902
2	136★	N. M. McVicker *and* G. D. McKenzie	Kent	Tunbridge Wells	1975
3	133	A. E. Knight *and* A. E. Davis	Sussex	Hove	1905

TENTH WICKET

1	228	R. Illingworth *and* K. Higgs	Northamptonshire	Leicester (GR)	1977
2	157	W. E. Astill *and* W. H. Marlow	Gloucestershire	Cheltenham (College)	1933
3	96	G. Geary *and* A. Skelding	Kent	Leicester (AR)	1925

(2) LIMITED-OVERS MATCHES

(a) John Player/Refuge Assurance League

Score	Batsmen	Opponents	Venue	Year
1st: 140	D. I. Gower *and* N. E. Briers	Derbyshire	Leicester (GR)	1982
2nd: 175★	D. I. Gower *and* N. E. Briers	Warwickshire	Leicester (GR)	1985
3rd: 152	J. J. Whitaker *and* D. I. Gower	Warwickshire	Leicester (GR)	1989
4th: 178	J. J. Whitaker *and* P. Willey	Glamorgan	Swansea	1984
5th: 115	T. J. Boon *and* J. D. R. Benson	Surrey	The Oval	1990
6th: 90	B. F. Davison *and* R. Illingworth	Surrey	The Oval	1970
7th: 96★	R. Illingworth *and* J. Birkenshaw	Somerset	Leicester (GR)	1971
8th: 57	M. E. J. C. Norman *and* G. D. McKenzie	Kent	Leicester (GR)	1969
9th: 53★	L. Potter *and* D. J. Millns	Nottinghamshire	Grace Road	1991
10th: 52	N. M. McVicker *and* K. Higgs	Nottinghamshire	Trent Bridge	1975

(b) Benson & Hedges Cup

Score	Batsmen	Opponents	Venue	Year
1st: 196	L. Potter *and* I. P. Butcher	Minor Counties	Leicester (GR)	1986
2nd: 160	T. J. Boon *and* J. J. Whitaker	Scotland	Grace Road	1991
3rd: 227	M. E. J. C. Norman *and* B. F. Davison	Warwickshire	Coventry	1972

336

4th: 146	P. Willey *and* J. J. Whitaker	Warwickshire	Edgbaston	1985
5th: 123	R. W. Tolchard *and* P. B. Clift	Worcestershire	Worcester	1976
6th: 80	P. Willey *and* M. A. Garnham	Essex	Lord's (Final)	1985
7th: 108	P. Willey *and* P. Whitticase	Derbyshire	Leicester (GR)	1987
8th: 52	J. F. Steele *and* G. J. Parsons	Northamptonshire	Leicester (GR)	1983
9th: 42	N. G. B. Cook *and* J. P. Agnew	Warwickshire	Leicester (GR)	1984
10th: 23	G. J. Parsons *and* K. Higgs	Surrey	The Oval	1981

(c) NatWest Trophy/Gillette Cup

Score	*Batsmen*	*Opponents*	*Venue*	*Year*
1st: 206	B. Dudleston *and* J. F. Steele	Staffordshire	Longton	1975
2nd: 139	J. J. Whitaker *and* D. I. Gower	Wiltshire	Swindon	1984
3rd: 209	P. Willey *and* D. I. Gower	Ireland	Leicester (GR)	1986
4th: 121	J. J. Whitaker *and* L. Potter	Northamptonshire	Northampton	1991
5th: 118	D. I. Gower *and* T. J. Boon	Derbyshire	Leicester (GR)	1984
6th: 70	R. W. Tolchard *and* J. Birkenshaw	Hampshire	Leicester (GR)	1976
70	J. C. Balderstone *and* P. B. Clift	Hampshire	Leicester (GR)	1978
7th: 97	P. Whitticase *and* P. A. J. DeFreitas	Lancashire	Leicester (GR)	1986
8th: 63★	R. Illingworth *and* P. Booth	Glamorgan	Swansea	1977
9th: 48★	J. C. Balderstone *and* K. Higgs	Somerset	Taunton	1973
10th: 40★	G. F. Cross *and* J. Cotton	Surrey	Leicester (GR)	1966

WICKETKEEPING RECORDS

(1) SIX DISMISSALS IN AN INNINGS

Ct	St	Keeper	Opponents and Venue	Year
4	2	P. Corrall	Sussex *at* Hove	1936
3	3	P. Corrall	Middlesex *at* Leicester (GR)	1949
6	–	R. W. Tolchard	Yorkshire *at* Headingley	1973
6	–	R. W. Tolchard	Hampshire *at* Southampton	1980
5	1	P. A. Nixon	Glamorgan *at* Hinckley (Leic. Rd)	1990

(2) EIGHT DISMISSALS IN A MATCH

Total	Ct	St	Keeper	Opponents and Venue	Year
10	7	3	P. Corrall	Sussex *at* Hove	1936
8	3	5	J. Firth	Kent *at* Folkestone	1952
8	7	1	J. Firth	Essex *at* Colchester (Castle Park)	1953
8	8	–	R. W. Tolchard	Middlesex *at* Leicester (GR)	1979
8	8	–	P. Whitticase	Derbyshire *at* Derby	1987
8	8	–	P. Whitticase	Northamptonshire *at* Leicester (GR)	1988
8	8	–	P. A. Nixon	Warwickshire *at* Hinckley (Leic. Rd)	1989
8	8	–	P. A. Nixon	Yorkshire *at* Sheffield	1990
8	8	–	P. Whitticase	Derbyshire *at* Derby	1991

(3) SEVENTY DISMISSALS IN A SEASON

Total	Ct	St	Keeper	Year
85	60	25	J. Firth	1952
79	72	7	R. Julian	1961
73	63	10	R. W. Tolchard	1967
73	69	4	P. Whitticase	1988
70	58	12	T. E. Sidwell	1921

(4) 400 DISMISSALS IN A CAREER

Total	Ct	St	Keeper	Career
903	794	109	R. W. Tolchard	1965–83
708	571	137	T. E. Sidwell	1913–33
563	379	184	P. Corrall	1930–51
444	353	91	J. Firth	1951–58
421	382	39	R. Julian	1953–71
410	325	85	J. P. Whiteside	1894–1906

Note:
A number of Tolchard's catches were taken whilst not keeping wicket.

FIELDING RECORDS

(1) FIVE CATCHES IN AN INNINGS

Fielder	Opponents	Venue	Year
H. Whitehead	Sussex	Leicester (AR)	1912
C. J. B. Wood	Warwickshire	Hinckley (Ashby Rd)	1919
W. E. Astill	Somerset	Weston-super-Mare	1920
R. L. Pratt	Derbyshire	Leicester (GR)	1961
M. R. Hallam	Northamptonshire	Leicester (GR)	1964
J. F. Steele	Nottinghamshire	Trent Bridge	1971
P. B. Clift	Worcestershire	Worcester	1976

(2) SEVEN CATCHES IN A MATCH

Fielder	Opponents	Venue	Year
R. L. Pratt	Derbyshire	Leicester (GR)	1961

(3) 40 CATCHES IN A SEASON

Total	Fielder	Year
56	M. R. Hallam	1961
41	M. R. Hallam	1955
40	H. Whitehead	1908
40	J. E. Walsh	1947

(4) 300 CATCHES IN A CAREER

Total	Fielder	Career
427	M. R. Hallam	1950–70
407	H. Whitehead	1898–1922
390	W. E. Astill	1906–39
375	C. T. Spencer	1952–74
368	G. Geary	1912–38
330	J. F. Steele	1970–83
309	J. H. King	1895–1925

FATHERS AND SONS WHO HAVE REPRESENTED LEICESTERSHIRE IN FIRST-CLASS MATCHES

Father	Son(s)
Sir A. G. Hazlerigg (1st Baron)	Sir A. G. Hazlerigg (2nd Baron)
A. Howard	J. H. Howard (brother A. R. Howard represented Glamorgan)
James King	J. W. King
G. F. Knew	G. A. Knew
J. Palmer	G. H. Palmer
E. Riley	H. Riley
G. E. Rudd	G. B. F. Rudd
A. T. Sharp	General Sir J. A. T. Sharp

BROTHERS WHO HAVE REPRESENTED LEICESTERSHIRE IN FIRST-CLASS MATCHES

F. J. Bowley, H. B. Bowley
J. C. Bradshaw, W. H. Bradshaw
J. H. Brown, L. Brown
J. Burgess, H. Burgess
R. T. Crawford, V. F. S. Crawford
G. C. Gill, E. H. Gill
F. M. Joyce, R. Joyce, J. H. Joyce
J. H. King, James King
A. Lorrimer, D. Lorrimer (B. Lorrimer played prior to first-class status)
V. S. Munden, D. F. X. Munden, P. A. Munden
W. W. Odell, E. F. Odell
C. W. C. Packe, R. J. Packe, M. St J. Packe
W. Shipman, A. W. Shipman
R. W. Tolchard, J. G. Tolchard

UNIVERSITY BLUES WHO HAVE PLAYED FIRST-CLASS CRICKET FOR LEICESTERSHIRE

Oxford University
G. Evans	1939
M. J. K. Smith	1954–56
F. W. Stocks	1898–99
C. H. Taylor	1923–26

Cambridge University
E. W. Dawson	1924–27
A. G. Hazlerigg	1930–32
D. Kirby	1959–61
H. H. Marriott	1895–98
W. N. Riley	1912
M. H. Rose	1963–64

340

BIBLIOGRAPHY

E. E. Snow *A History of Leicestershire Cricket* (Backus, 1949)
E. E. Snow *Leicestershire Cricket 1949 to 1977* (Stanley Paul, 1977)
D. A. Lambert *Leicestershire Cricketers 1879–1977* (ACS, 1977)
C. Gimson *Leicester Ivanhoe CC* (the Club, 1975)
J. R. Gimson *Leicester Ivanhoe CC* (the Club, 1923)
R. Illingworth *Yorkshire and Back* (Queen Anne Press, 1980)
B. K. Ward *Put Lock On* (Rigby, 1972)
Leicestershire CCC Year Book various years.
The following periodicals were also used: *The Cricketer, Cricket, Wisden's Cricketers' Almanack, Wisden Cricket Monthly, Playfair Cricket Monthly, The Cricket Field, Lillywhite Annual, Lillywhite's Companion.*

ACKNOWLEDGEMENTS

The writing of this book would have been exceedingly difficult without the research which had been undertaken over many years by Eric Snow, and published in his two volumes of Leicestershire Cricket history. Peter Wynne-Thomas assisted with the final manuscript and advised on various historical matters; Philip Thorn was kind enough to check the biographical details of players and add a number of new pieces of information. A number of members of the Association of Cricket Statisticians have, over the years, been of help in a variety of ways and their assistance has been most welcome. The statistics and records where applicable comply with the Association's Guides to First-Class cricket.

INDEX